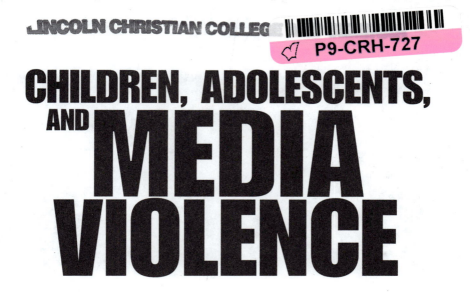

CHILDREN, ADOLESCENTS, AND MEDIA VIOLENCE

In loving memory of Helen Kirsh (a.k.a. Bubbie), and to my children, who wanted a horse and a go-cart but got this book instead.

CHILDREN, ADOLESCENTS, AND MEDIA VIOLENCE

A Critical Look at the Research

Steven J.
KIRSH

SUNY - Geneseo

SAGE Publications
Thousand Oaks ▪ London ▪ New Delhi

For information:

Sage Publications, Inc.
2455 Teller Road
Thousand Oaks, California 91320
E-mail: order@sagepub.com

Sage Publications Ltd.
1 Oliver's Yard
55 City Road
London EC1Y 1SP
United Kingdom

Sage Publications India Pvt. Ltd.
B-42, Panchsheel Enclave
Post Box 4109
New Delhi 110 017 India

Printed in the United States of America on acid-free paper

Library of Congress Cataloging-in-Publication Data

Kirsh, Steven J.
Children, adolescents, and media violence : a critical look at the
research / Steven J. Kirsh.
        p. cm.
Includes bibliographical references and index.
ISBN 0-7619-2975-4 (cloth) — ISBN 0-7619-2976-2 (pbk.)
    1. Mass media and children. 2. Mass media and teenagers.
3. Children and violence. 4. Youth and violence. 5. Violence in
mass media. 6. Aggressiveness in children. 7. Aggressiveness
in adolescence. I. Title.
HQ784.M3K5677 2006
302.23′083—dc22

                                                    2005020164

    06   07   08   09   10   9   8   7   6   5   4   3   2

Acquiring Editor:	Jim Brace-Thompson
Editorial Assistant:	Karen Ehrmann
Production Editor:	Sanford Robinson
Copy Editor:	Diana Breti
Typesetter:	C&M Digitals (P) Ltd.
Indexer:	John Hulse
Cover Designer:	Candice Harman

Contents

Preface

Children, Adolescents and Media Violence: A Critical Look at the Research provides a comprehensive review and critique of the research on media violence as it relates to children and adolescents. Thus, throughout the book, theories and research are evaluated from a developmental perspective. This perspective helps demonstrate the effects of media violence on youth as a function of age. More importantly, a developmental analysis of the research allows for identification of age-related "holes" in the literature. In fact, I think you will be surprised to find that across development, and for certain types of violent media (e.g., video games, music), very little research exists.

In each chapter, methodological and statistical concepts are introduced within the context of research. I do this for several reasons: first, it is my belief that methodological and statistical concepts are easier to grasp when introduced alongside an interesting study. Second, understanding such concepts is crucial in the analytical evaluation and understanding of any given study. Third, the relatively slow introduction of methodological and statistical concepts allows the reader to digest the material and apply the new understanding to studies as they are presented in each chapter. Finally, understanding research methodology so that one can be a *critical* consumer of research is a process that requires repetition.

The book is divided into three major sections: Understanding Aggression, Effects of Specific Forms of Violent Media on Youth, and Media Violence and the Concept of Risk. The first section places media violence in the context of aggression. Here, aggression is defined, theories of aggression are laid out and critiqued, the development of aggressive behavior is described, and the patterns of and reasons for violent media consumption are discussed. The second section begins with a discussion and review of the literature addressing the contention that violent media is actually good for youth. Once this contention has been disavowed, I evaluate the extant body of empirical research addressing the effects of the different types of violent media (e.g., video games, television) on children and adolescents. The third section addresses violent media consumption from a risk factor perspective. To understand the relative risk associated with violent media consumption, non-media-related risk factors for aggression in youth are reviewed. Subsequently, the relative risk associated with media violence exposure is addressed. Moreover, techniques for reducing the negative effects of violent media consumption are discussed. This section ends with a review and discussion of governmental and self-regulatory policies resulting from the perceived and actual threat of media violence consumption. Finally, because those interested in the effects of violent media on youth may also be interested in the effects of nonviolent media on youth, the last chapter of this book addresses the potential benefits and harm associated with nonviolent media consumption.

Acknowledgments

I would like to thank Carolyn Emmert, J. Martin Rochester, and Paul Olczak for their feedback on the manuscript. I am especially grateful to my father, Marvin Kirsh, and to Joan Ballard and Sudha Bakshi for their encouragement and support in writing this book.

PART I

Understanding Aggression

1

There and Back Again

A Media Violence Tale

*P*ow! Bam! Oomph . . . *thud!* As I lay on the ground, I thought to myself, "How did I get here?" At first it seemed obvious; my four-year-old son Daniel had just landed a very hard right hook to my . . . groin. As the pain subsided and the fog cleared, additional—not to mention more cogent— questions began to form in my mind. Why had he thrown the punch? Why was he smiling when he threw it? Should I tell him to step into the punch next time (after all, his form could use some improvement)? Where can I buy a cup? As it happened, I was lying on the ground facing the TV, and as my eyes began to refocus, I was able to make out the image on the TV: a gray uniform, a black cape and cowl . . . Batman. "No more *Batman* for you!" I said. My son's smile was replaced with anger, tears, and the ubiquitous tantrum. But on the bright side, I blocked his two-fisted, overhead, Hulk-like attempt to smash me. "Time out."

My interest in media violence started long before I was TKO'd by my son. I was a child of the very *first* video game generation. I remember being amazed at the wonders of *Defender, Asteroids, Centipede, Missile Command,* and other video game *classics.* I spent countless hours and countless dollars at video arcades. I was fortunate enough to have an Odyssey video game console and a friend with the competing video game console made by Intellivision. My steady diet of violent entertainment included hours of watching professional wrestling. I would root for BoBo Brazil and boo the Iron Sheik. I loved the spectacle of the matches, not to mention the power bombs! For a while, I even believed the matches were real. For me, violent entertainment was a common everyday occurrence. I'd watch classic 1950s horror movies with my mom (e.g., *Dracula, Frankenstein, Creature from the Black Lagoon*), 1970s "slasher" movies with my friends (e.g., *Halloween, Friday the 13th*), and Michigan football games with my dad (there is nothing more horrifying than watching a Michigan football team attempting to protect a lead at the end of a game). I read Stephen King novels voraciously, which subsequently led to a fear of clowns. I watched cartoons like *Speed Racer* and *Kimba the White Lion* and live action shows such as *Starsky and Hutch, Get Smart,* and the forever campy *Batman.* Yet, despite my heavy consumption of violent entertainment, I somehow made it through childhood and adolescence without getting in a single fight. Actually, in sixth grade, I *almost* got into a fight, but the other kid sat on me, and the "fight" was pretty much over after that.

My childhood experiences are similar to those of millions of children and adolescents around the globe today. Ostensibly, consuming copious amounts of violent media does not immediately cause youth to become hyper-violent. Millions of dollars are spent in video arcades every year, yet fights are not constantly erupting in these establishments. Even though one adolescent referred to slasher films as "educational" (Johnston, 1995), there has not been a rash of 16-year-olds slicing up their parents after watching slasher films. Nevertheless, just because *most* young consumers of media violence do not turn into serial killers or start their own "fight clubs" does not mean that they are not being influenced by the consumption of violent media. But just how are children and adolescents influenced by short-term and long-term exposure to violent entertainment? The purpose of this book is to answer that question. Prior to addressing the effects of violent entertainment on children and adolescents, however, it is necessary to place this issue in historical perspective.

A Look Through the Violent Sands of Time

Concerns over the impact of media on youth arose long before the first video game depicting decapitation, televised high-speed chase, radio program shootout, or illustrated bloody evisceration. In fact, long before Stephen King wrote about murders committed by demonic beings, aliens, werewolves, dogs, or evil twins, the spoken word raised alarm (Starker, 1989). In 339 BC, for instance, Socrates was jailed and executed, via hemlock poisoning, for corrupting the morals and values of Athenian youth (EyeWitness to History, 2003).

For centuries, storytelling was the primary medium for communicating the values, morals, and oral history of a culture. However, only those with access to the storyteller could receive such information. Over time, story details were easily changed or forgotten. Thus, once the alphabet was invented, storytelling gave way to story writing. However, writing stories on baked clay tablets, papyrus, or parchments was a labor-intensive and expensive chore. Thus, writing as a means of communication did not become widespread until the advent of the printing press in the fifteenth century. However, it was not until the eighteenth century that the Church cast the written word, which now constituted a true "mass media," as an *evil influence* (Starker, 1989). As used by Steven Starker, the term "evil influence" refers to the viewpoint that mass media, in its various forms (e.g., comic books, newspapers, novels, television video games, etc.), can be a source of wickedness, inflicting ills upon the world.

Criticism of the written word, however, goes beyond the Church. In the nineteenth century, learned scholars frequently labeled novels and newspapers evil influences. Novels were thought to overexcite the nervous systems of "frail" young women. And as Thomas Jefferson wrote, the reading of novels can lead to a distorted view of reality and a "bloated imagination" (Starker, 1989). Several of the most popular novels of that era would make today's readers take notice. In the late 1600s, autobiographical books describing settlers being captured, tortured, and killed by Native Americans were well read and well liked. Throughout the eighteenth and nineteenth centuries, the plots of the most popular novels involved seduction, attempted rape, and violence. As the popularity of the novels grew, so did the perceived threat to the individual. Starker aptly states, "The greater the audience, the greater the presumed threat to individual health and social order" (Starker, 1989, p. 53).

Similar to novels because of their low cost and widespread popularity, newspapers were also viewed as an evil influence. Newspapers contained a cornucopia of information, including stories, both serious and whimsical; pictures; comics; and advertisements. As viewed by critics, this potpourri of information was thought to cause rapid shifts of attention, placing the mental and emotional health of the reader at risk. This was especially true for the "penny papers," which, like the tabloids of today, reported highly sensationalized stories and were sold on the street, thus being available to all without a subscription. As with the novel, as the audience for newspapers and penny papers grew, so did the presumed threat to psychological well-being (Starker, 1989).

One section of the newspaper, in particular, came under fire for corrupting the morals of youth: the comics. As early as 1910, society regarded the comics as a "menace." Comics were thought to weaken the use of good manners, teach lawlessness, cheapen life, and increase the chance of mental illness. By the mid-1930s, bound versions of the comics told complete story lines; the golden age of the comic book had arrived. Comic books depicted burlesque, slapstick humor, crime, adventure, and, of course, superheroes. Although concern was raised over the tawdry nature of comic book characters, the glorification of violence as a means of problem solving, and the promotion of gay (e.g., Batman and Robin) and lesbian (e.g., Wonder Woman) lifestyles, it was the "Crime Comics" that were most often viewed as evil influences by society (Starker, 1989). Brandishing titles such as *Gangsters and Gun Molls, Crimes by Women,* and *March of Crime,* the story lines of crime comics involved stealing, murder, mayhem, torture, and other criminal activities. In the 1940s, nearly 50 cities attempted to ban the sale of crime comics (Starker, 1989).

Ten years later, critics were still concerned that violence in comic books would promote deceit, stimulate unhealthy ideas about sex, and increase aggression and delinquency in children (Wertham, 1954). Congress was aware of the public outcry against comic books, and in 1954 the Senate Subcommittee on Juvenile Delinquency initiated hearings on the topic. In addition to crime comics, comic books depicting themes of horror (e.g., *Tales from the Crypt* or *Haunt of Fear*) were vilified by the Subcommittee. As a direct result of the Senate hearings, the Comics Code Authority (CCA) was initiated. As a self-censoring agency for comic book content, the rules of the CCA were developed and enforced by the producers of comic books (Savage, 1990). This was not the first time that a rating system had been employed to assess media content, nor would it be the last.

In 1893, Thomas Edison invented the kinetoscope (Starker, 1989), a device that allowed viewers to peer through a peephole at the top of a cabinet and watch moving pictures. Within a year, James A. Bradley, a state senator from New Jersey, had lodged a public complaint against the vulgar content of a minute-long film that had the audacity to show the ankles of a Spanish dancer. Shortly thereafter, the Nickelodeon, the forerunner to the modern-day movie theater, was born. By the early 1900s, newspaper editorials across the country were denouncing films shown in these movie theaters as direct threats to the morals of children. Movie theaters were viewed as training grounds for criminals, offering children opportunities to watch acts of degradation and learn "values" not taught in Church or at home. Anecdotal evidence of the evil influence of motion pictures was reported in newspapers; mothers complained that films caused their sons to run away from home, steal money, or learn the art of burglary. As a result of these complaints, the National Board of Censorship of Motion Pictures was created to oversee the content of movies. After a period of self-regulation by the movie industry, the Hays Production Code was enforced to help curtail public complaints about the debauchery portrayed in movies. The code included prohibitions against swearing, vulgarity, the use of guns, sympathy for criminals, and revealing undergarments. The Hays Production Code was abandoned in the late 1960s and replaced with the modern-day rating system provided by the Motion Picture Association of America (Starker, 1989).

The advent of new media does not necessitate that it will be perceived as an evil influence, but a rise in its popularity does. Although the radio was invented in the late 1800s, it was not until the mid-1930s, when approximately 90% of American homes had one, that the medium of radio was viewed as a potential threat to children and adolescents (Starker, 1989). In addition to traditional radio fare, such as news and music, radio of the 1930s was replete with serial dramas. Shows such as *The Shadow, Green Hornet,* and *Sam Spade* were incredibly popular with youth. However, critics pointed out that the types of shows that children were listening to taught elements of crime and skullduggery. Kidnappings, beatings, espionage, extortion, threats, shootings, and arson were just a few of the serial drama story lines viewed as giving dangerous ideas to young children (Starker, 1989).

Today, the radio drama is a thing of the past. However, radio is not without restriction. Radio programs are heavily monitored by the Federal Communications Commission (FCC) for lewd content and vulgar language. Shock jocks such as Don Geronimo and Mike O'Meara of the *Don and Mike Show* and Howard Stern are broadcast with a delay for the purpose of giving the radio station a chance to prevent offensive content from airing. Similarly, when played over the terrestrial airways, offensive language in music is replaced with silence or bleeped out of existence. In an effort to protect children and adolescents from sexually explicit or violent lyrics, potentially offensive music sold in stores is voluntarily labeled by the record companies with a parental advisory warning sticker. However, the primary concern of parents and legislators has shifted from focusing on the effects of music on children and adolescents to television, and more recently, video games.

Starker's maxim that concern about media is directly related to its popularity is again illustrated by the rise of the television era. In the early 1940s, television sets were relatively expensive and were found in few homes. However, by the end of the decade, as the price of sets had become affordable to most and the variety of shows available increased, the popularity of TV skyrocketed. Warnings of the potential deleterious effects of television began as early as 1948, with magazines suggesting that watching TV would lead to the mental paralysis of children and was a pathway to juvenile delinquency. By the early 1970s, the U.S. Surgeon General warned of the susceptibility of children to the potential negative effects of violent television (U.S. Surgeon General's Scientific Advisory Committee, 1972).

In 1958, William Higinbotham programmed a computer to display on an oscilloscope a circle moving back and forth across a screen, with a small vertical line in the middle representing a net. The game was called *Tennis for Two,* and it signified the beginning of the video game era (Designboom, 2004). Some 13 years later, Nolan Bushnell released a revamped arcade version of *Tennis for Two* called *Pong.* However, the first violent video game, *Space Wars,* was developed at MIT in 1961. In *Space Wars,* two spaceships (a triangular wedge and a needle) with limited fuel try to destroy each other in a star-filled battlefield. The graphics were rough and the game was simple, but the significance was profound. The game was a huge hit at MIT and it spread like wildfire across ARPAnet, the precursor to the Internet (Designboom, 2004). By the mid-1970s, video games could be found in arcades and homes across the country. Currently, the popularity of video games has skyrocketed to more than $10 billion in sales annually. And as the popularity of video game play has increased, so too has concern over the effects of violent video game play on youth. Recently, research on the deleterious effects of violent video games on children and adolescents was presented to a U.S. Senate Commerce Committee (Anderson, 2000; Funk, 2000).

Evaluating the Evidence of Evil Influences

As our brief review of entertainment violence has shown, across decades and across modes of presentation (e.g., television, video games, etc.), violent entertainment has consistently been viewed as an evil influence on youth. Were these historical concerns valid? Are they still valid today? Prior to the 1930s, the moniker "evil influence" was based on conjecture and anecdotal evidence. Evidence of the harm to morals, values, and behavior would occasionally be presented, but in each instance, it would be anecdotal; the unsubstantiated, or poorly researched, report of a child gone wrong. However, as anyone who has bought a Ginzu Knife or a Popeil Pocket Fisherman can attest, testimonials can be very persuasive.

Critics would decry violent entertainment, but they would do so without providing any *empirical evidence* of the effects they were postulating. Empirical evidence refers to research conducted using the tenets of the scientific method. According to the scientific method, observations lead to the development of research questions (e.g., crime comics teach children how to steal). Next, based on what we know or what we think will happen, testable predictions, known as *hypotheses,* are made (e.g., adolescents reading crime comics will have more knowledge of how to commit crimes than adolescents who do not read crime comics). Those testable predictions are then evaluated through research in which a number of participants are studied (e.g., have one group of adolescents read crime comics and have another group of adolescents read Disney comics). During the testing of the prediction, care is taken to make sure that issues (e.g., criminality of parents) related to the phenomenon under study are taken into consideration, so that the likelihood of those issues affecting the results (e.g., knowledge of how to commit a crime) is reduced. Reducing the impact of variables that could potentially influence the research findings is called *control*. Finally, the findings of the study are compared with the prediction and conclusions about our predictions are drawn. Reasons for the results are then given, new predictions are made, and the process repeats itself. It is important to note that similar to anecdotal evidence, no one empirical study can be viewed as *proving* or *disproving* an effect. It is the accumulation of evidence over a period of years, using different methodologies and addressing the concerns associated with previous research, that leads to established conclusions or scientific facts about the area being studied.

The first empirical research addressing the effects of violent entertainment was undertaken between 1929 and 1932, in what has become known as the "Payne Fund Studies"(Jowett, Jarvie, & Fuller, 1996). The Payne Fund Studies assessed, among other things, the influence of movies on children's emotions, morals, sleep habits, attitudes, and behavior. Subsequently, hundreds of research studies have assessed the influence of media on children and adolescents, using the scientific method as a guide. Although early warnings of the potential negative effects of entertainment media were based on conjecture, over the past 70 years, voluminous amounts of research have been conducted, and the overwhelming conclusion is that the potential negative effects of entertainment media are more than just mere speculation; *they are scientific fact*. The effects of entertainment media have been shown to influence youth buying habits, sexuality, eating disorders, and drug use (Strasburger & Wilson, 2002). However, due in part to a rash of school shootings, the effects of entertainment violence have once again come under scientific, public, and political scrutiny. Thus, the primary focus of this book is to evaluate current research on entertainment violence, with particular attention paid to the effects of violent media on aggressive behavior and aggression-related constructs.

Aggressive Behavior and Aggression-Related Constructs

In front of a group of classmates, a 13-year-old girl makes fun of another girl's outfit; a 6-year-old boy hits another boy who tries to take his Ninja turtle; after being grounded, a 10-year-old boy tells his father to "F*%@ off"; and a 14-year-old boy walks into a classroom and begins shooting his classmates. Although the ages and genders of the perpetrators and victims may differ, and even though physical harm does not always occur, each of the above examples is an act of aggression. Aggression is defined as any behavior, be it physical, verbal, psychological, or emotional, intended to cause physical, emotional, or psychological injury to another human being. Of course, shooting a classmate is a more injurious form of aggression than is teasing another child. Thus, aggressive acts can also vary in intensity and severity. In fact, the term "violence" is typically reserved for extreme acts of aggression, acts that can lead to serious physical or psychological harm (Anderson, Berkowitz, et al., 2003). The distinction between aggression and violence, however, is a subtle one. For example, whereas kicking someone in the leg once may be an act of aggression, repeatedly kicking the leg to the point of it breaking would be considered an act of violence.

Although the dividing line between aggression and violence is difficult to determine, it is an important determination nonetheless. It is one thing to find evidence that playing violent video games or watching a violent television show increases the likelihood of an adolescent having nasty thoughts; it is quite another to find evidence that the consumption of violent entertainment increases the likelihood of that same adolescent shooting a classmate or beating him unconscious. Just as the intensity of an aggressive act can vary, so can the effects of violent media exposure. However, as the chapter on theories of media violence will illustrate, effects resulting from violent media exposure that seem far removed from violent behavior (such as an increase in aggressive thoughts) can, in the long run, set the stage for a pattern of aggressive behavior that could ultimately increase violent behavior in youth—the type of behavior that the public fears the most.

Types of Aggression

Violence and other aggressive acts resulting in damage to flesh and bone are considered acts of *physical aggression*. Examples of physical aggression include kicking, punching, shoving, stabbing, and shooting. Damage done to property, resulting from vandalism or willful destruction, is also subsumed into this category of aggression. However, aggression does not have to involve direct acts of physicality to be considered aggressive, nor does it have to produce physical harm. In fact, some acts of aggression occur over periods of days or weeks without any direct confrontation and without leaving any bruises. For instance, *relational aggression* involves attempts to hurt another person's social relationships or level of group inclusion

(Crick, Grotpeter, & Bigbee, 2002). Unlike physical aggression, relational aggression can occur in an indirect manner, in which harm occurs to the victim through a series of connecting steps. For example, a common occurrence in adolescence is for one person to spread nasty rumors about a classmate, resulting in a loss of friends for that person (Underwood, 2003). However, relational aggression can also occur in a direct fashion, in which the victim immediately experiences the aggressive act in the presence of the perpetrator. For instance, commenting on a classmate's "disheveled and outdated look" to a group of peers, in the presence of the victim, would be considered a direct act of relational aggression. At times, relational aggression is a form of *verbal aggression,* in which words are used to harm another. Teasing your little brother or swearing at that "idiot" who just cut you off in traffic are also examples of verbal aggression.

In contrast to acts of physical aggression, verbal and relational aggression leave no physical marks; nonetheless, marks are left. Recent research has shown that the part of the brain responsible for experiencing physical pain, the *anterior cingulate,* also registers the effects of social exclusion (Eisenberger, Lieberman, & Williams, 2003). Thus, the old adage "sticks and stones can break my bones, but names will never hurt me" may now be incorrect. It appears as if the brain processes nonphysical acts of aggression in a manner similar to physical acts of aggression. In other words, psychological pain resulting from verbal or relational aggression produces *real* wounds; it is just that these wounds lack visible bruises or broken bones.

Aggression-Related Constructs

In addition to linking consumption of violent media to aggressive behavior, a great deal of research has also looked at the influence of entertainment violence on aggression-related constructs. Whereas aggression involves causing harm to another, aggression-related constructs are those factors within an individual that influence the likelihood of that individual committing an aggressive act. The four major aggression-related constructs that presumably have the greatest effect on aggressive behavior are *aggressive emotions, aggressive personality characteristics, physiological factors associated with aggression,* and *aggressive thoughts.* Aggressive emotions include feelings associated with the onset of an aggressive act, such as anger, as well as feelings that follow aggressive acts, such as guilt. For instance, adolescent bullies tend to engender positive emotional states when picking on a victim (Warden & Mackinnon, 2003). Aggressive personality characteristics refer to those aspects of an individual's personality that might predispose a child or adolescent towards acting aggressively. Both the desire for thrilling experiences and the ability to control one's impulses have been associated with acting aggressively (Moeller, 2001). Aggressive personality characteristics arise as a result of both genetic and environmental factors. So, even though children may be predisposed to acting on their impulses, when parented in just the right way, the children can learn to control their desires to act without thinking (Johnston, 1996). Physiological factors associated with aggression include heart rate, blood pressure, and hormones. For instance, recent research on violent children suggests that the levels of the hormone cortisol are lower in violent children than in their nonviolent classmates (Walker, Walder, & Reynolds, 2001). Beliefs about the appropriateness of using aggression to solve problems, potential causes, and responses to acts of aggression are just a few of the many different cognitive processes encompassing aggressive thoughts. For instance, one of the key differences between aggressive and nonaggressive children is that when harm occurs (e.g., you get hit in the head with a ball), but the intent of the harm doer is unclear, aggressive children believe that they got hurt because the harm doer had hostile intentions. In contrast, nonaggressive children believe that getting hurt was an accident (Dodge, 1986).

Aggression-related constructs can be seen working in concert in the context of *provoked* and *unprovoked* aggression. In provoked aggression, a child acts aggressively in response to some negative event encountered in the world. For instance, in response to getting bumped, a child may angrily hit his classmate. In this instance, as in most cases of provoked aggression, the child is angry (aggressive emotion), lacks impulse control (aggressive personality), has increasing levels of the hormone cortisol (aggressive physiology), and exhibits a belief system that necessitates a response to provocation with force (aggressive thought). In contrast, unprovoked aggression occurs without any ostensible provocation from the environment. For instance, a child squishes another kid into a locker to make himself look "macho" in front of his friends. In this case, the bully is joyful (aggressive emotion), conniving (aggressive personality), excretes low levels of cortisol (aggressive physiology), and exhibits a belief system in which aggression is used to influence one's social standing (aggressive thoughts).

Violent Entertainment and Aggression-Related Constructs

In studying media violence, not only do researchers assess the impact of playing violent video games or watching violent movies on the incidence of aggressive behavior, but researchers also investigate the effects of media violence exposure on the previously mentioned aggression-related constructs.

Why should we care about aggression-related constructs? After all, it is *aggressive behavior* that causes harm to others. No one has been *directly* hurt by the aggressive thought of another, and a belief that aggression is appropriate to combat verbal taunts of others is just that, a belief. Although it is true that aggressive constructs do not directly cause harm, they may do so in an indirect fashion by influencing the likelihood of an individual committing an aggressive act. The *cause* of aggressive behavior is typically the result of events external to the child, such as a provoking event (e.g., a wedgie), and forces internal to the child, such as attitudes towards violence (or some other aggression-related construct). Differences in aggression-related constructs, therefore, can lead to different levels of aggressive behavior or even determine whether aggression occurs at all. For instance, whereas one child may respond to an extreme wedgie by punching the kid in the nose (an aggressive response), another child may respond nonviolently and with a question, "That hurt! What were you thinking?" Thus, anything that can modify an individual's aggressive-related constructs may indirectly influence the likelihood of a child engaging in provoked or unprovoked aggression. Certain environmental experiences, such as affectionate parenting and the use of rational discipline, may decrease the likelihood of children and adolescents acting aggressively. In contrast, other environmental experiences, such as harsh, physically punitive parenting, may increase the likelihood of youth engaging in aggressive behavior. But what about the effects of media violence exposure? How does it affect aggression-related constructs? In Chapter 3, I discuss theories of aggressive acts among children and adolescents and explore further the potential effects of violent media exposure on aggressive behavior and aggression-related constructs.

Answering Questions So New Questions Can Be Raised

Questioning the validity of research findings is important. Answering those questions with further research is science. Of course, some questions are easier to answer than others. For instance, "Did cavemen talk to each other through mental telepathy?" is a question that is impossible to answer with empirical evidence. From the very beginning, empirical findings that identified harmful effects of media violence consumption on youth were called into question. For instance, in the 1930s, the Payne Fund Studies were critiqued for the manner in which the data were collected and reported, thus lessening the impact of the findings (Jowett et al., 1996). In this section,

I address several commonly held beliefs about media violence research that have been raised over the years. Critical analysis of these commonly held beliefs will provide a framework for interpreting the research that will be presented in subsequent chapters.

1. Media violence does not affect youth because violent behavior is not observed after media violence exposure. One of the difficulties that social scientists face when explaining the effects of media violence on youth to skeptics is convincing them that violent entertainment can influence aggression. After all, knife fights, gun battles, and other acts of violence typically do not occur after one plays a violent video game or watches a violent movie. Then again, if the effects of exposure to violent media had that great an immediate impact, there would be no need for this book! The effects would be so apparent that video games, violent movies, and other forms of media violence would be legislated out of existence, available only on the black market. Violent Video Games Anonymous groups would pop up all over the country, and sheriffs would parade before the local news the most recent cache of Pokémon cards confiscated from the secret compartment of some unlucky 4-year-old's tricycle. However, exposure to media violence does not cause aggressive or violent behavior *by itself*. As Anderson and colleagues (2003) comment, exposure to violent media is not a "necessary or sufficient cause of aggressive behavior, let alone both necessary and sufficient" (p. 83).

Punching a beach ball causes it to roll (a direct link), but seeing someone punch a beach ball does not cause a child to immediately punch the nearest object. Media violence often affects behavior indirectly, through aggression-related constructs. Thus, if after seeing a video of a beach ball being punched, a child hits another child, he most likely did so because the various components of the child's aggressive constructs were already nearing the point at which aggressive behavior would be likely to occur. In this case, seeing the aggressive image of the ball being punched was the proverbial "straw that broke the camel's back." Chapter 13 will delve into this issue in more detail by presenting the concepts of relative risk and accumulation of risk factors.

2. The types of aggression displayed in the laboratory do not reflect what is happening in real life. Aggressive displays in laboratory settings are different from those in real life. In the real world, people kick, pinch, bite, spit at, punch, slap, push, tease, stab, sit on, restrain, shout at, swear at, or shoot one another. In the laboratory, aggressive behavior is shown by having participants administer electrical shocks or blast white noise into the ears of the "second participant" in the study (Anderson & Dill, 2000; Buss, 1961). The "second participant," often known as a *confederate*, works for the laboratory team and is trained to give certain responses, such as incorrect answers or a yelp in response to "being shocked." In reality, no one gets shocked or blasted during the experiment, but the participant doing the shocking or blasting does not know that. Some experimenters ask participants to respond to hypothetical scenarios in which aggression is one of several potential responses (Kirsh, 1998). In the real world, people do not typically walk around giving electrical shocks or noise blasts to those whom they want to assault. Nor do they respond to real life provocation with hypothetical responses written on paper. So, if the type of aggressive behavior exhibited in the laboratory is different from the types of aggression displayed in real life, why use laboratory experiments in the first place?

Ethics! It is unethical for researchers to inflict harm on participants. According to *The Publication Manual of the American Psychological Association* (5th ed.), research must be conducted "with due concern for the dignity and welfare of the participants" (American Psychological Association, 2001). However, researchers *are* allowed to conduct surveys and then connect the responses to actual incidents of aggressive behavior that have occurred in the past or that will occur in the future. In this case, the researcher is not inflicting harm on a participant or causing a participant to harm another. In contrast, you can not *really* shock a participant or blast noise into his or her ears. Nor can you have participants kick or hit one another. In order to investigate research in a controlled setting, researchers make use of deception; that is, they make participants *think* they are engaging in a behavior that they really are not. Since it is nearly impossible to use deception to fake kicking, pinching, biting, spitting at, punching, slapping, pushing, teasing, stabbing, and so on, hypothetical scenarios, aggressive shocks, and noise blasts are frequently used to measure aggression.

Of course, because laboratory aggression is different in form from real-life aggression, critics argue that laboratory studies waste time, squander resources, and provide data that could not possibly have any application in the real world. In other words, laboratory studies are said to lack *external validity* (Anderson & Bushman, 1997). External validity refers to the extent to which the empirical findings from one setting can be related to or generalized to other settings and populations. In the case of media violence research, critics believe that "aggressive displays" in the laboratory are so distinctly different from aggression in real life that the laboratory studies lack external validity and are therefore meaningless (Jones, 2002). Thus, critics might argue that although research shows an increase in "aggressive behavior" in the laboratory, you do not need to worry about similar effects at home because laboratory-based aggression is *different* from real-life aggression. But is it *really* different?

On the surface, laboratory and real-life aggression are different. Laboratory-based aggression typically does not occur in real life and, due to ethical concerns, real-life aggression is not allowed to occur in the laboratory. But on a conceptual level they are identical, for both laboratory and real-life acts of aggression depict the *concept* of aggression. Therefore, the conceptual similarity between laboratory and real-life aggression necessitates that the findings from the laboratory apply to real-world settings. In other words, laboratory experiments, because of conceptual similarities with the real world, have high external validity (Anderson & Bushman, 1997). The empirical findings from laboratory experiments, therefore, are of value and do provide worthwhile information. Increases or decreases in aggressive behavior or aggression-related constructs observed in the laboratory as a result of media violence exposure will also occur in real life. One of the difficulties of noticing these changes in real life, however, is that the real world does not provide the controlled environment of the laboratory.

3. **Children and adolescents consume violent media in the home and in the laboratory differently.** Not only is the nature of aggression different between laboratory, home, and other real-world settings, but the amount and nature of media violence exposure is different as well. In the laboratory, research on violent video games and violent lyrics in music requires that children and adolescents play a video game or listen to a song containing violent lyrics that *is not* of their choosing, for a period of time (typically 15–20 minutes) that is typically *out* of their control. For laboratory research involving movie and television violence, participants often watch a montage of disconnected clips depicting aggressive behavior or short, intact scenes devoid of plot. Once again, participants in these studies do not get to choose the television or movie selection that they will be watching (Jones, 2002). In contrast, in the home, consumers of violent media, be it television, movie, video game, or music, choose the type of violent media they will be consuming and have more say about the amount of time they will be playing, watching, or listening. Even if restrictions are placed on children in terms of violent media exposure, the amount of time exposed to violent themes will most likely be longer than the 5 to 20 minutes of violent media exposure shown in the laboratory. In fact, recent research has shown that adolescents watch violent television for hours per day, not minutes. Jones (2002) contends that the differences in the nature of violent media consumption in the laboratory and in the home call into question the external validity of the research.

Conducting research with children and adolescents is a time-consuming and often arduous process. Parents and their children need to be scheduled to come to the laboratory during a time in which the child does not have soccer practice, piano lessons, a test to study for, or some other extracurricular activity. As an enticement, participants are frequently paid for their participation in the experimental study. But, given the busy world of children and adolescents, most researchers try to have participants at the laboratory for no more than an hour or so. In that time, the experimenter needs to explain the study to the participant so that he or she understands what he or she has agreed to do (called *informed consent*), expose the child to the violent media, and do some assessment of aggressive behavior or an aggression-related construct. Given these limitations, media violence exposure is often limited to a brief, and often intense, exposure. The experience in the laboratory is not meant to *mimic* a real-world experience; it is meant to *approximate* one. Although violent media consumption in the laboratory and in the home differ in terms of surface presentation and exposure levels, they are similar with regard to the underlying concept of *violent media exposure.* Thus, as with aggressive behavior in the laboratory, laboratory exposure to violent media is externally valid.

However, as suggested by Jones (2002), is it possible that "forcing" children to consume violent media is the "real" cause of their increased level of aggressive responding (either in behavior or an aggression-related construct)? There is no doubt that the frustration associated with being forced to view violent media could influence aggressive responding (Berkowitz, 1993). But if that were the case, then children and adolescents would provide very negative ratings of the media they were exposed to, report high levels of frustration, and show their discontent to the experimenter. As it turns out, children and adolescents enjoy being exposed to most forms of violent media, and they enjoy their time in the laboratory (the reasons why children and adolescents enjoy violent media will be discussed in a later chapter). In fact, one of the advantages of conducting experimental research is that the experimenters can control for factors (called *extraneous variables*) that can potentially produce results similar to those elicited through naturally occurring violent media exposure.

On the Value of Research

In addressing the three major complaints commonly lodged against entertainment violence research, my goal has *not* been to suggest that research on media violence has been without flaw and that the empirical findings should be believed without challenge. Far from it. Science continuously provides more accurate and informative research by challenging earlier empirical findings. Not only do researchers need to illustrate an effect once, but they

Table 1.1   Challenging Commonly Held Beliefs About Media Violence

Beliefs About Media Violence Research in Need of Challenging:

Media violence does not affect youth because violent behavior is not observed after media violence exposure.

The types of aggression displayed in the laboratory do not reflect what is happening in real life.

Children and adolescents consume violent media in the home and in the laboratory differently.

need to illustrate it over and over again (called *replication*). In subsequent chapters, problems occurring in studies of violent media will be presented. At times, these problems identified will be minor, whereas in other instances, *fatal flaws* will be found. A fatal flaw is a problem in a study that is so severe that the findings of the study should be disavowed. However, one would be hard pressed to find any study that does not have some sort of flaw. Importantly, the presence of a flaw or flaws does not necessarily mean that findings of that study are worthless. For instance, the findings of video game research based on a sample of men may not be directly relevant to women; television research conducted on Caucasians may not apply to African Americans; and the effects of movie violence on the wealthy may be different from the effects of movie violence on the poor. In each case, the findings based on one group (e.g., males) may not *generalize* (extend) to another group (e.g., females). However, even though the findings may be limited to the sample from which they were collected, they are still valid for the group that generated the findings. In other words, the presence of flaws may limit the generalizability of any one particular research study. Subsequent research will either confirm the flawed finding or disprove it; that is the nature of science.

Preview of Coming Attractions

Early worries about the deleterious effects of violent media exposure on youth were based solely upon conjecture; science was nowhere to be found. Since those early days of public outcry against media violence, science has investigated the issue at great length. Those investigations suggest that the historical concern over violent media was not without merit. In the nascent years of media violence, critics of violent entertainment were prominent public figures, and public fears grew with the popularity of the new media.

Today, scientific researchers of violent entertainment focus on conceptual similarities between laboratory and real-life aggression and the generalizability of findings based upon those conceptual similarities.

In future chapters, different aspects of violent media consumption and concomitant effects will be addressed. However, in order to place those effects in an understandable framework, I will discuss patterns of developmentally normative aggressive behavior and the theoretical reasons for the negative impact of violent media on those normative patterns. To that end, it is important to operationalize the ages associated with the periods of development that will frequently be referred to throughout the book: early childhood, middle childhood, early adolescence, middle adolescence, and late adolescence. Early childhood (i.e., the preschool years) occurs between the ages of 3 and 5. Children between 6 and 10 years of age are classified as being in middle childhood (i.e., the elementary school years). Early adolescence refers to youth ranging in age from 11 to 13. Fourteen- to sixteen-year-olds comprise middle adolescence, and youth 17 to 19 years of age are considered to be in late adolescence.

Recently, Jones (2002) has forwarded the argument that media violence has no deleterious effects and that such consumption is actually *good* for children and adolescents. That argument will be addressed in detail with an eye towards evaluating the supportive research. Violent entertainment in its various forms (e.g., movies, TV, video games, etc.) will be examined in subsequent chapters. In each of these chapters, the reader will get a sense of the research that has been conducted and the importance of the findings. Of note, hundreds of studies on media violence have been conducted over the years. As such, it is impossible to review or describe each of those studies. In choosing studies to review, I have attempted to find research that illustrates new points, has historical significance, uses increasingly interesting or sophisticated methodology, or provides fascinating empirical data. The goal of this book is not to review all of the research ever conducted on entertainment violence. Instead, the goal is to cover a large variety of effects associated with media violence exposure. Throughout each chapter, I will identify areas in which more research is needed due to errors of commission (e.g., methodological flaws) and omission (i.e., the research has yet to be done). Similarly, important methodological and developmental concepts will be discussed in the context of the research. Additional chapters will focus on public policy and legislation associated with access to media violence for children and adolescents. Near the end of the book, media violence is placed in context with other factors that increase the aggressive behavior in youth and the magnitude of the effects will be discussed. Finally, the last chapter will address a variety of effects on youth associated with nonviolent media consumption.

Summary

- Entertainment violence has been viewed as an evil influence for well over 100 years.
- The perceived threat of violent media increases as the popularity of the media grows.
- Empirical evidence was lacking in early assessments of violent entertainment.
- An understanding of the differences between violence, aggression, and aggression-related constructs is critical in the evaluation of the effects of violent media on youth.
- Different types of aggression include physical, verbal, relational, provoked, and unprovoked.
- The major categories of aggression-related constructs include aggressive emotions, aggressive personality characteristics, physiological factors associated with aggression, and aggressive thoughts.
- When studying youth, it is important to evaluate the effects of violent media consumption on both aggression and aggression-related constructs.
- Beyond media violence, factors internal and external to youth can impact aggression and aggression-related constructs.
- Common misconceptions regarding media violence were raised and addressed: media violence does not have to produce violence directly after consumption to affect youth, and laboratory research and real-life experiences are conceptually similar.
- A variety of methodological issues were introduced, including confederates, control, deception, external validity, extraneous variables, fatal flaws, generalizability, informed consent, and replication.
- The ages associated with early and middle childhood and early, middle, and late adolescence were identified.

2

Exposing the Beast Within

Aggressive Behavior Across Development

When all goes well, babies come into the world crying. You would cry too if your head was forcibly misshapen during birth, you entered a cold room without any clothes on after spending months in the hot-tub-like amniotic environment, and to top it all off, you no longer have your nutritional supplements delivered via womb service! After experiencing the trauma associated with being born, newborns cry. What newborns do not do is act aggressively. Newborns will not strike at or attempt to kick the doctor, nor will they flail their arms about in tantrum or hurl obscenities at the nurse; they cry. Consider now the 2-year-old child who attempts to stick a self-removed dirty diaper into the DVD player. You calmly say to your child, "Dirty diapers are for the waste basket, they are not for the DVD player." Wham, Slam, Bam. Your toddler is now in the middle of a full-blown temper tantrum, complete with the throwing of objects (including the dirty diaper) and several attempts at assault and battery. Should you take this child directly to therapy? The answer is no, because the aforementioned behaviors, including the throwing of a dirty diaper, are all within the realm of normative development.

Normative Development and Individual Variation

Before the impact of entertainment violence on children and adolescents can be addressed, it is important to have an understanding of what is considered to be *normative aggressive behavior* across development and what contributes to *individual variation* in aggressive behavior and aggression-related constructs. Normative aggressive behavior refers to the typical amount and type of aggressive behavior displayed at any point in time during childhood and adolescence, such as the age during which relational aggression is displayed the most. The average number of verbal outbursts or acts of physical aggression such as hitting, pushing, and shoving expected for 3-, 5-, and 7-year-olds reflects normative aggressive behavior. In contrast, individual variation refers to differences between youth on some aspect of development. For instance, children vary in the amount of physical aggression they typically exhibit. Whereas some children exhibit physical aggression daily (high physical aggressors), others rarely exhibit this type of aggressive behavior (low physical aggressors). Thus, whether a child is a high or a low physical aggressor is an example of individual variation. Typically, individual variation is calculated as a subcomponent of normative aggressive behavior. In other words, at any given age, the average of the identified levels of individual variation (such as high, medium, and low relational aggressors) becomes the average for that age group as a whole (i.e., normative development).

As it turns out, the normative development of, and the individual variation in, aggression are influenced by a variety of sources. Some of these sources are internal to the child whereas others are environmental. Development is influenced internally through biological factors such as genes and hormones. In contrast, development is affected externally through environmental influences such as parenting, peers, siblings, and the media (Shaffer, 2000). The manner in which genetic inheritance (i.e., nature) and the environment (i.e., nurture) influence development is referred to as the *nature vs. nurture* debate. Historically, it was believed that developmental outcomes (e.g., aggressive behavior) were determined *either* by nature or by nurture. That is to say, nature and nurture were not believed to be intertwined. Thus, an aggressive child was aggressive because of either nurture (e.g., parenting) or nature (e.g., genes), but not both. Today, most researchers believe that nature and nurture are inextricably intertwined. In general, it is believed that nature predisposes a child towards certain types of behavior but that ultimately the environment determines which behaviors are displayed and how often they are performed (Plomin, DeFries, McClearn, & Rutter, 1997). For instance, children may inherit genes that predispose them to have poor impulse control and quick tempers. However, whether or not children become aggressive will be determined by the environment. Children experiencing parenting replete with affection, sensitive care, and rational discipline will most likely learn to control their impulses and temper. In contrast, children who experience parenting that is overly hostile and uses irrational or rigidly enforced discipline will most likely be unable to control their temper or impulses (Baumrind, 1991).

Whereas, when frustrated, the latter child will act rashly and aggressively, the former child will calmly assess the situation and then determine whether or not aggression is necessary.

The Developmental Pathway
From Anger to Conflict to Aggression

As was previously illustrated, youth do not have the capability to act aggressively when they are born. Instead, aggressive behavior develops over the course of early childhood. Although there are individual differences in the onset of aggression, most children follow a developmental pathway that starts in infancy with anger and progresses into physical aggression during the toddler years. Subsequent to that, new forms of aggression develop, gender differences become prevalent, and the potential for, and enactment of, violent behavior is seen.

Anger

During the middle of the first year of life, children begin to express true anger (DeHart, Sroufe, & Cooper, 2004). For instance, when a toy inadvertently goes out of reach or is removed by an adult, 7-month-olds will display facial expressions characteristic of anger, in which they press their lips together and turn their eyebrows inwards (Stenberg, Campos, & Emde, 1983). In addition, vocalizations often accompany infant expressions of anger, but instead of using profanity like many adults, infants will growl or fuss (Kochanska, Coy, Tjebkes, & Husarek, 1998). From this point forward, angry outbursts continue to increase, ultimately peaking at the end of the toddler period or in the early preschool years (Coie & Dodge, 1998). During the toddler period, angry outbursts typically center on the possession of toys. As children enter the preschool years, however, angry outbursts also result from interpersonal issues, such as a perceived lack of fairness. Thus, the seeds for aggression are planted at a very early age, for one of the key contributors to aggressive behavior is anger (Anderson & Bushman, 2002). Although infants do not typically aggress with intent to harm, they do engage in conflicts.

Conflict

Conflict refers to those situations where two or more individuals have desires, needs, or goals that are incompatible with one another (Shaffer, 2000).

And by the end of the first year, infants have begun to engage in conflicts with other 1-year-olds. Similar to the events precipitating anger, most often these conflicts revolve around the possession or use of toys. For instance, Caplan, Vespo, Pedersen, and Hay (1991) found that if a toy was desired, 1-year-olds would forcefully attempt to take the toy away from another infant. Over-powering another child for a toy is an example of *instrumental aggression* (Shaffer, 2000). Instrumental aggression refers to a type of aggression in which the main goal is to obtain an object, space, or privilege *without* intending to harm another person. In the Caplan and colleagues (1991) study, such acts of instrumental aggression continued to be demonstrated by infants even when those infants were given the opportunity to play with an identical toy. However, instead of playing with an available toy that was not in use, infants chose to take the desired physically identical toy out of the hands of another child. Thus, the "value" of a toy appears to be in direct proportion to whether or not it is being used by another child.

Typically, infant conflicts are resolved when one child overpowers the other or an adult intervenes. By age 2, the rate of inter-toddler conflict is similar (if not higher) to that of the conflict rate for one-year-olds. In fact, in sibling relationships, once the younger siblings enter toddlerhood, conflicts (both minor and major) can occur at rates as high as one conflict per minute (Dunn, 1993). However, in addition to resolving conflicts with force, toddlers are frequently able to resolve toy-related conflicts through sharing and negotiation (Caplan et al., 1991; Shaffer, 2000). Thus, although conflict does not have to result in instrumental aggression, engaging in conflict increases the likelihood that instrumental aggression will occur.

Normative Aggression in Preschool

Between the ages of 3 and 5 significant changes take place in the aggressive lives of children. First and foremost, new forms of aggressive behavior begin to appear. For instance, in addition to engaging in instrumental aggression, children begin to aggress with the intent to harm, a type of aggression referred to as *hostile aggression*. That is to say, preschoolers will hurt other children because they *want* to hurt other children. Interestingly, the means by which children hurt other children change notably throughout this period. As children age, physical aggression becomes less common, but verbal and relational aggression onset and become more prevalent (Crick et al., 1999; Hartup, 1974). Thus, in place of hitting and biting, preschool children will tease, name call, and try to socially isolate their peers. However, children have fewer confrontations overall at the end of the preschool period than they had at the beginning of it (Shaffer, 2000).

As children age, the perceived provocation that leads to acts of aggression changes. At the end of the toddler years and into early preschool, children are more likely to aggress against a parent asserting authority than against other children. For instance, the turning off of a television set or a refusal to let a child have a second fruit snack may result in a series of punches and kicks. However, by the end of the preschool period, children are more likely to aggress after engaging in a conflict with peers or siblings than against parents. Children will still aggress against their parents; it is just that the frequency of peer-related aggression has outpaced that of parent-related aggression (Shaffer, 2000).

Normative Aggression in Grade School

Consistent with the trend that began in preschool, as children enter grade school, the general amount of physical aggression engaged in continues to decline. However, when aggression does occur, it is more likely to be hostile in nature, rather than instrumental. Furthermore, demonstrating continuity across time, the proportion of acts of aggression that involve taunts, teasing, and social isolation continues to increase during the grade-school years (Crick et al., 1999; Hartup, 1974). *Indirect aggression* increases throughout childhood as well (Tremblay et al., 1996). Indirect aggression refers to aggressive behavior that involves an attempt to harm another child, but without a face-to-face encounter. For instance, spreading nasty rumors about another child's hygiene (a form of relational aggression) would be an example of indirect aggression, whereas telling that same child in front of friends that he or she smells (another form of relational aggression) would not.

In contrast to the preschool years however, grade-school children are more likely to act aggressively in response to a threat to the *sense of self*. The sense of self refers to an individual's beliefs about who one is, what one likes, what one is skilled at, and any learned behaviors that make one feel good about the self (Fiske & Taylor, 1991). For example, after losing a foot race and being called a "loser," a child may hit the provocateur. The combination of losing the race and being teased inflicts pain on the child's sense of self. In turn, in order to protect the "threatened" sense of self, the child may engage in *retaliatory aggression*. Retaliatory aggression refers to aggressive behavior that occurs as a result of a real or perceived threat. Whereas a "real" threat consists of a physical attack (e.g., getting hit) or a verbal threat of attack (e.g., "I'm going to pound you"), a perceived threat refers to the child's *interpretation* of the situation as threatening, regardless of whether or not there is a true threat present. In fact, the situation may not involve a threat at all. Consider the following situation: after losing a foot race, an 8-year-old boy looks at the victor and sees a smile on her face. The boy then interprets the girl's smile as a taunt, and therefore considers it to be a threat to his sense of self. The boy then teases the girl in retaliation against this perceived attack. Not only does retaliatory aggression increase across the grade-school years, but it is consistently viewed by most children as an *appropriate* response to an attack (Sancilio, Plumert, & Hartup, 1989).

Normative Aggression in Adolescence

Adolescence provides an interesting paradox with regard to aggression and violent behavior. Although actual physical aggression (e.g., fighting), parent-teen conflict, and relational aggression peak early in adolescence and then decrease as individuals enter late adolescence, the incidence of *violent* behaviors increases throughout adolescence (Loeber & Stouthamer-Loeber, 1998; Steinberg, 2001). In fact, recent research has found that nearly 30% to 40% of adolescent males and 16% to 32% of adolescent females report having committed a serious violent offense (e.g., assault, robbery, gang fights) by the age of 17 (U.S. Department of Health and Human Services, 2001). It should be noted, however, that although hundreds of thousands of acts of violence are perpetrated yearly by adolescents, the vast majority of adolescents are nonviolent. Unfortunately, instead of lauding the positive contributions that teens make to society, the headlines focus on these serious offenses, giving the *impression* that today's youth are out of control.

Interestingly, there is one significant change that occurs as youth enter adolescence: when acts of aggression or violence occur, they increasingly involve the collective actions of a group of adolescents. For instance, a group of boys may bully a younger peer into giving up his lunch money, or a group of girls may tease and humiliate another girl because of her choice of clothing. Collective aggression becomes even more organized and dangerous when adolescents become members of gangs, a phenomenon that also begins early in adolescence (Loeber & Hay, 1997). Yet it is adolescent school shooters, acting alone (e.g., Kip Kinkel, Springfield, OR) or in pairs (e.g., Eric Harris and Dylon Klebold, Littleton, CO) who worry parents and teens the most.

School Shooters

In 1998, there were approximately 18 million incidents of bullying, 1.5 million fights, 260,000 serious injuries, and 35 deaths in American schools (see Gentile, 2003). Although bullying is far more prevalent and can have a significant and negative impact on the psychological well-being of youth, it is the heinous and deadly nature of school shootings that creates the image that teens are increasingly violent. Additionally, similarities between the crimes committed and the content of violent media enhance the idea that media violence is one of the primary contributors to the teens' violent and deadly actions. For instance, Klebold and Harris were known for wearing long black trench coats similar to the one worn by Keanu Reeves's character "Neo" in *The Matrix*. Furthermore, the Columbine killers murdered their classmates in a manner similar to a fantasy scene depicted in the Leonardo DiCaprio film *The Basketball Diaries*. In response to these atrocities, many schools have imposed *zero tolerance* policies regarding threats against other students.

Zero tolerance policies typically state that *all* violations of a policy, regardless of their severity, result in the same punishment. For instance, under zero tolerance policies, bringing a squirt gun to school will result in the same punishment as bringing a loaded semi-automatic assault rifle to school. The following is the actual zero tolerance policy for "Threats/ Assaults Upon Students and Employees" as defined by one school district located near Pittsburgh, PA.

> The Board of School Directors advises all persons that it views very seriously threats directed to and/or assaults upon students and employees of the School District, and that the Board of School Directors has no tolerance for threats and/or physical attacks directed toward its students and employees, regardless of the source of the threat.

However, because of the vagueness of such policies (e.g., there is no definition of the word "threat") and the fact that zero tolerance policies mandate expulsions or suspensions if violated, nonviolent youth have been removed from schools for actions that many people would not necessarily perceive as threatening. For instance, 14-year-old Rachel Boim was expelled from school after a story written in her private journal was read by her teacher. The story was considered "threatening" because a character in the story dreams about shooting her math teacher.

Assessing Threats Made by Youth

To help thwart future school shootings while at the same time preventing administrators from overreacting to creative writing assignments involving adolescent angst, the FBI created a *threat assessment procedure*. This procedure helps educators, mental health professionals, and law enforcement officers evaluate the seriousness of identified threats made to one or more individuals at school.

Threat assessment procedures are meant to identify the credibility and seriousness of threats, the intent and motivation of the threatener, and the availability of weapons to carry out threats. Such assessments do not create a "profile" of the typical school shooter because no such profile exists. At times, school shooters have acted alone; at other times, they have acted in pairs; some school shooters were loners whereas others were not; and revenge was a motivating force in some school shootings but not others. In fact, the FBI has concluded that there is no single profile of a school shooter that would help identify future school shooters. Furthermore, the FBI discourages the profiling of adolescents, as checklists of behaviors tend to result in ascribing the labels of "dangerous" or "disturbed" to students when such labels are not typically warranted. According to the FBI, the credibility and seriousness of threats can be subdivided into three levels of risk: *low level of threat, medium level of threat,* and *high level of threat.*

Low-level threats are unrealistic, vague, indirect, and contain inconsistent, implausible, or missing details. The likelihood of carrying out such threats is perceived to be low. An example of a low-level threat would be an e-mail stating, "You're a dead man!" Medium-level threats are more detailed than low-level threats, in that they provide a general indication of a time and place (e.g., "Next week after band practice, you're dead."), refer to violent books or movies to indicate purpose (e.g., "I'm going to pull a *Matrix* on your butt!"), suggest that preparatory steps have been taken (e.g., "I know where I can get a gun!"), and contain a specific statement of purpose (e.g., "I'm not kidding, I really mean this!"). Finally, high-level threats are direct, specific, and plausible. Furthermore, the threat details the steps that have been undertaken, thereby increasing the credibility of the threat and the likelihood that it will be carried out. An example of a high-level threat is as follows: "Tomorrow, at 10 a.m., I'm going to shoot my math teacher right as he's leaving the faculty lounge. I stole a gun from my dad's collection and have been shooting squirrels in the woods with it. I'm going to teach him about what happens when you give me an F."

After a threat has been made and the level of risk is identified, the threat is then evaluated in terms of four "prongs." These prongs represent factors that influence the intent and motivation of a threatener: *personality traits and behaviors, family dynamics, school dynamics,* and *social dynamics.* Personality traits and behaviors refer to those characteristics and actions that are associated with violence. The FBI lists 28 traits and behaviors, including poor coping skills, low tolerance for frustration, lack of resiliency, failed love relationships, depression, alienation, narcissism, feelings of injustice, dehumanizing others, lack of empathy, sense of entitlement, attitude of superiority, exaggerated need for attention, blaming of others for failings and shortcomings, anger management problems, intolerance, inappropriate humor, manipulation of others, lack of trust, closed social groups, changes in behavior, rigid and opinionated, unusual interest in sensational violence, negative role models, behaviors relevant to carrying out a threat (e.g., practicing with firearms), and leakage (e.g., clues to violent fantasies or intentions revealed in writings, drawings, and words). Additionally, a fascination with *violence-filled entertainment* is listed. Repeated watching of a violent movie, repetitive play of violent video games (with a primary focus on the violence and not the winning of the game), constant reading of material with themes of violence and hatred, and surfing the Internet for violence-related sites all reflect a fascination with violent imagery. As you can see from this list, the traits and behaviors listed describe many adolescents, even nonviolent ones. Therefore, it is important to remember that such traits are (1) evaluated only *after* a threat has been made, and (2) evaluated in connection with the other three prongs.

The prong "family dynamics" refers to identifiable problems within the family system (e.g., parent-child relationship, sibling relationships). These problems include turbulent relationships with parents, a lack of family intimacy, acceptance of unusual behaviors as normal (e.g., extreme fascination with death is considered "typical" for an adolescent), access to weapons, lack of parental involvement (e.g., the adolescent has an inordinate amount of privacy and the parents have no idea what their child is doing), and few limits on conduct (with no consequences for rule violations). Additionally, this prong includes problems related to parental monitoring of their children's media use (e.g., TV and Internet), such as the amount of, or quality of, media consumed.

The school dynamics prong refers to the student's self-perception of the role that one plays in the school culture. This prong focuses on the adolescent's level of detachment from the school (and concomitant detachment from students, teachers, and activities). Additionally, included in this prong are the student's perceptions of (1) the school's tolerance for disrespectful behavior; (2) the adequacy of discipline imposed for infractions; (3) the school culture with regard to behaviors, values, and relationships; (4) the treatment of students in high- versus low-prestige groups; and (5) the level of perceived safety in confiding in teachers regarding the behavior of other students. Finally, the level of unsupervised computer access (often used to play violent video games and surf the Internet for hate group material) constitutes the last component of this prong.

The final prong used to evaluate adolescent threats against others, "social dynamics," addresses broad social influences that adolescents encounter. The adolescent's general access to media and entertainment technology; the

Table 2.1   FBI Threat Assessment Procedure

Aspect	Descriptor
Types of Threat Identified	
Low	Unrealistic, vague, and indirect
	Inconsistent, implausible, and lacking in detail
Medium	Indicates time and place
	Refers to violent books or movies
	Suggests that preparatory steps have been taken
	Contains a specific statement of purpose
High	Direct, specific, and plausible
	Details the steps that have been undertaken
Threat Evaluation Prongs	
Personality and Behavior	Personal characteristics and behaviors that are associated with violence
Family Dynamics	Identifiable problems within the family system
School Dynamics	Student's self-perception of the role that one plays in the school culture
Social Dynamics	Broad social influences that adolescents encounter

level of fascination of the adolescent's peer group with violence, hate, and extreme beliefs; general attitudes towards and use of drugs (and recent changes to those); the level of interest in activities outside school; and recent media coverage of violence that could result in adolescents mimicking those acts (typically referred to as "copy-cat" crimes) are all subsumed in this prong.

According to the FBI, students who demonstrate problems in each of the four prongs mentioned above may have the motivation to carry out the threat. However, the FBI also states that beyond motivation, such youth may already have begun the process of carrying out the threat (e.g., procuring a weapon), or, at the very least, they may have begun to fantasize about acting out the threat. (See Table 2.1 for a summary of the FBI Threat Assessment Procedure.)

Evaluating Current Threat Assessment Procedures

There are several aspects of threat assessment that need to be addressed. First, the threshold for determining the critical number of personality and behavioral characteristics (in each of the four prongs) that will predict extreme violence is not defined. Therefore, the policy could be implemented differently in different locations. Second, threat assessments are not diagnostic of future violence. According to the FBI criteria, after reaching some undefined critical level, adolescents may act violently or they may simply be fantasizing about violent actions, with no real intent to harm. Finally, although violent media exposure is listed as a criterion in each prong, violent media exposure is only one of many factors used to determine the intent and motivation of the threatener.

Singling out violent media because of similarities between real-life acts of violence and acts of violence portrayed in the media oversimplifies the problem of school shootings. Moreover, by focusing on media violence alone, attention is diverted away from issues that may be of greater importance, such as peer rejection, parent-child relationships, and mental illness. Media violence is one of many influences on adolescent behavior, but it is generally *not* thought of as causative of extreme violence (Gentile & Anderson, 2003).

Correlation

In order to investigate patterns of aggression throughout development, researchers have relied heavily on a statistical tool called *correlation*. Correlation is a statistical procedure that mathematically determines how two variables are empirically related to each other. In other words, correlation assesses the degree to which two different variables fluctuate together, if at all. For instance, recent research has shown that increases in the stork population near the German city of Berlin (variable #1) are associated with increases in out-of-hospital deliveries (variable #2; Hofer, Przyrembel, & Verleger, 2004). Because both variables (i.e., stork population and birth rates) fluctuate in the same direction, the relationship is defined as a *positive correlation*. In contrast, when one variable increases and the other variable decreases, the relationship is defined as a *negative correlation*. For instance, the association between maternal smoking during pregnancy and the newborn's birth weight represents a negative correlation, in that increases in maternal smoking are associated with decreases in newborns' weight at birth (Kirchengast & Hartmann, 2003).

In addition to providing the directionality of the effect (i.e., positive or negative), correlational analyses also provide a number that describes how strongly the two variables are related. This number is referred to as the *correlation coefficient*. When there is no relationship at all between two variables, the correlation coefficient is zero. That is to say, a change in one variable is unrelated to a change in the other variable. Any relationship greater than zero but less than or equal to +1 describes a positive correlation. For a negative correlation, the correlation coefficient ranges somewhere between 0 and −1. The strongest positive correlation is +1 and the strongest negative correlation is −1. Additionally, the closer the correlation coefficient is to +1 or −1, the more consistently the two variables change together. For instance, consider the hypothetical situation based on a sample of 20 media violence students, in which a positive correlation exists between beer consumption and pizza consumption. If, for each student, the number of slices eaten matched the number of beers downed, then a perfect +1 correlation would be found. However, if the majority of students eat one slice per beer, but several students eat pizza without drinking beer and a few others drink more beer than they eat pizza, then the correlation coefficient will fall somewhere between 0 and +1. Furthermore, the strength of a correlation coefficient is determined by the absolute value of the number. So, a correlation of .5 is equal in strength to a correlation of −.5, and both of these correlations are weaker than correlations of −.75 or .75. Finally, correlation coefficients (and their absolute values) ranging from 0 to .2 are considered *slight*; coefficients ranging from .2 to .4 are considered *small*; coefficients ranging from .4 to .7 are considered *moderate*; and coefficients ranging from .7 to 1 are considered *large* (Guilford, 1956).

Correlation Is Not Causation

Of utmost importance when interpreting correlations is the issue of causality. Just because two variables are correlated does not mean that one variable *causes* a change in the other variable. Storks do not bring babies, no matter how strong the correlation is. In order to establish a cause and effect relationship, it becomes necessary to demonstrate that event A (pushing a child) preceded event B (child falls down). Correlational analyses tell us nothing about the time ordering of events. Instead, people artificially impose a time order to the events in order to interpret the findings in a manner that makes the most sense. For instance, eating chocolate is positively correlated with weight gain. It makes sense to assume that the sequencing of events is as follows: eating chocolate (event A) followed by weight gain (event B). However, when assessed through a correlation, it is equally likely that the weight gain preceded eating chocolate. A person might think to himself, for example, "I might as well eat what I like, since I'm getting fat anyways."

Furthermore, for any observed correlation, an unseen and unmeasured third variable could account for the mathematical relationship between the two variables—a situation commonly referred to as the *third variable problem*. Take, for example, the relationship between chocolate consumption and weight gain. It is possible that a medical condition (such as hyperphagia, which is characterized by excessive eating) could account for the increase in chocolate consumption and the concomitant weight gain.

Associations among variables that are, in fact, *not* causally linked are referred to as *spurious correlations*. The third variable problem is one of the most common causes of spurious correlations. The difficulty in using correlations to establish cause and effect relationships is that time ordering and the third variable problem *always* leave open the possibility that the relationship identified in the correlation is spurious in nature. However, correlations are valuable in that they help identify areas of research that need to be investigated in order to discover causal relationships. Furthermore, with each successive study, more and more potential third variables can be eliminated as a source of the relationship. In summary, correlations can help identify and describe relationships between variables, but they cannot provide causal explanations for that relationship with total certainty.

Individual Variation in Aggressive Behavior

Loeber and Hay (1997) have identified four distinct patterns relating to the onset and stability of aggressive behavior throughout childhood and adolescence: *desisting, stabilizing, escalating,* and *onsetting*. For stabilizing youth, the level of aggressive behavior displayed remains consistent across time; for desisting youth, aggressive behavior decreases during childhood and adolescence; for escalating youth, aggressive behavior increases in frequency and severity, ultimately resulting in violent behavior; and for onsetting youth, previously nonaggressive children become noticeably more aggressive and violent adolescents.

Desisting

As previously stated, for most children the amount of physical aggression displayed decreases throughout childhood and adolescence (Loeber & Hay, 1997). However, children who frequently get into fights with other children in childhood are actually more likely during early adolescence to desist in fighting than to maintain the same high level of fighting (McCord, 1983). Thus, the general pattern of desistance that is apparent for the average child is also present for physically aggressive youth. It should be noted, however, that not all forms of aggressive behavior desist across childhood.

In fact, relational aggression and other forms of indirect aggression tend to increase over time. Indirect aggression is a more socially acceptable form of aggressive behavior than is physical aggression. Children are told that "sticks and stones can break my bones but names can never hurt me." In essence, the onus is placed on the victim to cope with being indirectly aggressed against as opposed to placing blame on the aggressor. In contrast, when a child is physically aggressive, the aggressor is chastised for his or her behavior and support is given to the victim. Additionally, the punishments handed out for indirect aggression are far less serious than those handed out for physical aggression. Furthermore, the increasing verbal and cognitive abilities of older children and adolescents make indirect aggression a more viable means of hurting another person than when they were younger.

Stabilizing

Over the last 25 years, numerous studies have correlated the amount of aggressive behavior displayed at one point during childhood with aggressive behavior displayed at later points of development. Consistently, the correlations produced from such assessments are in the moderate to strong range (e.g., .40 to .77), with a general pattern of stronger correlations appearing as children get older (Olweus, 1979; Van Beijsterveldt, Bartels, Hudziak, & Boomsma, 2003). For instance, Van Beijsterveldt and colleagues found that the correlational stability of aggressive behavior between 4 and 7 years of age was .40 but that the stability of aggressive behavior increased between ages 7 and 12 to .66. Thus, as children age, there is a greater likelihood that the level (low vs. high) of aggressive behavior currently displayed will remain the same.

However, these data need to be qualified and interpreted in the context of desisting. Remember, aggressive behavior is desisting for most children from childhood through adolescence. Thus, it is the relative *rank ordering* of children in terms of their aggressive behavior that remains stable. Rank ordering refers to the process by which children are ranked from low to high (or vice versa) on some behavior. In comparison to their peers, children ranked as highly aggressive at age 6 are likely to be ranked as highly aggressive children at age 15. However, the total amount of aggressive behavior displayed for these "highly aggressive" youth (as well as for "low aggressors") has actually decreased across time. Finally, it should be noted that within the realm of normative development, most aggressive children do not become aggressive adults (Robins, 1978).

Escalating

For many adults, acts of violence (e.g., shooting, stabbings) were preceded by years of aggressive behavior during childhood and adolescence that, over time, became incrementally more and more severe. In fact, the pathway to violence in adulthood appears to start in childhood with seemingly mild forms of aggression, such as purposely engaging in annoying behavior. However, without intervention, more severe forms of aggression may soon follow, such as bullying of peers. Bullying may escalate into frequent bouts of physical fighting, and, subsequently, the possibility of joining a gang and engaging in gang-related violence becomes more likely (Loeber & Hay, 1997). In fact, a study conducted in the late 1970s found that nearly 70% of 21-year-old violent felons had been rated as highly aggressive in early adolescence (Farrington, 1978).

In evaluating the association between early aggression and later violence, investigators made use of a methodological technique known as *postdiction*. Postdiction refers to identifying a group of participants characterized by a common attribute (in this case, violent felons) and tracing their behavior backwards though time. The problem with postdictional research is that it does not involve a random sample of participants (e.g., everyone in the sample is a known violent felon). As such, aggressive youth who did not commit violent crimes as adults, or aggressive youth who became violent adults but had yet to be caught, were not included in the sample. Thus, the strength of the association between early aggression and later violence could change dramatically depending upon how many of the aforementioned youth were omitted from the study.

Onsetting

Very little research exists regarding the onset of physical aggression late in adolescence in which there is no prior evidence of aggressive behavior during childhood. Furthermore, the research that has been conducted is limited to samples of boys and to violent adult male offenders who had been incarcerated. For instance, in an investigation of Canadian youth, Brame, Nagin, and Tremblay (2001) found that boys who were highly aggressive in childhood were more likely to continue to be highly aggressive in adolescence than were boys who engaged in lower levels of physical aggression in childhood. Thus, there is little evidence supporting the contention that late onset of high levels of physical aggression is commonplace (Brame et al., 2001). However, there is some evidence that late onset of violence is associated with certain personality characteristics. For instance, for a small proportion of men who had been jailed for violent crimes, there was no history of aggressive behavior during childhood and adolescence. In order for these men to act aggressively, the instigation needed to be of such intensity that it overrode their strong inhibitions to aggress (Blackburn, 1993). Furthermore, these late onset aggressors tended to be exposed to more life stress and have a higher incidence of psychopathology than nonaggressive adults (Windle & Windle, 1995). Similarly, many of the youth who have committed acts of violence in school (and afterward had their atrocities linked with media violence) had no prior history of aggressive behavior. However, the vast majority of these late onset violent youth were under extreme duress (typically from being bullied) and occasionally suffered from diagnosed psychopathology (Vossekuil, Fein, Reddy, Borum, & Modzeleski, 2002), just like the late onset incarcerated males.

Individual Patterns of Aggression as a Function of Violent Entertainment

The frequency and intensity of aggressive and violent behavior may remain stable, increase, or decrease throughout development. However, research on the relative impact of violent media exposure on these antisocial patterns of behaviors is limited. The studies that have been conducted suggest that exposure to violent media early in life is a precursor to increased aggressive behavior later in life (Anderson, Berkowitz, et al., 2003). For instance, Anderson and colleagues summarize several research studies indicating that high levels of media violence consumption, such as watching violent TV in childhood, was linked with increased levels of aggressive behavior in adolescence. These findings remain statistically significant even after taking into consideration the fact that highly aggressive children and adolescents like violent media more than do less aggressive youth. So, the findings cannot simply be explained away as a spurious correlation based on the fact that aggressive youth do and like aggressive things. Although this research is compelling in its demonstration that media violence consumption contributes to an escalation of aggressive behavior, the research was primarily designed to identify overarching links between media violence and escalation in aggressive behavior through positive correlations. Subgroups of children who desisted, stabilized, or had a late onset of aggression were not looked at separately from the other children. As such, it is difficult to know whether media violence affected these children differently than the children for whom a positive correlation between media violence and aggressive behavior was identified. Thus, future research should take into consideration individual differences in patterns of aggressive behavior throughout development and assess the relative impact of media violence on those patterns.

Sex Differences in Aggressive Behavior Across Development

"Girls are made of sugar and spice and everything nice," or so the saying goes. But as many little brothers will tell you, and as recent research suggests, some of the nastiest sibling interactions are perpetrated by older sisters against their younger brothers. Are these sibling-related aggressive acts artifacts of watching the animated television program *The Powerpuff Girls,* in which three sisters use their superhero powers to beat up primarily male adversaries, such as the Rowdyruff Boys? Possibly, but it should be pointed out that while the Powerpuff Girls primarily use physical aggression to destroy their enemies, older sisters tend to use relational aggression against their younger brothers (DeHart, personal communication). In fact, from the preschool years on, girls are more likely than boys to antagonize others using verbal aggression, indirect aggression, and relational aggression. In contrast, as early as the toddler period, boys are more likely than girls to aggress against others in a physical manner, a pattern that remains constant throughout childhood and adolescence (Leschied, Cummings, Van Brunschot, Cunningham, & Saunders, 2000).

Sex Differences in Aggression and Violent Entertainment

Consistently, research has shown that boys and girls differ in the frequency of physical and relational aggression displayed, as well as the primary mode of aggressing, with boys more likely to act physically aggressive and girls more likely to act relationally aggressive over time. However, the fact that boys and girls typically use different forms of aggression is significant in that the majority of studies assessing the impact of entertainment violence on youth aggression use physical aggression as the dependent variable. Although few gender differences are found in terms of the effects of violent media on physical aggression (Anderson, Berkowitz, et al., 2003), most studies have failed to assess indirect forms of aggression. Interestingly, one of the few studies conducted that used both physical and indirect forms of aggression as the dependent variables found that whereas early media violence exposure affected males primarily on the dimension of physical aggression, for females, early media violence was primarily related to indirect aggression (i.e., nonphysical; Huesmann, Moise-Titus, Podolski, & Eron, 2003). Perhaps media violence has the greatest impact on the type of aggressive behavior that a person uses the most (e.g., physical, verbal, relational), regardless of the nature of the aggressive and violent content observed.

Why should we expect to see violent media displaying one form of aggression (e.g., physically aggressive Powerpuff Girls) affect a different, and non-depicted, type of aggressive behavior (e.g., relationally aggressive older sisters)? According to Bushman (1998), exposure to media violence can activate associations among aggressive thoughts, aggressive memories, provocational stimuli, potential responses to provocations, and concomitant emotions. Importantly, the content of the aggressive stimuli (e.g., hitting, kicking) involved in activating linked associations does not have to be related to the observed aggressive behavior (e.g., threat, gossiping) because once aggressive associations are activated, the likelihood of any type of aggressive behavior occurring increases. Therefore, the choice of which type of aggression to enact is left up to the individual. For boys, the aggressive behavior of choice is often physical in nature, whereas for girls relational and indirect forms of aggression are typically performed.

Aggressive Behavior in the Context of Development

As the previous review illustrates, aggressive behavior does not develop in a linear pattern with ever-increasing amounts of aggression. In contrast, the levels of aggression go through a series of peaks and valleys, each of which coincides with the *developmental tasks* associated with that age group. Developmental tasks refer to challenges that must be met in order for development to proceed normally (Gentile & Sesma, 2003). The tasks that toddlers are faced with include establishing autonomy from caregivers and independently exploring their world. The emergence of behavioral and emotional self-control and compliance to the commands of others are developmental tasks that are not typically mastered until the early preschool years. As such, toddlers display more aggression than any other age group (DeHart et al., 2004). Then, in response to learning that aggressive behavior is punished, children learn to control their impulses; as a result, aggression decreases. The increase in aggressive behavior in early adolescence coincides with a series of psychosocial and behavioral changes experienced by adolescents. Specifically, early adolescents are faced with developmental tasks surrounding changes in the parent-child relationships, a surge and need for independence, pubertal changes that affect emotionality (e.g., emotional reactivity) as well as physiology, and school-related changes. Furthermore, early adolescents cognitively respond to these new challenges using the emotion centers of their brains more so than the cognitive centers. As such, a second peak in aggressive behavior occurs during this stage, as early adolescents tend to respond with emotions (which at times increase the likelihood of aggressive behavior) but with limited amounts of impulse control and cognitive intervention. However, with development, cognition supercedes emotion, impulse control is stabilized, and adolescents adapt to their new physiology, social relationships, and environment. Consequently, normative aggression decreases throughout the teen years and into early adulthood.

Developmental Tasks and Violent Entertainment

It becomes clear that when viewed in the context of developmental tasks, youth aggression is influenced by the challenges of dealing with new physical, psychological, and social aspects of development. What is less clear, however, is whether violent media has varying effects (i.e., more or less deleterious) on youth at different points in development. Gentile (2003) argues that media violence should impact children and adolescents differently depending on their current developmental tasks. For instance, when faced with the developmental task of controlling impulses, playing violent video games may reduce impulse control as many violent games require quick decisions and random firing of guns. However, others have suggested that media violence does not impact youth any differently than it impacts adults. In fact, current research supports the contention that media violence does not impact children any differently than it impacts adults or adolescents. It is important to remember, however, that a lack of evidence for developmental differences does not mean that violent media exposure is *good* for youth. Instead, it may be that the negative consequences associated with violent media consumption do not vary by age; they are equally bad for everyone.

Despite the fact that Gentile's argument makes theoretical sense, there is currently little empirical evidence to support his contention. One reason for the lack of consistency between theory and empirical findings may be that the theory is incorrect. That is to say, media violence effects may not vary as a function of developmental task. Along with theoretical failings, however, methodological reasons might explain why few media violence–related effects are evident across development. For instance, it may be that there *are* differences across development; it is just that the findings are very subtle and that the current methods used are not designed to detect the differences.

If this were true, then it may be that the findings are not *robust*. Findings that are robust occur across a wide range of conditions and assessment protocols and, therefore, are not affected by idiosyncratic details. Second, it may be that researchers have not identified and researched the domains for which real developmental differences appear. Additionally, it may be that research attempting to find developmental differences has used samples with an insufficient number of participants necessary to detect the differences. In other words, many of the research studies conducted lack the *statistical power* necessary to detect a difference. Statistical power refers to the ability to detect an effect when an effect actually exists. More research, conducted with sufficiently large samples, is needed to help clarify this issue.

Excessive Aggression in Youth

At times, children do not have the capability or resources to cope with the daily challenges and developmental tasks they face. When such failings occur frequently, children's behavior may no longer fall within the normal range associated with their age group and gender, resulting in the characterization of their behavior as "abnormal." According to Moeller (2001), there are both *qualitative* and *quantitative* differences between "normal" and "abnormal" forms of aggression. Qualitative differences are variations in the characteristics or qualities of something (e.g., the physical characteristics of a caterpillar are different from the physical characteristics of a butterfly). When abnormal aggression is qualitatively different, the qualities of the aggressive behavior deviate significantly from their peers. For instance, whereas it is normal for an adolescent to swear or get into a fight, it would be considered qualitatively different and abnormal to torture a pet or set fires. Similarly, school shootings are considered abnormal because they are qualitatively different from the types of aggression typically displayed by adolescents.

Quantitative differences, on the other hand, refer to differences in the amount of something (e.g., the characteristics of a small snowball and a large snowball are identical, in that both are round; they simply differ in terms of the amount of snow). With regard to excessive aggression, quantitative differences occur when the frequency of aggressive behavior outpaces the frequency of aggressive behavior that is considered to be developmentally appropriate. It is important to remember that in defining abnormal aggression, both qualitative and quantitative differences are contrasted with behavior that is considered to be normal for a particular age group and gender. Thus, what is considered to be normal for a 13-year-old (e.g., relational aggression) could be considered abnormal for a 2-year-old (e.g., relational aggression). Similarly, what is considered developmentally appropriate for boys of a particular age (e.g., physical aggression) may be considered abnormal for same-aged girls.

Additionally, abnormal aggression, more so than normative aggression, negatively impacts the lives of youth in three distinct ways. First, abnormal aggression tends to interfere with children's ability to cope with developmental tasks that are unrelated to the management of aggression. For instance, children who display quantitatively more aggression than normal children (i.e., hyper-aggressive youth) tend to have difficulty interacting with their peers and engaging in appropriate behavior (i.e., nonviolent) in other social settings. In this case, hyper-aggressiveness would interfere with the developmental task of establishing intimate peer relationships. Secondly, abnormal levels of aggression can negatively impact the behavior of others. For instance, a child seated next to a hyper-aggressive youth in school may have difficulty focusing on schoolwork, either due to having become a victim or fearing that he or she will be victimized. Finally, in addition to affecting the behavior of others, hyper-aggressive youth may negatively impact others by destroying or damaging their property (Moeller, 2001).

Aggression and Developmental Psychopathology

Excessive aggression in childhood and adolescence is characteristic of a group of children who suffer from a class of psychological disorders (i.e., psychopathology) known as *disruptive behavior disorders* (DBD). Approximately 5% of school-aged children suffer from DBD (American Psychiatric Association, 1994). Subclassifications within this disorder include Conduct Disorder (CD), Oppositional Deviant Disorder (ODD), and Attention Deficit Disorder (ADD). Youth suffering from ODD demonstrate a pattern of behavior replete with defiance, disobedience, and hostility towards authority figures. Children and adolescents with CD continually violate societal norms and the rights of others through the destruction of property and aggression towards people and animals. Finally, ADD involves a long-standing pattern of inattention, impulsivity, and hyperactivity. Although aggression is not necessarily characteristic of these youth, their significant lack of impulse control often results in aggressive behavior (Moeller, 2001).

Developmental Psychopathology and Entertainment Violence

For about 5% of the children, aggressive behavior is enacted due to the presence of psychopathological conditions such as DBD. In subsequent chapters, the specific effects that *different* types of violent media have on children and adolescents will be addressed. In contrast, the focus here is to assess whether violent media in general have different effects on children suffering from DBD in comparison to non-diagnosed youth. Very few studies have investigated this important issue. However, the limited amount of evidence that does exist suggests that those suffering from psychopathology are affected to a *greater* extent by violent images than those not suffering from DBD. For instance, Grimes, Vernberg, and Cathers (1997) found that after watching 45-second clips of violent acts taken from one of three different movies (*Regarding Henry, In the Line of Fire,* and *Grand Canyon*), 8- to 11-year-old youth with DBD endorsed the appropriateness of the portrayed violence more so than did the non-disordered children. Furthermore, DBD-diagnosed children reported being *less* emotionally affected by the witnessed violence than did the group of children without a DBD diagnosis. Similarly, Grimes, Bergen, Nichols, Bernberg, and Fonagy (2004) found that after watching the aforementioned movie clips, 8- to 12- year-old boys with DBD were less physiologically aroused (e.g., skin conductance, heart rate, respiration) than were youth without DBD. Moreover, the DBD-disordered group manifested more facial expressions of anger while watching the violent clips than did the non-disordered group.

When these findings are looked at together, Grimes et al. contend that youth diagnosed with DBD are far more susceptible to the negative effects of consuming violent media than are psychologically normal children. In order to understand why this is the case, the concepts of *behavioral inhibition* and *behavioral activation systems* need to be introduced. The behavioral inhibition system generates feelings of anxiety (often indicated by high physiological arousal) in certain situations, such as those involving fear, non-reward (i.e., a behavior is not rewarded), and punishment. Thus, when individuals think about acting aggressively, the behavioral inhibition system increases the feelings of anxiety surrounding the aggressive course of action. As such, the individual is less likely to act aggressively due to the anxiety caused by the negative consequences associated with the potential aggressive act. For instance, the anxiety associated with "being grounded" for hitting another child helps prevent that child from acting aggressively.

In addition to activating the behavioral inhibition system, Grimes and colleagues posit that violent imagery activates the behavioral activation system. However, in contrast to the behavioral inhibition system, the *behavioral activation system* increases the likelihood that aggressive behavior will occur after perceiving *cues* of reward and non-punishment (i.e., a behavior is not punished). For instance, after witnessing a television character praised for hitting a peer, a young boy acts by hitting his sister after she teases him.

The findings of Grimes and colleagues (2004) can now be placed in the proper perspective. For both psychologically normal and DBD-diagnosed youth, violent media may activate the behavioral activation system, thus increasing the likelihood that these youth will act aggressively. However, the violent imagery also activates the behavioral inhibition system in psychologically normal youth, thus putting the brakes on aggressive behavior, reducing the likelihood that aggression will occur. In contrast, the behavioral inhibition system is not activated in youth with a DBD diagnosis, as evidenced by the fact that DBD-diagnosed children and adolescents express anger when watching violent media but are not physiologically aroused by it. Furthermore, because DBD-diagnosed youth are more likely than psychologically normal youth to value the use of aggression to solve problems and because they function without the fear of consequences associated with aggressive acts (generated by the behavioral inhibition system), violent imagery may have greater putative effects on DBD-diagnosed youth than non-diagnosed youth. However, it is important to remember that psychologically normal children do experience negative effects after consuming violent media—effects that happen to be of a lesser magnitude than for DBD youth, but effects that are present, nonetheless.

In addition to demonstrating quantitative differences in response to violent media, it is important to note that youth with psychopathology also prefer violent media more than do children without psychopathology (Dorr & Kovaric, 1980). Funk et al. (2002) suggest that the preference for violent media and the concomitant effects of violent media exposure are examples of *bidirectional effects*. Bidirectional effects refer to situations in which environments affect individuals (e.g., increase aggression) *but* personal characteristics (e.g., psychopathology) cause individuals to prefer and seek out the environments (e.g., violent media) that are causing the negative effects. Thus, as Funk et al. suggest, violent media consumption may be a "high risk" activity for youth with psychopathology. Importantly, it needs to be stated that there is *no* evidence to suggest that violent media cause children and adolescents to develop psychopathology (Grimes et al., 2004).

Summary

- The concepts of normative aggression and individual variation in aggression were introduced.
- During infancy and toddlerhood, anger and conflict precede aggression.
- Instrumental aggression is typically the first form of aggression that children display, an accomplishment that occurs in infancy.
- During the preschool period, hostile aggression commences and indirect aggression begins to replace physical aggression, a trend that will continue throughout childhood.
- In grade school, perceived threats to the sense of self can induce aggressive responding, and retaliatory aggression becomes acceptable.
- Aggressive behavior peaks in early adolescence and then declines. Violent behavior increases across adolescence, but most adolescents are nonviolent.
- In response to bullying behavior and school shootings, "zero tolerance policies" have been instituted across the country. However, many of the policies are vague and treat rather innocuous behavior as having the same level of severity as extremely violent behavior.
- The FBI has developed a threat assessment procedure for identifying potential school shooters. The procedure attempts to identify the credibility and seriousness of threats, the intent and motivation of the threatener, and the availability of weapons to carry out such threats. Threats are evaluated in terms of the intent and motivation of the threatener.
- Throughout development, aggressive behavior can onset, stabilize, desist, or escalate. Most youth, even aggressive ones, desist in engaging in physical aggression across development. Research on the influence of violent entertainment on youth has focused on escalating aggression across development. Little research has assessed how violent entertainment influences desisting, stabilizing, or late onset aggression.
- Boys are more likely than girls to engage in physical aggression during childhood and adolescence. In contrast, girls are more likely than boys to use indirect, verbal, and relational forms of aggression. Research on media violence, however, has typically assessed physical aggression as the dependent variable.
- Developmental tasks help explain why aggressive behavior peaks during toddlerhood and during early adolescence. At this time, there is no empirical evidence to suggest that violent media impact youth in relation to developmental tasks.

- Quantitative and qualitative criteria can be used to identify excessively aggressive youth. Excessive aggression is typical among children and adolescents with disruptive behavior disorders. Violent media appear to influence youth with DBD to a greater extent than youth without psychopathology. The concepts of behavioral inhibition and behavioral activation systems can be used to explain this finding.
- As a result of bidirectional effects, youth with psychopathology prefer violent media more so than other youth.
- The methodological concepts of rank ordering, correlation, spurious correlation, robustness, statistical power, and postdiction were introduced. Remember, correlation is not causation.

3

Understanding
the Beast Within

Theories of Aggressive Behavior

In the 1988 combined cartoon and live action comedy *Who Framed Roger Rabbit,* Jessica Rabbit says in a distinctive Mae West style, "I'm not bad, I'm just drawn that way." Unfortunately, the reasons that youth act aggressively are far more intricate than the application of ink to animation cells. In either its benign or malevolent form, the complexity of human behavior is not so easily understood. Why is it that docile and cherubic neonates turn into hitting, kicking, teasing, screaming, pushing, and swearing children and adolescents? In an effort to explain how the seeming innocence of infancy can transform into the aggressiveness of youth, social scientists have relied on *theories.*

Understanding Theories

A theory refers to an integrated set of ideas that can be used to explain, predict, and control a particular phenomenon. Thus, theories of aggression explain why aggressive behavior occurs, predict the circumstances under which future acts of aggression will take place, and prescribe a means of reducing aggressive acts. Over the past 100 years, multiple theories of aggression have been raised. Theoretical explanations for aggressive behavior have ranged from instinct to learning to the processing of information related to social relationships. In this chapter, theories of aggression most relevant to the study of media violence are explored. But why are there so many theories in the first place? Why cannot social scientists stick to one theory? The answer lies in the nature of science and the development of good theories.

Valid Theories

Not all theories are created equal; some are "better" than others. In science, theories are evaluated on specific criteria, and the result of that evaluation is used to identify *valid* theories. The following statements characterize a valid theory: (1) the theory explains what is currently known about a subject; (2) the theory is continually supported by new research; (3) the theory provides a guide for future research, including the generation of hypotheses (i.e., testable predictions); and (4) the theory is *falsifiable,* that is, *capable* of being proven wrong. Over time, the validity of a theory is called into question when it can no longer adequately meet any of the four criteria mentioned above (e.g., the theory is contradicted by new data). At that time, the theory is either modified to become valid (e.g., changed so it can explain new data) or categorized as invalid.

Pseudoscientific Theory

Any theory that is presented to the public as scientific but that is, in fact, not falsifiable is considered a *pseudoscientific theory.* An example of pseudoscience involves the theory of *psi.* Psi is posited to be the factor underlying all psychic phenomena, such as extra-sensory perception (ESP). According to psi theory, ESP disappears in the presence of *skeptics,* a phenomenon known as the *shyness effect.* Proponents of psi theory contend that skeptics produce *inhibitory psi,* that is, psychic energy that counteracts psychic phenomena. Thus, failed laboratory attempts to find evidence of psychic abilities occur because of inhibitory psi generated by skeptics watching the experiments. Although psi theory can possibly meet three of the four criteria mentioned above (psi explains psychic phenomena; psi could be supported by new data; and psi theory can provide a guide for future research), psi theory is not falsifiable. Because inhibitory psi can be used to explain away *any* failure to find evidence of ESP, there is no way to prove the theory wrong, and as such, it cannot be falsified.

Theories of Aggression

Psychoanalytic Theory of Aggression

According to Sigmund Freud, *thanatos* (i.e., the death instinct) is responsible for *all* acts of aggression. Freud posits that thanatos seeks to end life

Table 3.1   Theories of Aggressive Behavior

Psychoanalytic Theory of Aggression
Frustration Theory
Social Learning Theory
   Excitation Transfer
Social Information Processing Theory of Aggression
Script Theory
   Cognitive Neoassociation Theory
Self Control Theory
Social Control Theory
General Aggression Model

but often takes a self-destructive course (i.e., suicide). However, the instinct for death can be redirected away from the self and towards others, and when redirection takes place, aggressive behavior results. But just how is thanatos able to enforce its nefarious agenda? While it may be true that you have to eat to live, Freud contends that you have to eat to die. That is, energy from food is converted into energy for aggression—aggression that can then be directed towards the self or others. Over time, aggressive energies build up, and if not released, can cause self-destructive behavior (e.g., suicide, self-mutilation) or extreme acts of violence against others (e.g., murder). Thus, in an effort to reduce dangerous levels of aggressive energies, individuals engage in less extreme acts of aggression, such as fighting, teasing, and vandalism. Furthermore, through aggressive play, youth are able to release aggressive energies (Shaffer, 2000).

Evaluation of the Psychoanalytic Theory of Aggression

Currently, there is no research to support the major tenets of Freud's theory of aggression. Although some youth and adults are suicidal, there is no evidence for the presence of a universal death instinct (Shaffer, 2000). Furthermore, there is no empirical evidence for the generation and accumulation of aggressive "energies" or that engaging in lesser acts of aggression reduces the likelihood of violent behavior (Bushman, 2002). Even if there are genetically preprogrammed aggressive instincts in humans, aggressive behavior can still be modified through experience. Finally, thanatos is not a falsifiable construct. It is impossible to detect or measure the presence of a death instinct. As the previous review illustrates, Freud's theory of aggression has multiple problems, including the theoretical "kiss of death," the fact that it is not falsifiable. As such, Freud's concept of thanatos is generally considered to be an invalid theory of aggression.

Application of Psychoanalytic Theory to Media Violence

According to Freud's theory, violent media consumption would serve as a mechanism for the release of aggressive energies. In particular, violent video games involving aggressive actions, such as hitting, kicking, and shooting, would clearly constitute aggressive play, and thus should result in a reduction of the need to act aggressively. However, current empirical data do not support the contention that acting aggressively during play releases pent-up anger and aggressive feelings (Bushman, 2002). Although Freud's instinct theory has been invalidated, the idea that aggressive energies can be released though play is frequently used as a justification by parents, school officials, and others for the acceptance of aggressive play and consumption of media violence (Carnagey & Anderson, 2003).

Belief in Invalid Theories. Why does the public so wholeheartedly accept invalid theories? Michael Shermer (1997) contends that people believe weird things (such as invalid theories) due to wishful thinking. Thus, if a child plays lots of violent video games, the parents may be *hoping* that by exposing their child to virtual violence, the amount of aggression their child engages in will be reduced. Moreover, despite evidence to the contrary, people continue to believe in invalid concepts because of unwillingness to alter their preconceived notions. In other words, people do not want to admit they are wrong. Finally, belief in the invalid occurs because people like to have thoughts that make themselves feel comfortable and safe, even if such thoughts are wrong. Comfort thoughts related to media violence might include, "violent television makes children fear aggressive behavior" or "violent video game play keeps my child off the streets."

Frustration Theory

Have you ever had to wait in line when you were in a hurry, and no matter what line you moved into, it was always the slowest? Have you ever received a poor grade because the *test* was unfair? If you answered "yes" to either of these questions, then you know what it is like to feel frustrated. When you felt frustrated, did you strike out in anger against the source of the frustration? According to the *frustration-aggression hypothesis*, you most definitely should have acted aggressively. The original version of the frustration-aggression hypothesis had two basic propositions. First, when goals are thwarted and frustration ensues, you *must* act aggressively. Second, aggression is *always* caused by frustration (Dollard, Doob, Miller, Mowrer, & Sears, 1939). However, social scientists quickly realized that not everyone who is frustrated acts aggressively and that people will act aggressively even when they are not frustrated. As such, Berkowitz (1965) fashioned a revised version of the frustration-aggression hypothesis.

According to Berkowitz, frustration does not directly cause aggression. Instead, frustration creates a "readiness to aggress," that is, feelings of hostility or anger. In addition to frustration, an attack by another person or the presence of existing aggressive habits also can cause a readiness to aggress. In order for an individual to act aggressively once a condition of readiness has been established, the individual needs to come into contact with an *aggressive cue.* An aggressive cue is any object or event that has previously become associated (i.e., linked) with an act of aggression. Objects traditionally associated with aggression (e.g., guns, knives) serve as aggressive cues, but so, too, can toy replicas of these objects. In fact, any object, even seemingly benign objects (e.g., feathers, tissue paper), can become associated with aggression and serve as an aggressive cue. Similarly, events traditionally associated with aggression (e.g., hockey games) and events not traditionally associated with aggression (e.g., Scrabble tournaments) have the potential to become cues for aggression. However, under conditions of *extreme* anger (i.e., extremely high readiness), a person will act aggressively even without the presence of aggressive cues. Finally, enacted aggressive behaviors and existing aggressive habits operate in a feedback loop, with new acts of aggression reinforcing old aggressive habits and helping in the creation of new aggressive habits (Berkowitz, 1993).

Evaluation of Frustration Theory

Berkowitz's revised frustration-aggression hypothesis stresses the importance of learning with regard to aggression, in that both aggressive cues and aggressive habits develop through experiences with the world. However, as Shaffer (2000) contends, the theory provides little explanation as to how aggressive habits develop or how stimuli develop into aggressive cues. Furthermore, what exactly constitutes an aggressive cue is idiosyncratic and, as such, makes empirical testing difficult. For instance, as a result of sibling torment, objects not typically thought of as being associated with aggression, such as feathers and tape, could become aggressive cues. Finally, the role of cognition in aggression is not addressed.

Application of Frustration Theory to Media Violence

Under the Berkowitz revision of the frustration-aggression hypothesis, violent entertainment can serve as an aggressive cue. Whether it is watching *The Power Rangers* on TV or playing the violent video game *Soul Calibur,* violent media are thought to become associated with aggression in real life.

As such, when frustrated and in the presence of a media violence–based aggressive cue (e.g., playing a violent video game), youth should act aggressively. Given the nature of violent video games, it is possible for violent video game play to be both the source of frustration (e.g., die during game play) and the aggressive cue. Several studies on children have provided support for the aggressive cue hypothesis. For instance, acts of aggression unrelated to game play are more likely to occur when children play with toy guns and swords than when they play with toy trains and farm animals (Feshbach, 1956). However, the presence of media violence alone is not enough to cause youth to become aggressive when frustrated.

Social Learning Theory

Albert Bandura's (1986) social learning theory posits that behavior is learned in a social context. The colloquial phrase "Do as I say and not as I do" is antithetical to Bandura's theory, for children and adolescents learn aggression by observing the behavior of others. *Observational learning*, as it is formally called, refers to the cognitive process of attending to and remembering behaviors performed by others. In the context of aggression, actions speak louder than words. More so than admonitions, it is the actions of others on which youth focus their cognitive resources. Aggressive behavior also is acquired through direct experience with *punishments* and *reinforcements*. Whereas punishments are consequences (e.g., time out) for actions (e.g., hitting) that result in a decrease in behavior (e.g., hitting), reinforcements (e.g., high five) are consequences for actions (e.g., kicking) that result in an increase in behavior (e.g., kicking). Thus, future acts of aggression are dissuaded when youthful acts of aggression are punished. In contrast, aggressive behavior that is reinforced will most likely increase in the future.

In addition to explaining how aggressive behavior is acquired, social learning theory clarifies how aggressive behavior is maintained (or becomes habitual) over time. First, aggressive behavior is maintained when it is successfully used to satisfy personal needs that do not necessarily require the use of aggression. For instance, instead of taking turns, a child aggressively pushes others to get a desired object. Second, aggressive behavior resulting in the termination of another person's annoying behavior helps make aggression habitual. So, if in response to the ubiquitous little sibling question, "What are you doing?" the big sibling gives the little sibling a wedgie and the annoying questioning stops, the big sibling's response has been reinforced. Consequently, the big sibling's aggressive behavior is likely to be maintained. Third, aggressive behavior is maintained when it is socially sanctioned by peers. Finally, aggressive behavior is maintained when it becomes intrinsically rewarding (i.e., self-reinforcing). That is to say, when aggressive behavior becomes a source of personal pride, it is likely to continue.

To a lesser extent, frustration, anger, and other forms of internal arousal also play a role in the production of aggression. Specifically, Bandura suggests that any form of arousal, even arousal not associated with aggression (e.g., sexual arousal), increases the likelihood of aggressive action if the individual cognitively interprets (or reinterprets) the arousal as frustration or anger. Consider, for example, two children at the beach. While one child tans peacefully for an hour, the other child swims. Next, both children get sand kicked into their faces. According to Bandura's theory, the child who went swimming would be more likely to respond aggressively than the child who tanned. The reason? In contrast to tanning, swimming causes physiological arousal which can then be reinterpreted as anger *after* being sprayed in the face with sand.

Excitation Transfer: A Related Arousal Concept. Similar to Bandura's contention that any form of arousal can be reinterpreted as anger is Zillmann's (1983) idea that physiological arousal can be transferred from one event to another. *Excitation transfer* is based on the premise that physiological arousal is slow to dissipate. As such, when two events are temporally close, arousal generated during the first event can be added to the level of arousal generated during the second event, resulting in a heightened level of arousal for the latter occurrence. Thus, because of excitation transfer, the total amount of physiological arousal experienced during the second event is higher than it would have been if the second event had occurred alone. In relation to aggression, if the second event involves anger or frustration, the arousal from the first event (no matter what the origin) will make the person angrier or more frustrated during the second event.

Evaluation of Social Learning Theory

In contrast to the frustration-aggression hypothesis, social learning theory (Bandura, 1986) explains how aggressive behaviors are acquired and maintained, and elaborates on the role of cognition in aggression. However, critics such as Shaffer (2000) contest Bandura's notion that aggressive children act aggressively primarily because they value the outcomes associated with aggression. Furthermore, Bandura's theory provides little detail as to how aggressive and nonaggressive youth cognitively process information. Similarly, the interpretation and decision-making process leading to aggressive behavior are not clearly specified.

Application of Social Learning Theory to Media Violence

Whether shown on TV, played on a video game console, or read in a comic book, violent media provide ample opportunities for observational learning. For instance, when children view Batman beating up Joker and receiving accolades from Commissioner Gordon, they are witnessing the reinforcement of aggressive action. Similarly, when youth see 90-pound weaklings getting sand kicked in their faces and then ridiculed for not fighting back, they are witnessing the punishment of passivity. Furthermore, video games provide direct experience with both acting aggressively and feeling the consequences of aggression. For instance, most violent video games include reinforcement for good behavior (e.g., killing the right people) in the form of bonus points and punishments for bad behavior (e.g., killing the wrong characters) in the form of lost points or lives. Additionally, research on media violence has shown that the consequences that the media-based aggressor experiences influence the likelihood that the viewer will act aggressively, with punishments decreasing aggressive behavior and reinforcements increasing aggressive behavior (Bandura, 1965). Finally, based on both Bandura's contention that arousal gets reinterpreted as anger and Zillmann's (1983) concept of excitation transfer, the arousal stimulated by media violence should increase the likelihood that aggressive actions will follow temporally close to events involving frustration or provocation.

Social Information Processing Theory of Aggression

The central tenet of social information processing theory is that children *create* their own rationales to explain the behavior of others during social encounters. In turn, these self-generated interpretations influence children's responses in their ongoing social interactions. Consider, as an example, the following situation: While walking to class, an 11-year-old girl gets tripped by a smiling peer. In order to create a rationale to explain why she was tripped, the preteen girl would process information related to the social behavior (e.g., attending to a peer's smiling face), impose her own interpretation of the situation (e.g., the peer pushed me on purpose), and react to the observed behavior based on her interpretation (e.g., hit the peer).

In applying social information processing theory to aggression, Kenneth Dodge has formulated a six-step model that can explain both aggressive and nonaggressive reactions to provocations (Crick & Dodge, 1994; Dodge, 1986).

Step 1: Encoding Social Cues. In the first step, the child identifies information related to the experienced provocation (e.g., getting hit with a ball).

For instance, children will look at the facial expressions of others (e.g., are they smiling or frowning?) and assess the physical make-up of their surroundings (e.g., large open space or small enclosed space).

Step 2: Interpret Social Cues. After identifying relevant cues, children interpret those cues to be evidence of either benign or hostile intent on the part of the provocateur. For instance, after being hit with a ball and seeing the thrower smiling, children might interpret the facial expression to be a show of one-upmanship.

Step 3: Formulate Social Goals. Next, children need to formulate a social goal. That is, children need to figure out what to do in order to resolve the situation. For instance, children could decide to ignore the transgression and walk away, confront the thrower with questions, or respond with force.

Step 4: Generate Problem-Solving Strategies. After a social goal has been formulated, youth now generate a list of potential strategies to accomplish that goal. For instance, if children choose to use force in response to provocation, then the potential strategies generated could include throwing the ball back hard, yelling verbal insults, or engaging in fisticuffs.

Step 5: Evaluate the Effectiveness of the Strategies, Then Choose One. Children evaluate the strategies in terms of their ability to effect the desired goal, and based upon that evaluation, choose a strategy. For instance, when responding with force, children might decide that throwing the ball back hard will not work well because they cannot throw well, or that the hurling of verbal insults will be ineffective given their lack of slang vocabulary. As such, children may choose fisticuffs.

Step 6: Enact a Response. Children engage in the behavior that was chosen in the previous steps. Thus, children choosing to physically fight another based on the evaluation done in Step 5 will, at this point, start to throw punches.

Throughout the six-step process, children's *mental state* can affect the processing of information (Crick & Dodge, 1994; Lemerise & Arsenio, 2000). Mental state refers to the following: knowledge of social rules (e.g., what is acceptable behavior with peers during arguments), knowledge gained based on past social experiences (e.g., the offense was intentional if the perpetrator smiles at you when you are hurt), expectations for one's behavior in social settings (e.g., I'm supposed to be tough), and the ability to regulate emotions (e.g., the ease with which one gets angry or upset and the amount of time it takes to cool down). Furthermore, it is believed that mental states can bias the processing of information towards or away from hostile/angry/aggressive cues, interpretations, and so on at each step.

Thus, in response to the *same* provocation, individual differences in mental states result in disparate information processing in terms of the encoding of information, interpretation of social cues, formulation of social goals, problem-solving generation and evaluation, and enactment of behavior. Take, for example, the situation in which a child gets hit in the back of the head with a ball. A child who believes that it is OK to defend oneself, has a history of being attacked, has a reputation for toughness, and is quick to get angry will be more likely to *search for cues* with a bias towards hostility-validating information, interpret situations as being of hostile origin, formulate an aggression-based resolution, generate aggressive strategies, evaluate the best aggressive choice, and then choose and enact an aggressive action. In contrast, in response to the same provocation, a child who believes it is important to resolve issues peacefully, has a history of peaceful interactions with others, is thought to be nice, and is rarely angry will be more likely to search for cues pointing towards a nonaggressive cause; interpret the provocation as stemming from benign intent; and ultimately generate, choose, and enact a nonaggressive response.

It should be pointed out that the concept of mental states is part of a feedback loop in which current social information processes come to affect future social information processes. Following the harmful actions of provocateurs, children progress through each of Dodge's six steps, the end result being enacted behavior. Next, the provocateur responds in kind. The entire interaction then, from peer provocation to response to peer response, becomes part of children's "past social experiences" that, in turn, will be used to influence future social interactions involving this six-step process.

Evaluation of Social Information Processing Theory

In support of this theory, research has shown that the social information processing of aggressive children is replete with aggression-laden (i.e., aggressively biased) perceptions, interpretations, and decision making (Dodge & Crick, 1990). Although social information processing theory adequately describes individual differences in the processing of aggression-related social information, the mechanisms by which such variations develop in the first place are unclear. Furthermore, the theory neither posits how children became aggressive in the first place (Shaffer, 2000) nor adequately addresses the relative contributions of differing environmental experiences (e.g., with peers, parents, teachers) in the development of aggressive behavior. Moreover, environmental factors that can decrease aggressive behavior are not addressed.

Application of Social Information Processing Theory to Media Violence

Given that mental states operate in a feedback loop, it is possible that all social experiences, including those involving violent media, could influence social information processing. For instance, violent video game play could constitute a past social experience, affect knowledge of social rules (e.g., violence is an appropriate response to provocation), influence social expectations (e.g., violence is a necessary response to provocation), and alter emotion regulation. In fact, research has supported the contention that mental states are influenced by violent media. For instance, Kirsh (1998) found that after playing a violent video game, 3rd- and 4th-grade children demonstrate biases in social information processing by perceiving hostility in situations where hostility was not overtly portrayed.

Script Theory

At times, art violently imitates life. At other times, life violently imitates art. Huesmann's (1986, 1998) script theory is perfectly suited to explain the latter situation. According to Huesmann, aggressive scripts are personal screenplays in which the beginning, middle, and end of interpersonal altercations are clearly and explicitly illustrated. Such scripts develop as a result of observational learning and direct experience. From instigation to outcome, scripts provide not only detailed information of event sequencing but also the appropriateness of an action given a particular situation. In fact, whether or not children act out a script depends on the content of the script in relation to the likelihood that enacting the script will lead to the desired consequences. Furthermore, it is believed that youth will primarily enact scripts that are consistent with their beliefs about social norms (i.e., what is considered to be socially acceptable behavior). In order to handle any given situation, similarities between the current situation and programmed scripts determine which scripts are retrieved from memory. Ultimately, the choice of which script to enact is based upon the appropriateness of the script for the current situation, anticipated consequences of script enactment, and beliefs about social norms. Thus, evaluation differences between aggressive and nonaggressive children are the result of any combination of (1) script content, (2) script appropriateness, (3) anticipated consequences, and (4) social norms. Additionally, Huesmann contends that once in place, aggressive scripts are resistant to change, and therefore continually influence aggressive behavior throughout development in a similar fashion.

Different situations require different scripts. However, scripts not only function as independent guides for behavior; they are believed to cluster together and form a network of social behavior emphasizing similar action. For instance, although the playground may require different aggressive scripts than the hallways of school, which in turn require different aggressive scripts than those used by siblings on long car trips, because each script stresses using aggressive action, the child develops a cognitive network of scripts which accentuate aggressive responding. Similarly, Berkowitz's (1993) *cognitive neoassociation theory* contends that aggressive behaviors, aggressive emotions, and aggressive thoughts are linked together in memory.

Cognitive neoassociation theory posits that *aversive events* produce negative emotions. Aversive events refer to events that individuals would like to avoid, such as frustrating situations, being accosted by another person, or hot temperatures. Once a negative emotion has been induced by an aversive event, similarly valanced (negative) thoughts, emotions, and physiological responses arise. For instance, the negative feelings of being stuck in a long lunch line while famished may give rise to negative feelings that occurred when you were bullied on the playground. The end result of this spreading activation of negativity is that *flight or fight* tendencies are set in motion. Whereas the flight tendency gives rise to fear, the fight tendency gives rise to anger. Although Master Yoda says, "Fear leads to anger. Anger leads to hate. Hate leads to suffering," Berkowitz believes that fear inhibits aggression. In contrast, the fight response of anger increases the likelihood that aggression will occur.

Script theory (and cognitive neoassociation theory, for that matter) posits that repeated use or activation of associated concepts/scripts strengthens the connections between the concepts/scripts. Moreover, strong connections are not only easily accessible in memory but are activated by a greater number of stimuli than are weak connections. The ease of activation and the large number of situations that can activate these pathways result in scripts becoming chronically assessable, and chronically assessable scripts are used as a primary means of dealing with new situations. Thus, children and adolescents with chronically aggressive scripts will tend to process new information as though it were aggression related, even if it was not.

Evaluation of Script Theory

Huessmann's script theory provides a detailed explanation of how children and adolescents develop aggressive solutions to the problems they face. One of the most unique contributions to the understanding of aggression this theory makes is that it stresses the importance of internalized standards (in terms of the child's understanding of social norms) in deciding whether or not to engage in acts of aggression. The implication of this contention is powerful, for it suggests (1) that factors that influence social norms influence the likelihood of acting aggressively, and (2) that youth will seek out environments that are consistent with their beliefs. Thus, aggressive children will seek out aggressive friends, stimuli, and opportunities to use aggression, all of which have been verified by empirical research.

Application of Script Theory to Media Violence

Violent media can provide both direct learning and observational learning of aggressive scripts. For instance, watching the Powerpuff Girls defeat their arch enemy, Mojo Jojo, with hitting and kicking increases the likelihood that children will learn scripts with hitting and kicking as the primary means of problem solving. Additionally, violent entertainment may skew children's and adolescent's beliefs about social norms to be more accepting of aggressive solutions to social problems. Furthermore, children with well-established aggressive scripts can use violent media to validate the social norms that they believe in, even if they are receiving contradictory information about the use of aggression from parents, teachers, or even their peers. Certain forms of violent media, such as violent video games, not only give the individual practice at using aggressive scripts, which in turn strengthens them, but the outcomes associated with those scripts are also reinforced (e.g., scores go up when violence is used).

Control Theories

Antisocial behavior is defined as any action that conflicts with conventional ethical, moral, and legal principles (Moeller, 2001). Antisocial behaviors can impact others (such as with theft) or the self (as is the case with drug abuse). Likewise, both aggressive and violent behaviors are also subsumed within this concept. In an effort to understand antisocial behavior, Hirschi and colleagues have forwarded two theories involving the interactive roles of self and society: *self-control theory* and *social control theory* (Gottfredson & Hirschi, 1990; Hirschi, 1969; Hirschi & Gottfredson, 1994).

Self-Control Theory

According to Hirschi (1969), self-control is the ability to avoid engaging in an antisocial behavior whose long-term consequences are more problematic than the momentary pleasure it brings. For instance, although hitting a teacher who gave you an "F" on your term paper might feel satisfying for a moment, the long-term consequences of getting kicked out of school for the aggressive act will result in greater problems in the long run (e.g., lower pay for not having a high school diploma). Hirschi and colleagues contend that youth who engage in antisocial behavior (such as aggression) experience intense pleasure from antisocial behaviors while at the same time paying little attention to the long-term consequences of their antisocial actions. As such, these youth are said to lack self-control. Hirschi's self-control concept is similar to the developmental concept *delay of gratification*, which is the ability to hold out for a better, delayed reward by forgoing an immediate, lesser reward.

Social Control Theory

According to Hirschi's (1969) social control theory, youthful acts of aggression (and other antisocial acts) are naturally occurring behaviors that require societal intervention in order to bring them under control. The aggressive tendencies of youth are thought to be governed by an emotional bond with society called a *social bond*. There are four aspects to social bonds: *attachment, commitment, involvement,* and *belief.*

Hirschi defines attachment as an affection and sensitivity to groups (e.g., school, family) and specific individuals. The three primary attachments of youth are parents, school, and peers. Note, this concept varies somewhat from John Bowlby's (1969/1982) definition of attachment, which focuses solely on the emotional bonds of children with their parental figures (e.g., parents, daycare providers, etc.). Hirschi suggests that strong attachments reduce antisocial tendencies of children and adolescents by instilling a desire to uphold conventional (e.g., nonaggressive) values.

Commitment refers to the extent to which conforming to societal values produces greater benefits than those achieved by not conforming to societal conventions. Social control theory posits that antisocial behaviors are reduced when children are motivated (through positive reinforcements) to maintain societal values. In contrast, children who lack commitment engage in antisocial behavior because the payoff for such behaviors outweighs the benefits of conformity.

Participating in school groups, after-school programs, and like activities valued by society are posited by Hirschi to instill a sense of involvement. Hirschi contends that the more involved youth are in society, the less likely they are to engage in antisocial actions because they are becoming increasingly invested in societal values. Additionally, Hirschi believes that involvement in conventional activities keeps youth occupied, thereby reducing opportunities for antisocial behavior.

The last component of social control theory, beliefs, focuses on the acceptance of societal values. According to theory, if society promotes a shared value system, then youth will come to accept the beliefs within that system. However, when children and adolescents fail to perceive a cohesive set of values, they will seek out other sources to provide them. Furthermore, youth are more likely to conform to social values when they believe in them.

Evaluation of Control Theory

Self-control theory stresses the importance of short-term gains (i.e., pleasure) versus long-term problems in determining acts of aggression. This theory is partially useful in explaining bullying behavior (e.g., bullies like the outcome associated with aggression). However, there is little research to support the contention that youth go through such an evaluation process before every act of aggression. For instance, this theory has problems explaining why children aggress in response to attack or frustration. What is the pleasurable outcome in this situation? Thus, self-control theory can not explain acts of aggression in the absence of short-term gains.

Social control theory brings to light the importance of society, and more specifically, the child's connection to society in determining aggressive behavior. Moreover, the theory identifies important contexts within a child's life (such as home and school) that had been given less attention in other theories. However, social control theory provides little explanation as to how social controls develop over time and the specific circumstances under which attachments, commitments, involvements, and beliefs become favorable. Finally, the theory lacks the organization needed to connect the various components of social bonds to the likelihood that youth will engage in aggressive behavior.

Application of Control Theory to Media Violence

In relation to Hirschi's (1969) notion of self-control, violent media often model an "act now, deal with the consequences later" attitude. As such, through media violence, youth could validate their own pattern of seeking rewards available immediately and not concern themselves with long-term consequences. This would be especially true for children with weak social bonds who lack a socially based belief system and were seeking out values elsewhere. Furthermore, certain forms of media violence, such as violent video game play, give youth practice at receiving immediate rewards for aggressive behavior, while at the same time failing to consider the long-term consequences of their actions.

Under social control theory, violent media serve as a source of values for youth to seek out and adopt. Additionally, violent media could potentially weaken attachment bonds by reducing sensitivity to others. Given that certain forms of violent media promote the benefits of antisocial behaviors, and that children get rewarded for their aggressive actions, violent media have the potential to weaken youth's commitment to society. Finally, excessive consumption of violent media reduces involvement by decreasing the likelihood that children and adolescents will join in socially sanctioned activities, such as playing soccer or belonging to a religious youth group.

General Aggression Model

In an effort to create a unified theory of aggression, Anderson and Bushman (2002) have drawn on the tenets of the above-mentioned theories (with the exception of psychoanalytic theory) and posited the General Aggression Model (GAM). According to GAM, *input variables, routes,* and *outcomes* cyclically interact to affect aggression (see Figure 3.1).

Input Variables. Input variables are composed of *person* and *situational* variables. Person variables refer to those person-based characteristics that determine an individual's overall preparedness to act aggressively.

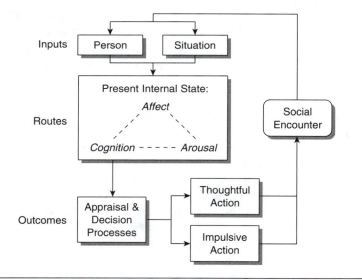

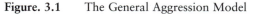

Figure. 3.1   The General Aggression Model

Aggression-related genetic predispositions, personality characteristics (e.g., level of hostility; impulse control), scripts, attitudes, and belief systems are subsumed within the person variable. Simply put, person variables are stable aspects of an individual's personality, thoughts, and feelings that are brought into new situations. In comparison, the situational variable is composed of the physical environment the individual is currently in along with any inter-actions taking place within that environment. Thus, in contrast to the more stable person variable, the situational variable is context dependent. As youth move from setting to setting, they may or may not encounter situation-based variables such as frustrations, provocations, drugs, pain, and cues for aggression.

Routes. Person and situational variables do not directly influence aggressive behavior. Instead, input variables directly affect an individual's appraisal of situations by altering the *present internal state.* Ultimately, the route from input variable to aggressive action goes through an individual's present internal state. Anderson and Bushman (2002) have identified three main pathways within an individual's present internal state: *cognition, affect,* and *arousal.* The cognitive route involves the activation/creation of hostile thoughts and scripts. The affective pathway entails the induction of nega-tive moods (e.g., hostility) and emotions (e.g., anger). Arousal refers to the manipulation of physiological arousal, the excitation transfer of arousal, and the reinterpretation of arousal as anger. GAM theory also posits the notion that cognition, affect, and arousal are interconnected. That is, they influence one another. For example, hostile feelings may increase hostile thoughts, which in turn increase levels of physiological arousal, ultimately resulting in the reinterpretation of the arousal as anger.

Outcomes. After traveling through GAM routes, the filtered information is used to appraise the current situation, make a decision regarding which action to take, and finally enact that decision. The GAM posits the presence of two appraisal processes that influence the decision to aggress. The first type of appraisal, *immediate appraisal,* involves the automatic, spontaneous, and unconscious interpretation of the information coming from one's present internal state. Similar to the aggression-related constructs presented in Dodge's (1986) social information processing model, immediate appraisals provide information on the affect (e.g., angry or happy), intent (malevolent or benign), and goals (e.g., retaliation or peaceful resolution) of the parties involved (e.g., self and provocateur). Furthermore, through immediate appraisals, behavior is enacted without conscious thought, in a manner that can best be described as impulsive. For instance, if while swimming a child gets splashed in the face with water, the immediate appraisal (based upon aggressive scripts) could result in yelling nasty epithets at the other child. However, if sufficient resources are present and the immediate appraisal meets one of the following two conditions, (1) the appraisal comes to an unsatisfying conclusion (e.g., you realize you'll get your butt kicked), or (2) the decision is considered to be important to the individual (e.g., you view violence to be reprehensible), a second appraisal, called a *reappraisal,* will take place. However, if one of the two conditions is not met or the individual lacks the resources to engage in a reappraisal, then the outcome, as determined by the immediate appraisal, will be enacted. Behavior enacted as a result of immediate appraisal is referred to as *impulsive action.*

Reappraisal goes beyond impulse and actively engages conscious cognitive thought. During the reappraisal process, the individual actively searches for more information relevant to the current predicament. Memories of previous altercations are referenced, and outcomes associated with past decisions are brought to mind. Moreover, potential responses and outcomes to those responses are consciously thought about. In the end, a decision is reached, and the person chooses to act aggressively or to take another course of action. Regardless, if the individual aggresses or not, the outcome of the reappraisal process is considered to be *thoughtful action.*

The Cyclical Features of the GAM. The GAM is a feedback loop–based theory. The loop starts with input variables (i.e., person and situational variables), which in turn impact the child's present internal state (i.e., current affective, arousal, and cognitive states), which then influences outcomes (i.e., appraisal, decision making processes). The confluence of GAM processes then affects the current social encounter. In turn, this social encounter affects the individual's input variables, thus completing the cycle of aggression.

Evaluation of the General Aggression Model

GAM processes influence the perception and interpretation of information as well as decision making and action. Furthermore, GAM theory posits that aggression is the result of environmental experience and intrapersonal processes. These processes become automated with use, guide future interactions with others, and influence aggressive responding to a wide range of provocations. As such, GAM is compatible with theories proposed by Bandura (1986), Berkowitz (1965), and Dodge (1980). Although the GAM has received empirical support (Anderson & Bushman, 2001; Lynch, Gentile, Olson, & van Brederode, 2001), additional research is necessary to validate the interactive nature of the various GAM components, as well as to establish the ability of the GAM to predict aggressive behavior. Furthermore, the importance of social control and its various components is not clearly defined within GAM.

Application of GAM to Media Violence

According to GAM, violent entertainment influences aggressive behavior through short-term and long-term effects. In the short term, violent entertainment (such as video game play) functions as a situational variable, resulting in an increase in aggressive cognitions, affects, and arousal. Anderson and Bushman (2001) have recently produced a meta-analytic review that provides empirical support for the contention that violent video games lead to aggressive behavior ($r_+ = .19$), aggressive cognitions ($r_+ = .27$), hostile affects ($r_+ = .18$), and increased physiological arousal ($r_+ = .22$). In the long term, violent entertainment is hypothesized to influence aggressive behavior by promoting aggressive beliefs and attitudes and creating aggressive schema, aggressive behavioral scripts, and aggressive expectations, as well as desensitizing individuals to aggression. In turn, these factors bias an individual's personality towards aggression. At this point, the theory is partially supported, in that while the long-term effects of violent television on behavior have been demonstrated, little research exists for other forms of media violence. For instance, currently there are no longitudinal data to support the proposed negative long-term effects of exposure to video game violence. However, Anderson and Bushman believe that given the similarities between video game violence and television violence, and the fact that long-term exposure to television violence is significantly associated with increased aggressive behavior (Strasburger, 1995), the long-term impact of violent video games should correspond to GAM predictions.

Theories of Aggression and Developmental Considerations

In the following chapters, research on children and adolescents will be presented with an eye towards understanding individual differences in aggression and the normative development of aggression. Thus, it is necessary to assess aggression theories as a function of development. Like traditional theories, *developmental theories* focus on explaining, predicting, and controlling behavior. However, developmental theories also focus on changes in behaviors that occur over time. Because youth are different physically, socially, cognitively, and emotionally at different ages, varying explanations, predictions, and control options are forwarded for each age group. Furthermore, developmental theories explain the course of development, including transitions from one age group to the next. In other words, developmental theories not only provide age-specific explanations for behavior; they also explain why developmental differences occur.

What is intriguing about the aforementioned theories of aggression is that none of them meets the criteria for a developmental theory (Miller, 1989). Absent from social information processing theory, frustration theory, script theory, control theory, social learning theory, and the GAM are varying explanations, predictions, and control options forwarded as a function of physical, cognitive, social, and emotional developmental changes. Additionally, none of the aforementioned theories specifically addresses the reasons *why* changes in aggression occur across development. By adding developmental explanations, theories would better be able to accurately explain, predict, and control aggressive behavior throughout development.

Consider, for example, the following integration of developmental considerations with GAM components in addressing the impact of violent video games across adolescence. Violent video games negatively influence socioemotional functioning during the adolescent period (Anderson & Bushman, 2001). However, given that biological and psychosocial changes occur during adolescence, exposure to violent video games should differentially affect the processes operating within the GAM during adolescence. By the time children reach adolescence, person and internal state components of the GAM, such as cognition, affects, and arousal, are already in place. However, between early and late adolescence, these variables will continue to develop and be influenced by current environments. The general increase in aggression that accompanies early adolescence (Loeber & Stouthamer-Loeber, 1998; Steinberg, 2001) should affect the internal state variables of the GAM by reinforcing and increasing aggressive cognitions, aggressive affects, and arousal. Exposure to violent video games should further affect the aggressive nature of the adolescent by creating or reinforcing aggressive cognitions and scripts, by creating or reinforcing hostile affects, and by increasing aggression-related arousal. According to the GAM, cognitions, affects, and arousals directly influence one another. Thus, the increases in physiological arousal (Lynch et al., 2001), aggressive cognitions, and hostile affects (Anderson & Bushman, 2001) that follow violent video game play should interact with one another to negatively bias internal state variables. Although violent video game play will impact early, middle, and late adolescents, the influence of violent video games should be more pronounced in early adolescence than in middle and late adolescence. For instance, the heightened physiological arousal experienced by early adolescents (Spear, 2000) should interact with internal state arousal caused by violent video games to create a cumulative level of internal state arousal that is higher than in middle and late adolescence, resulting in more aggressive behavior.

The decision-making processes of the GAM may also function differently throughout adolescence. Cognitive deficiencies may result in more aggressive responding in early adolescence than in middle and late adolescence. Early adolescents should act impulsively and with little cognitive evaluation during emotionally laden (e.g., stressful) situations. This effect should be heightened following violent video game play since the aggressive nature of video games should result in increased internal state arousal (e.g., limbic system activity and adrenal hormone release). In contrast, as individuals enter late adolescence, the decision-making portion of the GAM will become more rational and evaluative. Thus, even if a state of heightened arousal accompanied by hostile cognitions and affects occurs following violent video game play, late adolescents should be less likely than early adolescents to act aggressively due to late adolescents' increased cognitive ability and relatively lower levels of limbic system activity and adrenal hormones. However, even if violent video games affect early, middle, and late adolescents' internal state variables (i.e., cognition, affect, and arousal) similarly, early adolescents should experience a greater increase in aggressive behavior than older adolescents because of impulsive behavior and poor decision-making processes.

As the previous example illustrates, the ability to understand, predict, and control aggressive behavior is enhanced when developmental issues are taken into consideration. Not only does integrating development into theories of aggression result in an increase in the applicability of the theory throughout development, but areas of research that have yet to be explored can be more easily identified.

Summary

- Theories are integrated sets of ideas that can be used to explain, predict, and control behavior.
- Valid theories explain what is currently known about a subject, are supported by new research, provide a framework for future research, and are falsifiable.
- Pseudoscientific theories, like psi theory, present themselves as if they were valid but are not falsifiable.
- According to psychoanalytic theory, thanatos is responsible for aggressive behavior towards the self and others. The periodic release of aggressive energy, through aggressive play or violent video game play, is thought to prevent

monumental acts of aggression. Currently, there is no empirical support for this theory.

- People believe in invalid theories due to wishful thinking, an unwillingness to alter preconceived notions, and because they want to have thoughts that make themselves feel comfortable and safe.

- The frustration-aggression hypothesis states that all acts of aggression are the result of frustration. Recent revisions of this theory contend that although frustration leads to a readiness to aggress, it does not directly lead to aggression. When in a ready state, the presence of an aggressive cue stimulates aggressive behavior. It is possible for violent video games to be both the source of frustration and the aggressive cue.

- Social learning theory contends that through observational learning and direct experience, youth learn aggressive behaviors and maintain current levels of aggressiveness. Both reinforcement and punishment of aggressive behavior determine what will be learned and maintained. Both physiological arousal and excitation transfer increase the likelihood that youth will act aggressively. Entertainment violence offers ample opportunities for observational learning and direct experience with the punishments and reinforcements associated with aggressive behavior.

- Social information processing theory posits that children create their own rationales to explain aggression-related behaviors. In response to provocations, children go through a six-step process in order to determine the appropriate behavior. The child's mental state influences the processing of social information throughout each step. Media violence may influence mental state processes, such as social rules, social expectations, and emotion regulation.

- Aggressive scripts describe the specifics of aggressive altercations, from beginning to end. The enactment of scripts depends on the content of the script in relation to the likelihood of achieving the desired consequence. Youth are thought to primarily enact scripts that are consistent with their beliefs about social norms. Youth with chronically aggressive scripts will tend to process new information as though it were aggression related. Violent media consumption has the potential to create, alter, or strengthen aggressive scripts and skew children's and adolescents' beliefs about social norms.

- According to self-control theory, a lack of self control can lead to aggressive behavior. Youth who lack self-control derive pleasure from antisocial activities and fail to consider the long-term consequences of their actions. Through media violence, youth can validate the pattern of seeking rewards available immediately and not concerning themselves with long-term consequences.

- Social control theory contends that youth act aggressively due to weak social bonds. The four aspects of social bonds are attachment, commitment, involvement, and belief. Entertainment violence is thought to weaken each of these aspects.

- According to the GAM, input variables, routes, and outcomes cyclically interact to affect aggression. Input variables are composed of person and situational variables. The route from input variable to aggressive action goes through an individual's present internal state, which is composed of cognition, affect, and arousal. Appraisal and decision-making processing include impulsive and thoughtful action. Violent entertainment functions as a situational variable, resulting in an increase in aggressive cognitions, affects, and arousal. In the long term, violent entertainment is hypothesized to influence aggressive behavior by altering aggressive beliefs, attitudes, scripts, and expectations.

- Developmental theories explain why children change over time. Current theories of aggression do not meet the criteria for a developmental theory. The ability to understand, predict, and control aggressive behavior is enhanced when developmental issues are taken into consideration.

4

Dining on Death and Destruction

The How Much and
Why of Violent Media Consumption

When I was a kid growing up in the 1970s, one of my dad's favorite expressions was "You're making a mountain out of a molehill!" Apparently, he felt I tended to exaggerate the significance of certain events by giving them more credence than they actually deserved. Given the lack of documentation in the matter, it is currently unclear whether my dad's assertion was true or not. But for the record, it *is* a big deal when your sister cheats at the home version of "Name That Tune"; there *is* nothing more embarrassing than having your parents look in your general direction, from 50 feet away, when you're talking to a girl you want to ask out but probably will not because you are not really talking to her; and several months of mourning *is* an appropriate response to the cancellation of the vaunted television series *The Love Boat*.

Today, there are many who believe that the controversy surrounding violent entertainment does, in fact, make a mountain out of a molehill. For instance, Freedman (2002) dismisses the voluminous amount of research connecting violent media to aggressive behavior and aggression-related constructs, and Jones (2002) believes that media violence is actually good for youth. Thus, to the naysayer, the Surgeon General's warning against excessive television watching (U.S. Surgeon General's Scientific Advisory Committee, 1972), the testimony of media violence experts on the potential health threats of violent video games (e.g., Anderson, 2000; Funk, 2000), and the hundreds of empirical articles that have been written on the issue are all simply exaggerations of insignificant effects surrounding benign playtime fun. Because one person's mountain is another person's molehill, the mountain or molehill nature of media violence exposure is not a question that can be answered with data. As such, it is not an *empirical question*. However, the amount of violent media consumption across childhood, the reasons for violent media consumption in youth, and the effects of violent media consumption on children and adolescents *are* empirical questions. In the current chapter, I address the first two issues dealing with the amount of, and reasons for, violent media consumption. In the remainder of this book, the effects of violent media consumption on youth will be reviewed.

Media Violence Consumption Across Development

Before discussing patterns of media consumption across development, it is crucial to understand how such data are collected, for if the data collection process was flawed, then the results of the study may be incorrect or biased—simply stated, meaningless. As the old statistical saying goes, "Garbage in (data), Garbage out (results)"! Thus, it is imperative that the merits of the assessment procedure are evaluated *before* the importance and implications of the data collected are determined.

Survey Research

The *survey method* has been the primary means for collecting data on media consumption by children and adolescents. In the survey method, participants are asked about their attitudes, behaviors, beliefs, opinions, and so on, concerning a topic such as their favorite television shows. The questions can be asked and answered on the Internet, over the phone, in person, or as a part of a questionnaire. Surveys can be worded to ask about the past, present, and future. Thus, because of the ease of administration and flexibility of content, surveys are the most frequently used tool to assess children's and adolescents' media consumption habits.

However, an alternative way to assess media consumption would be to eschew the survey method and, instead, engage in *unobtrusive recordings*. In such procedures, behavior is monitored in a natural setting (e.g., home, movie theaters, video arcades) without the individuals knowing they are being watched. For each individual being observed, the type of violent media consumed and the length of consumption would be recorded without being influenced by self-reporting biases, such as social desirability. The data, therefore, would provide an accurate, unbiased recording of media consumption in youth. However, because we do not live in the Orwellian society of *1984*, doing unobtrusive recordings in private settings without the consent of the participant is unethical. Consequently, this type of methodology is not done in media consumption research.

Although it is considered ethical to use unobtrusive recordings in public situations (such as video arcades), if limited to that setting alone, the data collected would not be representative of youth as a whole. For instance, youth who do not play video games at all and youth who only play video games at home would not be included in the sample. Consequently, the sample would be considered to be *biased* and, therefore, not representative of the population. Regardless of the methodology employed, sampling bias has the potential to confound any study. However, data collected through surveys are especially vulnerable to this type of bias. To illustrate, several different survey methods and the problems associated with each will be explored.

Varieties of Survey Methods and Problems

The *intercept interview* involves obtaining participants by standing around in a location (e.g., outside a video arcade) and asking individuals who go by to fill out a survey or answer some questions. The researcher chooses the participants, and therefore the sample is subject to both the conscious (e.g., "looks like a gamer") and unconscious (e.g., "looks like a potential date") biases. This type of method is not used very often in violent media research as parental consent is needed to collect information from youth under 18 years of age.

In *mail-in surveys*, researchers mail questionnaires to potential participants and request that they send the survey back to the lab. Here, there is a potential for bias because *response rates* are quite low. A response rate is the percentage of individuals who return a mailed survey. When response rates are low, the possibility that those who respond are systematically different from those who do not respond is enhanced. For instance, in an assessment of media violence consumption, it is possible that the greatest number of responses will come from parents who expose their children to little media violence because they are concerned about the effects of violent entertainment on their children. In contrast, those parents not concerned about the adverse effects of violent entertainment and who, accordingly, let their children consume a great deal of media violence may find the survey unworthy of a response. If this were the case, then due to the preponderance of "caring parents" who responded, the survey would give the impression that media violence consumption is lower than it actually is. Given the amount of time and effort it takes to complete and send back a survey, a response rate of 70% or above is considered high. In contrast, a response rate at or below 30% is considered low. Importantly, if there is a consistent difference between those who respond and those who do not (e.g., non-respondent is too busy playing violent video games to mail back the form), the potential for bias is still present, even when the response rate is high.

Other survey methods include interviewing a subject in person, as is done in the *face-to-face interview*, over the telephone (i.e., *telephone survey*), or over the Internet (i.e., *Web-based survey*). Face-to-face interviews produce extremely high response rates (upwards of 80%). However, given that subjects are interviewed individually and that this type of interview is very time consuming and expensive, it is seldom used today. The telephone interview is one of the most popular survey methods used in industrialized countries. In the United States, telephones are in nearly every household, so there is little chance of producing a biased sample based on subjects selected by the researcher. However, response rates can still be affected, for it is easy for potential participants to refuse to participate by hanging up or failing to answer the phone. More and more research is assessing attitudes, behaviors, and opinions through surveys conducted over the Internet. However, these Web-based surveys are not without their own unique problems. For instance, questionnaires are visually different when displayed using different Internet browsers or on different computer monitors. Therefore, respondents may see different views of the same question, possibly resulting in the reader perceiving the question differently. Additionally, different levels of computer expertise may affect errors or responses to questions (Gunn, 2004).

Social Desirability

Response rates and issues specific to the mode of assessment are not the only challenges of using survey data. With surveys, you need to keep in mind the following quote: "There are two types of people, those who stare at objects and try to make them move and those who *say* they don't." This quote relates the potential effect that *social desirability* has on the veracity of collected survey data. Social desirability refers to the situation in which participants respond to questions by giving socially acceptable answers, as opposed to what they are really thinking. Typically, when answering survey questions, people tend to make themselves look good. For instance, several years ago, I studied the influence violent video games have on how grade-school children interpret different types of situations. When asked about the number of video games played, one boy said, "I'm not allowed to play video games." His mother, who was present in the room during the questioning, beamed. By chance, this boy was assigned to play the very violent video game *Mortal Kombat* (a martial arts game involving hand-to-hand combat).

Although the child stated that he had never played this game before, he proceeded to have his character, Sub-Zero, rip out the spine of his opponent. This type of "fatality" move involves a series of key presses done in a particular order within a particular time frame. Thus, it is extremely unlikely that the "fatality" occurred by chance. The most plausible explanation is that the child responded in a socially desirable manner in order to avoid getting in trouble for playing video games prohibited by his mother. Furthermore, given the negative publicity that violent media have in the press, it is reasonable to assume that parents may respond to questions in a socially desirable manner as well. Such socially desirable responding would lead to an under-reporting of children's exposure to media violence.

Patterns of Media Consumption

Media Ownership

According to Comstock and Paik (1999), by the time youth finish high school they will have watched upwards of 20,000 hours of TV but will have only been in the classroom for 14,000 hours. However, the total amount of media exposure is greater than what was reported by Comstock and Paik, as playing video games, accessing the Internet, attending movies, listening to music, and reading for enjoyment were not included in the analyses. In fact, there is typically no shortage of media options for children and adolescents. Virtually all families own at least one TV, and 75% of families report owning three TVs. In fact, nearly two-thirds of 8- to 18-year-olds report having a TV in their bedroom. Moreover, 80% of surveyed families report owning a video game console, and 50% of youth report keeping a video game console in their bedroom. Finally, almost 75% of families have computers with Internet access, with around 20% of youth having access to the World Wide Web and the World Live Web (e.g., blog, instant messaging) in their bedrooms (Roberts, Foehr, & Rideout, 2005).

As children and adolescents get older, the types of media found in their bedrooms changes. For instance, adolescents are more likely to have radios, CDs, and tapes in their bedrooms than are children. In contrast, youth in middle childhood and early adolescence are more likely to have video game consoles in their bedrooms than are youth in late adolescence. Across development, with increasing age comes increasing bedroom-based computers and Internet access. However, regardless of age, the percentage of youth with TVs in their room remains the same. Figure 4.1 shows the percentage of youth reporting TVs, video game consoles, CDs/tapes, computers, and Internet access in their bedrooms, as a function of age. In short, youth are

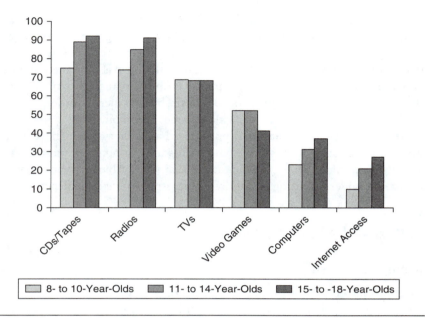

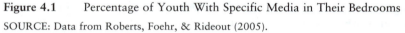

Figure 4.1   Percentage of Youth With Specific Media in Their Bedrooms

SOURCE: Data from Roberts, Foehr, & Rideout (2005).

exposed to thousands upon thousands of hours of media, a process that begins in infancy (Roberts et al., 2005).

Media Consumption During Childhood

Rideout, Vandewater, and Wartella (2003) surveyed several thousand parents and found that electronic media, in its various forms, is a staple in the daily diet of experiences of young children. On an average day, children up to the age of 6 spend two hours watching television (including video tapes and broadcast programming) and one hour listening to music, and adults read to them for about half an hour. In general, media consumption increases throughout childhood, with a recent study finding that by the time children are 8 years old, they consume nearly eight hours of media per day (Gentile, Lynch, Linder, & Walsh, 2004). Given that parents report that their children play outside for two hours per day, children are more likely to experience the world through the media than through the outdoors. In fact, nearly one-third of children begin watching television before the age of one.

Whether it is alone, with a sibling, or with a parent, very young children are exposed to violent media. For instance, according to parental report, nearly 4% of 2- to 7-year-olds have played an action/combat video game, and approximately 5% have recently viewed an action movie (which almost always contain violence), with another 1% having seen a horror movie (Roberts, Foehr, Rideout, & Brodie, 1999). The level of violence exposure, however, was probably under-reported, as the Roberts et al. survey most likely included cartoons in the comedy genre. Cartoons are replete with acts of aggression. In fact, in 1967 the typical cartoon contained nearly three times as many acts of aggression as did the typical adult drama (Gerbner, 1972).

Across the board, children's programming (i.e., programming aimed at children under 12 years of age) contains a constant barrage of violence. Recently, Wilson, Smith, and colleagues (2002) found that 69% of all programs aimed at children 12 years of age or younger contained frequent acts of violence, with an average of 14 acts of violence per hour. Furthermore, certain subgenres of children's programming were particularly likely to contain violence. For instance, 100% of slapstick shows (e.g., *Animaniacs, Bugs Bunny, Road Runner*), 97% of superhero shows (e.g., *Captain Planet, Power Rangers, Spiderman*), 89% of adventure and mystery shows (e.g., *Garfield, Scooby Doo, Timon & Pumbaa)*, and 48% of shows focusing on social relationships (e.g., *Allegra's Window, Care Bears, Rugrats*) depicted acts of aggression. However, the total amount of *violent* media consumed on a daily basis during childhood is not known. Clearly, this is an area in need of research.

Media Consumption During Adolescence

Media consumption increases as children approach adolescence and then stabilizes. Across adolescence, nearly one-third of the day is spent consuming media. Roberts (2000) reported that 8- to 13-year-olds spent 8 hours per day using media (e.g., TV, movies, radio), which was just slightly higher than the 7.5 hour per day consumed by 14- to 18-year-olds. However, more recent data by Roberts et al. (2005) suggest that across adolescence nearly 9 hours of media are consumed daily. Clearly, with such high levels of media consumption, adolescents will be exposed to violent media daily. However, the total amount of *violent* media consumed per day has yet to be determined.

Throughout adolescence, the viewing of screen media (e.g., television shows, videos, DVDs, movies) is the most popular form of media consumption. For instance, a recent survey of 607 8th and 9th graders found that adolescents watch TV 25 hours per week, listen to music 21 hours per week, play video games 9 hours per week, and read for fun 3 hours per week

(Gentile et al., 2004). However, not all media retain the same daily level of consumption during the teen years. Roberts and colleagues (2005) report a slight decrease in video game play as youth become older. In contrast, during adolescence, computer use and music become increasingly popular venues for media consumption. How popular does music become during adolescence? Consider the following: Roberts et al. (2003) asked adolescents which form of media (e.g., TV, music, video games, computer, newspapers, magazines) they would take with them if they had to be stranded on a desert island. Nearly half of 11th graders chose music, in comparison to 44% of 9th graders and 40% of 7th graders. Moreover, Roberts and colleagues (2005) report that music consumption more than doubles from middle childhood to late adolescence.

Gender Differences in Media Consumption

Childhood

Between 2 and 7 years of age, boys tend to consume slightly (i.e., 21 minutes) more media on a daily basis than do girls. Differences arise because boys are watching more TV and playing more video games than girls (Roberts, Foehr, et al., 1999). Furthermore, gender-based differences are evident in the genre of media consumed. In particular, boys, more than girls, tend to prefer media laden with violence. For instance, Valkenburg and Janssen (1999) found that 1st- through 4th-grade Dutch and American boys, more than girls, preferred television shows with violence. Similarly, Collins-Standley, Gan, Yu, and Zillman (1996) demonstrated that 2- to 4-year-old boys preferred fairy tales replete with violence, whereas same-age girls preferred romantic fairy tales.

Adolescence

Similar to the pattern evident in childhood, across adolescence boys and girls consume the same amount of media. Once again, what differs between genders is the type of media consumed. Specifically, between the ages of 8 and 18, boys tend to play more computer games than do girls. In contrast, on a daily basis, girls tend to listen to slightly more music and read more books than boys (Roberts et al., 2005). For instance, Gentile et al. (2004) found that 8th- and 9th-grade boys play video games nearly twice as much as same-age girls. Roberts et al. (1999) report that this pattern holds throughout childhood and adolescence. It is worth noting, however, that although adolescent boys play video games for more hours than adolescent girls, both male and female adolescents play video games on a regular basis (Dill & Dill, 1998).

Across adolescence, gender differences also are found in the media genre preferred. Consistently, males prefer violent media more than females do. Cantor (1998a) found that adolescent boys are more interested in violent TV than are adolescent girls. Similarly, Sargent et al. (2002) found that 10- to 14-year-old boys watch more extremely violent movies than girls do. Similar findings have been shown for video games. In fact, Walsh, Gentile, Gieske, Walsh, and Chasco (2003) report that among 13-year-olds, 87% of boys compared with 46% of girls play M-rated games. M-rated games contain intense violence and strong language and are thought to be suited for individuals 17 years and older (Entertainment Software Rating Board [ESRB], 2004). Additionally, 78% of 13-year-olds rate M-rated games in their top five favorites, with 40% saying that an M-rated game is their favorite. Not surprisingly, Dietz (1998) found that 80% of the most popular video games on the market today are violent in nature. Similarly, in a large survey of 5,000 10- to 14-year-olds, Sargent and colleagues (2002) found that 59% of 10-year-olds, 56% of 12-year-olds, and 70% of 14-year-olds had previously watched a movie rated as extremely violent (e.g., *Scream, I Know What You Did Last Summer*). It is worth noting that 80 of the 89 extremely violent movies included in the sample were rated R. As Sargent aptly states, researchers interested in media violence could not do research on the effects of these types of movies on children and adolescents, as the showing of R-rated movies to youth would be considered unethical.

Reasons for Consuming Violent Entertainment

As the above review illustrates, children and adolescents spend countless hours consuming violent media. Across development, youth will bear witness to, or virtually partake in, the murder, assault, or battery of countless numbers of people of varying gender, age, and ethnicity. Using a variety of violent entertainment media, children and adolescents will be exposed to mean-spiritedness, foul language, bullying, and the hatred and humiliation of others. Guns, machetes, knives, cars, and body parts are just some of the many instruments of destruction that youth will encounter. And most of the time, children and adolescents will actively seek out the death and destruction they will devour. One of the least-researched areas in the field of media violence research addresses the reasons children and adolescents have such a voracious appetite for violence. However, the *uses and gratifications perspective* has provided a framework for understanding the varied reasons for violent media consumption.

According to the uses and gratifications perspective, individuals use TV, movies, video games, and other forms of media to have rewarding experiences (Palmgreen, Wenner, & Rayburn, 1980). According to this perspective, therefore, violent entertainment must *somehow* provide fulfillment for children and adolescents. But just what are the "needs" of youth and how does consuming violent media provide such fulfillment? Sparks (2001) provides a list of the most frequently cited needs/gratifications, including *arousal, companionship, escape, habit, learning, passing time,* and *relaxation.* Although this list was originally put forth to explain the consumption of media in general, these gratifications can be applied to violent entertainment.

Uses and Gratification of Violent Media

Companionship

"Oh man, that was so cool. Did *you* see the top of his head fly off?" "Yep, that was sweet!" According to Goldstein (1999), youth (especially boys) most often consume violent entertainment in groups, regardless of whether consumption takes place in a video arcade, at the theater, or sitting around the family room. However, there are no data to indicate how often violent media are consumed alone or in groups, and there are no data to assess whether group consumption varies across development. Given that prevailing attitudes often become more extreme when discussed in groups, a phenomenon known as *group polarization,* it is possible that attitudes towards violence and the use of aggression to solve problems may vary as a function of the number of people consuming violent media at the same time and the consensus of the group regarding the consumed media. Goldstein (1999) also suggests that even if youth are consuming violent media alone, they most certainly are discussing what they saw, heard, or did with their friends. Anecdotal evidence was used to support his claims; given that such evidence lacks generalizability, additional assessments are warranted.

Table 4.1   Reasons Why Youth Consume Violent Media

Companionship	Escape	Habit
Learning	Passing Time	Relaxation
Sensation Seeking	Vicarious Aggression	Identity Formation
Defiance of Restrictions	Empowerment	Social Status
Mood Management		

Escape

Sparks (2001) suggests that individuals may use media to escape from the reality of everyday life. The extent to which youth use violent media to accomplish this goal, however, is largely unexplored. It may be that in an effort to divert one's thoughts from school work, peer problems, and issues of youth, children and adolescents play violent video games, watch violent movies, or read violent comic books. Research by Johnston (1995) suggests that this might be the case when adolescents watch horror films, as watching this form of media violence was used by adolescents when lonely, angry, or in an effort to avoid problems. Furthermore, the behavior of using media violence for escapism was also significantly associated with another escapist behavior, drug use.

Habit

Research over the last several decades has pointed to the fact that some forms of media, such as television and video games, not only are habit forming but also may reflect an addiction (Salguero & Moran, 2002; Smith, 1986). According to Kubey and Csikszentmihalyi (2002), addiction in general and TV addiction in particular are characterized by the same criteria: (1) using the substance a great deal, (2) using the substance more than one intended, (3) making unsuccessful attempts to reduce use, (4) giving up important activities to use the substance, and (5) experiencing withdrawal when usage stops. However, not all scientists are convinced that media are addictive in the same way that heroin, cocaine, and alcohol are addictive. For instance, Sparks (2001) points out that the term "addiction" may not directly apply to TV use (or video games, the Internet, etc.) but that individuals display behaviors that resemble addictive behaviors but do not quite reach the criteria for an addiction. Furthermore, whether youth play *violent* video games or watch *violent* TV out of habit or addiction is unanswered. It may be that youth are not addicted to any one particular genre of media (such as violence or comedy) but instead demonstrate addiction or habitual behavior towards media (e.g., TV or video games) in general.

Learning

As described in Chapter 1, for nearly 70 years the critics of entertainment violence have claimed that by playing violent video games, watching violence on TV and in movies, and by listening to angry and misogynistic music, youth are being taught that aggression is an appropriate way to solve problems, and they are receiving instructions on how to tease, bully, and assault others. For instance, Grossman and DeGaetano (1999) contend that violent video games involving hand-held guns teach kids not only how to use, aim, and shoot weapons but also how to overcome the natural hesitancy that is associated with killing. However, in the aforementioned situations, the knowledge gained is an artifact of media consumption and not something that was sought out as part of the child's original intention when deciding to consume violent media. According to the uses and gratification perspective, in contrast, youth specifically and intentionally seek out violent media for information. As one adolescent so aptly stated, "slasher movies are educational" (Johnston, 1995). Unfortunately, there were no follow-up questions for this eager-to-learn teen, so it is unclear which of the following aspects of slasher films were perceived as instructive: screaming techniques; the practical uses of chainsaws and kitchen knives; or the proper approach to stalking a victim so that although the victim runs away in horror, you are still able find a way to catch and kill him or her without breaking a sweat.

To date, the educational opportunities youth seek out when consuming violent media are largely unexplored, and as such, are ready for further investigation. Understanding what children and adolescents expect to learn from violent entertainment would make possible appropriate interventions to mitigate the harmful effects of violent media exposure while providing youth with the knowledge that they seek. For instance, if a teen wishes to learn about the physiological responses to being shot, the graphic illustrations frequently depicted on the TV show *CSI* would allow the child to see an unjustified, non-reinforced portrayal of a shooting. Furthermore, the negative consequences of the shooting for the victims and their families are frequently shown on *CSI*. In contrast, witnessing hundreds of people being shot in the movie *True Lies* will also provide a depiction of physiological response to being shot, except the shootings in this case are portrayed as being justified, with the shooter reinforced and the negative consequences to the victims not addressed. Anderson and colleagues (2003) contend that justified and unpunished violence, in which the consequences to the victims are overlooked, may produce more harmful effects to the viewer than if the violence is shown as being unjustified, punished, and associated with negative consequences.

Passing Time

"Are we there yet?" Say it three times really fast, wait one minute, repeat. If you've ever traveled long distances with children, the four most-repeated words that you will hear are, "Are we there yet?" To make the time pass more quickly for their children on long trips, and to retain their own sanity, parents allow (and at times exhort) their children to listen to music, play video games on their Game Boys, and watch movies on their factory-installed DVD player. "I'm hungry." Say it three times really fast, wait one minute, repeat. To a parent, the time between ordering food in a restaurant and receiving the food can seem like an eternity. As such, some parents promote the use of quiet entertainment, such as listening to CDs with headphones, reading comic books, and playing Game Boys (with the sound turned off). Just like nonviolent entertainment, violent entertainment can make long waits pass more quickly, thus reducing any negative effects associated with being frustrated, such as anger and hostility (Zillman, 1998). Although consuming violent media is associated with increased levels of anger and hostility, no research has assessed the use of violent entertainment to relieve boredom in children and adolescents. For instance, it would be interesting to know what causes children to become more angry and hostile, boredom while waiting for an event to occur (e.g., food to be delivered, arriving at a destination) or playing violent video games. It may be that proximately, violent video game play is the "lesser of two evils." However, it should be pointed out that ultimately, violent video game play could be the "greater of two evils." For instance, in the short term, the child may be less frustrated after playing a violent video game, but in the long term, the child may never learn to cope with being bored. As such, when placed in circumstances that are boring, without the distraction of media the child may be unable to effectively cope with the situation.

Relaxation

After a long school day involving standardized testing, standardized instruction, and standardized cafeteria food, what could be more relaxing than blowing away a few zombies in *House of the Dead* or watching the dismemberment of others, as is done in *Dawn of the Dead?* With each exploding head or disembowelment, you can feel the tension melt away. In actuality, it is non-arousing media, such as classical music or educational television, that can lead to feelings of relaxation (Sparks, 2001). In contrast, most forms of violent media cause physiological arousal (e.g., elevated heart rate and blood pressure), not relaxation. Unfortunately, there is no research to address whether youth *seek out* violent entertainment to relax. That is, in an attempt to relax, youth may seek out violent media even though the relaxation effects that they seek may not occur.

Sensation Seeking

Children and adolescents may seek out violent entertainment to gratify their need for new experiences, excitement, and physiological arousal, a phenomenon known as *sensation seeking* (Zuckerman, 1994). In comparison to those low in sensation seeking, individuals high in sensation seeking have a preference for activities that lead to physiological arousal, such as raves, drug use, amusement park thrill rides, and sky diving (Slater, 2003; Sparks, 2001). Additionally, several studies using adolescent participants have found that teens high in sensation seeking prefer violent media (e.g., violent TV, movies, and Web sites) more than teens low in sensation seeking (Aluja-Fabregat, 2000; Slater, 2003). Most of the research linking sensation seeking with media violence has done so by correlating sensation seeking with violent media consumption. Although this type of research has shown positive correlations between violent media consumption and sensation seeking, the motivation behind the consumption was not directly assessed. As such, the previous studies did not address whether youth were *using* violent media as a means of gratifying their need for sensation (Johnston, 1995). However, in one of the few studies conducted that actually asks youth directly why they like certain forms of violent media (i.e., slasher movies), Johnston (1995) found direct evidence that violent media gratifies sensation-seeking needs. Johnston assessed adolescent motivations for watching graphic horror movies. One subgroup of youth, labeled "Thrill Watchers," reported sensation-seeking behavior, such as watching horror movies to "have fun," "freak themselves out," or because they "like to be scared" (p. 536).

Although violent movies, TV, and video games are inherently action oriented, and thus replete with sensation, action movies, TV, and video games *do not* have to be violent. In fact, Valkenburg and Janssen (1999) found that 6- to 11-year-old children perceive the action and violence in television programs as separate characteristics. However, there is currently no research that assesses whether youth *perceive* action with violence and action without violence as differing in or containing the same amount of sensation. Furthermore, research on visual attention has produced contradictory results with regard to children's attentional preferences for violence or action. For instance, Potts and colleagues found that preschool children attended more to cartoons depicting high action than cartoons containing little action (Potts, Huston, & Wright, 1986). However, action-oriented programs did not receive more visual attention than violence-oriented programs. In a somewhat contradictory fashion, research on elementary school–age children has shown that television programs high in violence attract more visual attention than television programs depicting little violence. Once again, however, violence- and action-oriented programs did not differ in the amount of visual attention received (Alvarez, Huston, Wright, & Kerkman, 1988). If the action does predominate over violence, then the sensation-seeking needs of youth could be met without exposing them to unwanted depictions of violence. More research is required using different modes of violent media, such as video games and live-action movies, before any definitive conclusions can be drawn.

Gratifications Specific to Violent Media

As the above review illustrates, the uses and gratifications perspective is a general model of media consumption. As such, the reasons youth consume *violent* media may be different from the reasons youth consume nonviolent media, such as romantic or comedic movies. Recently, Cantor (1998a) has forwarded reasons specific to the use of violent media by children and adolescents, including *vicarious aggression* and *defiance of restrictions*.

Vicarious Aggression

"People are for hugging, not hitting!" "It's OK to be angry; it's not OK to hit!" "I told you not to hit your sister! Time out!" As each of the above quotes illustrates, children are socialized to inhibit acts of aggression. Moreover, failure to show appropriate restraint often results in punishment. Thus, Cantor (1998a) contends that youth are attracted to violent media because they can "act" aggressively through vicarious participation. Similarly, vicarious aggression may be prominent in youth who are small for their age or physically weak.

The fascination that many youth have with outlaws and bad boys fits this perspective. In third grade, I wrote a report about the *greatness* of the noted outlaw of the Old West, Jesse James. After all, Jesse James robbed banks and did what he wanted! My teacher responded with a poor grade and a handwritten note stating that Jesse James was a ruthless killer, and therefore, "He really wasn't that great." At the time, the point was lost on me. Today, children are still fascinated by those who do what they want to do without restriction. For instance, in *Star Wars I: The Phantom Menace,* the evil, seven-horned warrior Darth Maul was on screen for a short period of time, uttered only five lines, and died at the end of the movie. Yet, he was one of the favorite characters from that movie, with Halloween costumes, action figures, and bicycles bearing his likeness. Why was he so popular? It may be that it was because he was a virtually unstoppable force who answered to no one but himself (and the Emperor of the Dark Side, of course). Darth Maul did not have to show restraint and he did not have to eat his vegetables.

It is important to note that there is virtually no published research directly assessing vicarious aggression. Cantor reports that in one unpublished study (Bruce, 1995), nearly 50% of middle-school students surveyed imagined or pretended to be "a person in the show who was violent." Furthermore, there is some research that suggests that youth often *identify* (i.e., adopt the characteristics or beliefs of another) with media-depicted aggressors (Cantor, 1998a). However, identification is different from vicarious experiences. For instance, although I do not identify with Darth Maul's beliefs about the Dark Side, I can experience vicarious aggression when he kicks Jedi butt! In short, identification is a process through which individuals determine who they are and who they want to become, whereas vicarious aggression is a short-term emotional experience involving desires to act in a forbidden manner or in a way that is impossible for the individual. However, youth may be consuming violent media for the purpose of identity formation, and in doing so they may experience identification with the aggressors.

Identity Formation: Individual Identity

Individual identity consists of a person's view of the traits (e.g., smart), characteristics (e.g., nice), and personal appearance (e.g., tall and beautiful) comprising the self. As part of figuring out who they are, validating their personal characteristics, or attempting to make themselves feel good about who they are, youth may seek out violent movies in which characters similar to themselves are reinforced for their aggressive behavior. For instance, adolescents who perceive themselves to be "riotous" may seek out violent media in which youth create havoc. Interestingly, the research on adolescent identity formation has focused on how media influence different aspects of children and adolescents' identities (e.g., sex roles, body image; Arnett, 1995; Huntemann & Morgan, 2001) without actually asking youth whether they purposefully seek out certain types of media to help clarify their identity. In other words, whether identity formation is the result of a passive influence from media exposure or an active process involving confirmation of who one is through the media, or a combination of both, has yet to be determined.

Identity Formation: Social Identity

Social identity refers to knowledge of social group membership, along with the value and emotional significance attached to that membership. In an effort to strengthen their identification with a particular social group (e.g., goths, jocks), or in an effort to view the social group to which they belong in a more positive light, youth may seek out media portrayals of the group with which they identify (Harwood, 1999). For instance, youth who identify with "computer nerds" may seek out violent movies in which "computer nerds" get revenge against the students who had bullied them at school. According to Arnett (1995), adolescents use music to establish a sense of social identity. By listening to punk, heavy metal, or rap music, youth are attempting to actively express their view of the world and validate their beliefs.

Defiance of Restrictions

A recent headline in *The Journal Gazette* read, "Advisory Labels Stimulate Sales" (De La Paz, 2004). The premise of the article was that "parental advisory" warning labels, such as "strong language" or "sexual content," result in increased sales for marked CDs. Unfortunately, the article does not discuss who is buying the CDs: underage youth, adults for themselves, or adults for underage youth. Similar warning labels appear on video games, with ratings such as "T" (acceptable for teen use) and "M" for mature (17 years of age or older). Even television shows are labeled with age restrictions.

Cantor (1998a) contends that *parents* believe that restrictive warning labels result in restrictive desires in their children. But what is the empirical effect of warning labels on children's desires to consume restricted media? According to the *forbidden fruit theory,* warning labels increase the attractiveness of violent media for youth. In contrast, the *tainted fruit theory* posits that warning labels decrease the attractiveness of violent media for children and adolescents (Bushman & Stack, 1996). Unfortunately, there is a dearth of research on the effects of warning labels on children's desire for warned-against media. Research using undergraduates, however, has clearly demonstrated that warning labels increase interest in violent programs for both males and females (although at times, the effect is more significant for males than females). In youth, however, restrictive labels appear to produce a tainted fruit effect for girls and a forbidden fruit effect for boys. For instance, Sneegas and Plank (1998) found that pre-adolescent boys preferred television programs labeled as age inappropriate more than television programs labeled as age appropriate. In contrast, pre-adolescent girls preferred television programs labeled as age appropriate. Cantor, Harrison, and Nathanson (1997) also demonstrated a forbidden fruit effect for boys, but not girls, with regard to the desire to view age-inappropriate television programming.

Gender Differences and Forbidden Fruit. Why is it that boys tend to demonstrate a forbidden fruit pattern of media violence consumption whereas girls tend to consume media in an approach consistent with the tainted fruit perspective? One significant contributor to the aforementioned differences may be the manner in which boys and girls are socialized. Boys are socialized to adopt an *instrumental role* that involves being assertive, competitive, dominant, goal oriented, and independent. In contrast, girls are socialized to adopt an *expressive role,* resulting in behavior that is cooperative, kind, nurturing, and sensitive to the needs of others (Parsons, 1955). Additionally, research has shown that in response to the requests and demands of authority figures, such as parents and teachers, boys tend to be less compliant than girls (Feingold, 1994). Thus, the pattern of noncompliance and instrumental role activity that boys exhibit may result in a forbidden fruit effect for warning labels. After all, being independent and dominant means that you do what you want to do, not necessarily what you are told. In contrast, the characteristics of the expressive role, such as cooperation and the tendency to be compliant, may result in a tainted fruit effect for girls.

Furthermore, Bushman and Stack (1996) found that college students with a tendency to rebel against authority showed greater interest in violent programs with warning labels than did undergraduates less likely to rebel against authority. This finding is consistent with the fact that socially devalued music (e.g., heavy metal rock) is preferred by delinquent youth. What is less clear, however, is whether youth are choosing to listen to socially devalued music because it is a "forbidden fruit," simply because they like it, or some combination of both.

Empowerment and Social Status

Additionally, Zillmann (1998) has suggested that youth, and boys in particular, are motivated to view violence in an effort to feel empowered or to elevate their social status. For instance, after watching gory and violent movies, adolescents report feeling "brave," "mature," and "different" (Johnston, 1995). Thus, by overcoming their own fears, a "rite of passage" has taken place and subsequently youth may feel empowered by the experience. Furthermore, Zillmann (1998) contends that violent media consumption is a social event, in which adolescents prove that they are "fearless" and that they can "take it." Similarly, Goldstein (1999) reports that violent entertainment is primarily consumed in the presence of others and when consumed alone is almost universally talked about with peers at some point in the future. Through the process of *social comparison,* in which youth define and evaluate themselves by comparison to others, violent media consumption may contribute to the elevation of their social status. Specifically, by pointing out to the group that they have accomplished something that their peers have not, their position within the group may be elevated (Zillmann, 1998).

Mood Management

Zillmann contends that youth consume violent entertainment in an attempt to create a particular mood state (e.g., happiness) or to modify a currently experienced mood state. In support of this contention, research by Hakanen (1995) found that African American adolescents report using rap music to "get pumped up." Although mood management can occur with any form of violent media, it is particularly prominent in the medium of music. Moreover, adolescents will listen to music that matches the mood state they are currently in. For instance, youth will listen to upbeat music when they are happy, thrashing music when angry, and somber music when sad. However, gender differences abound. Whereas adolescent boys use music to increase their level of arousal, adolescent girls tend to use music to reduce feelings of loneliness and isolation, or for contemplative purposes. With regard to mood matching, males tend to use music to match negative moods (and in particular anger) while girls listen to music to match somber moods (Roberts & Christenson, 2001).

The Importance of Understanding Why Youth Consume Violent Media

Understanding why youth watch violent movies, play violent video games, and so on is important, for the gratifications that youth gain when consuming violent media may influence the impact of that consumption on their health and well-being. For instance, youth who watch violent movies to elevate their social status may, in fact, be more likely to adopt aggressive behaviors (in an effort to further increase their social status) than those who watch violent movies for educational purposes or out of curiosity. In support of this notion, Johnston (1995) found that the motivation for watching slasher films was related to the effects that those films had on the adolescent's cognitive and affective state. As an example, Johnston reports that youth who watch slasher films for sensation-seeking purposes report more positive emotion, before and after viewing graphic horror, than youth motivated to watch movies in an effort to engage in mood management. Little is known, however, about the factors (e.g., parenting, peers, siblings) that influence the particular uses and gratifications that violent media provide for children and adolescents. Furthermore, changes in patterns of uses and gratifications of violent media consumption require further exploration, as there is no research in this area.

Violent Media Consumption as a Function of Development

Adolescents consume violent media with the greatest frequency during the developmental period in which they respond to provocation situations with the greatest frequency of aggression. Why violent media consumption and developmental changes in adolescent aggression correspond is intriguing. One possibility is that as adolescents become more aggressive, they become more attracted to activities that involve aggression. Previous research supports this contention. For instance, highly aggressive boys have been shown to prefer violent media (e.g., toys, video games, television) more than less aggressive boys (see Goldstein, 1998). It follows that as psychosocial and biological factors trigger adolescents' aggressive tendencies, adolescents should become drawn to more violent activities. Later, developmental changes resulting in a decrease in aggressive behavior may lead to decreases in preference for aggressive activities such as video games. A second possibility is that because video game play is action oriented, it creates a high level of arousal. According to Goldstein, individuals who have a high need for sensation or arousal are attracted to violent imagery. In support of this contention, McCauley (1998) suggests that individuals who are high in sensation seeking find violence in television and film more appealing than do their low sensation-seeking counterparts. Recent research by Lynch (1999) has shown that following violent video game play, individuals high in trait hostility show greater increases in epinephrine than individuals low in trait hostility. Additional research has shown that increases in heart rate and blood pressure accompany violent video game play (Anderson & Bushman, 2001). Thus, research indicates that violent video games result in an increase in physiological arousal. Early adolescence is a time of increased risk taking and novelty seeking. Spear (2000) suggests that adolescents may be less affected by moderate stimuli than children or adults. Consequently, adolescents may seek out sensation-producing activities, such as video game play, for rewarding experiences. Thus, violent media consumption may be an attempt to provide the adolescent with acceptable levels of arousal. However, more research is necessary to determine the exact reasons why adolescents are attracted to violent media.

Summary

- Empirical questions are answered with data.
- Across childhood and adolescence, the survey method is the most frequently used technique to collect data on media consumption. It is unethical to engage in "Big Brother"–type monitoring of media consumption.
- Survey data can be collected using intercept interviews, mail-in surveys, face-to-face interviews, and Web-based questioning. Care needs to be taken during the data collection process to avoid bias. Low response rates, unrepresentative samples, and social desirability can lead to inaccurate survey data.
- Children spend more time consuming media than they spend outside. By the time most children enter 3rd grade, they will spend close to 8 hours per day consuming media.
- The vast majority of children are exposed to media violence through television programming aimed at youth under 12 years of age. A relatively small percentage of young children are exposed to violent media meant for older adolescents and adults. A much larger percentage of early adolescents are exposed to violent media intended for adults. Media consumption peaks in early adolescence.
- Across development, boys consume more media, and more violent media, than do girls.
- There are many uses and gratifications associated with consuming violent media. Youth consume entertainment violence for companionship, to relax, to pass time, to learn something, and to escape reality for a brief period of time. Some youth consume out of habit and others do so because they seek excitement.
- Additionally, youth consume violent media in order to experience aggression vicariously, to defy authority, to alter their mood, to increase their social status, and to help in the establishment of social and individual identities.
- In an effort to dissuade youth from media violence consumption, warning labels and ratings systems have been instituted. However, restrictive labels appear to produce a tainted fruit effect for girls and a forbidden fruit effect for boys. The instrumental and expressive roles can help explain why such gender differences occur.
- The gratifications that youth gain while consuming violent media may influence the impact of that consumption on their health and well-being.
- Adolescents consume the greatest amount of violent entertainment during early adolescence, the developmental period in which they tend to be the most aggressive. The reason for this finding remains unclear.

PART II

Effects of Specific Forms of Violent Media on Youth

5

Violent Media and the Need to Feel Strong and Powerful

Over the course of the history of science, new research has periodically contradicted what the scientific community had thought to be an established fact. For instance, for over 1400 years it was a *known* fact that the Earth was the center of the universe. Now we know the Earth revolves around the Sun (Jonstone, 1999). Prior to the 1950s, doctors used X-rays to evaluate the health of developing fetuses because of the scientific fact that the uterus shielded the unborn infant from all environmental influences; of course, given the tragic health consequences that followed, we now know that moderate and large doses of radiation can cause birth defects and cancer (DeHart et al., 2004). Recently it was thought that eating meat was bad for your health, but now, under the Aktins Diet, juicy steaks served medium rare are viewed as a healthy staple. And in his controversial book *Killing Monsters: Why Children Need Fantasy, Super Heroes, and Make-Believe Violence*, Gerard Jones (2002) argues that nearly 70 years of scientific evidence on media violence is fatally flawed and that the connection between violent media exposure and aggression is tenuous at best. In fact, not only does Jones believe that there is little convincing evidence linking violent entertainment and aggression, but he also believes that such exposure is *good* for children and adolescents and, at times, a *necessary component* of healthy development.

For most parents, the health and well-being of their children is of paramount importance. Parents want their children to have high levels of self-esteem and feel in control of their destinies. Parents want their children to work hard and endeavor to succeed in the face of challenges. Parents want to help children deal with their fears and show them how to appropriately handle their anger. Although it would be nice to think that all the experiences youth have are healthful (or at the worst neutral), sadly, that is not the case. Poverty, neglect, abuse, peer rejection, and sibling rivalry negatively affect the health of children and adolescents (Dehart et al., 2004). The nature of media violence exposure as a health risk will be dealt with in subsequent chapters. In this chapter, the nature of media violence as a promoter of health is addressed.

Historical Proponents of Media Violence

Suggesting that violent media research is flawed and that the so-called effects are weak is nothing new; others have made the same critique. For instance, the "Payne Studies" of the 1930s were criticized for an "anti-movie tone" and the "minimizing of points" that would demonstrate the benefits of movie watching (Jowett et al., 1996). More recently, Freedman (2002) summarizes laboratory research on media violence research by stating that the evidence "does not demonstrate that exposure to media violence affects aggression" (p. 195). The idea that exposure to entertainment violence might have some benefits can be traced back to Aristotle and his notion of *katharsis*. Katharsis refers to the purging of emotion through pity and fear. In fact, Aristotle was probably one of the first proponents of media violence, for katharsis occurred in response to viewing dramatic tragedies, which were replete with violent imagery and death. However, what is new, and what is most intriguing about Jones's thesis, is the notion that children and adolescents benefit from exposure to *all* forms of media violence, and the benefits are more than a simple release of emotion.

Bruno Bettelheim championed the power of violent imagery in *The Uses of Enchantment* (Bettelheim, 1967), in which he promoted the therapeutic benefits that children experience through hearing or reading fairy tales that contain imagery of violence and gore. According to Bettelheim, fairy tales such as *Hansel and Gretel,* in which kidnapped children ultimately kill their captor, lead to a reduction of aggressive behavior due to the purging of aggressive desires. However, Bettelheim's view of the benefits of fairy tales was limited to that particular genre. Modern-day works of written fiction, and other forms of mass media, were viewed as potentially harmful to children (Jones, 2002). In contrast, for Jones, the benefits of media violence transcend the images created in one's mind when reading fairy tales to include the more grotesque and vivid displays of violence and gore depicted in slasher films. For instance, movies posited to be beneficial to youth could include *Halloween,* in which an adolescent boy gets stabbed through the heart and pinned to a wall with his feet dangling several feet off the ground, blood trickling from his toes. According to Jones, youth could also benefit from playing violent video games—video games like *House of the Dead,* in which the protagonist shoots zombies and assorted demonic creatures; bullets entering the target's body result in exploding heads, dismembered body parts flying through the air, and blood pooling at the feet of a now-headless corpse, all of which happens within the first minute of the game. Developmental well-being may be promoted, according to the tenets of Jones, by having adolescents listen to misogynistic lyrics frequently found in rap music; lyrics in which women are referred to as "bitches" and the degradation and rape of women are advocated. So, what are these benefits that Jones proclaims develop after violent media consumption, and exactly how strong are the empirical data used to support these claims?

The So-Called Modern-Day Benefits of Media Violence

According to Jones, violent media consumption engages a child's fantasies—fantasies that can be used to create a *more* mentally sound child. As such, he posits that playing violent video games can help children feel strong, powerful, and in control. For instance, watching violent movies is thought to reduce feelings of anger and anxiety. Jones suggests that reading violent comic books or listening to violent lyrics in music can help children deal with the emotional challenges associated with facing violence in the real world. Similar to the presentation of "scientific fact" in Bettelheim's (1967) treatise, in *Killing Monsters* Jones relays vivid accounts of teenagers and their concomitant teenage angst. Jones contends that with the help of violent video games, violent comic books, or some other form of violent media, youth can overcome problems to become healthier, more nonviolent individuals. For instance, in the first chapter of his book, "Being Strong," Jones describes his encounter at a comic book convention with a young adolescent girl named Sharon. Sharon was a highly timid, tensely angry, slightly depressed fan of the comic book *Freex. Freex,* written by Gerard Jones himself, conveys the adventures of runaway teen superheroes. When engaged in reading the comic book, Jones reports, Sharon can see the passion of the characters, a passion that in turn makes those characters powerful. And since when she reads the comic book she becomes the character she is reading about, *she* in turn becomes powerful. Thus, according to Jones, comic book violence can lead to feelings of passion and the feelings of passion lead to feelings of power.

With the help of a violent comic book, a characteristically shy girl becomes powerful. Later, in that same chapter, Jones tells the story of Jimmy, a young adolescent boy who, filled with anxiety and labeled a behavior problem at school, becomes "calmer and more confident after spending a while with his games" (Jones, 2002, p. 17). Incidentally, "Jimmy's games" were the first-person shooter video games *Doom* and *Quake. Doom,* of course, was made infamous because it was the preferred video game of Dylan Klebold and Eric Harris, the Columbine killers. Note that by linking *Doom* with the horrific events that occurred at Columbine High School, I have used a single experience to support the argument that violent video games increase aggression for all. Similarly, in support of the benefits of violent media consumption, Jones relies heavily on this type of *anecdotal evidence* to support his claims. But is anecdotal evidence really "evidence" of the claims being made?

Anecdotal Evidence: Is It Scientific?

Anecdotal evidence is information presented in favor of an argument that is based on casual observations rather than data collected using the scientific method. Typically, anecdotal evidence involves the presentation of vividly detailed and emotional stories—stories that are enthusiastically told and retold by several different people. Infomercials are filled with such presentations. And much like horoscopes, the details of anecdotal stories are general enough so that a great number of people can relate to some aspect of the account. Most of the time, anecdotal stories are chosen because not only are they memorable, but they emphatically and unilaterally support the argument being presented. Jones excels at presenting this type of information. Nearly every anecdotal story presented throughout his book is wonderfully vivid and reflects feelings and/or experiences that are generally true of everyone. At times, anecdotal evidence is presented that goes against Jones's prevailing argument (i.e., media violence is healthful). However, in those cases, the information is quickly discredited as being nonscientific or belittled by pointing out the flaws of anecdotal evidence. Those flaws include the following: anecdotal evidence is *inaccurate*, filled with *bias*, and findings based on it are not *generalizable.*

Anecdotal evidence is often inaccurate because the information reported was not recorded in an objective manner and, therefore, may not reflect what actually happened. For example, Jimmy may not have actually been calmer after playing violent video games. Jimmy's mother, because she was thinking retrospectively, may have remembered the information incorrectly. Many studies have shown that reported "memories" of events never actually occurred, even though people believe that they have provided factual information (Fiske & Taylor, 1991). Additionally, anecdotal information is subject to bias because the observer's interpretation and reporting of a behavior may be influenced by the individual's preconceptions about the causes of that behavior. In fact, observations that contradict expectations are often ignored, dismissed, or changed (Fiske & Taylor, 1991). For example, Sharon may be reporting feeling "powerful" because she *wants* to be powerful and is, therefore, ignoring the many times in which she felt powerless after reading *Freex*. In support of this contention, research has shown that when children who have traditional beliefs about male and female occupational roles are shown pictures of male nurses and female firefighters, they remember the pictures as depicting female nurses and male firefighters (Liben & Signorella, 1993). That is, children's preconceived conceptions about gender roles result in a memory bias for information consistent with their gender role beliefs. Finally, because anecdotes are interesting stories that relay a singular experience, the findings illustrated in those stories may not apply to the public as a whole; that is, they will not be *generalizable*.

But what about the fact that Jones reports multiple anecdotes, all of which point to the same conclusions? First, each anecdote is subject to the flaws mentioned above, and simply having more of them does not mean that the findings from each anecdote are less flawed. Secondly, Jones specifically and calculatedly chose each story to prove his point about the benefits of violent media. However, there may be hundred of stories that go against Jones's contentions, but they were not reported. Thus, simply reporting that a large number of individuals have similar experiences does not necessarily mean that a phenomenon has been reliably demonstrated. Reliable demonstration comes from research in which the likelihood of biases and inaccuracy clouding the data has been controlled. That is, the research involved is conducted using the scientific method.

The Use of Flawed Data

So, why use anecdotal evidence if it provides flawed data? The answer is simple. When you do not have well-researched, empirical data to support your beliefs, use anecdotal evidence. Because of its emotional power, anecdotal evidence can appear to strengthen an argument, even though the "evidence" supplied may be incorrect. Anecdotes relay "real-life" stories—stories that everyone can relate to and understand. Anecdotes provide stories that give concrete examples of the phenomenon being reported, examples that are devoid of jargon (e.g., reliability, validity, generalizability), and examples that are easily remembered and provide a clear "take home" message, such as "Superheroes, video-game warriors, rappers, and movie gunmen are symbols of strength. By pretending to be them, young people are being strong" (Jones, 2002, p. 11). These messages, however, are more style than substance, more emotion than logic, and more speculative than definitive. The following question, however, has yet to be addressed. Is there evidence in support of the contention that violent media is good for kids?

Evaluating the Empirical Evidence Presented by Jones

Jones contends that media violence can (1) help children feel strong, powerful, and in control; (2) reduce negative emotions and aggression; and (3) help children deal with their anxieties and fears. Although intriguing, the anecdotal evidence cited by Jones is too flawed to either support or disconfirm his arguments. However, by evaluating the scientific literature, the answers to each of the aforementioned questions can be explored. Prior to evaluating the research in these areas, a bit of new psychological terminology needs to be introduced. Developmental psychologists studying children's social and emotional changes use different words to describe the same concepts to which Jones is referring. In place of "strong," "powerful," and "competent," developmental psychologists use the term *self-efficacy*. In place of "in control," psychologists use the verbiage *locus of control*.

Does Media Violence Increase Feelings of Strength, Power, and Competence?

Self-Efficacy

Self-efficacy is the sense of being able to independently and successfully complete a variety of tasks. For children and adolescents, these tasks include activities such as riding a bike, mastering algebra, or even controlling negative emotions (Bandura, Caprara, Barbaranelli, Gerbino, & Pastorelli, 2003). Youth high in self-efficacy believe that they can successfully complete such tasks by themselves, whereas youth low in self-efficacy believe that they will most likely fail when left to their own devices. Importantly, youth with high and low levels of self-efficacy demonstrate different outcomes on various measures of social, emotional, and cognitive aspects of development.

Table 5.1   Is Media Violence Good for Youth?

Can media violence consumption
  help children feel strong, powerful, and in control?
  reduce negative emotions and aggression?
  help children deal with their anxieties and fears?

For children and adolescents, high self-efficacy has been associated with success in school, expressing anger in positive ways (such as through discussion; Ausbrooks, Thomas, & Williams, 1995), and resisting the power of peer pressure. In contrast, children and adolescents with low self-efficacy are more likely to experience depression, anxiety, poor academic achievement, and drug use (Caprara, Regalia, & Bandura, 2002). Additionally, and specifically relevant to the issue of aggressive behavior, low levels of self-efficacy have been linked with aggressive and violent behavior in adolescents. Caprara et al. (2002) demonstrated that for both adolescent boys and girls, self-efficacy for emotion regulation (i.e., the ability to stay in control of strong positive and negative emotions) predicted self-reported levels of violent behavior at the time of the initial assessment as well as two years later. Specifically, adolescents reporting high levels of self-efficacy were less likely to engage in violent acts than adolescents with low levels of self-efficacy. Thus, self-efficacy—or, as Jones calls it, being strong, competent, and powerful—does appear to be an important contributor to healthy development across childhood and adolescence. The question that remains, however, is whether violent media consumption can also positively influence the child's level of self-efficacy.

Media Violence and Self-Efficacy

It is one thing to suggest that youth need to feel self-efficacious (or strong, powerful, and competent, according to Jones); it is quite another to suggest that virtually blowing off the head of a soldier, watching graphic disembowelments, or listening to music advocating homicide and cannibalism can positively increase self-efficacy. In order to answer this divisive question, it becomes necessary to examine the variables that influence child and adolescent self-efficacy.

Factors That Influence Self-Efficacy. One of the leading researchers in the area of self-efficacy is Albert Bandura. Bandura (1986) posits that there are three major factors influencing self-efficacy: *mastery experiences, social modeling,* and the *evaluative feedback of others.* Mastery experiences refer to excelling at some ability (such as tying one's shoe, riding a bike, or learning how to swim) through hard work and practice. Thus, actual success generates feelings of success, and with those feelings comes the belief that one can continue to master that task as well as other tasks yet to be faced. Social modeling refers to imitating the behaviors of models, such as other children or make-believe characters who are perceived to be similar to the self. For example, after witnessing a peer receive an accolade for winning a chess tournament, a child may be motivated to believe that she too can succeed when playing chess. Additionally, directly receiving positive feedback from others, such as praise for high marks on a test, helps foster the belief that one can accomplish great things (Caprara et al., 2002).

Violent Media and the Factors That Influence Self-Efficacy. Based on the above criteria, it is possible that experiences with certain types of violent media could impact a child's sense of self-efficacy. For instance, success at video game play *could* constitute a mastery experience; the characters in the video games *could* serve as social models, as could the peers being cheered on at an arcade; and receiving positive feedback from peers regarding one's video game prowess *could* constitute evaluative feedback. Furthermore, even though violent media exposure is linked with negative emotions such as anger (Anderson & Bushman, 2002), mood changes do not appear to influence perceived self-efficacy (Cervone, 2000). Unfortunately, there is no research examining whether *violent* media exposure can alter perceived self-efficacy.

There is, however, some indirect research addressing the relationship between issues of self-efficacy and media violence exposure. For instance, in an investigation of 183 junior high school students, Funk and Buchman (1996) found that girls reporting higher levels of video game play (be it violent or nonviolent) in an arcade or at home rated themselves as less competent (i.e., less efficacious) in settings involving academics, athletics, or social interactions. Furthermore, as girls' video game play increased, their overall level of *self-esteem* decreased. Self-esteem refers to an individual's evaluation of the self in terms of a variety of attributes, including academic (e.g., school performance), physical (e.g., appearance, athletic prowess), psychological (e.g., aggressiveness, shyness), and social (e.g., peer and love relationships) abilities. Individuals with high self-esteem feel good about themselves, whereas individuals with low self-esteem feel poorly about themselves. Self-esteem and self-efficacy are related in that self-efficacy (i.e., believing that you can accomplish tasks on your own) is taken into consideration when evaluating the self (Fiske & Taylor, 1991).

Media Violence and Discounting. Funk and Buchman (1996) contend that a course of action known as *discounting* may explain why decreases in self-efficacy were associated with increases in violent video game play. Coined by Susan Harter (1986), discounting refers to the process of valuing competencies (i.e., things you are good at) in areas that are not traditionally valued by others (e.g., skateboarding, music trivia from the 1970s) in order to *minimize* the significance of competencies in areas that are traditionally valued by others (e.g., academics, athletics, social interactions). Adolescents will engage in discounting when they do poorly in competencies valued by the majority of adolescents (Harter, 1987). For instance, a boy doing poorly in school may devalue the importance of academics to his future because he is a "rad" skateboarder who will turn his passion into a profession. Adolescents are thought to engage in the process of discounting to help maintain positive self-esteem. However, if competencies in valued areas drop below "socially acceptable levels," then discounting may lead to a drop in self-esteem (Harter, 1987). Funk and Buchman (1996) contend that girls may have engaged in video game play in order to discount other important areas of competence. Unfortunately, the girls' discounting behavior appeared to have been ineffective, given that higher levels of video game play were associated with lower levels of self-esteem.

Although the findings from Funk and Buchman's study were based on *general* video game play, as opposed to *violent* video game play, they do suggest that Jones's (2002) contention may find both corroboration and contradiction. Jones states that children and adolescents engage in violent video game play in an effort to feel strong, powerful, and competent. In fact, what Jones may be describing is the process of discounting. In corroboration of Jones, children may seek out violent media in an effort to feel competent in traditionally less valued areas (such as video game play) because they are doing poorly in traditionally valued competencies. However, the research also suggests that this discounting process has a limited range of usefulness. Thus, for some kids, the process of using violent media in an effort to discount other competency domains may contradict Jones's contentions that children will end up feeling strong and powerful. Instead of increasing a positive sense of self, children may be actually decreasing their overall self-worth. However, because the empirical evidence necessary for a proper evaluation has yet to be conducted, the impact of violent media on self-efficacy is an area requiring further exploration before any definitive conclusions can be drawn.

Does Media Violence Increase Feelings of Control?

Locus of Control

Jones (2002) contends that in addition to feeling strong and powerful, children and adolescents need to feel in control and that violent media can help children do just that. Psychologists have identified two types of control that are associated with aggressive behavior: *internal* and *external locus of control*. Youth with an internal locus of control believe that they can control their own fate. In contrast, youth with an external locus of control believe others have control of their fortune (Rotter, 1966). Positive outcomes, such as higher levels of academic achievement and better problem-solving abilities, are associated with internal locus of control. On the other hand, aggressive behavior and delinquency have been associated with an external locus of control (Halloran, Doumas, John, & Margolin, 1999). As these findings suggest, feeling in control has many psychological benefits, whereas lacking such feelings is associated with psychological detriments. Consequently, psychologists have tried to identify factors that promote an internal locus of control.

Media Violence and Locus of Control

Experiences in which practice leads to improved performance and hard work results in positive outcomes help children and adolescents develop an internal locus of control (DeHart et al., 2004). Certain forms of media, therefore, could potentially help children develop an internal locus of control. Just as studying for a spelling test may result in better spelling scores, so too may repeated video game play result in higher video game scores. By their very nature, video games require practice in order for success to be attained. In fact, in a study of incarcerated juvenile felons, playing the video games *Pac Man* and *Donkey Kong* resulted in improvements in the felons' levels of internal locus of control (Kappes & Thompson, 1985). Thus, it is plausible that if video game play in general can increase feelings of internal locus of control, violent video game play, and other forms of violent entertainment that require hard work, could lead to similar improvements. Once again, more research is necessary to confirm this contention.

In summary, the empirical data suggest that, in line with Jones's contention, violent entertainment could potentially lead to increases in feelings of self-efficacy (being strong and powerful) and locus of control (feeling in control). However, even if violent entertainment leads to these improvements, is associating self-efficacy and locus of control with aggressive and violent actions necessarily a good thing for children and adolescents? Unfortunately there is no direct research on this topic. However, research on bullies suggests that the negatives may outweigh the positives when using violent media to improve aspects of the self.

Bullying and Media Violence: What Are the Similarities? "Eighteen million" is a fantastic number if you've hit the lotto, but equally horrifying when you find out that *18 million* refers to the number of incidents of bullying that occur annually (Gentile & Sesma, 2003). Children who are victimized by bullies tend to be rejected by their peers, have low self-esteem, and experience higher rates of anxiety and depression (Griffin & Gross, in press). Given the staggering numbers of children and adolescents who are bullied, and the fact that demonstrable health concerns are associated with being victimized, the reasons why children bully have been investigated. As it turns out, many of the reasons for bullying are similar to the reasons that Jones (2002) gives when explaining why children play violent video games or immerse themselves in a world of violent imagery.

So, what is "gained" when children bully others, and how is it similar to Jones's rationale for the benefits of violent media consumption? Children who bully enjoy the domination and control associated with their aggressive acts, and they highly value the fruits of their aggressive labor (Shaffer, 2000). Children who play violent video games, by design, are dominating and controlling virtual characters and receive points for appropriately crafted violent acts. Thus, bullies feel strong, powerful, and in control when they bully, and according to Jones (2002), children feel strong, powerful, and in control when they play violent video games. Bullies tend to hang out together and praise each other for their aggressive acts (Shaffer, 2000). Praise, in this case, is a type of *reinforcement*. Reinforcement is the process by which rewards increase the likelihood that a behavior will increase in the future. Similarly, the process of reinforcement occurs in video game play, as points are given to reinforce a violent job well done. Although it was once believed that bullies suffer from low self-esteem, that notion has since been disproved (Griffin & Gross, in press). The self-esteem of bullies is typically at levels consistent with their non-bullying classmates. However, unlike their classmates, bullies use aggression to maintain their current level of self-esteem (Moeller, 2001).

Although aggressive competencies can be used to maintain high levels of self-esteem, as the problems associated with discounting suggest, children and adolescents would be better off using nonviolent competencies as a source of self-esteem. In support of this claim, a recent study found that by age 24, 70% of former junior high school bullies had been *convicted* of at least one crime. Furthermore, in comparison to their classmates, bullies are more likely to suffer from depression and be referred to mental health professionals for counseling (Griffin & Gross, in press). Thus, the long-term costs of bullying are more detrimental than the short-term gains garnered from bullying. Similarly, even if Jones is correct in his contention that violent media may give children and adolescents a sense of strength, power, and control in the short term, the long-term consequence of such aggressive associations may result in more harm than good. This is not to say that violent video games, and other forms of violent media, are going to cause a child to bully. As stated in Chapter 1, the effects of violent media exposure are more indirect than direct and more subtle than observable. However, although a child may not become a bully after playing a violent video game, violent media exposure may increase the likelihood that a child engages in aggressive behavior in the future. As a final note of comparison, research has shown that in comparison to children and adolescents who do not bully, it is easier for bullies to act aggressively (Moeller, 2001). And as Lt. Col. David Grossman contends, just as the army trains soldiers to shoot their weapons with ease, playing violent video games trains children and adolescents to use aggression with ease (Grossman & DeGaetano, 1999).

Does Media Violence Consumption Make Youth Less Likely to Aggress?

Catharsis

In Stephen King's classic horror novel *The Shining*, Jack Torrance, his wife, and his son spend the winter months alone at the remote and isolated Overlook Hotel. As caretaker of the hotel, Jack's primary responsibility is to periodically release the pressure building up inside the hotel's aging boiler. But as Jack succumbs to the evil lurking within the hotel, he slowly becomes murderous and maniacal, and he loses touch with reality. And as Jack spends the last few hours of his life trying to murder his wife and son, the boiler, not having been purged of its pent-up pressure for quite some time, explodes in a ball of fire. If only he had released the pressure; the hotel would be in one piece, and Jack would still be alive. Of course, if alive, Jack would then murder his wife and son, but that is beside the point.

The point, according to Jones, and Freud before him, is that aggressive urges build up over time, just as pressure can build up inside a boiler. Left unchecked, these urges can reach a fevered pitch, ultimately resulting in violent outbursts. The process of ridding oneself of this volatile pent-up anger and aggressive feelings is known as *catharsis*. Furthermore, a cathartic release is thought to be brought about by engaging in aggressive actions or by watching aggressive behavior (Bushman, 2002). What better way to blow off steam than to blow away some virtual bad guys, right? Feeling frustrated? Feeling angry? Why not play *Manhunt*, one of the bloodiest, goriest, and most violent games out on the market today? During the game, executions are rated on a five-star scale, with the most gruesome assassinations receiving the highest ratings. According to catharsis theory, as you release the blood of your victim from his body, you will be releasing the anger from your own. Okay, so maybe you prefer to get your daily intake of violence more voyeuristically. Why not watch *Reservoir Dogs,* in which carjackings, shootings, and torture are all graphically depicted? Catharsis theory contends that as you watch Mr. Blonde cut the ear off a captured police officer with a straight razor, you will cut away your own captured anger. The motto for catharsis theory could be "Violence, it does the body good!" But is there empirical evidence in support of catharsis?

Media Violence and Catharsis

In promoting the benefits of catharsis, Jones (2002) relies heavily on anecdotal evidence: Jimmy, the son of a drug addict, is described as being calmer after playing violent video games; Nicky, after smacking his head on a picnic table, releases his anger by becoming a bloodthirsty dinosaur; and 15-year-old Mary, still reeling after the death of her father, experiences a cathartic release after watching *Friday the 13th.* However, as mentioned above, no matter how much an anecdote resonates with personal experience and no matter how much the emotion of the story pulls at your heart strings (and then pulls it out of your body, in the case of violent media), anecdotal evidence is not valid empirical evidence.

A great number of controlled studies have investigated the theoretically proposed benefits of cathartic release. For instance, in 1956, Seymour Feshbach recorded the amount of inappropriate aggressive play engaged in by 5- to 8-year-old children while playing with neutral (e.g., trains, farm animals) or aggressive (e.g., guns, swords) toys. Inappropriate aggressive play was defined as taunting, striking, or hitting that was *not* part of one of the four aggressive themes (cowboys, Indians, soldiers, pirates) that children were required to play. Aggressive play in line with the aggression-laden, dramatic themes was considered to be appropriate aggressive play. Children also had opportunities to engage in thematic play ostensibly devoid of aggression, such as trains, circus, farm, and store. According to the catharsis hypothesis, children should demonstrate less inappropriate aggression after playing with the aggressive toys than with the nonaggressive toys, because the aggressive toys afford a cathartic release. However, the results contradicted the catharsis hypothesis in that more inappropriate aggression was seen during play involving aggressive themes than in play involving nonaggressive themes (Feshbach, 1956).

For the last 50 years, not only has research consistently failed to empirically support the catharsis effect, but frequently the opposite effect has been found, in that aggressive experiences result in increases in aggressive behavior. Furthermore, along with aggressive actions, both talking (i.e., venting) and thinking (i.e., ruminating) about frustrating or anger-provoking experiences fail to produce catharsis (Bushman, 2002). Thus, although the commonly held belief is that venting, ruminating, and acting out aggressively can release pent-up anger and aggressive feelings, the empirical data do not support that contention.

Does Media Violence Consumption Help Youth Deal With Anxiety and Fear?

Blue flying monkeys! Ugh, I still shudder when I think of them swooping down and scooping up Dorothy in *The Wizard of Oz*. I lived in fear of those flying monkeys during my youth. They flew! You just never knew when one of those monkeys could sneak up on you and grab you from behind. Of course, my individual experience is an anecdote, and as such, it is subject to bias, inaccuracies, and a lack of generalizability. I'm sure that there are thousands of people who loved those flying monkeys. It just so happens that I'm not one of them. Furthermore, my own anecdotal experience with (*gulp*) flying monkeys, in which my anxiety increased, is in direct contradiction to the anecdotal experiences presented by Jones (2002), in which anxiety is allayed.

In addition to claiming that violent media consumption produces a cathartic release of aggression for children and adolescents, Jones contends that exposure to media violence, such as watching heads roll, viewing eviscerations, and virtually creating copious amounts of bloodletting, can *reduce* anxiety and fears. Jones contends that fantasy, especially the violent fantasies portrayed on television and movies and in comic books and video games, can help children calm themselves down in the face of real violence. As Jones (2002) states, "being shocked by an image within the safe confines of fantasy can help them learn not to be so shocked in reality" (pp. 101–102). To support his contention, Jones describes his encounter with Andrew, who in the aftermath of the Columbine massacre became anxiously preoccupied with school shootings. However, with the help of repeated viewings of the incredibly violent and gory movie *Natural Born Killers*, Andrew's fear about school shootings diminished. Once again, vividly powerful and salient anecdotes are presented to support his viewpoint, but what does the empirical literature suggest?

Research on Media Violence-Induced Fear

In comparison to the number of studies on the effects of violent media on aggressive behavior, relatively few studies have assessed the effects of violent media on children's level of fear and anxiety (Valkenburg, Cantor, & Peeters, 2000). However, the studies that have been conducted produce characteristically similar findings—findings that suggest that for children and adolescents, levels of fear and anxiety *increase* following media violence consumption (Valkenburg et al., 2000). Incidentally, memories of media-induced fear during childhood are so powerful that they have been empirically demonstrated to last into adulthood (Harrison & Cantor, 1999). *Damn you flying monkeys!* Developmental differences across childhood have been shown as well. Whereas children tend to be more frightened by fantasy violence (e.g., *Incredible Hulk, Wizard of Oz*) than adolescents, adolescents tend to be more frightened by realistic violence (e.g., television news) than children (Cantor & Sparks, 1984). However, less support has been found for developmental differences in the level of fear associated with realistic violence (Valkenburg et al., 2000). At times, children and adolescents are equally frightened by reality.

Part of growing up is learning what is plausible and what is impossible. If a dehumidifier can magically take water out of the air, why cannot monsters magically appear from under the bed? Even as children are being told, "There is no such thing as monsters. Now go to sleep," they are also being told to place their recently lost tooth under the pillow so that the tooth fairy can come and find it. "Be good," kids are warned during December, "or else Santa will bring you coal." If the beneficent tooth fairy and Santa Claus can magically do good deeds, why cannot demons magically do bad ones? At some point during childhood, usually between the ages of 6 and 10 (DeHart et al., 2004), children are able to firmly grasp the distinction between fantasy and reality. Once the *fantasy-reality distinction* has been made, fantasy is less frightening, because children are less likely to believe that fantasy can be turned into reality. However, even fantasy violence can still be frightening, as the images, unrealistic though they may be, activate the part of the brain responsible for fear (Murray, 2001).

There are some limitations to the fear-related findings mentioned above. First, there is little, if any, research on the effects of violent video game exposure on anxiety in children and adolescents. However, research on adults suggests that as the level of video game violence increases, so too does the player's levels of anxiety (Anderson & Ford, 1986). Thus, similar increases in anxiety would be expected for children and adolescents because, on average, children and adolescents report more fear than adults. Additionally, the research presented does not take into consideration the motivation of the watcher/player. Jones (2002) contends that when used to battle one's fears, violent media exposure can effectively reduce those fears. In support of this contention, research has demonstrated that adolescents watching violent movies, in an effort to exhibit mastery over fear, show positive emotions but not negative emotions (such as fear) after watching a violent film (Johnston, 1995). However, these same individuals demonstrated high levels of positive emotions *before* they watched the movie. Thus, the adolescents claiming to watch violent movies to master their own fears were not actually feeling afraid at the time they viewed the violent movie. Although there is currently a lack of evidence supporting the use of violent media to reduce anxieties, such reductions have been demonstrated using virtual reality.

Virtual Reality and Phobias

In most video games, the player controls a virtual character who moves about and interacts with a virtual two-dimensional environment. In virtual reality, an individual dons goggles to view a three-dimensional environment in which he or she can move about and interact with the objects within the setting. Research on virtual reality has demonstrated that virtual environments can help individuals suffering from extreme fears known as *phobias*. A phobia is an intense and irrational fear of an object or situation that goes beyond what most individuals typically experience. For instance, when standing on a ledge, many people get a little nervous, but the person suffering from a fear of heights (acrophobia) may experience symptoms similar to those of a heart attack, such as chest pains and difficulty breathing (Bernstein, Penner, Clarke-Stewart, & Roy, 2003). To help the acrophobic overcome his fears, a virtual environment is created in which the individual can move around and expose himself to different heights. Through a process known as *systematic desensitization*, in which the patient learns to associate a calm state with incrementally increasing levels of the fear stimulus, the acrophobic then learns to calm himself down in the face of ever-increasing heights. Jones (2002) claims that just as virtual reality can reduce anxieties, virtual violence can help children and adolescents deal with violence in the real world, by "calming themselves down in the face of an imaginary version of it" (p. 102). Just like acrophobics can be desensitized to real heights through virtual heights, so too can children and adolescents be desensitized to real violence through virtual violence. However, whereas reducing or eliminating the fears that phobics experience is considered to be a health benefit, reducing or eliminating the distress associated with virtual violence has been postulated to be a health risk (Huesmann et al., 2003).

Most people have an emotional reaction when they first view depictions of extreme violence: grimaces appear when watching a head explode; eyes avert when seeing an arm tearing away from a body, blood spurting into the air; and hearts palpitate and blood pressure rises when virtually tearing a spine out of the back of a fallen foe. That is to say, there is a physiological reaction to media violence (Anderson & Bushman, 2001). However, after a while, the emotional impact of seeing such gruesome depictions of violence wanes: eyes no longer avert, grimaces no longer appear, and respiration and heart rate remain steady. Researchers in media violence call this reduction in physiological distress *emotional desensitization*. According to Huesmann and colleagues (2003), the health risk of consuming copious amounts of violent media lies in the fact that the likelihood of having aggressive thoughts or even acting aggressively increases when depictions of violence no longer cause an emotional reaction. Although it has yet to be firmly established that desensitization to violent media increases violent behavior in children and adolescents (Anderson, Berkowitz, et al., 2003), there does appear to be cause for concern.

A Final Dagger into the Heart of Sexy Vampire Slayers

In one of the more provocative chapters of *Killing Monsters,* titled "Vampire Slayers," Jones (2002) alleges the benefits to adolescent girls of watching provocatively dressed heroines kick their opponents' butts. According to Jones, heroines such as Buffy (the vampire slayer), Xena (the warrior princess), and Lara Croft (the tomb raider) are positive role models for girls because they promote the idea that not only can girls be strong and powerful, but they can look sexy, too. No longer are women simply objects of desire. Now, they are *violent* objects of desire. This is a dramatic change from the slasher films of the 1970s, in which female victims were portrayed as being terrified (T) and airy (A). No longer will females simply be viewed as lambs going to slaughter, nor will they be associated with the old meaning of T & A. Now, according to Jones, T & A has a new meaning: tough and attractive.

Adolescence is a time of dramatic physical change, and with those changes come a whole host of new issues. With respect to the issue of sexuality, girls need to adjust to the new adult-like proportions of their bodies and to sexual advances from boys. Jones (2002) suggests that heroines such as Buffy and Xena demonstrate to girls the importance of being in control of their sexuality, that is, having power over it. The question remains, however, whether modeling aggression in the context of sexuality promotes healthy development for girls. Jones believes that it does, as the following quote about Buffy illustrates:

> She's the perfect symbol of a girl taking power over sexuality not by bottling it up . . . . But by facing, loving it, and then outsmarting it. It's important, then, that girls find Buffy impossibly cool and that they know boys drool over her. (pp. 156–157)

But what does the empirical evidence suggest?

Research on Media Violence and Body Image

In general, media images displayed on TV, in movies, and in magazines depict an unrealistic view of the female body—a view that is desired by many adolescent girls, nonetheless. Nearly 70% of girls report wanting to adjust their appearance to look like a character on TV, with nearly 50% of those girls actually doing so by changing their clothing or hair style (Signorelli, 2001). More disturbing is the relationship between media images and *affective body image*.

Affective body image can be conceptualized as the positive and negative feelings that children and adolescents have toward their bodies' appearance (Cash & Green, 1986). Although there are many influences on affective body image (Banfield & McCabe, 2002), such as peers and family, media consumption also makes a contribution. For instance, one study found that the more times female adolescents are exposed to female images in the media, the more likely they are to be dissatisfied with their bodies. Given that models depicted in magazines weigh 23% less than the average woman and Playboy centerfolds meet the body mass index criteria for anorexia, the dissatisfaction that girls face with regard to their bodies places them at risk for an eating disorder (Brown & Witherspoon, 2002). So powerful are the images on TV that 10-year-old girls become dissatisfied with their bodies after briefly watching Britney Spears music videos (Mundell, 2002). Furthermore, a recent study found that for some boys, viewing of thin body images in TV commercials increases the importance of girls being slim and attractive (Hargreaves & Tiggemann, 2003). With regard to sexuality, media portrayals fare no better. In an average year, adolescents will view nearly 14,000 sexual references on TV (Lowery & Shidler, 1993). Women in music videos are typically portrayed as objects to be desired, and magazines tell girls how to attract boys (Brown & Witherspoon, 2002). Furthermore, the media presentation of female sexuality may have an impact on girls' sexual behavior by normalizing sexual activity for adolescents (Strasburger, 1995). In fact, several studies found links between watching MTV and sexual experiences (Peterson & Kahn, 1984).

To date, little research has addressed the impact of media violence laden with sexually provocative female characters on adolescent well-being. However, the evidence that does exist suggests that Jones's (2002) contention may prove difficult to substantiate. First, as the previous review illustrates, current depictions of female sexuality in the media have a negative effect on adolescent girls' body image and sexuality. Second, violent media exposure is associated with a host of negative outcomes for adolescent girls, such as increased aggressiveness. As such, there is no reason to believe that the combination of sexuality and aggressiveness would somehow produce positive effects. Two wrongs do not make a right, no matter how good they look in cut-off jeans and a belly shirt. In fact, it was recently found that girls who frequently watched sexually provocative heroines on TV (such as those seen in the 1970s hit *Charlie's Angels*) as children were more likely to act aggressively 15 years later than girls who watched fewer violent shows depicting female champions (Moise & Huesmann, 1996).

Summary

- Jones (2002) contends that violent media plays a crucial role in the healthy development of children and adolescents.
- Watching violent movies, playing violent video games, and listening to violent lyrics are posited to empower youth and reduce anxiety, thus enabling them to handle the constant uncertainties of life. Through aggressive fantasies, children and adolescents are thought to be able to release the anger from within, avoiding future acts of extreme violence.
- In support of his contentions, Jones relies heavily on rhetoric and anecdotal evidence. Anecdotal evidence is not scientific data; it is filled with bias, inaccuracies, and it is not generalizable.
- Research on related developmental concepts of self-efficacy and locus of control can be used to address Jones's contentions.
- Mastery experiences, social modeling, and the evaluative feedback of others influence self-efficacy. Violent media have the potential to influence each of these areas. Currently, there is no research examining whether violent media exposure can alter perceived levels of self-efficacy. However, youth who play a lot of video games tend to have low levels of self-efficacy. The process of discounting can explain this finding.
- An internal locus of control develops through practice and hard work. Certain forms of media violence offer both of these things. Research on felons suggests that video game play could increase levels of internal locus of control.
- Promoting health benefits is not just a subject of debate, nor anecdote; it is a subject of empirical research. Unfortunately, the research necessary to corroborate or contradict the health benefit issue has not been directly conducted. Thus, investigating the potential effects of violent media consumption on self-efficacy and locus of control is an area for future research.
- Although little research has addressed the potential positive effects of media violence consumption, research on related areas suggests that violent media could potentially influence self-efficacy and locus of control. However, when media violence becomes a primary contributor to the self, much as it does for bullies, self-efficacy and locus of control may become enveloped in aggressive behavior and aggression-related constructs.

- Based on the empirical findings, the strongest conclusions can be made with regard to the issue of catharsis. In short, there is little, if any, support for the contention that venting, ruminating, or smashing things in the real world or in the virtual world results in a decrease in aggressive behavior.

- Although virtual reality has been used to reduce the extreme fears faced by individuals suffering from phobias, there is no research to suggest that fears are abated after exposure to violent media. If anything, anxiety levels increase after media violence exposure.

- Finally, media portrayals of sexuality and female bodies do not appear to provide a health benefit to children and adolescents. Furthermore, adding aggression to the already sexually characterized female does not appear to reduce aggressive behavior; in fact, the opposite appears to happen.

6

Watching the Playful Beast:

Sports Violence and Aggression

I had never seen anything like it! With a flurry of devastating punches, Mike Tyson sent his adversary reeling to the canvas. In 1985, Tyson repeatedly demolished the opposition, knocking out 11 fellow combatants, each in less than one and a half minutes (Sports Illustrated, 2004). Many sports fans live for such moments—moments in which unbridled power is unleashed mercilessly upon a foe. Mike Tyson was a modern-day gladiator. Observing sanctioned physical force as sport, however, is as old as the gladiators themselves.

By all accounts, the gladiatorial games of ancient Rome were well liked by the populace. In fact, in an effort to increase or maintain their popularity, Roman emperors would pit gladiator against gladiator in epic battles to the death. At times, mock wars would be staged using thousands of combatants. Completed in 80 C.E., the Roman Coliseum seated 50,000 fans, each of whom came to watch the bloody gladiatorial games. "Games," however, is too kind a word. Unlike Parcheesi, the designated outcome of most gladiatorial combats was death. Spectator participation was also an inherent part of these deadly games. After suffering a severe injury, a gladiator could request mercy. Although the decision to spare the life of the gladiator was ultimately left up to the Emperor (or a steward in his place), spectators yelled out their desired outcome and indicated their lethal or non-lethal preferences by sticking their thumbs up or down (Guttmann, 1998).

As with modern-day sports, the gladiators themselves could become popular. Just as a baseball player's status increases with each home run hit, so, too, did a gladiator's popularity rise with the number of opponents slain. In fact, the most popular gladiators slew the greatest number of combatants (Guttmann, 1998). Of course, given that the least popular gladiators were dead, it was better to be popular. Somewhat surprisingly, there is evidence that children collected parchments that depicted their favorite gladiators. One wonders if two kids ever got into a fight because one kid felt "ripped off" after trading two "Flavius" parchments for a rookie "Spartacus" parchment, only to find out later that Spartacus had been disemboweled the previous day.

Aggression in Modern Sport

Contact sports today are neither as violent nor as bloody as Roman gladiatorial games, and the goal of modern-day sport is to win, not to kill or even maim (with the exception of boxing, kickboxing, etc.). However, modern-day contact sports display copious amounts of aggression. For instance, physical aggression occurs every time a football is snapped. Even on extra points, offensive and defensive linemen "battle it out" for position. Hockey players "check" one another into the boards, "drop the gloves," and get in an occasional fist fight. Hockey teams often have designated "enforcers" whose job it is to "protect" teammates from the unfair play of others. Basketball players push and shove to get into position to rebound an errant shot. Boxing, by its very design, is replete with aggressive acts. Boxing fans are even known to let loose a chorus of "boos" if there is not enough "action." However, there are limits to what is considered to be an acceptable act of physical aggression during competitive sport. For instance, during a professional football game, contact that puts the player at risk for serious injury, such as spears and chop-blocks, can result in penalties during the game and substantial fines levied after the game.

Aggressive behavior in sport is not limited to acts of physical aggression. *Trash talking* is also part of modern sport. Trash talking, a form of verbal aggression, involves enthusiastically lauding one's own abilities and disparaging the abilities of the opposition. However, just as there are limits to acceptable levels of physical aggression, there are also limits placed on what is considered to be an acceptable form of verbal aggression. For instance, whereas it may be appropriate to belittle the opponent's ability to cover a receiver, it is not appropriate to denigrate that player's mother (even if she *really* is as big as a house). There are rules to modern-day sport. These are rules that, when violated, can result in aggressive behavior that is not central to the game. However, whether or not sport aggression is a designated part of the game, fans witnessing these acts are observing acts of *aggression*. Thus, given that contact sports are replete with aggressive acts and that millions of children and adolescents bear witness to those acts, the impact on youth of watching sports-related aggression is of interest.

There Was No "Second Spitter" Hidden on a Grassy Knoll for Roberto Alomar

In the now classic 1992 *Seinfeld* episode titled "The Boyfriend," Kramer and Newman convey to Jerry their mutual dislike of professional baseball player Keith Hernandez. This dislike arose because Hernandez allegedly spit on Kramer and Newman following an altercation at a baseball game. In accord with the Oliver Stone movie *JFK*, Hernandez contends that there was a "second spitter" and that he is actually innocent of the alleged malicious expectoration. Sometimes art imitates life and sometimes life imitates art. In 1996, while arguing a "bad" call, Roberto Alomar spit into the face of the umpire, John Hirschbeck. This time, however, there was no second spitter behind a grassy knoll (or behind the pitcher's mound, for that matter). Alomar's act of aggression was replayed over and over again on ESPN, for both young and old to see. Ultimately, Alomar was suspended from play for his actions. However, the punishment was delayed until the beginning of the following season (a relatively unimportant time during the 162-game baseball schedule), allowing Alomar to participate in the playoffs that year. For many, Alomar's "punishment" was tantamount to a "free pass."

The following summer, anecdotal evidence that children and adolescents playing Little League baseball were spitting at umpires surfaced, a behavior that had *never* been seen before. Or had it? Alomar's act stood out because it was completely different from the acts of aggression that umpires had previously experienced. In other words, it was an act of aggression with a high degree of *salience*. Saliency refers to the degree to which an object or event stands out from its surroundings (Fiske & Taylor, 1991). For years, players and coaches have stood nose to nose with umpires, yelling obscenities at them or kicking dirt onto their legs. But spitting—well, that was unheard of! Alomar's aggressive act was so distinct, so different, so *salient*, that it ended up focusing the attention of the public on acts of spitting. Because when an event is salient people tend to *believe* it occurs more often than it really does,

Little League acts of spitting came easily to people's memory (Pryor & Kriss, 1977). We will never truly know if the incidence of spitting in Little League was greater following Alomar's infamous act because there are no objective records of spitting behavior in youth baseball. Without objective evidence of spitting, an accurate determination of a change in spitting behavior cannot be made, no matter how salient an event is. Although anecdotal reports should not be construed as empirical evidence, because of their salience, anecdotes can help "bring to life" a concept. Additionally, such stories can provide the social scientist with potential avenues to pursue in future research. In this case, Alomar's transgression can be used to help illustrate the role of modeling and consequences in influencing aggressive behavior in youth and highlight an area of research that has been greatly understudied.

Modeling Aggression and Its Consequences

"Do as I say, not as I do!" Parents often make this admonition (or some variant thereof) in an effort to dissuade their children from engaging in the "bad" behavior—behavior that the parents themselves had performed some time earlier. For instance, "hypothetically," it took my daughter Michelle until the age of 4 to realize that the University of Michigan football team was called the "Wolverines" and not the "F@#$ing Wolverines," *despite* my best efforts at using admonitions. The process of learning by observing another (i.e., the model) is referred to as *observational learning*. For over 40 years, observational learning has been one of the foremost concepts used to explain the acquisition and maintenance of aggression as well as the reduction of aggressive behavior in children and adolescents. Simply put, children and adolescents can learn and unlearn aggressive behavior by observing the consequences experienced by the aggressor.

Laboratory Experiments

To investigate the role of observational learning in the acquisition of aggressive behavior in youth, researchers have made use of the *laboratory experiment*. In the laboratory experiment, children are assigned to either the *experimental group* or the *control group*. Youth in the experimental group get "manipulated" in some way, whereas youth in the control group experience no manipulation. For research on violent media, *manipulation* refers to exposing children to media violence, such as playing violent video games or watching violent movies. Thus, whereas participants in the experimental group get to watch or play with violent media, participants in the control group do not get to play with or watch violent media at all. When designing an experiment, special care is taken to make sure that the only observed difference between the experimental group and the control group is the manipulation. For instance, if the experimental group was exposed to media violence in a *hot room* with very *hungry* children, but the control group (which is not exposed to any media violence whatsoever) had a *comfortable* room temperature and *well-fed* children, any difference between the experimental group and the control group could be due to any of the following: media violence exposure, being uncomfortable, or being hungry. When factors other than the manipulation can plausibly account for the results of the study, the study is said to be *confounded*. Finally, to ensure that there are no differences between the experimental group and the control group based on personality characteristics related to aggression (e.g., aggressiveness, hostility levels, or sensation seeking), youth are *randomly assigned* to a group (e.g., they are assigned by chance). Random assignment helps prevent the unwanted situation of having the characteristics of the individuals in the experimental group differ from the characteristics of those in the control group. For instance, if children playing a violent video game were characteristically hostile and children playing the nonviolent video game were characteristically passive, any observed differences in aggression between the two groups could be due to either the type of video game they played or the personality differences between the groups (i.e., hostile vs. passive). When done properly, a laboratory experiment is designed such that the *only* relevant difference between the experimental group and the control group is the manipulation (e.g., exposure to media violence). Therefore, at the end of the experiment, any observed differences between the experimental group and the control group can be viewed as being *caused* by the manipulation (e.g., exposure to media violence).

Laboratory Experiments and Observational Learning

In the history of psychology, Albert Bandura has conducted some of the most famous laboratory experiments involving the acquisition of aggression in children. Several of Bandura's famous experiments involved a five-foot-tall inflatable "Bobo" doll that wobbled back and forth when hit. In 1961, Bandura and his colleagues demonstrated that after observing an adult strike the Bobo doll on the head with a mallet; throw it and kick it about the room; and say verbally aggressive statements such as, "Sock him in the nose," "Throw him in the air," and "Kick him," preschool children mimicked those aggressive actions toward the doll during a period of free play (Bandura,

Ross, & Ross, 1961). In contrast, a second group of preschool children who did not witness the adult verbally and physically assault the hapless Bobo doll failed to aggress against the doll in the manner described above.

Having demonstrated that children can learn aggressive behavior through observation, Bandura assessed the role that consequences experienced by the *adult* model play in determining the *child's* learning of aggression. The learning of new behaviors following the observation of an aggressive action has been referred to by Bandura as a *learning effect* (Bandura, 1973). For instance, in an act of aggression, if a child had never thrown a mallet before, doing so following the witnessing of such an act exemplifies a learning effect. In contrast, *performance effects* refer to the circumstances that influence the likelihood that a person will enact an already learned aggressive behavior. For instance, whether or not an observer mimics a behavior is influenced by the consequences experienced by the model.

In 1965, Bandura *replicated and extended* his earlier research. That is, he repeated the essence of the original study but changed it so that additional issues could be investigated. In this latter experiment, preschool children were randomly assigned to one of two experimental conditions, "model-rewarded" and "model-punished," or the control condition, "no consequences." In the "model-rewarded" condition, children witnessed an adult get rewarded for hitting and kicking the doll. The reward consisted of being given candy and soda and being called a "strong champion" by the experimenter. In the "model-punished" condition, children observed the adult getting punished for brutalizing the doll. The adult model who was punished was verbally chastised (i.e., "You quit picking on that clown. I won't tolerate it."), sat on, and spanked with a magazine. Finally, in the "no-consequences" condition, children were spectators to the model's severe maltreatment of the doll, but no rewards or punishments were doled out. Children were then given the opportunity to play with the Bobo doll. Interestingly, children in the "model-reward" and "no-consequences" condition imitated more of the modeled aggressive acts than children in the "model-punished" condition. Stated differently, *doing nothing* about aggressive behavior produced the same results as *rewarding* aggressive behavior. Next, Bandura offered children a monetary reward to demonstrate the various acts of aggression that they had seen levied against the now battered and bruised Bobo doll. At that point, the evidence indicated that children, regardless of condition, performed equally well. Thus, although children in the "model-punished" condition demonstrated few acts of aggression during play, they, in fact, had *learned* the modeled acts of aggression. However, they had also learned that those same aggressive acts had negative consequences, and as such, children in the "model-punished" condition used those aggressive behaviors sparingly (Bandura, 1965).

Observational Learning and the Roberto Alomar Incident

In applying the results of Bandura's study to the Roberto Alomar incident mentioned earlier, we can conclude that failing to punish aggressive behavior is akin to a tacit approval of that behavior. Accordingly, because Alomar was still allowed to participate in the American League playoffs that year, Alomar's act of aggression can be viewed as either being "rewarded" or, at the very least, receiving "no consequences." Thus, through the process of observational learning, children and adolescents could conclude that spitting is an appropriate behavior on the baseball diamond, thereby increasing the probability that they themselves would engage in that behavior in future altercations. Furthermore, in applying the second of Bandura's findings to the Alomar case, we could conclude that even if youth do not exhibit spitting behavior, by witnessing spitting in action, they have added it to their repertoire of potential ways to express aggression. Although theoretically sound and based on related research, the above statements have not been tested empirically. Consequently, before any definitive conclusions can be made regarding the influence of punishing (or not punishing) the "on the field" transgressions of professional athletes on subsequent youth behavior during sporting events, more research needs to be done.

On the Importance of Rough-and-Tumble Play

Differentiating Rough-and-Tumble Play and Aggression. One of the major critiques levied against Bandura's "Bobo doll" studies has been that the children in the study were engaged in *rough-and-tumble play* and not aggressive behavior aimed at hurting someone (Freedman, 2002; Jones, 2002). Rough-and-tumble play is a high action form of play involving running, chasing, jumping, and wrestling. Prior to assessing the impact of observing sports aggression on the aggressive behavior of youth, it is important to place rough-and-tumble play in an appropriate context in relation to aggression. In fact, there are marked differences between aggressive behavior and rough-and-tumble play. First, children smile when engaged in rough-and-tumble play. During acts of aggression, children display angry faces. Second, in rough-and-tumble play, children cooperate and take turns. In contrast, during acts of aggression, cooperation and turn taking are lacking. Third, when rough-and-tumble play stops, children stay together and begin other activities, such as cooperative play. Aggressive interactions, on the other hand, typically result in the various participants parting ways. Unlike aggressive interactions in which the role of aggressor and victim seldom reverses, alternating of roles takes place during rough-and-tumble play. Finally, whereas rough-and-tumble play does not typically lead to injury, aggressive behavior frequently leads to physical or psychological pain (Moeller, 2001;

Pelligrini, 2002). See Table 6.1 for a side-by-side comparison of the attributes characteristic of rough-and-tumble play and aggression.

Situations in Which Rough-and-Tumble Play Turns Into Aggression. Given the high level of arousal and physicality of rough-and-tumble actions, such play behavior can lead to actual aggression under certain circumstances. Pelligrini (2002) suggests three reasons for the onset of aggression during rough-and-tumble play: honest mistakes, a show of dominance, and social/ emotional immaturity. Honest mistakes, such as inadvertently pushing or hitting during play, can lead to the accidental injury of a playmate. Typically, the "aggressor" in this case is both surprised and apologetic. In an effort to exert social control over others, some youth purposefully go beyond the accepted guidelines of rough-and-tumble play and aggress against their peers. For instance, Pelligrini (1995) has found that youth who are gaining in dominance use this strategy to continue their rise in the hierarchy of peers. Finally, for some youth, the inability to read social signals associated with play, or control their impulses during play, results in reactive aggression. However, it should be pointed out that for most children, rough-and-tumble play does not escalate into aggression, nor does it typically co-occur with aggression (Pelligrini, 1988). For instance, one study found that during the elementary school years, rough-and-tumble play leads to acts of aggression less than 3% of the time (Pelligrini, 1989).

Gender and Developmental Differences. Significant gender and developmental differences have been identified with regard to the quantity and function of rough-and-tumble play. Across a variety of primate species, males engage in rough-and-tumble play with greater frequency than do females. Humans are no different. Boys not only engage in rough-and-tumble play more frequently than do girls, but they are more likely to initiate it as well.

Table 6.1   Differentiating Rough-and-Tumble Play From Aggressive Behavior

	Rough-and-Tumble Play	*Aggressive Behavior*
Affect	Positive	Negative
Cooperation	Present	Absent
Behavior Afterwards	Continued Play	Separation
Role Reversal	Present	Absent
Injury	Uncharacteristic	Characteristic

In contrast, girls are more likely than boys to withdraw from the typical playground rough-and-tumble fare (Meaney, Stewart, & Beatty, 1985). Furthermore, across development, rough-and-tumble play appears to have different functions. Whereas rough-and-tumble play appears to promote positive peer affiliations among children, similar behavior in adolescence is primarily related to establishing or maintaining dominance during same-sex peer interactions. Interestingly, adolescents engaging in rough-and-tumble play involving mixed sex groups of youth tend to do so in an effort to establish heterosexual relationships (Pelligrini, 2003).

Managing Aggression Through Play. Over time, children who participate in rough-and-tumble play become skilled in physical movements, are better able to distinguish between real and feigned aggression, are more adept at recognizing different emotional expressions, and learn to regulate the activities of others (Pelligrini, 2002). Furthermore, in direct contrast to the playing of violent video games, the reading of violence-laden comics, and the viewing of aggressive displays on television, rough-and-tumble play *allows* children to learn how to manage aggression, that is, how to stay in control in the face of aggressive impulses.

Moreover, the management of aggressive behavior that can be learned during rough-and-tumble play provides an alternative argument to catharsis. That is, as opposed to the cathartic notion that rough-and-tumble play reduces aggressive behavior as a result of a release of emotion, it may be that rough-and-tumble play has the potential to reduce aggressive behavior because it facilitates control over aggressive impulses. Although rough-and-tumble play is not associated with increased aggressive behavior during childhood (Pelligrini, 2002), there is no evidence to suggest that it reduces it either. However, in order to prevent aggression, youth need to learn skills to manage aggressive thoughts and feelings. Consequently, the potential benefits of rough-and-tumble play in teaching children how to control their aggressive impulses and manage highly arousing situations requires further investigation.

Media Violence and the Management of Aggression. In contrast to rough-and-tumble play, violent entertainment provides models for aggression and practice at acting aggressively but does not typically provide opportunities to manage aggression. Blowing away virtual characters, viewing mutilation and decapitations on television, and reading about eviscerations do not teach youth what to do when feeling hostile and angry. Nor do they provide youth with practice at controlling aggressive behavior. Thus, the proposed benefits of rough-and-tumble play do not extend to media violence.

The Bobo Doll Studies Revisited. In the Bandura studies mentioned above, it is quite possible that the "aggressive behaviors" children directed at the Bobo doll were actually incidents of rough-and-tumble play. Bandura (1965) found that children exhibited fewer aggressive acts in the punishment condition than in the other conditions. This finding demonstrates that even in the context of play, by observing others, children can learn what behaviors are *acceptable* and *unacceptable*. Sport is child's play. And as such, children can learn acceptable and unacceptable forms of behavior in sport by observing adult athletics. Additionally, some kids get too rough during rough-and-tumble play or actually become aggressive in an effort to dominate others. For these kids, the line between play and aggression is blurred, and the role of observed rewards and consequences becomes even more important (Moeller, 2001). Finally, although real-world aggression does not typically involve beating the living daylights out of an inflatable doll, based on the underlying concept of "modeling of aggression," Bandura's experiment can be applied to real-world settings involving modeling. In other words, because children and adolescents can learn aggressive behaviors in the laboratory by watching others, they can also learn aggressive behaviors by watching others in the real world.

Watching Aggression in Sport and Sports Entertainment: Effects on Aggressive Behavior

Sports Violence and Hostility

There is very little research on the effects of sports aggression on children and adolescents, but the research that has been done suggests that aggression-related constructs, such as *hostility,* are affected by observing violence in sport. Hostility refers to negative beliefs and attitudes about others (e.g., mistrust, cynicism), accompanied by unpleasant emotions, such as anger, rage, and irritation (Matthews, 1997). Becoming hostile is considered to be a risk factor for aggression because individuals who are characteristically hostile tend to engage in more aggressive acts than do individuals low in trait hostility (Moeller, 2001). Thus, environmental influences that raise hostility levels in youth have the potential to increase the risk of subsequent aggressive behavior. One such environmental influence is sports violence. For instance, Celozzi, Kazelskis, and Gutsch (1981) found that characteristically hostile high school seniors reported higher levels of hostility after viewing a 10-minute professional hockey game in which hard checking, stick fighting, body checking, and fist fighting were shown. Interestingly, the effect of the video did not impact levels of hostility for high school seniors who were characteristically low in hostility. Thus, the effects of sports violence on hostility may vary as a function of an individual's baseline level of hostility.

Sports Violence and Gender

Research findings suggest that viewing contact sports may affect boys and girls differently. For instance, Lefkowitz, Walder, Eron, and Huesmann (1973) found for girls, but not for boys, that watching a lot of contact sports in 3rd grade predicted higher levels of aggressive behavior 10 years later. Lefkowitz and his colleagues used a technique called *peer nomination* to assess the relationship between the viewing of contact sports in childhood and aggressive behavior 10 years later (Lefkowitz et al., 1973). In peer nomination assessments, children are asked to name classmates who engage in particular types of behavior. For Lefkowitz, the focus of the peer nominations was on aggressive behavior (e.g., pushing). Peer nomination techniques provide useful information as to how children *perceive* their classmates' behavior. Such assessments are subject to biases, in that a child's reputation can result in negative nominations even if the reputation is unwarranted. Children's reputations can have significant impact on the type of interactions they have with others. For instance, children with a reputation for being aggressive are subject to more unprovoked attacks by their peers than children without such reputations (Shaffer, 2000). However, studies have shown that even preschool children can rate their peers' physical aggression in a manner consistent with teacher ratings (McEvoy, Estrem, Rodriguez, & Olson, 2003).

Although Lefkowitz et al.'s (1973) study found differential effects of viewing contact sports on boys and girls, other studies have not. For instance, Graña and colleagues (2004) found that the viewing of televised bullfights led to increases in hostility for both boys and girls. Although the effects of viewing contact sports has yet to produce consistent gender differences *during* childhood, the long-term effects of watching violent media in childhood has produced some interesting gender differences in adulthood. For instance, childhood consumption of violent media (e.g., television, video games, and music) influences physical aggression in adulthood for males and relational aggression in adulthood for females (Anderson, Berkowitz, et al., 2003). These findings correspond with additional research that has shown that physical aggression is expressed proportionally more by males than females and, conversely, that relational aggression is expressed proportionally more by females than males (Shaffer, 2000).

Longitudinal Research

On a separate methodological note, Lefkowitz and colleagues' (1973) study is an example of *longitudinal research*. In such studies, a group of children are followed over an extended period of time. The primary advantage of a longitudinal design is that it allows the researcher to examine factors (e.g., SES, gender, birth order) that influence different developmental outcomes (e.g., academic achievement, relationships with peers; DeHart et al., 2004). For Lefkowitz and colleagues (1973), the *factor* of interest was viewing contact sports and the *developmental outcome* was aggressive behavior. However, a primary concern when conducting a longitudinal study is *attrition*. Attrition refers to the loss of participants over a period of time. The reasons for attrition are many: children move away, refuse to participate, or have scheduling conflicts that prevent them from future participation. If the attrition is random, then all is well, and the findings of the study are not influenced by the loss of subjects. However, if there is *systematic attrition*, that is, a group of children all drop out for the same reason, then the study's findings are influenced by the loss of subjects. For instance, if most of the "aggressive kids" dropped out of a study, then, overall, the level of displayed aggression would be less than it would have been if the "aggressive kids" had stayed in the study. Attrition is a potential confound for the Lefkowitz study, for only half of those assessed in 3rd grade were reassessed 10 years later. However, the dropout did not appear to be systematic in that *both* peers nominated as aggressive and nonaggressive in 3rd grade participated in the follow-up study.

Laying the Smack Down on Sports Entertainment

With a referee's count of "1 . . . 2 . . . 3," Vince McMahon, the owner of the World Wrestling Federation (WWF; currently referred to as the WWE) pinned Triple H to win the World Heavyweight title. In professional wrestling, events that would be considered atypical in sports occur on a weekly basis. Inept referees are unable to find a set of brass knuckles hidden in the wrestler's way-too-tight bikini shorts; third parties frequently interfere with the match by distracting the referee or slyly pulling the legs out from under the opponent of their compatriot; and specialty moves, such as the "People's Elbow," the "Walls of Jericho," and "The Pedigree," can incapacitate the opposition (even when the previous, and seemingly powerful, 50 blows to the head have not). Only in the world of professional wrestling can an owner of a sport hold a championship belt without both the players and fans revolting. However, Vince McMahon himself would be the first to state that professional wrestling does not constitute sport. Instead, it constitutes *sports entertainment*. But is Vince McMahon correct in his assertion that professional wrestling is not sport? In the 1980s, the state of New Jersey believed so, for the state formally defined professional wrestling as entertainment and not athletic competition. But just how does sports entertainment differ from sport? Sport involves three components: (1) physical activity; (2) an actual contest; and (3) rules to govern play. By analyzing the WWE in terms of each of these components, the true nature of "sport" in sports entertainment wrestling is revealed.

The Nature of Physical Activity in Sports Entertainment

There is a tremendous amount of physical activity in professional wrestling. Wrestlers jump from the top of three ropes, flip, and then land on their opponent. At times, wrestlers will hurl their opponents out of the ring, drop them through tables, or smash chairs into their heads, all of which can leave visible dents in both the inanimate objects and the wrestlers. Wrestlers frequently get hit with the forearm of a combatant and knocked to the ground in a controlled fall called a "bump." In essence, professional wrestling involves a series of coordinated stunts—stunts, however, that at times can be very dangerous. "Stone Cold" Steve Austin, Kurt Angle, and "The Lethal Weapon" Steve Blackman have all broken vertebrae in their necks while wrestling. Mick "Mankind" Foley fell off a steel cage and through a table, creating a hole just beneath his bottom lip that was big enough to fit his tongue through (which he was kind enough to show to the worldwide audience). Wrestlers frequently get concussed or tear muscles in their biceps and legs. The athleticism involved in professional wrestling definitely is not fake, and the chance of injury is all too real.

Competitive Contests in Sports Entertainment

In professional wrestling matches, there are winners, losers, ties, and disqualifications. However, unlike football, baseball, or other competitive athletics in which the winner of the contest is not preordained (with the occasional exception of boxing and ice dancing), there *is* a predetermined winner in professional wrestling. In fact, professional wrestling matches follow a makeshift "script" in which the wrestling moves, trash talking, and winner are decided before the match takes place. Thus, there are no true contests in professional wrestling matches.

Rules That Govern Play in Sports Entertainment

Professional wrestling gives the appearance of lawlessness. During matches, it seems as though almost "anything goes" (e.g., spitting, raking of fingernails, ripping off clothes, hitting with chairs, brass knuckles, sledge hammers, and the continuation of a beating long after the bell has sounded). However, there is, in fact, one simple rule: follow the script. Failing to follow the predetermined course of a match can result in "fake"-looking moves (e.g., having a kick land two feet short of its target, but the wrestler falls to the ground anyway) or injury. However, professional wrestling does have fake rules—"rules" enforced by "referees" that players must ostensibly follow. In true sporting competitions, the breaking of rules results in penalties or fines. In contrast, the breaking of a wrestling-related "rule" will only result in a "penalty" if it is a designated part of the storyline. The penalty, however, is not meant to punish the transgressor; instead, it is meant to manipulate the emotions of the public or give the wrestler an excuse to leave for a vacation or to film a movie.

Based on the three criteria of sport, it is clear that professional wrestling is sports entertainment and not sport. However, sport or not, children and adolescents watch professional wrestling contests (fixed though they may be) every week, and they attend live shows *staged* in arenas. In 2002, the WWE sold over $100 million in wrestling-related toys, video games, and other products frequently purchased by and for children and adolescents. In support of these products, the WWE advertising targets their broad-based audience of adolescent and young adult males (World Wrestling Entertainment, Inc., 2003). Given that professional wrestling is similar to sport in physical activity, mimics the nature of a sporting contest, has the semblance of rules, and is frequently viewed by youth, the effect of professional wrestling on children and adolescents is of interest.

Research on the Effects of Viewing Professional Wrestling

Noble (1975) provided some of the first evidence that the viewing of professional wrestling can impact aggressive behavior in youth. Prior to the viewing of violent media, the amount of interpersonal conflict exhibited in a free play session was calculated. Next, boys either watched professional wrestling or a violent Western movie for a total of 15 minutes. Free play behavior was once again evaluated. Results indicated that the amount of time spent conflicting with classmates doubled after watching professional wrestling but only showed a slight increase after watching the violent

Western. However, it is unclear whether the conflict assessed in the study represented true conflict or rough-and-tumble play.

In a more recent study, Bernthal (2003) assessed the imitation of professional wrestling moves, vulgar language, and vulgar gestures by children and adolescents. The data for Bernthal's study was obtained through *teacher reports*. Teacher report is a form of data collection in which teachers provide information about their students. This method has been demonstrated to be a valid assessment of child behavior for behaviors and emotional states that are easily observed, such as expressed aggression. Teacher ratings become problematic when attempting to garner information on behaviors or emotional states that are more difficult to observe, such as anxiety and depression (Epkins, 1993).

Professional wrestling is theater. And as such, the behaviors, gestures, and language used by professional wrestlers are all extreme. For example, the Undertaker demonstrates extreme physicality when he lifts another wrestler into the air by the throat and slams that wrestler to the mat (i.e., the "choke slam"). The Rock demonstrates extreme language when he uses a microphone to challenge or make fun of another wrestler, using phrases such as "The Rock will layeth the smacketh down on all their candy asses!" or "What do you think? It doesn't matter what you think!" Goldberg demonstrates an extreme gesture when, after driving another wrestler to the mat with his signature move, "The Spear," he drags his finger across his throat in a slashing manner. Given that wrestling moves, gestures, and language, such as the ones mentioned above, are easily observable when imitated, teacher reports can provide useful information as to the presence of such behavior *in school*.

Bernthal reports that nearly 30% of teachers report seeing some sort of "body slam" (e.g., slamming body against wall or ground) during the school day. An additional 21% of teachers report seeing neck-related moves, such as a "clothesline" (i.e., hit person just below the neck with a forearm) and "choke holds" (i.e., choke opponent with hand or arms) during school. Nearly 25% of teachers report hearing WWE-related vulgar language, such as "Stone Cold" Steve Austin's signature phrase, "Give me a hell, yeah." Finally, nearly 30% of teachers report vulgar gestures, such as one performed by the now defunct tag-team "Degeneration X," in which crossed arms are repeatedly thrusting over the pelvis, accompanied by the phrase "suck it." The level of imitation seen in children and adolescents in the United States has been replicated in other countries. For instance, a similar percentage of imitated WWE wrestling moves has been reported for Israeli children (Lemish, 1998). See Figure 6.1.

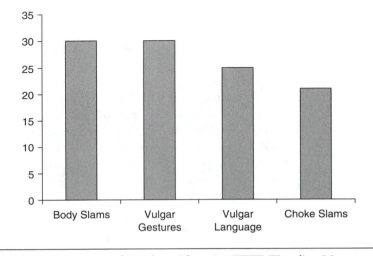

Figure 6.1   Percentage of Teachers Observing WWE Wrestling Moves
in School

SOURCE: Data from Bernthal (2003).

The confines of the school setting limit the nature of the professional
wrestling activities that can be aped. In contrast, the home environment
allows for greater freedom of expression. However, whereas many children
and adolescents are satisfied with simply imitating a few moves in the com-
forts of their dining room, a few adolescents have begun staging "backyard
wrestling" matches that mimic an entire professional wrestling evening of
performances. These "amateur" matches include chair smashing; jumping
off roofs and onto an opponent lying on a table; and assorted flips, bumps,
and other extremely dangerous activities (Furtado, 2005). Often, backyard
wrestling matches are performed before an audience of adolescent peers.

Factors That Influence
Imitative Behavior in Youth

Every day children and adolescents imitate the behavior of others. When my
daughter, Michelle, was 9, she loved to watch the television programs shown
on the cable channel *Animal Planet*. *Animal Planet's* television line-up
includes talent shows for animals (*Pet Stars*), wildlife exploration (*The
Crocodile Hunter*), and even an animal version of *Cops*, entitled *Animal*

Precinct, in which the ASPCA rescues abused animals and incarcerates their owners. But one of her favorite programs to watch was *Emergency Vets,* a show in which injured animals are taken to a veterinary hospital and treated in the ER—treatments that, at times, included graphic footage of operations. One evening, I found Michelle doing surgery in her room. One of her stuffed animals, who we'll call "Fluffy" to protect its anonymity, had been ripped apart at the belly after a run-in with a real-life dog. Michelle had meticulously added beads to Fluffy's belly to replace her lost stuffing and sewed her back together. I'm happy to report that Fluffy pulled through. Since that day, Michelle has built up a very successful stuffed-animal veterinary practice.

Was I concerned that Michelle's imitation of the veterinarians shown on *Animal Planet* would extend to real-life animals? Not at all. Michelle loves animals too much to hurt them. Rarely do psychologically healthy children and adolescents willfully engage in imitative behavior that seriously hurts another. However, children and adolescents will engage in imitative behavior that is potentially harmful or even deadly to the self and others. For instance, Bernthal (2003) found that nearly 40% of teachers reported that children were injured as a result of imitating professional wrestling moves. The most common of these were bruises and scrapes. However, a little over 5% of teachers reported broken bones. Although extremely rare, the imitation of a wrestling move has even resulted in a child's death (Barton, 2004). So, why do children and adolescents imitate the dangerous wrestling moves and various forms of vulgarity displayed by professional wrestlers?

Power, Similarities, and Consequences

Youth are most likely to imitate adults who pay attention to them or have power over them, such as teachers and parents. Similarities between the model and the child influence imitation as well, for children are likely to imitate those of the same sex, age, and race. Thus, children are more likely to imitate the behaviors of their friends than their non-friends (DeHart et al., 2004). As the Bandura study described above illustrated, the rewards and punishments that a model's behavior elicits influence whether or not children will imitate those behaviors. Finally, youth are likely to imitate successful individuals whom they admire, such as athletes and celebrities (Anderson, Berkowitz, et al., 2003).

Identification

Professional wrestlers are celebrities, and their actions can be perceived as being rewarded every time they appear on television, regardless of the outcome of the match. Furthermore, the aggressive behaviors enacted during a match are reinforced or punished by the audience's reaction. Additionally, the psychological phenomenon known as *identification* can help explain why children and adolescents imitate the behaviors of professional wrestlers.

Identification refers to the process by which an individual desires, either consciously or unconsciously, to pattern the self after another. Youth will imitate the behaviors of those with whom they identify. As such, identification with professional wrestlers is of potential concern, because research has shown that viewers who identify with aggressive, victorious, and powerful characters act more aggressively following short-term exposure to media violence than do viewers who do not identify with individuals displaying those characteristics (Geen & Thomas, 1986). Huesmann et al. (2003) found that identification with same-sex aggressive television characters in childhood significantly predicted levels of physical aggression 15 years later. However, more research is necessary to demonstrate that watching violent sports entertainment can result in an increase in aggressive behavior for children and adolescents.

Personal Fable

Additionally, the phenomenon known as the *personal fable* can be used to explain why youth will fearlessly, and at times foolishly, engage in dangerous activities. The personal fable refers to an adolescent's exaggerated beliefs in his or her uniqueness (DeHart et al., 2004). For instance, the pain and suffering that an adolescent experiences upon being "dumped" by his first girlfriend cannot possibly be understood by that boy's father (even if Dad was left at the altar in his first attempt to get married and he is currently going through his third divorce). A feeling of invulnerability and indestructibility often accompanies the personal fable of adolescents. Such Achilles-like beliefs lead youth to minimize concerns for personal welfare. And because adolescents discount the likelihood of getting injured, they engage in risky behaviors such as drinking and driving too fast. Thus, the invulnerability component of the personal fable allows adolescents to mimic the behaviors of professional wrestlers with little regard for their own personal safety or the safety of others.

Effects of Watching Aggressive Behavior on Youth Aggression During Sport

Although there is no direct empirical evidence linking on-the-field transgressions to similar offenses in youth, there is evidence that watching violence prior to playing a game can increase the level of aggression displayed during sport. Josephson (1987) randomly assigned nearly 400 2nd and 3rd graders to watch a violent television show (i.e., police officers shooting and capturing snipers) or a nonviolent television program (i.e., motocross racing) and then play a game of floor hockey. In addition, children were randomly assigned to play floor hockey under two conditions: floor hockey alone or floor hockey with a prop from the television show. In this latter condition, the referee carried a "walkie talkie" similar to the one that had been prominently displayed in the *violent* television show. During the floor hockey game, research assistants tallied the total number of excessive physical acts of aggression (e.g., hitting, elbowing, tripping, hair pulling). That is, only acts of aggression that would typically result in a hockey penalty were noted. Such behaviors go beyond the level of acceptable behavior during rough-and-tumble play.

Importantly, the research assistants tallying the aggressive acts were unaware of (i.e., *blind*) the television program (e.g., violent or nonviolent) that the children had watched. Keeping research assistants blind to the child's participation in an experimental or control condition is of crucial importance because it prevents *observer bias*. Observer bias refers to any preconceived notions or beliefs that may bias an observer's judgment in favor of the researcher's hypothesis. For instance, if a researcher believes that media violence causes aggressive behavior, she may be more likely to view a physical interaction between hockey players as resulting from purposeful aggression as opposed to accidental contact. Thus, keeping the researcher blind to condition prevents the incorporation of biased beliefs into the experimental findings.

In the case of the Josephson (1987) study, the experimental findings indicated that characteristically aggressive boys who had watched a violent television program *and* played hockey in the presence of the movie prop demonstrated more acts of extreme physical aggression than children in any of the other conditions. Additionally, in the absence of the prop, characteristically aggressive boys watching the violent television program acted more aggressively than characteristically aggressive boys watching the nonviolent television program. Of note, television violence, with or without cues, did not result in an increase in aggressive behavior for characteristically nonaggressive boys. These findings suggest that watching violence on television, even if it is not sports related, can influence sports-related aggression in youth who are already predisposed to act aggressively. It follows, then, that watching modeled sports violence on television should produce a similar effect in youth. It has yet to be determined, however, whether the effects of watching sports violence are the same when the modeled sport and the sport played by youth match, in comparison to when they are different. For instance, does watching aggression modeled by professional baseball players have a bigger impact on aggression during youth baseball games than during youth football games? Interestingly, the findings revolving around the "walkie talkie" in the Josephson study can help resolve this question.

Generalizing From Observed Sport to a Different Sport

After watching a violent television program, boys playing hockey in the presence of a referee holding a walkie talkie acted more aggressively than boys playing hockey with the same referee sans walkie talkie (Josephson, 1987). At first glance this seems odd, for there is nothing inherently "aggressive" about a walkie talkie. People do not get shot, stabbed, or disemboweled by walkie talkies; there are no mythical creatures for which the walkie talkie can cause instant death; and there are no video games in the arcade titled *House of the Dead Walkie Talkies* or *Grand Theft Walkie Talkie!* However, because the walkie talkie was used in the context of aggression, the walkie talkie became linked with aggressive behavior. That is to say, the walkie talkie became an aggressive cue. An aggressive cue refers to any object or event that can evoke thoughts or feelings related to aggressive behavior (Berkowitz, 1993). For instance, traditional objects used in acts of aggression, such as guns, knives, machetes, and weapons of mass destruction, all function as aggressive cues because they evoke thoughts and emotions related to acts of aggression. In fact, any object or event has the potential to become an aggressive cue; the only requirement is for that object or event to occur in association with acts of aggression. Thus, if used to hurt or torment another, even feathers could become an aggressive cue.

As it turns out, toy replicas of objects used in real-life acts of aggression have been shown to increase aggressive behavior in children. For instance, Turner and Goldsmith (1976) found that preschool children exhibit more acts of aggression and rule breaking when playing with toy guns than when playing with toy airplanes. Similar effects have been shown for older children, as well. As reported in Chapter 5, Feshbach (1956) found that 5- to 8-year-old children displayed more acts of inappropriate aggression (i.e., aggression that was not part of the game) while playing with toys that were replicas of objects used in real-life aggression (e.g., guns and swords) than when playing with replicas of objects not typically associated with aggression in real life (e.g., trains or farm animals). Thus, the presence of aggressive cues during play increases the level of inappropriate aggressive behavior. But how is this possible? Why would the mere presence of a toy or walkie talkie increase aggressive thoughts, emotions, and behavior in children? To answer this question, it becomes necessary to understand the concept of *priming*.

Priming

Priming refers to the *activation* of related thoughts, emotions, and concepts residing in memory. Think of activation as a "readying process." Activation makes related information that had been unavailable accessible for immediate use. Such information includes thoughts, ideas, emotions, concepts, and so on. Because these elements are cognitively linked with one another, the entire association of information becomes activated once primed. For instance, when I hear the words "Michigan football," I am primed in the following manner: memories surrounding the games are readied for use (e.g., standing in line to buy a hotdog); thoughts regarding Michigan football are activated (e.g., Michigan players eat their cereal on plates, because if it was served in a bowl, they'd lose it!); emotions accompanying the viewing of a Michigan football game (e.g., anxiety, anger, despair) begin to surface; and concepts related to Michigan football are activated (e.g., the concept of a "good season," which is currently conceptualized as any season during which Michigan beats Ohio State).

"Yogi ran through the woods bare naked." Now, quickly think of an animal. Anybody think of a rabbit? How about a bear? Due to priming, information that is situationally, conceptually, semantically, or phonetically linked is activated. Thus, in the "Yogi" sentence mentioned above, the word "bare" activated the homonym of bare, "bear." Yogi, an animated bear, activates the related concept of real-life bears. And because bears live in the woods, the word "woods" also activates "bear." Thus, due to priming, people are more likely to mention a bear than a rabbit. However, information that is "accessible" is not necessarily consciously remembered. Just as a football player can be activated for a game only to sit on the bench for four quarters, information can be activated through priming but not brought into conscious memory. In contrast to the activated but benched football player who has no influence over the outcome of the game, information that has been primed can affect the interpretation of new information. For instance, after reading violent comic books, college students were more likely to believe that harm occurring under ambiguous circumstances (e.g., a child gets tripped, but it is unclear why he got tripped) was the result of hostile intent (e.g., he did it on purpose) than benign intent (e.g., it was an accident) on the part of the harm doer (Kirsh & Olczak 2000). Thus, reading and visualizing depictions of violence *primed* aggressive thoughts and emotions, which, in turn, influenced the interpretations of situations involving ambiguous provocations.

Aggressive Networks

As a result of priming due to aggression-related stimuli, associations among aggressive thoughts, memories, and emotions are formed. These associations are commonly referred to as an *aggressive network*. As the comic book example illustrated, an activated aggressive network can aid in the processing and interpretation of social information (Bushman, 1998). Factors that make an aggressive network accessible include frequent use (e.g., habitual aggressive behavior) or priming (i.e., exposure to aggressive stimuli). Furthermore, the more often children and adolescents experience aggression, be it in word or deed, by action or by observation, the more likely it is for an aggressive network to be activated at any one point in time. Given that an activated aggressive network influences individuals' perception and interpretation of their current experiences, such individuals may come to view the world through *"Mortal Kombat"*–colored glasses; that is, a bias towards perceiving and interpreting situations as being caused by aggression. Thus, when faced with a novel situation, setting, or experience, those with activated aggressive networks will be biased towards aggressive interpretations of their encounters with others. For instance, when bumped into a wall, a child with an activated aggressive network will assess the situation from a starting point biased towards aggressive interpretations and assume that the bump was meant to harm (Dodge, 1986). In contrast, when bumped into a wall, a child without an activated aggressive network will *begin* the assessment process from a more balanced vantage point—the bump could be either an accident or on purpose, but more information is needed.

Priming and the Josephson Study

The stimulus that primes an aggressive network does not have to be identical to the resulting aggressive behavior, thought, or emotion. For instance, watching a *physically* aggressive sport can activate an individual's aggressive network, resulting in that person demonstrating an increase in *verbal* aggression. I like to refer to this particular phenomenon as the *Wolverine Priming Effect,* as I frequently find myself swearing at my dog during University of Michigan football games. As it turns out, priming effects can explain the Josephson (1987) findings relating the presence of walkie talkies to higher levels of aggressive behavior during a hockey game. The presence of the walkie talkie appeared to have been a contributing factor to the activation of the characteristically aggressive boys' aggressive networks. Interestingly, for nonaggressive boys, the priming effect was not strong enough to increase aggressive behavior. Thus, these findings suggest that certain children and adolescents may be more at risk from violent media exposure than others, a fact that will be addressed in greater detail in a later chapter.

Earlier, I suggested that the Josephson study could help determine whether watching aggression modeled by professional athletes has a bigger impact on youth aggression during the same type of athletic competition in which the aggressive behavior was modeled than during a different type of athletic competition. In addition to objects (such as walkie talkies) priming an aggressive network, so, too, can the context or setting in which a sport takes place prime an aggressive network. As a result, aggressive behavior during sport should occur more often in the setting in which it was modeled than in a different setting. However, this hypothesis has yet to be assessed in the literature and thus warrants future research.

Summary

- From Roman gladiatorial games to modern-day sport and sports entertainment, aggression has become an integral part of athletic competition.
- Whether the aggression is game-related or incidental, children and adolescents observe frequent acts of physical and verbal aggression during sporting events.
- The perceived frequency of salient events is often higher than their actual level of occurrence.
- The concepts of learning effects and performance effects were introduced. Bandura's research on observational learning has shown that the rewards and punishments experienced by others influence the types of behaviors that children learn and the types of behaviors that children are willing to enact.
- Although research has demonstrated that sports violence can influence children's behavior in a non-sports setting, and that aggression displayed outside of sport can influence aggressive behavior during sport, no research has addressed the impact of aggressive behavior in sport on youth behavior during sport. Future research should endeavor to investigate this issue.
- Rough-and-tumble play differs from aggression in terms of the emotions displayed, the behaviors enacted, and the behaviors that follow it. For some children, rough-tumble-play can easily turn into aggressive behavior. Gender and developmental differences are evident in the frequency of, and reasons for, engaging in rough-and-tumble play. Rough-and-tumble play, unlike media violence, may teach children how to manage aggressive thoughts and feelings, thereby reducing aggressive behavior.
- Observing sports violence may influence current levels of hostility, but the effects may vary as a function of an individual's baseline level of hostility.

- Viewing contact sports may affect boys and girls differently. However, more research is necessary.
- Sports entertainment is not sport, but it can influence youthful rough-and-tumble play.
- Power, similarities, consequences, identification, and personal fable influence whether or not a behavior will be imitated.
- In addition to the importance of observational learning in the acquisition and maintenance of aggressive behavior, the concepts of priming and aggressive networks were introduced.
- The following methodological concepts related to laboratory experiments were defined in the context of research on media violence: experimental group, control group, manipulation, confound, random assignment, replication, and extension. Methodological concepts related to the study of child development include peer nomination, teacher report, observer bias, longitudinal research, and attrition.

7

Violence-Laden Imagination

Comic Books, Fiction, and Toys

As I read over my tattered copy of Todd McFarlane's comic book *Curse of the Spawn*, I was struck by two things. First, the drawings were visually stunning. Glossy, lifelike, richly colored, artistically drawn figures glinted up at me, captivating my attention. Second, I found the depiction of a severed head hanging there in midair, blood frozen in mid-spurt, tissues and sinews dangling in places they should not be, both grotesque and disturbing. Although modern comic book drawings are often realistic, they are still caricatures of real life—motionless caricatures. However, the lack of movement depicted within the violent imagery of comic books should not be construed as a lack of influence from exposure to the violent imagery within. Thus, in the first section of this chapter, the effects of reading violent comic books will be examined.

The brutality depicted in modern-day comic books is often matched in novels. Although there are no data to support this contention, I suspect that novels directed at youth are less graphic and gory than comic books. At times, however, significant events of violence take place in children's novels. Consider, for example, the following occurrences from the phenomenally successful *Harry Potter* series by J. K. Rowling. Over the course of the first five novels, an ethereal creature kills and drinks the blood of a unicorn; both a popular adolescent boy and Harry's godfather are killed; excruciating pain is inflicted on Harry through the use of an "unforgivable curse"; a hand is cut off in order to complete a ritual to regenerate the evil Lord Voldemort; and Harry kills a Basilisk (a giant, snake-like monster) with a sword.

Widespread incidents of riotous behavior following the reading of the *Harry Potter* books have not been reported, nor would they be expected to happen. So, just what is the impact of violence-laden written material on youthful aggression? To answer this question, the second section of this chapter will address the effects of reading violent content, such as that found in fairy tales and children's novels, on aggression across childhood.

In the final section of this chapter, a third type of entertainment violence will be explored. Similar to comic books and novels, this activity engages the imagination. But unlike violent media involving reading, this particular form of violent entertainment engages the child's physicality. Previously, the connection between rough-and-tumble play and aggressive behavior in childhood was assessed. Here, we address the relationship between war toy play and aggression.

Comic Book Violence

Comic Book Sales

Over the past two decades, voluminous research has focused on media influences on aggression, with the vast majority of research focusing on television, movies, and more recently, video games. An additional, yet understudied, source of media violence that children and adolescents may frequent is comic books. Recent statistics show that approximately $400 to $500 million in comic books (at around $2 per comic) are sold annually with a top-selling comic producing around 150,000 copies in advance orders per month. An additional $200 million in annual sales comes from the purchase of long-form comic books (i.e., at least 48 pages in length), commonly referred to as graphic novels (Antonucci, 1998; Gustines, 2005; Reid, 2005). Historically, the target audience for comic books has been 10- to 14-year-old boys; however, recent estimates suggest that comic book readers vary greatly in age. Antonucci (1998) reports that as much as 25% of comic book sales may be made to individuals over age 40.

Comic Book Content

In the 1950s, concern that violence in comic books might increase aggression in children (Wertham, 1954) led to the development of a Comics Code Authority, a self-censoring agency for comic book content developed and enforced by the producers of comic books (Savage, 1990). However, the overwhelming majority of comic books available today still contain violent themes (see *Diamond Comics*, 1999 for a list of the top 100 selling comic books, by month), and many comic books are laden with graphic gore and sexual themes. For instance, comic books such as *Homicide, Spawn,* and *Evil Ernie* frequently depict brutal acts of violence. These acts include graphic illustrations of bloody decapitations, vivid eviscerations, and sinewy amputations. The weapons used to commit these heinous acts range from machine guns to machetes and an array of body parts, including fingernails, toenails, and teeth. In fact, finding a comic book without any acts of aggression is nearly impossible. Even comic books that are meant to be funny (e.g., *The Simpsons, Rug Rat Adventures*) contain acts of aggression. More often than not, the violence drawn in humorous comic books is of a *slapstick* form.

Slapstick Humor

Slapstick humor is a type of comedy in which the humor derives from physical action. Acts of aggression-related slapstick humor include being pushed into a door, getting hit with a hammer, and being poked in the eye. Such events can occur as a result of hostile aggression (e.g., a poke in the eye for punishment) or instrumental aggression (e.g., an attempt to sit in a chair). Slapstick humor does not have to involve overt acts of aggression, just pain and injury. For instance, slipping on a banana peel involves accidental, painful, and injurious behavior. Of note, the impact of violence portrayed in a comedic manner will be discussed in the next chapter detailing the effects of cartoon violence on youth.

Comic Book Violence Compared to Other Types of Media Violence

Although television, movies, and comic books may all contain portrayals of violence, the manner in which violence is presented in each of these media differs. Violence on television and in movies is presented in a continuous narrative form, and the portrayals of violence are passively consumed by the viewer; imagination and thinking are limited. Comic books, unlike television and video games, do not provide a continuous story in which all of the action relevant to the storyline is displayed. In comic books, the storyline is told in partially connected frames. Thus, continuity between frames must be inferred by the reader. For instance, in one frame of a comic book, a lone hero is shown brandishing a sword in an attack arc. The next frame depicts a warrior lying on the ground, the hero standing over him. Although the actual duel to the death is not shown, the reader must infer that the hero killed the warrior with his sword.

This type of disconnected presentation of information forces readers to engage their imaginations (McCloud, 1993). Thus, in order to witness the death of the warrior mentioned above, readers will need to visualize it in their heads. When doing this, the frames of the comic books become starting and end points for the visualization. All readers need to do is connect the two frames using their imaginations. As the previous example illustrates, when reading violent comic books, individuals are not simply witnessing depictions of aggressive behavior; they are, in fact, becoming active participants in the creation of the aggression-laden storyline (McCloud, 1993). For instance, when reading *Curse of the Spawn,* I had to visualize the hapless corpse's head being unceremoniously detached from its body. It was difficult to do at first, but with practice, I became quite good at it.

When reading comic books, individuals can self-regulate the intake of information by adjusting the speed at which they read. Individuals can spend as much time as they like reading dialogue and viewing pictures. The ability to self-pace the reading of a comic book may afford a detailed encoding of the stimulus material. Given that individuals read comic books at a comfortable, self-guided pace, and that they become actively engaged in the storyline of comic books, the potential influence of this medium seems great (Potenza, Verhoeff, & Weiss, 1996). However, to date, there are very few studies that have assessed either the benefits or drawbacks of comic books (Potenza et al., 1996). Thus, the question remains: Do comic books affect aggressive behavior in youth? To address this issue, research from the late 1940s and onward will be evaluated.

Comic Book Violence and Aggressive Behavior in Youth

Early Research

The best-known research on the impact of violent comic books on youth was conducted more than 50 years ago by Fredrick Wertham (1954). Reported in Wertham's book *Seduction of the Innocent* were the effects of reading comic books on reading ability, attitudes towards others, psychosexual development, and delinquency in youth. Wertham felt that the empirical evidence was clear: comic books were detrimental to the health and well-being of children and adolescents. In particular, Wertham reports that reading violent comic books promoted the following: illiteracy; prejudicial beliefs towards others; deviant sexual beliefs; and the endorsement of and desire to follow a lifestyle of delinquency, which includes criminal behavior and acts of violence. Moreover, Wertham felt that frequent readers of comic books would inevitably develop a *comic book syndrome.* Children suffering from comic book syndrome were described as displaying the following characteristics: (1) feelings of guilt surrounding the reading of violent comic books; (2) having sadistic and violent fantasies as a result of reading violent comic books; (3) reading comic books in a surreptitious manner; (4) lying about reading "crime comics" and stating that one only reads "Disney Comics"; and (5) buying comic books with money meant for something else or stealing money in order to buy comic books.

So just what was the evidence that Wertham used to support his claims regarding the health hazard of comic books and the development of comic book syndrome? Wertham's (1954) treatise on the evils of comic books on youth starts out reasonably enough with a statement on the nature of scientific research.

> Anyone wishing to study scientifically the psychological causes of human behavior must always be on guard against the error of assuming that something has causal significance just because it happened in the past. He must think in terms of psychological processes and developments which connect cause and effect. And he can hold a new factor responsible only if he has taken into account all other possible factors, physical, individual, psychological and social. (p. 86)

Essentially, Wertham is suggesting that conclusions regarding the effects of reading violent comic books on youth cannot be firmly established until all of the various risk factors related to violence have been taken into consideration. Unfortunately, Wertham did not take his own advice when conducting his research, at least not as his research was reported in *Seduction of the Innocent*. For Wertham's "findings" are reported as narrative anecdotes or data-less correlations. For instance, Wertham relates the story of an adolescent boy who gets the idea to run down a policeman with his car from comic books. He further suggests that comic book reading played "an important contributing factor" in the shooting of one teenager by another (even though the shooting was officially ruled as an accident). As mentioned in Chapter 5, anecdotal evidence is often inaccurate, biased, and lacking in generalizability. Moreover, when Wertham does report correlational findings, he does so by describing the correlation rather than by providing empirical data (i.e., a correlation coefficient). In addition, Wertham fails to report important details of the study. Particulars that go unreported include the gender and age of the participants and the measures and methodology used to conduct the research. In fact, when looked at closely, Wertham's research does not meet the criteria for scientific research.

Criteria for Scientific Research. The four criteria that characterize science are *solvable problems, falsifiable hypotheses, systematic empiricism*, and *publicly verifiable knowledge*. The solvable problems criterion refers to the fact that science attempts to understand phenomena that can be understood using currently available methods. Determining whether human beings are inherently good or evil is not a solvable problem. As such, this question is not within the realm of science. However, discerning the effects of violent comic books on youth is a solvable problem and, therefore, is within scientific purview. Falsifiable means that an idea is *capable* of being proven wrong. Thus, findings contrary to the hypothesis that violent comic books negatively affect youth would provide falsifiable evidence. Research does not have to find such evidence to meet the falsifiability criterion; it just needs to be *capable* of finding such evidence.

Methodical recording of behavior and attitudes that follow scientific guidelines surrounding the collection of data comprises the third aspect of science, systematic empiricism. Scientific research provides a detailed recording of how the experiment was conducted. Moreover, systematic empiricism follows the guidelines of the scientific method: observations, development of hypothesis, data collection, hypothesis testing, and evaluation of the theory. With systematic empiricism, the observations are structured and findings are objective. Anecdotal evidence does not meet this criterion of systematic empiricism, as it is biased and subjective; therefore, it is not scientific.

Finally, publicly verifiable knowledge means that the researchers publish the methodology and results of their studies in journals and books with such specificity that another researcher could replicate the study. Moreover, by making the study available to the public, the research reported within can be evaluated and criticized by the scientific community based on its scientific merit. In contrast, unscientific research, such as that frequently reported in an infomercial, bypasses the normal channels of scientific peer review and publication. Instead of making their research available to the public for critique, such unscientific endeavors report their "findings" in the media. However, such reports are general and lacking in scientific empiricism.

Although Wertham's (1954) research easily meets the first two criteria for scientific research, it fails in the final two. As stated earlier, Wertham's use of anecdotal evidence to support his claims about the evils of comic books does not constitute scientific research. Likewise, Wertham fails to give details about the sampling procedure used to garner his subjects, the age and gender of those involved in his correlations, and the measures used to assess his outcomes. Based on the reporting of his data, it would be impossible to replicate Wertham's research. Thus, although Wertham presents engaging and compelling arguments, he does not report scientific research.

Modern Research

Over the past 50 years, only a handful of studies that meet the criteria for scientific research have been conducted on the effects of violent comic books on youth. Of the few studies that have been conducted, the vast majority have failed to support the contention that reading violent comic books increases aggressive behavior in youth. In one of the first empirical studies conducted on comic books following the release of *Seduction of the Innocent,* Blakely (1958) found that the reading of comic book violence was unrelated to 7th graders' levels of behavior problems, as rated by their teachers. Tan and Scruggs (1980) failed to find a relationship between measures of physical and verbal aggression and exposure to violent comic books among middle school children. Similarly, Brand (1969) was unable to connect comic book reading with aggressive feelings among 12-year-old boys and girls. In contrast, Hoult (1949) found that compared to a matched group of non-delinquent youth, delinquent (i.e., arrested for delinquency) 10- to 17-year-old boys and girls read more comic books with depictions of criminal activities and violent acts. However, no such group differences were evident for the reading of comic books deemed harmless by the researcher.

Quasi-Experimental Designs. It is worth noting that only Hoult's study used a *quasi-experimental design.* The word *quasi* can be defined as "resembling something;" consequently, a quasi-experimental design resembles an experimental design. One form of quasi-experimental design, referred to as a *non-equivalent groups design,* is identical to a true experiment with one exception: participants are not randomly assigned to the experimental and control conditions. Instead, pre-existing groups of individuals comprise the experimental and control groups. For instance, comparing physically abused children to non-abused children on measures of aggression involves non-equivalent groups.

Non-equivalent groups designs are used when it is either impossible (e.g., you cannot randomly assign fetuses to male or female status) or unethical (e.g., you cannot randomly assign youth to engage in delinquent or non-delinquent activities) to use random assignment. However, because random assignment is not used, any differences emerging between the experimental and control groups could occur due to factors associated with the pre-existing condition and not the experimental manipulation. Experimenters try to account for as many pre-existing conditions as possible by *matching* individuals within the experimental and control groups on a variety of other issues. For instance, if there are four 12-year-old white females with insecure attachments in the control group, then the experimenter will make sure that there are four 12-year-old white females with insecure attachments in the experimental group. Hoult's study is a quasi-experiment because he tests the effects of comic book exposure on an intact group of non-delinquents (the control group) and delinquents (the experimental group). Thus, even though participants wer matched on a variety of issues, because there was no random assignment to condition, it is possible that the aforementioned significant differences had nothing to do with comic book reading. Instead, such differences may have occurred due to some unrelated variable on which the researcher failed to match the groups.

Research Using Matched Designs. In one of the most comprehensive studies of the time, Belson (1978) attempted to establish a causal relationship between violent media exposure and violent behavior. To accomplish this goal, detailed survey data were collected from 1,565 randomly selected 12- to 17-year-old adolescent boys. Belson asked the boys questions about the type of violent media they consumed earlier in life and how often they had consumed it. For instance, the boys were given a list of 68 television shows and asked to identify which ones they had seen. Similar questionnaires were developed for comic books, with a total of 21 violent comic books being presented to youth. Boys were simply asked to check off the comic books they had previously read.

This type of research involves the assessment of *retrospective memory,* because participants are being asked to recall information about the past. Unfortunately, this type of research is flawed in that the memories are often unreliable and impacted by the current mood state of the individual. For instance, participants in the Belson study may have forgotten many of the comic books that they had read during their youth. Based on their responses to the retrospective questionnaire, the boys were divided into low and high consumers of violent media. Using a sophisticated matching procedure, which controlled for over 200 different variables that could be related to aggression (such as social class and education), the boys who were light consumers of violent media were matched with boys who were heavy consumers of violent media. In addition to exposure to violent movies and television, the reading of violent comic books was assessed. The results indicated that in comparison to youth who read few violent comic books, youth who read many violent comic books engaged in more acts of serious (e.g., fighting, throwing bricks, beating dog) and less serious (e.g., making sister cry, teasing, irritating others) aggression.

Research on Late Adolescents and Young Adults

Recent research on late adolescents and young adults has found that short-term exposure to comic book violence can influence *social information processing.* Social information processing refers to the processing of information (e.g., attention to, memory for) related to social relationships (e.g., peer relationships, parent-child relationships). For instance, determining whether or not an act of transgression, such as being pushed into a wall, was done on purpose or not requires that cues to the cause be detected and processed and that a judgment be made. Dodge (1986) contends that individuals act aggressively and perceive hostility (when none is present) due to biases in social information processing. Moreover, Dodge (1980) purports that aggressive children act aggressively, in part, due to a type of aggression-related construct known as a *hostile attribution bias*. A hostile attribution bias refers to the situation in which an individual infers hostile intent in the actions of another, even though the intent of that individual is unclear. For instance, after getting pushed into a wall, a boy with a hostile attribution bias will come to the conclusion that he was pushed on purpose, even in the absence of clear evidence. When exposed to a frustrating social stimulus (e.g., being hit in the back with a ball), a hostile attribution bias is thought to distort the cues surrounding the cause of the incident, rendering such clues as indicating the presence of hostile intent. For instance, a smile, or the lack thereof, could be perceived as being indicative of maliciousness. Thus, because the child perceives himself to be under attack he responds with aggression (Dodge & Frame, 1982).

Research on hostile attribution bias has focused primarily on aggressive children (Dodge, 1980; Dodge & Frame, 1982). Consistently, Dodge and his colleagues have found that when harm occurs under ambiguous circumstances (i.e., the intent of the harm doer is unclear), aggressive children ascribe hostile intent to the harm doer. Of note, both aggressive and nonaggressive children interpret obviously hostile or benign circumstances in the same way. It is only when the circumstances are unclear that differences arise. Dodge contends that socialization experiences lead to the formation of a hostile attribution bias. For instance, frequently aggressive children (i.e., children who display a hostile attribution bias) are raised by parents who display little warmth and rely on physical punishment as a source of discipline (Parke & Slaby, 1983). One source of socializing experiences that may influence youth comes from mass media exposure, and relevant to the current chapter, violent comic books.

Using a laboratory experimental design, Kirsh and Olczak (2000) found evidence in young adults of a hostile attribution bias surrounding ambiguities associated with overt acts of aggression after they read extremely violent comic books. Specifically, participants read either an extremely violent comic book (e.g., *Curse of the Spawn*) or a nonviolent comic book (e.g., *Archie*) for 15 minutes. After reading the comic books, the participants were asked to respond to a series of hypothetical scenarios in which harm occurs to a child (e.g., being hit with a ball), but the intent of the harm doer was unclear. After each story, participants were asked a series of questions about the provocateur's intent, potential retaliation toward the provocateur, and about the provocateur's emotional state. For this task, participants were asked to respond to the questions as though they were a 10-year-old child. Results indicated that male participants reading the extremely violent comic books responded more aggressively to the ambiguous stories than did males reading the nonviolent comic book.

Although Kirsh and Olczak's (2000) initial research on overt aggression suggested that violent comic books may have a bigger negative impact on the social information processing of males than that of females, more recent research suggests that *type* of aggressive conflict assessed may also be important. Kirsh and Olczak (2002) investigated the effects of reading extremely violent comic books and nonviolent comic books on the interpretation of overt and relational ambiguous provocation situations. Two hundred forty nine introductory psychology students read either extremely violent or nonviolent comic books. After reading the comic books, participants read hypothetical stories in which an overt or relational aggression occurred, but the intent of the provocateur was ambiguous. Once again, participants were asked a series of questions about the provocateur's intent, potential retaliation against the provocateur, and about the provocateur's emotional state. Responses were coded in terms of amount of negative and aggressive content. Regardless of the type of aggression, participants reading the extremely violent comic books responded more negatively than participants reading nonviolent comic books. However, gender differences were evident: males responded more negatively to the overt scenarios than females; females responded more negatively to the relational scenarios than males. These findings are consistent with previous research suggesting that the presence or absence of aggression-related gender differences may be related to the type of aggressive conflict under study (e.g., relational or overt aggression; see Bartholow & Anderson, 2002). Moreover, the findings are consistent with the fact that males tend to use overt aggression and females tend to engage in relational aggression (Crick et al., 1999).

Additionally, participants' characteristic level of hostility, known as "trait hostility," was significantly related to hostile responding, with the more hostile individuals providing the most aggressive content. These findings are in line with previous research, which has demonstrated positive correlations between trait hostility and increases in hostile attributions (Epps & Kendall, 1995). These findings support Bushman's (1998) contention that an individual with a chronically aggressive network (e.g., a person high in trait hostility) will typically demonstrate aggressive biases in social information processing. Taken together, these findings indicate that social information processing of ambiguous material appears to be affected by a number of variables, including gender, trait hostility, and environmental stimuli such as violent media.

Projective Tests. In asking late adolescents to respond to the hypothetical scenarios like 10-year-old children, the researchers were making use of an assessment procedure known as a *projective test*. A projective test is designed to yield information about the characteristics of an individual based on his or her responses to ambiguous objects or situations. Thus, in the Kirsh and Olczak studies, participants' responses were meant to reflect their current state of mind with regard to hostile/non-hostile perceptions. Whereas some participants would respond negatively, others would respond neutrally or positively. The positive/negative perceptions associated with participants' "child-like" responses were, in fact, meant to be projections of the participants' current cognitive state. Unfortunately, projective tests typically have questionable *reliability* and *validity,* and they are subject to contextual effects such as demand characteristics.

Validity refers to the extent to which a test measures what it is intended to measure. Thus, when a test is low in validity, as is the case in projective tests, there is no guarantee that what the researchers think they are measuring is actually what they are measuring. For instance, what late adolescents think 10-year-olds believe may differ from what late adolescents, themselves, actually believe. If this were the case, then the projective test would not be projecting the inner dynamics of the individual that the researchers are hoping for. *Reliability* refers to the extent to which a test provides consistent results across time. When a test is low in reliability, there is no guarantee the experimental manipulation is causing the observed results.

The Future of Media Violence Research May Be Written in Comic Books

As the previous review of the literature revealed, there is little evidence to support the contention that reading violent comic books influences aggressive behavior or feelings. However, there is evidence that violent comic books influence social information processing. It may be that different forms of media violence (e.g., comic books, video games) differentially influence aggressive behavior and aggression-related constructs. However, with so little research done on violent comic books across childhood and adolescence, additional evidence is needed before any hard and fast conclusions can be drawn. Interestingly, all of the aforementioned studies that failed to find significant differences between exposure to violent and nonviolent comic books involved early adolescents. It may be that comic books influence aggression or aggression-related constructs at certain points in development more than at others. Of course, the paucity of research surrounding the interaction of age and comic book exposure necessitates the need for further investigations in this area.

If the intention of media violence research is to understand the influence of violent imagery on youth, then future researchers may wish to use comic books in their experimental designs. In fact, there are several advantages of using comic books to assess the impact of media violence on children and adolescents. In contrast to playing video games, comic book reading is not confounded by motor movement physiological arousal. Although much of the arousal associated with violent video games will come from the violent components of video game play, the arousal associated with motor movements becomes an unwarranted artifact that has the potential to confound data. In contrast, the physiological arousal experienced by a comic book reader will most likely be due to the images in the comic books alone or an interaction of the images with the individual's personality characteristics. Furthermore, comic books may be less likely than video games to cause the participants to feel frustrated. Assessments of video games typically require participants to play a video game for 5 to 20 minutes and then stop, regardless of where they are in the game. It is possible that participants feel frustrated from having to stop playing the game prematurely. In contrast, when using comic books as the medium of media violence, an individual typically gets to read an entire comic book. In addition, the outcome (e.g., winning or losing) of the video game being played can cause frustration. For instance, Kirsh (1998) found that children who tied a basketball video game gave more hostile responses to ambiguous provocation questions than did children either winning or losing a basketball video game. Furthermore, it is difficult to find a sample of participants who do not play video games regularly. Estimates suggest that 84% of adolescents play video games frequently (Funk, 1993). In contrast, because comic books are not nearly as popular as video games, the impact of previous exposure to the experimental stimuli is mitigated. Thus, the outcomes associated with reading violent comic books may be less likely than video games to be influenced by confounds such as motor arousal, frustration, and previous exposure to the stimuli.

Violence in Literature and Youthful Fear and Aggression

When my daughter was 6 years old, I started to read her *Harry Potter and the Sorcerer's Stone*. I did not get very far. During the first two chapters, she became agitated and scared. She did not sleep well that night either. Scary Harry Potter–related images were in her head—images that were *not* shown in the book. The lack of imagery when reading prose requires that youth engage their imagination to visualize the elements of the story. To help illustrate this point, try to visualize the following original prose that I wrote for this book (Warning: Gore and Extreme Violence):

> With a smile on his face, the demonic creature dug his 5-inch-long sharpened fingernails deep into the cheek of his screaming victim. Tender strips of flesh followed the path of his fingers as they made their way towards the suffering victim's now-slackened jaw. Without hesitation, the Creature took the tender and bloody strips of flesh and gently lobbed them into a frying pan. The remains of what was once a beautiful face sizzled like bacon, only the smell was much worse: it was a stench of death.

If you were successfully able to imagine the above paragraph *and* found it somewhat disturbing, then you have been affected by media violence. Similar to reading comic books, reading novels engenders a high degree of involvement with the content of the story, resulting in the potential to influence the reader's level of emotional and cognitive states.

Frightening Stories and Fear

The idea that media images can influence the emotional states of children is not new. Orbach, Vinkler, and Har-Even (1993) found that the frightening elements in stories increased the level of anxiety in 6- to 9-year-olds. Research conducted on other mass media demonstrated similar findings. For instance, Cantor (2002) has repeatedly shown that violent and scary images on television and in movies can cause immediate fright reactions and memories of such fearful stimuli in young children for decades to come. My own experience with the flying monkeys from the *Wizard of Oz* exemplifies this latter point.

Bettelheim (1967) contended that the anxiety caused by fearful stories afforded children the opportunity to master—that is, gain control over—this particular emotional state. In fact, Orbach and colleagues (1993) found some evidence in support of this contention. Orbach created three versions of the Grimm Brothers' fairy tale *Rapunzel:* a frightening version with a happy ending, a frightening version with an unhappy ending, and a neutral version with the frightening elements removed. Results indicated that the frightening version with the unhappy ending yielded the greatest amount of anxiety in children. Interestingly, despite the high level of anxiety created by hearing it, the frightening story with the unhappy ending also received the greatest number of requests to be read again. Orbach and colleagues suggest that these findings indicate an attempt by children to gain mastery over fearful content. However, children in Orbach's experiment heard the frightening story on two separate occasions, and in each instance, their anxiety level went up after hearing the frightening version of the story (and not down, which would be indicative of control over anxiety). Thus, there is no evidence that children actually mastered their feelings of anxiety. If not for mastery purposes, why, then, would children prefer the frightening story?

Children's preference for the frightening story with an unhappy ending may simply reflect the fact that this particular version of the story was edited in a more entertaining way, in comparison to the other versions of the story. What remains to be seen, therefore, is if children who become anxious after hearing a story request to hear that same story when given the opportunity to hear non-frightening stories that are just as entertaining. Children may, in fact, use scary stories as a means of mastering fears. To date, however, there is no clear evidence of this in the scientific literature.

Aggressive Stories and Aggressive Behavior

Although research has consistently shown that mass media can cause a fearful response in youth, less is known about the effects of violent story content on aggressive behavior and aggression-related constructs across development. In fact, there is no substantive research on this issue. One reason why there is so little research on the effects of reading on aggressive behavior across development may be because of the empirically supported viewpoint that leisure reading positively influences academic achievement. For instance, research has consistently found the amount of free reading done outside of school is positively correlated with the level of achievement in vocabulary, reading comprehension, verbal fluency, and general information (Anderson, Wilson, & Fielding, 1988; Cunningham & Stanovich, 1991). Thus, in contrast to television, video games, movies, comic books, and popular music, leisure reading is not considered by most media violence researchers to impose a negative influence on children and adolescents. That is *not* to say, however, that those outside of academe agree with this position.

Despite a lack of research connecting the reading of violent material with deleterious outcomes, between 1990 and 2000, books from the *Harry Potter* series and over 700 other books deemed violent were challenged in an attempt to ban them from school libraries across the country (American Library Association, 2003). Even if research were to demonstrate that reading violent material negatively affects the behavior of youth at certain ages more so than others, censorship is still not the answer. Instead, a rating system (like that used for the television and the movies) could be employed to help parents make appropriate reading choices for their children.

War Toys and Aggression

In the following section, the term "war toy" will be used to refer any toy that resembles weaponry and is used in rough-and-tumble play or fantasy aggression. In addition to miniaturized versions of guns, knives, and so on constituting toys of war, toys transformed from their original intent into weaponry will also be classified as war toys. Thus, clay shaped into the form of a gun, dolls contorted into makeshift knives, and wads of crumbled paper used as hand-grenades would constitute war toys. So, too, would snowballs and dirt clods; I've even seen a feather turned into a light saber. To be considered a war toy, then, the object being played with needs to be manipulated in a manner that mimics an act of real-life violence.

Comic books, novels, and toys all engage the imagination of youth. However, only war toys allow for the practice of aggressive scripts and the enactment of aggressive behaviors. Therefore, in comparison to the other two forms of entertainment violence, war toy play has the potential to greatly impact aggressive behavior (Sanson & DiMuccio, 1993). Of no minor consequence, though, is the fact that when playing with toys of violence, youth may also learn how to practice controlling aggressive impulses, allaying fears and anxieties, and resolving conflicts (Goldstein, 1995). So, which is it? Does playing with toys increase aggressive behavior or teach children how to control aggressive impulses?

War Toy Research

Given the controversy surrounding war toys, it is somewhat surprising to note that there are few empirical papers on the topic. In fact, fewer than 15 papers addressing the impact of war toy play on behavior have been published in the last 50 years. Despite the limited amount of research, three basic findings regarding the negative effects of war toys on youth have been demonstrated: (1) war toy play leads to aggressive play; (2) war toy play can influence aggressive behavior; and (3) gender differences in war toy play abound.

First, when aggressive toys are present, aggressive play will typically follow (Goldstein, 1995). For instance, Hellendoorn and Harinck (1997) found that among 4- to 7-year-olds, a preexisting preference for war toys and the use of weapons during a free play session were both significantly correlated with make-believe aggression. Of note, aggressive play differs from actual aggression in that while the former is associated with fun, joint laughter, and continued play, the latter is associated with negative affect, the stoppage of play, and avoidance of the play partner afterwards.

Second, the differentiation between aggressive play and aggressive behavior is an important one, since the literature linking war toy play with aggressive behavior is less clear than the research on aggressive play. For instance, several studies have failed to find a significant relationship between the use of war toys and aggressive behavior (Sutton-Smith, Gerstmyer, & Meckley, 1988; Wegener-Spohring, 1989). Other studies purporting to link aggressive toys with real-life aggression failed to include aggressive play in their coding of aggressive behavior (e.g., Potts et al., 1986; Sanson & DiMuccio, 1993). As such, it is impossible to tell if the reported acts of real-life aggression were, in reality, acts of aggressive play. At the very least, the conclusion that war toys increased aggressive play in these studies can be drawn.

However, several studies have successfully linked war toy play with increases in aggressive behavior. Turner and Goldsmith (1976), Watson and Peng (1992), and Hellendoorn and Harinck (1997) differentiated make-believe aggression from real aggression in their studies, and in each instance, war toy play was found to significantly increase non-play-related aggressive behavior. These findings occurred even after including additional environmental variables, such as parental attitudes towards war toys and socioeconomic status. However, the presence of contradictory research suggests that additional research is needed to validate the hypothesized negative effects of war toy play on aggressive behavior in youth.

With regard to the positive aspects of war toy play, only one empirical paper has been published in a *peer-reviewed journal*. Bonte and Musgrove (1943) found that following the bombing of Pearl Harbor during World War II, Hawaiian youth engaged in more war toy play but experienced a reduction in aggressive behavior. Bonte and Musgrove contend that this finding reflects an attempt to cope with anxieties and a release of aggression through catharsis. However, none of the articles accepted for publication in peer-reviewed journals since that time has replicated this finding. Articles accepted for publication in such journals go through a peer-review process in which the article is evaluated based on its contribution to the field, methodological soundness, and overall adherence to the scientific method. In contrast, when empirical findings are published in books or made public in the form of a press release, there is no guarantee that the article meets the standards of the scientific method.

The third and final finding that has been consistently shown across studies is that the effects of war toys on aggressive play and behavior are more consistently found for boys than girls. And when significant effects are evident for both genders, they tend to be stronger for boys (Goldstein, 1995).

A Closer Look at Gender
Differences in War Toy Research

Why effects of war toy play are found for boys and to a lesser extent for girls is an intriguing question. To start, let us review general gender differences in play that occur across development. Starting in the toddler period, preference for sex-typed toys occurs (Caldera, Huston, & O'Brien, 1989), with boys preferring tanks, soldiers, trucks, and action figures and girls preferring dolls, stuffed animals, and other objects that can be nurtured (Singer & Singer, 1990). These sex-typed patterns of play continue throughout childhood. In general, boys tend to prefer toys and activities that allow a great deal of active play, and girls tend to choose more sedate activities. As such, the need for arousal and excitement may, in part, account for the sex-typed toy choices mentioned above. Interestingly, where there are consistent violations of sex-typed play, biological factors, such as exposure to prenatal hormones, appear to play a critical role. Boys and girls exposed prenatally and perinatally to high levels of androgens (i.e., the "male" hormones) prefer toys traditionally meant for boys during early and middle childhood. Complimentary to this finding is that prenatal exposure to a synthetic version of progesterone (i.e., "female" hormones) is associated with lower levels of rough-and-tumble play among boys and girls (Berenbaum, & Snyder, 1995; Meyer-Bahlburg, Feldman, Cohen, & Ehrhardt, 1988). However, environmental experiences play an important role in toy preference as well. In particular, children who engage in sex-typed play are reinforced by their peers for such actions though positive exchanges and increased opportunities for play (Eisenberg, Tryon, & Cameron, 1984).

There are many potential reasons to explain why gender differences in war toy play occur. The arousal and excitement that follows war toy play complements boys' desire for physically stimulating activities. An additional possibility is that because boys, more than girls, are socialized to be assertive, competitive, dominant, goal oriented, and independent (i.e., adopt the instrumental role), they seek out play that affords such opportunities (Parsons, 1955). War toy play, therefore, allows the expression of instrumental characteristics. Along this same line, Goldstein (1995) contends that in response to pressures to suppress emotions and intimacy, when engaged in emotional and intimate moments (which can arise during play) boys overcompensate and become hyper-masculine, resulting in aggressive play.

The *practice hypothesis* has also been forwarded to explain the aforementioned gender differences. The practice hypothesis contends that in preparation for adulthood, youth practice the activities in which they may have to frequently engage in the future (Humphreys & Smith, 1984). In support of this contention, Regan (1994) has found that in times of war, in which adult soldiers (who are predominantly male) are actively engaged in combat, there is an increased interest in war toys among youth. Thus, seeing and hearing about war on TV may arouse in youth a desire to practice for the future.

Although the exact reasons for gender differences in war toy play are not known, one thing is certain. The differences that occur are real, and the reasons for those differences arise from a variety of factors. It is also worth noting that because boys and girls are differentially influenced by war toys, a general indictment of such toys as evil or detrimental to all is not warranted. As will be continually shown throughout this book, violent entertainment alone does not influence aggressive behavior; instead, it is one of many potential risk factors for aggression. One limitation to this research, however, is that measures of aggressive behavior typically focus on acts of physical aggression. As previously stated, girls are more likely to engage in relational aggression than physical aggression. As such, additional research investigating the influence of war toys on more indirect forms of aggression is necessary before any definitive conclusions regarding the disproportionate effect of war toy play on boys can be validated.

Critique of the War Toy Literature

One of the major limitations of war toy research is that it has almost exclusively focused on the effects of war toys during early childhood. Little is known about war toy play beyond this particular developmental period. Given that the preschool period is a time when children are beginning to gain control over their aggressive impulses, it may be during this period that war toy play is most likely to affect aggressive behavior. However, aggressive toy play continues across childhood, adolescence, and even into adulthood. But instead of playing with faux light sabers, spongy arrows, and plastic darts, older children, adolescents, and adults play dodge ball, shoot bottle rockets at one another, and play paint ball. Unfortunately, there are no studies that

Table 7.1   Explaining Gender Differences in War Toy Play

War toy play may meet the needs of boys by allowing them to

- engage in physically stimulating activities.
- be dominant, assertive, and independent.
- suppress emotions and become hyper-masculine.
- prepare for adult roles.

assess the impact of war toy play during middle childhood and adolescence. Additionally, the research that has been conducted has focused on aggressive behavior. Little is known about the effects of war toy play on other aggression-related constructs across development.

Moreover, the studies that have assessed the immediate impact of war toy play on aggressive behavior suggest that the effects are short-lived. Once the child leaves the setting in which the war toy play occurred, the heightened levels of aggressive behavior begin to abate (Turner & Goldsmith, 1976). Thus, the aggressive behavior that started in the play setting does not appear to carry over into other settings. Furthermore, little is known about the effects of repeated exposure to war toy play and aggressive behavior across development. Does a pattern of war toy play increase aggressive behavior over days, months, or years? This is a question in need of an answer. However, several studies have indicated that aggressive children, more than nonaggressive children, prefer war toys over nonaggressive toys (Jenvey, 1992; Jukes, 1991). In each instance, trait levels of aggression appear to be the connecting element. Once again, aggressive behavior appears to be the result of a multitude of factors. There is no single "magic bullet"—or plastic magic bullet, for that matter—to account for aggressive behavior in youth.

Summary

- Slapstick humor involves both aggressive and nonaggressive actions.
- In comic books, the disconnected presentation of information forces readers to engage their imaginations.
- Initial research on the effects of comic book violence on youth was based on anecdotes and did not meet the criteria for science. The vast majority of studies conducted on youth have failed to support the contention that reading violent comic books increases aggressive behavior. However, using a matched, quasi-experimental design, one study found that the reading of violent comic books was correlated with aggressive behavior in adolescent boys. Recent research on late adolescents and young adults has found that short-term exposure to comic book violence can influence social information processing.
- Compared to other forms of violent entertainment research, comic book research has several advantages: no arousal artifact, no frustration, and reduced familiarity.
- Frightening stories can cause fear in children and adults alike—fears that can last for years to come. There is no evidence that hearing or reading frightening stories helps children master feelings of anxiety.
- There is no research on the effects of violent story content on aggressive behavior and aggression-related constructs across development.

- War toy play consistently leads to aggressive play in preschool children. At times, war toy play results in an increase in aggressive behavior. Boys prefer war toy play and appear to be affected by it to a greater extent than girls. Little is known about war toy play beyond the preschool years.
- The following methodological concepts were discussed: quasi-experimental design, non-equivalent groups design, matching, projective tests, reliability, and validity. Additionally, the definition of a peer-reviewed journal was provided.

8

Animating the Beast

Cartoon Violence

Although I am rarely disturbed by the violent media I consume, I was disturbed by Quentin Tarantino's critically acclaimed, ultra-violent ode to martial arts films, *Kill Bill: Vol. 1*. The opening of the movie, during which Beatrix Kiddo (a.k.a. Black Mamba) gets shot in the head, startled me, but I was not bothered by it; I found the sequence of events in which Black Mamba uses a Samurai sword to annihilate the many members of The Crazy 88s (a Japanese gang of hoodlums) over-the-top in its use of blood but not too troubling to watch; and the scene surrounding the death of O-Ren Ishi, in which the top of her head falls to the ground as if it were a flake of snow, had a strange cinematic beauty to it. To me, the most disturbing events in *Kill Bill: Vol. 1* (or *Kill Bill: Vol. 2*, for that matter) were those shown in animation. During these extremely violent animated sequences, O-Ren Ishi's parents are killed; O-Ren seeks bloody revenge against the per-petrators; a sword is propelled through O-Ren's father's head; ammunition rips though flesh like it was paper; fists pummel into a man's face with authority and authenticity; and a sniper's bullet creates a peephole through the head of a unknown dignitary. The *Kill Bill* movies were appropriately rated R and therefore are unlike most of the animated movies and television programs directed towards youth. Nonetheless, as the following sections will reveal, the violence depicted in cartoons does, in fact, influence youthful viewers, even if the violence is not as extreme as that depicted in *Kill Bill*.

Cartoons: A Brief Historical Overview

Animated films and television shows have been entertaining children and adults for over 80 years. The first true animated star was 1920s feline icon Felix the Cat. Felix was also the first animated character to be heavily merchandised to the American public, with watches, dolls, toys, baby oil, and cigars bearing his likeness (FelixTheCat.com, 2004; Chapter 15 will address further the impact of advertising on children). Soon thereafter, Walt and Roy Disney launched the Disney Brothers' Cartoon Studios. By the early 1930s, characters such as Mickey Mouse, Donald Duck, and Pluto were making their way onto the silver screen and international fame in a cartoon series called *Silly Symphonies*. The historical popularity of animated movies cannot be understated. From the start, animated films were box office juggernauts. As evidence, consider the following: Disney's first feature-length film, *Snow White and the Seven Dwarfs,* is still one of the ten top grossing films of all time (when inflation is taken into consideration). Some 70 years later, animated films are still as popular as ever. For instance, the 2004 Dreamworks animated film *Shrek 2* generated nearly $900 million in box office receipts and millions more in DVD sales (Box Office Mojo, 2004).

In the mid-1950s, the violence-laden *Popeye the Sailor* dominated the television airways, generating millions of dollars in advertising revenue. Following the success of Popeye, studios such as Hanna-Barbera began to produce made-for-TV animated series, and in 1960 *The Flintstones* became the first cartoon to air during prime-time hours (8:00–11:00 P.M.). A slate of cartoon series soon followed, with shows such as *Rocky & Bullwinkle, Speed Racer, Jonny Quest,* and *Scooby Doo Mysteries* garnering a large viewership among children. Currently, animated film classics and new television series can be seen on cable/satellite channels such as *Boomerang, Cartoon Network,* and *The Disney Channel.*

Violence in Cartoons

Since the inception of animation, violence has been an integral part of cartoon content. Be it in dramatic or comedic form, the amount of violence is higher in cartoons than in other types of programming (Potter & Warren, 1998). A little-known fact is that children and adolescents are more likely to witness acts of media-depicted violence during Saturday morning cartoons than during prime-time television hours (Gerbner, Gross, Morgan, & Signorelli, 1994). However, the nature of dramatic and cartoon violence frequently differs. Cartoon violence on television tends to involve minor acts of violence; death is rarely animated, and rapes are never televised (rightly so, given that most animated shows are meant for children). Additionally, cartoons *sanitize* the outcomes of violence. That is, victims are rarely shown suffering in realistic pain. In contrast, prime-time dramas regularly involve major acts of violence (e.g., rape and murder), and the pain and suffering of the victim is often highlighted (Potter & Warren, 1998).

Although the term "cartoon" connotes the presence of comedic elements, not all cartoons portray violence in the context of comedy; some cartoons just portray the violence. For instance, cartoons such as *Samurai Jack*, *X-Men Evolution,* and *Batman: The Animated Series* relay stories in which, in the absence of comedy, violence is used to start and resolve conflicts. Haynes (1978) refers to this latter form of cartoons as "authentic," due to their portrayals of authentic-looking characters. The presence or absence of comedic elements in media violence is an important consideration when evaluating the effects on youth of viewing cartoons, for many researchers posit that comedy has the potential to camouflage and trivialize depictions of violence (King, 2000; Potter & Warren, 1998).

The Effects of Comedy on the Perception of Cartoon Violence

Very few studies have assessed the impact of humor on youths' perception of violence in mass media. Snow (1974) found that 27% of 4- to 8-year-olds and 16% of 9- to 12-year-olds correctly identified violent behavior in

Table 8.1   Factors That Influence the Perception of Violence in Cartoons

Cartoons With Comedic Elements:

Cognitive Transformations
Schematic Processing
Priming
Contextual Factors

Cartoons Without Comedic Elements:

Graphicness
Perceived Actuality
Perceived Similarity
Perceived Reality

an animated cartoon (i.e., *Roadrunner*) as violent. In comparison, nearly 70% of youth in Snow's sample classified the television Western *Gunsmoke* as containing violence. Regardless of age, all children correctly identified news clips of the Vietnam War as containing violent imagery. Contrasting these findings, Haynes' (1978) investigation of 5th- and 6th-grade boys and girls revealed that cartoons with comedic elements were perceived as more violent than cartoons without comedic elements, even though both cartoons contained the same amount of violence. Studies on adults' perceptions of humorous cartoons have been a bit more consistent. Howitt and Cumberbatch (1975) found that most adults do not perceive humorous cartoons as violent. Similarly, Gunter and Furnham (1984) found violence depicted in humorous cartoons is perceived as less violent than the same behavior enacted by live actors. Given the contradictory findings and paucity of research using children, more studies are needed to establish facts regarding the perception of violence in comedic and authentic cartoons across development.

Despite the lack of evidence suggesting that children perceive humorous cartoons as less violent than other media forms, there are theoretical reasons to believe that comedy does, in fact, camouflage or trivialize depictions of violence.

Cognitive Transformation

Humorous elements in cartoons are thought to signal the viewer that the seriousness of the events they are watching should be downplayed. As a result, a cognitive transformation occurs, rendering material that might otherwise be considered grave as whimsical (Kane, Suls, & Tedeschi, 1977). With regard to depictions of aggression, in the context of humor such acts are transformed from solemn and gruesome events into comical ones. In fact, the more the violence deviates from reality (as is the case in cartoons, science fiction, and fantasy), the less likely it is that the act of violence will be taken seriously by the viewer. Potter (2003) suggests that in order for viewers to perceive violence in media, a feeling of personal threat must occur. For instance, if the viewing of a homicide causes an individual to worry about his or her own safety, then the violence that caused the murder will be perceived. Given that comedic cartoons deviate significantly from reality, and it is therefore difficult for the viewer to make a connection between the onscreen violence and a personal threat of violence, the level of violence associated with the viewed media is diminished. For instance, the high level of realism in the animation sequences in *Kill Bill: Vol. 1* make it difficult for the viewer to *not* consider it violent.

Schematic Processing

Schemas are cognitive structures that organize responses to experiences (Fiske & Taylor, 1991). With each new encounter, schemas are thought to guide us through the experience by providing a template of expectations for rules, behaviors, and outcomes. When watching an episode of *Law and Order,* for example, it is expected that the show will start with two unsuspecting people stumbling upon a lifeless body; the murder will mirror a real-life event; within the first 20 minutes of the show, the police will identify and arrest the killer; and during the remainder of the show, the legal team will struggle with their own issues of morality while attempting to convict the alleged killer. Of course, 45 minutes into the show some unseen and unpredictable twist will occur. According to Potter and Warren (1998), schemas are formed for different media genres, such as Westerns, action/adventure, drama, and comedy. Schemas for comedies are thought to contain expectations and rules regarding the type and pacing of jokes, the variety of characters involved, and the typical endings. In fact, with comedies, the viewer expects levity throughout the entire show. The schema changes, however, if the show is introduced in the following manner: "Tonight, on a very special . . ." Such an introduction tells the viewer that the rules of comedy have changed and that there will be some somber and dramatic moments during the episode. And in all likelihood, such a preface is also an indication that the show has "jumped the shark"—that is, from now on, the quality of the show will get worse, not better.

Although schemas are updated for accuracy, such modifications rarely take place in situations of *low involvement.* During such instances, minor discrepancies between the experience and the schema are ignored, and the schema is applied to the situation in an all-or-none fashion. Thus, any elements within the show that contradict the expected pattern are not processed. However, large discrepancies between the show and the schema can effect a change in the schema. Potter and Warren (1998) suggest that the viewing of comedic television is a low-involvement activity for youth. As such, minor discrepancies between the program and the schema are ignored because the schema is being applied in an all-or-none manner. Moreover, Potter and Warren contend that schemas for comedies *exclude* violence. As such, when violence occurs in comedies, the viewer ignores it. In other words, schematic processing causes violence in comedies to be camouflaged. Of course, in order for this camouflaging effect to happen, the violence depicted needs to involve minor acts of aggression, which, as mentioned above, frequently happen in cartoons. Viewers would be hard pressed to ignore the brutality, blood, gore, and sinew of *Kill Bill: Vol. 1,* even if it were shown during Saturday morning cartoons. In this case, the violence is not minor, and therefore the schema cannot ignore it.

Priming

In Chapter 6, the concept of priming was presented. Essentially, priming is a reading process in which related thoughts, emotions, and concepts residing in memory are activated. When aggressive acts are presented alone, as is the case in violent dramas, the activation of aggressive thoughts, feelings, and concepts primarily occurs. However, when comical events are paired with acts of violence, as is the case in comedic cartoons, priming not only occurs in aggression-related thoughts, concepts, and feelings but in humor-related thoughts, concepts, and feelings as well. As a result of this dual priming, the perceived level of violence may be lessened.

Contextual Factors

Contextual factors are the circumstances surrounding the depiction of an act of violence. For instance, the moral justification for an act of violence can influence the perceived seriousness of that act. Two of the most frequently cited contextual factors viewed as influencing the perceived level of violence in a media offering are *consequences* and *legitimation* (Potter & Warren, 1998). The consequences to both the victim and the perpetrator appear to influence the interpretation of a violent act. Specifically, when the victim shows a high degree of pain and suffering, it becomes difficult for the viewer to trivialize the televised violence. Moreover, when the perpetrator acts remorseful and sorrowful following an act of violence, the violence is perceived as more serious than when the perpetrator does not express such emotions (Gunter, 1985).

Elements in a story that help the viewer determine the morality of a violent act define the concept of legitimation. Potter and Warren (1998) contend that acts of violence that are rewarded or go unpunished are perceived as moral. At the very least, such acts are viewed as not wrong. As a result of such interpretations, depictions of violence become trivialized in the mind of the viewer. As it turns out, contextual factors in comedic cartoons foster the trivialization of violence. In particular, the perpetrators of cartoon violence are frequently rewarded (i.e., legitimized) and unremorseful. Moreover, the pain and suffering of the victims are often minimized, absent, or comedically presented.

Non-comedic Cartoons and Perceived Violence

Although comedic elements in cartoons may result in the trivialization of violence, cartoons that lack humor are also perceived to be less violent than live-action forms of media violence. In this section, I address the factors influencing the perception of cartoons without comedic elements.

Graphicness

One would be hard pressed to find a significant number of people who would equate the level of violence depicted in an animated fistfight, such as those shown during *Batman: The Animated Series,* with the brutality and graphicness of a fistfight cinematically portrayed in the live-action Brad Pitt offering, *Fight Club.* In fact, the more graphic the depiction of blood and gore during scenes of violence, the higher the level of violence attributed to that scene (Potter & Berry, 1998). Given that most cartoons viewed by youth contain little in the way of graphic blood and gore, animated violence is often overlooked by the viewer. Similarly, the more an act of violence generates feelings of uneasiness in the viewer or lessens the viewer's enjoyment, the higher the associated level of perceived violence of that act (Potter, 2003). Thus, violent content that is perceived to be offensive is rated as more violent than less offensive content. Once again, cartoons readily available for youthful viewing are rarely perceived as offensive. As such, youth discount the violence depicted.

Perceived Actuality

Perceived actuality is the degree to which a viewer perceives media-depicted portrayals of events, settings, and characters as existing, or being able to exist, in the real world. The more a viewer believes that what he or she is seeing on television or in movies could actually happen in real life, the higher the degree of perceived actuality. Consider as an example the differences between Batman and Superman. Batman is a crime-fighting hero who fights on the side of justice using his wit, martial arts training, and technical achievements. In contrast, Superman, an alien from another world, relies on super powers (such as superior strength and being able to fly) to defeat the bad guys. Although both Batman and Superman are make-believe characters, Batman has a higher level of perceived actuality than Superman, because a Batman-like individual is more likely to occur in real life (improbable though it may be) than a Superman-like character (remember, super powers do not really exist). Perceived actuality is thought to be an important factor in determining the influence of media violence. The more viewers perceive that what they are seeing could actually happen in real life, the greater the likelihood they will attend to, remember, and be motivated to perform similar acts of aggression (Bandura, 1965). In essence, youth can learn more about real-life aggression (e.g., appropriateness of use, consequences) when the models and circumstances surrounding acts of aggression could exist in reality.

Perceived Similarity

Perceived similarity refers to the degree of similarity between the viewer and media-depicted events, settings, and characters. The more similarities perceived between the viewer's life and the content of the viewed media, the greater the level of perceived similarity. In comparing Batman and Superman to a typical male viewer, differences in perceived similarity are evident. For instance, Batman is human, as are the viewers; Superman has super powers, whereas the viewers do not. Based on these criteria, Batman would have a higher level of perceived similarity with the viewer than would Superman. Programs high in perceived similarity are posited to influence aggression in youth to a greater extent than programs low in perceived similarity. As perceived similarity increases, the following are thought to occur: the amount of priming of aggression-related constructs increases, emotional arousal swells, observers expect to experience similar events in their lives (thereby enhancing modeling influences), and there is a greater chance of identification.

Perceived Reality

Together, perceived actuality and perceived similarity make up the *perceived reality* of a media offering. The greater the perceived actuality and perceived similarity of a violent media offering (movie, video game, etc.), the more realistic that violent media offering is perceived to be. Moreover, regardless of media form (e.g., animated, live-action, video game), depictions of violence with little realism are rated as less violent than more realistic depictions of violence (Atkin, 1983). It is worth noting that perceived reality is individually determined. As such, it is possible for two youth watching the same show to be impacted differently by it because of differences in perceived actuality and perceived similarity. By the nature of their presentation, cartoon characters are less realistic than actors in live-action shows. Moreover, the activities portrayed in modern, non-comedic cartoons tend to have a strong fantasy component. Shows containing a high degree of violence, such as *Teenage Mutant Ninja Turtles, X-Men,* and *Justice League Unlimited,* depict creatures that do not really exist (such as talking turtles and superheroes) engaging in activities that are unrealistic in nature (e.g., flying, X-ray vision).

Development and the Fantasy-Reality Distinction. Developmental issues appear to moderate the perceived reality of a television program or movie. In particular, as children age their ability to correctly differentiate fantasy from reality improves, an ability that is referred to as the *fantasy-reality distinction.* At first, children believe that what they see on television is real. Two-year-olds will attempt to clean up an egg that was broken during a televised program and 3-year-olds believe that if a television is turned upside down, the contents of a televised bowl will spill. By age 4, children no longer make these mistakes. However, the ability to differentiate fantasy from reality is still developing. Because scene cuts and replays violate real-world possibilities, 6- and 7-year-olds may incorrectly identify "real" information as fantastical. By age 9, regardless of editing, children realize that news shows and documentaries present real information (Flavell, Flavell, Green, & Korfmacher, 1990; Huston & Wright, 1998; Jaglom & Gardner, 1981; Wright, Huston, Reitz, & Piemyat, 1994).

Fantasy-Reality Distinction, Cartoons, and Aggression. The fantasy-reality distinction may impact the potential influence of cartoons on youthful aggression. To understand why this may occur, it is necessary to briefly review how the realism (or lack thereof) of a show tends to influence the aggressive behavior of children and adolescents. In general, realistic portrayals of media violence engender greater levels of aggressive behavior in viewers than unrealistic media depictions (Huesmann, Lagerspetz, & Eron, 1984). For instance, adolescents report a greater likelihood of acting aggressively against another person following a provocation if they had previously witnessed acts of violence during a television newscast than if the same acts of violence were viewed as part of a commercial for an upcoming television drama (Atkin, 1983). Thus, given that the ability to correctly distinguish fantasy from reality does not become reasonably accurate until late childhood (starting around age 8; Wright et al., 1994) and that misidentifications of fantasy as reality could result in higher levels of aggressive behavior in youth, many are concerned cartoons could disproportionately influence the behavior of young children. In fact, research has shown that preschool-aged children are more frightened by animated images than are older children. Witches and wizards casting deadly spells are just as frightening to preschoolers as are depictions of bullies and burglars (Cantor & Sparks, 1984).

Although cartoons and animated movies may frighten youth, this genre of media is one of the first to be recognized by children as being unreal. In fact, 5-year-olds clearly understand the unreality of cartoons; that is to say, they recognize them as fantasy (Wright et al., 1994). Thus, by the end of the preschool years, the threat of aggressive behavior due to cartoons is reduced because they are no longer perceived as real. It appears, then, that the contention that young children's inability to distinguish fantasy from reality as a risk factor for aggression is not supported.

Fantasy-Reality Distinction, Cartoons, and Fear. But what about the finding that televised fantastical entities cause fear in children? Here, there appears to be an apparent contradiction: children are frightened by what they know to be fantasy. It may be that *stating* that some entity is fantastical (e.g., monster under the bed) and being *sure in your belief* that the entity is, in fact, fantastical are two separate things. As Woolley (1997) states, "Children may understand that these entities generally are not real, but may be less good at saying 'it's not real' to themselves and comforting themselves with this knowledge" (p. 1007). Although children recognize cartoons as unreal at the end of the preschool years, their belief in fantastical beings in general (e.g., Santa Claus, Easter Bunny, Tooth Fairy, Dragons) does not decline until age 8 (Woolley, Boerger, & Markman, 2004). Moreover, children classify something as fantasy or reality on a case-by-case basis. For example, although 5-year-old children may believe that there are no monsters under their own bed, there in fact could be monsters under Grandma's bed. Thus, even though young children recognize that cartoons are unreal, the content of those cartoons (e.g., monsters and wizards) could still be real; as such, they may trigger fears of fantastical entities.

Cartoons and Aggressive Behavior: The Evidence

Given the importance ascribed to perceived reality in influencing aggressive behavior, it is not surprising that not only are cartoons rated as less realistic than live-action media forms (Bandura, Ross, & Ross, 1963), but the impact of violent cartoons on aggressive behavior is typically less than that of programs containing a higher degree of realism. However, the fact that cartoons influence aggressive behavior and aggression-related constructs to a lesser extent than live-action shows should not be construed as suggesting that there is *no* effect of cartoon violence on youth. Quite the contrary, as research has consistently shown that animated violence influences youthful aggressive behavior.

Disinhibition

At times, acts of aggression resulting from violent media consumption exemplify the concept of *disinhibition*. Disinhibition refers to situations in which youth readily enact *previously learned* aggressive behaviors. In other words, the viewing of violent media can remove/reduce (i.e., disinhibit) reservations that youth might have with regard to performing aggressive acts already in their repertoire. Thus, the witnessing of Wile E. Coyote being blown to bits by dynamite (made by ACME, of course) has the potential to disinhibit unrelated acts of aggression in viewers, such as pushing, shoving, and hitting. The concept of disinhibition is important to research on cartoon violence because the elements of cartoon violence are fantasy laden. Children cannot pick up anvils and drop them on the head of another person; youth do not have access to TNT explosives, which when detonated leave only a pair of blinking eyes; and most children lack the strength to punch someone with enough force to turn their head completely around. As Hapkiewicz (1979) states, "It is often impossible for the viewer to model the novel responses displayed by imaginary characters in imaginary situations" (p. 30). From more realistic types of cartoons, however, children can learn acts of aggression that are possible in real life. But the concept of disinhibition diminishes the argument that unrealistic cartoons cannot affect the aggressive behavior of children because the behaviors displayed in the cartoons are impossible to reproduce in real life.

Laboratory Research in Early Childhood

Almost 50 years ago, the first laboratory experiment on the impact of violent cartoons on aggressive behavior in youth was conducted. In that experiment, a humorous and violent Woody Woodpecker cartoon was shown to young children (Siegel, 1956). Siegel paired preschool children with one another and exposed them to either a violent or a nonviolent cartoon. Following the animated media consumption, youth were observed during *dyadic free play* (i.e., they were free to play how they wished), in which the number of aggressive acts towards the peer-partner, toys, or self were counted. The following week, the children returned to the laboratory and viewed a cartoon of an opposite valence from the week before (e.g., if they watched a violent cartoon the first week, they watched a nonviolent cartoon the second week and vice versa). The results of the study indicated that the amount of aggressive behavior displayed did not vary by the level of cartoon violence observed by preschool children. Studies exposing children in middle childhood to cartoons with comedic violence have also failed to show increases in *peer-partner* aggression (Hapkiewicz & Roden, 1971; Hapkiewicz & Stone, 1974).

In contrast, three laboratory experiments have found that violent cartoon exposure does, in fact, negatively influence preschool children. For example, children viewing animation involving human-like figures that hit and bite one another chose to play with an aggressive toy (i.e., a hitting doll) as opposed to a nonaggressive toy (i.e., a ball in a cage) in a greater percentage than children seeing a nonviolent cartoon (Lovaas, 1961). Bandura and colleagues (1963) found that exposure to a violent cartoon resulted in greater aggression (e.g., hitting and kicking) towards a Bobo doll than did the screening of a nonviolent cartoon.

Comedic and Non-comedic Violence

There are two equally compelling reasons for the contradictory findings mentioned above. First, whereas the studies that failed to find significant effects of cartoon violence on aggression used animation depicting comedic violence, the studies that were able to demonstrate significant effects of cartoon violence on aggressive behavior used cartoons replete with violence but lacking in comedy. Thus, the presence of comedy during the cartoons may have camouflaged the violence depicted within, thereby reducing its influence on aggressive behavior in youth. Thus, although there is concern that when preschoolers watch comedic violence they will come to learn that violence is funny (Nathanson & Cantor, 2000), thereby increasing their aggressive tendencies, the research has yet to validate this concern.

Object-Oriented and Person-Oriented Aggression

A second possibility concerns the object of aggression assessed during the experiments. The majority of the studies finding significant effects of watching cartoon violence on youth measured object-oriented aggression (e.g., hitting Bobo doll; selection of aggressive toy). In contrast, the studies that failed to find significant effects measured peer-related aggression. Given that interpersonal aggression among youth is frowned upon by society, and that acts of interpersonal aggression are punished, the preschoolers in these studies may have been concerned about social disapproval by the experimenters and reduced the level of aggression displayed. In contrast, because there is less social disapproval associated with object-oriented aggression during play, disinhibition effects may be easier to detect.

This explanation leaves open the possibility that preschoolers' desire to act aggressively increased following media violence exposure, but socialization experiences caused them to control their behavior. It follows, then, that if youth lack appropriate socialization experiences, and if the controls set in place to limit the use of aggression are absent, the effects of violent media will be more pronounced. Such is the case with children suffering from certain childhood psychopathologies in which the ability to control one's behavior is compromised. Consider the following: recent research suggests that children in middle childhood with Disruptive Behavioral Disorders are affected to a greater extent by violent imagery than youth without this form of psychopathology (Grimes, Vernberg, & Cathers, 1997).

Field Experiments in Early Childhood

In addition to the laboratory studies mentioned above, the impact of violent cartoons on preschool aggression has been assessed using *field experiments*. Field experiments are similar to laboratory experiments in that there is random assignment, a control group, an experimental group, and a manipulation of the independent variable (e.g., the presence or absence of violent media).

Ecological Validity

The primary difference between field and laboratory experiments is that field experiments take place in natural settings (such as the playground, home, or school) and not in the laboratory. As such, field experiments are high in *ecological validity*. That is, because field experiments are conducted in real-world settings, the findings of such experiments should generalize to similar events taking place naturally.

Demand Characteristics

Moreover, field experiments are thought to reduce *demand characteristics* associated with experiments (Freedman, 2002). Demand characteristics are cues in an experiment that make participants aware of the hypotheses of the experiment or how the experimenter expects them to behave following the presentation of a stimulus. As such, participants alter their behavior to match the expected outcome of the study. Although the cognitive limitations of youth decrease the likelihood that prior to middle or late adolescence participants will figure out the hypothesis of the study, the possibility that demand characteristics are present is not completely eliminated. For instance, it is possible that savvy adolescents or insightful children may wonder why they were brought to the laboratory to watch a violent cartoon. Even if youthful participants do not figure out the hypothesis that violent media increases aggressive behavior, they could assume that the experimenter, at the very least, likes violent cartoons or violent actions and adjust their behavior accordingly. Because field experiments take place in natural settings, participants are less likely to figure out the purpose of the study or the anticipated results. However, Anderson and Bushman (1997) contend that the consistency of results between laboratory and field experiments on a variety of factors that influence aggression (e.g., alcohol, provocation, temperature) diminish the importance of demand characteristics in laboratory research.

Debriefing and follow-up questioning could help assess the presence of demand characteristics in media violence research. Debriefing refers to the process during which the experimenter provides participants with an explanation of the scientific goals of the study and potential value of findings for science. Thus, future research should engage in debriefing of youthful participants, followed by questions designed to determine whether, in fact, youth were responding in a manner consistent with perceived experimenter expectations.

Face Validity

With regard to assessing the impact of cartoon violence on preschoolers' aggressive behavior, two field experiments have been conducted. In addition to occurring in a natural setting, these experiments differed from laboratory research in that children were exposed to cartoon violence on multiple occasions. Media violence is often critiqued for presenting violent stimuli to children for short durations in assessments that do not mimic real-world settings (Freedman, 2002; Jones, 2002). In other words, Jones and others suggest that many media violence studies lack *face validity*.

Face validity refers to the "common sense" notion that the study looks, at face value, as if it is assessing what it is supposed to be assessing. Laboratory studies on media violence often lack face validity because of their contrived nature. However, given that many field experiments involve the repeated showing of media to youth in a manner consistent with how they typically view media, they tend to have higher face validity. Studies with face validity tend to be more persuasive to the public than those without. However, determining whether or not something has "face value" is subjective, and therefore psychometricians typically do not rely on this concept when evaluating the validity of a measurement (Lacity & Jansen, 1994).

The Research

Research on Early Childhood

As previously mentioned, there has been limited field experiment–based research on children in early childhood. Friedrich and Stein (1973) exposed preschool children to either 20 minutes of *Batman* and *Superman* or to a series of neutral live-action films. Regardless of condition, youth viewed their assigned media selections three times a week for four weeks. At the end of the experimental period, physical and verbal aggression towards peers, rule obedience, and tolerance for delay were assessed. Youth watching the violent cartoons were more disobedient and less tolerant of delay. Moreover, youth who exhibited high levels of aggression prior to the experiment became more aggressive if they watched the violent cartoons than if they watched the nonviolent cartoons. Similarly, Steuer, Applefield, and Smith (1971) found that 11 daily 10-minute sessions of watching Saturday morning programs (which had a preponderance of unspecified cartoons and occasional live-action programs) resulted in greater physical aggression towards peers in comparison to young children watching a series of non-violent cartoons. Interestingly, the amount of physical aggression displayed by the children who watched Saturday morning programming increased throughout the course of the experiment.

Steuer et al. (1971) did not list the cartoons viewed by youth, thereby making it impossible to know the percentage of cartoons viewed containing humor. However, Friedrich and Stein (1973) showed children cartoons lacking comedic elements. Thus, in contrast to the laboratory experiments that failed to show an association between comedic violence exposure and interpersonal aggression, the field experiment of Steuer et al. (1971) demonstrated that non-comedic violence can increase interpersonal aggressive behavior. However, it is unclear if the aforementioned effects were due to the repeated viewing of cartoon violence over a period of days and weeks or because there were so few comedic elements in the cartoons that the screened violence was not camouflaged by comedy. What remains to be seen, then, is whether repeated exposure to cartoons with comedic violence negatively impacts interpersonal aggression in early childhood.

A Study That Combines Object- and Peer-Oriented Aggression

In addition to the research mentioned above, Silvern and Williamson (1987) conducted an interesting field experiment involving cartoon violence and 28 preschool boys and girls. The experiment, which took place over a three-day period, involved the assessment of baseline aggression during dyadic play with a classmate; the viewing of the humorously violent cartoon *Road Runner;* and the playing of the now classic arcade game *Space Invaders,* which served as the violent video game. The results pertaining to violent video game play will be discussed in greater detail in Chapter 11.

During the first day of the experiment, *baseline* aggression during dyadic play was assessed. Baseline observations are data collected prior to the experimental manipulation that are used for comparison or control. During the second day, half of the children played the video game for six minutes and the other half watched the six-minute long cartoon. Children were then observed in a free-play session with the toys that were available during the baseline condition. During the third day, youth who had watched the violent cartoon the day before played the video game and youth who had played the video game watched the violent cartoon. Once again, a free play session with the familiar toys took place. Prosocial behavior and fantasy play were assessed during each of the three free play sessions. Additionally, the amount of peer-related physical and verbal aggression and the frequency of object-oriented aggression were assessed. For each individual, the amount of aggressive, fantasy, and prosocial behavior was compared between the baseline condition and the free play session following each of the two separate exposures to media violence.

The results indicated that relative to baseline levels of responding, after watching the comedically violent cartoon, preschool youth demonstrated higher rates of aggressive behavior and lower rates of prosocial behavior. Unfortunately, the breakdown of peer-oriented and object-oriented aggression was not reported. Therefore, it is impossible to determine whether the data fit into the pattern mentioned above. It may be that, consistent with previous research, peer-related physical and verbal aggression were not affected by the media violence exposure but object-oriented aggression was. Moreover, because there was no control group, it is impossible to determine whether aggressive behavior would have increased and prosocial behavior would have decreased during the second and third play sessions with familiar toys, regardless of whether they had been watching a violent cartoon or playing a violent video game. It is possible, for instance, that the frustration of playing with the same child and the same toys over a period of days caused the aforementioned changes in behavior.

Within- and Between-Subjects Designs and Field Experiments

Silvern and Williamson's (1987) study is also of interest because of the methodology employed and, in particular, the fact that the children served as their own controls. No two children are alike. Some have greater levels of sensation seeking, some have greater levels of hostility; some have very little impulse control; and some are more likely than others to strike out in anger. Participants differ, and they differ greatly.

In many of the studies presented earlier, participants were randomly assigned to either the experimental or control group. Such experiments are referred to as having a *between-subjects design,* because participants in the experimental and control groups experience the experiment differently. Participants in the experimental group get exposed to the independent variable whereas participants in the control group do not. Thus, in between-subject designs, individual differences among participants have the potential to invalidate the findings of the experiment. That is to say, differences in the dependent variable may occur due to preexisting differences between the experimental and control conditions, instead of the experimental manipulation. Because it should theoretically equate the characteristics of the individuals in the experimental and control groups, random assignment helps diminish the effects of individual differences in a between-subjects design. Moreover, statistical analyses take into consideration such differences by considering them to be error. The more error that is present, the harder it becomes to establish statistical differences between the experimental and control groups. However, chance occurrences can result in the experimental group and the control groups differing prior to exposure to the independent variable. And with small sample sizes, random assignment becomes less effective at equating the experimental and control groups.

In the Silvern and Williamson (1987) study, children were exposed to video games and cartoons on subsequent days. The same participants were used in both conditions, and the comparison between conditions was made with each of the participants. Whether or not youth were high or low in aggression prior to the experiment was irrelevant. All that mattered was whether aggressive behavior went up or down relative to each child's baseline starting point. Thus, the results indicated how much a child's behavior changed, regardless of his or her preexisting levels of aggressive behavior. Moreover, due to children serving as their own controls, the effects of preexisting differences in personality and other factors that could influence aggression were mitigated.

Silvern and Williamson's (1987) study involved children experiencing all potential incarnations of the independent variable (e.g., video game and TV exposure) over a course of repeated assessments. As such, this study is referred to as having a *within-subjects design* (also referred to as a repeated measures design). Although within-subjects designs have the advantage of removing the amount or error due to individual differences, the fact that subjects are repeatedly assessed could result in *carryover effects* and *fatigue*. A carryover effect is an effect that "carries over" from one experimental condition to another. That is to say, the observed behavior is due to the lingering effects of an earlier exposure to an independent variable. For instance, the effects of watching a violent television show on one day of an experiment might cause children to behave more aggressively to any stimulus on the second day of the experiment. A fatigue effect is when participants' responses decrease or become less enthusiastic with repeated assessment.

The design of Silvern and Williamson's study adequately accounts for carryover effects. Because half of the participants saw the cartoon during the first experimental session while the other half played the video game, and then they reversed for the second treatment exposure, the lingering effects of being exposed to either a violent cartoon or a video game on subsequent days could be assessed. As it turns out, the analyses testing for carryover effects were non-significant. However, fatigue effects cannot be completely ruled out. Because a control group in which children played together on three consecutive days was not used, it is possible that participants simply became less enthusiastic about the experiment, resulting in greater levels of hostilities with their peer-partner. In fact, the reported reduction in prosocial behavior across sessions supports the contention that fatigue was taking place: participants may have been getting too fatigued to be prosocial.

Research on Middle Childhood

Aggressive Behavior

Research on the effects of comedic and non-comedic cartoons on children in middle childhood mirrors the effects found for early childhood. Laboratory experiments using cartoons with comedic violence failed to demonstrate significant differences in interpersonal aggression among peers (Hapkiewicz & Roden, 1971; Hapkiewicz & Stone, 1974); laboratory experiments using non-comedic, violent cartoons demonstrated increases in aggressive behavior towards inanimate objects (Mussen & Rutherford, 1961); and field experiments consistently found that the viewing of violent cartoons without comedic elements resulted in increases in aggressive behavior (i.e., physical and verbal) towards peers (Ellis & Sekyra, 1972; Liss, Reinhardt, & Fredriksen, 1983; Sanson & DiMuccio, 1993).

Aggression-Related Constructs

In contrast to the null findings associated with the viewing of comedic violence in cartoons, Nathanson and Cantor (2000) found that the viewing of a humorous, violent cartoon increased aggressive responding to hypothetical questions for boys between 2nd and 6th grades. Thus, cartoons with violent and comedic elements appear to affect aggression-related constructs in young children, such as aggressive thoughts and desires, but fail to alter actual aggressive behavior. Such a finding supports the contention that aggressive behavior is the result of a multitude of factors and that some factors may affect only certain aspects of aggression (such as aggressive thoughts) while failing to significantly alter other aspects of aggression (such as aggressive behavior). Of course, with so few studies done in this area, additional research is necessary to validate this contention.

Research on Adolescence

To date, little research has been conducted on the effects of cartoon violence during early, middle, and late adolescence. Perhaps the paucity of research is due to the fact that cartoon watching is thought to be the domain of childhood. Moreover, as children age, they become more interested in live-action shows laden with more "adult" themes and content. Aluja-Fabregat and Torrubia-Beltri (1998) conducted one of the few adolescent studies specifically designed to assess the impact of non-comedic violent cartoons on aggression. In an assessment of over 400 8th-grade boys and girls, personality characteristics (such as sensation seeking and anxiety levels), ratings of extremely violent Japanese anime, and teacher reports of adolescent *aggressivity* were correlated. Aggressivity is a composite variable that describes a person's overall level of aggression. Included in this variable are name calling, fighting, and disrespectful attitudes. The results of the study indicated that for boys, but not girls, the perception of extremely violent cartoons as being funny and thrilling was related to higher levels of teacher-rated aggressivity. In line with these results, Belson (1978) found that the viewing of cartoon violence among adolescent boys was associated with increases in minor acts of violence. Girls were not assessed in the Belson study.

If comedy does, in fact, camouflage violence, then the perception of *non-humorous* violent media as funny should reduce the perceived severity of that violence. By viewing violence as humorous (even in the absence of humor), it becomes less disturbing and less harmful to the victim. As it turns out, bullies tend to perceive their own acts of violence in a manner consistent with how they perceive violent cartoons. Bullies tend to dehumanize their victims; they do not perceive their own acts of aggression as particularly harmful; and they tend to have a positive attitude towards the use of violence (Moeller, 2001). Thus, it should be of no surprise that aggressive adolescents perceive humor in violent cartoons that are *lacking* in comedic elements. They tend to enjoy violence, be it in reality or animated fantasy.

The failure of Aluja-Fabregat and Torrubia-Beltri (1998) to find significant effects for girls may be due to the fact that their measure of aggressivity was biased towards aggressive behaviors that are easily detectable by teachers, such as name calling and fights. Less observable acts of aggression, such as those frequently seen in relational aggression, are harder to detect in a classroom. It is this type of aggression that is most common among adolescent girls. Thus, the null findings for girls may simply reflect the fact that the type of aggressive behavior that girls typically engage in was not assessed. Clearly, more research is warranted.

Summary

- The amount of violence in cartoons is higher than in other types of television programs.
- Adults typically perceive cartoons with comedic elements as less violent than authentic cartoons. Similar research conducted on youth, however, has produced contradictory findings. More studies are needed in order to establish whether children and adolescents perceive the violence in comedic and authentic cartoons differently.
- Humorous elements in cartoons may trigger cognitive transformations. Such transformations result in the reinterpretation of serious events as inconsequential.
- Violence in cartoons may be ignored because schemas for comedies do not include violence.
- Comedies may simultaneously prime both violent and humorous information, thereby reducing the level of perceived violence.
- Contextual factors in comedic cartoons, such as legitimization and consequences to the victim, trivialize the depicted violence.
- Graphicness influences the perception of violence in cartoons. As graphicness decreases, so too does the level of perceived violence.
- Relative to live-action programs, the perceived actuality, perceived similarity, and perceived reality of cartoons are low.
- By age 5, children understand that cartoons are fantasy, not reality. The contention that young children's inability to distinguish fantasy from reality is a risk factor for aggression is not supported.
- Although young children recognize that cartoons are unreal, the content of those cartoons may trigger fears of fantastical entities.
- Disinhibition refers to the enactment of previously learned aggressive behaviors.
- Laboratory research in early and middle childhood has failed to find that the viewing of violent cartoons with comedic elements influences interpersonal aggression. However, non-humorous violent cartoons have consistently been shown to influence object-related aggression.
- Field experiments have linked comedic violence with interpersonal aggression. However, flaws in the studies prohibit the conclusion that comedic violence caused the observed effects.
- Cartoons with violent and comedic elements have been shown to influence aggression-related constructs in children but not aggressive behavior.
- During adolescence, boys who perceive extremely violent cartoons as humorous are rated by teachers as aggressive. The non-significant findings for girls may be the result of the failure to assess indirect forms of aggression.
- The following methodological concepts were introduced: field experiments, debriefing, ecological validity, face validity, demand characteristics, baseline, within-subjects design, between-subjects design, carryover effects, and fatigue.

9

Listening to the Beast

Violence in Music and Music Videos

When I was 14 years old, I was rudely awakened early one Saturday morning (1:00 P.M.) by classical music blaring from the site of my neighbor's indoor pool. I did what any adolescent boy who had repeatedly been denied access to a neighbor's indoor pool would do: I moved my speakers to the window, turned them outward, cranked the volume to 11, and let loose Rush's classic album *Moving Pictures*. By the time "Tom Sawyer" had finished, all was quiet; not even the birds were chirping. Using music as a weapon, I had acted aggressively. Although the use of music to enact aggression is interesting, there is no research on the topic. Instead, media violence research has consistently focused on the relationship between violence in music and music videos and the likelihood that youth will act aggressively (Anderson, Carnagey, & Eubanks, 2003).

Historical Overview

In what could be described as the first instance of music provoking violent behavior during the twentieth century, the staging of a pagan sacrifice along with the "brutal and violent" music that accompanied it led to fisticuffs and near-riot among those witnessing the production. Did these unseemly proceedings happen in a mosh pit, in which pushing, shoving, and body slamming are the norm? Was the violence incited by murderous lyrics, inspiring the listener to engage in homicidal behavior? Did the acts of interpersonal

179

aggression follow the screening of a Rage Against the Machine music video? The answer to all these questions is "No." The events described above occurred during the 1913 premier of Igor Stravinsky's ballet *The Rite of Spring* (Wikipedia, 2004).

Upon closer inspection, the events surrounding the melee at the ballet suggest that the link between the violence depicted in the choreography, overall "violent" musical tenor, and subsequent insurrection is tenuous, for it has been reported that a group of insurgents may have been hired to disrupt the ballet's premiere (Wikipedia, 2004). This finding reminds us of the importance of not assuming causality prior to investigating a phenomenon. However, the tendency to "rush to judgment" often follows prominent acts of violence involving youth. For instance, immediately following the tragedy at Columbine High School, newspapers around the country were attempting to identify a single cause for the tragedy. Some focused on peer rejection and bullying, others focused on antidepressants, still others attempted to blame violent video games and music (Wikipedia, 2004). In the end, acts of aggression and violence, even tragic ones, are the result of a multitude of factors. In this chapter, music as a risk factor for aggressive behavior will be explored.

The Focus of Modern-Day Research on Music Violence

Currently, one would be hard-pressed to find a single researcher who would consider classical music to be a threat to the mental health and well-being of youth. Instead, such considerations are levied against Heavy Metal and Rap music.

Heavy Metal

The term "Heavy Metal" was first coined during the 1960s to describe loud, guitar-driven, bass-laden, amplified music (Pareles & Romanowski, 1983). The popularity of groups such as Led Zeppelin and Black Sabbath helped bring Heavy Metal into prominence. Today, there are many different subgenres of Heavy Metal, with the sound and lyrical content differentiating subgenres from one another (see Table 9.1). Some subgenres relay lyrics involving morbid imagery or anarchist ideals, while others focus on death and violence. The commonality among all of these subgenres, however, is driving music and the presence of dark and sexually explicit themes (Walser, 1993).

Table 9.1   Selected Subgenres of Heavy Metal

Subgenre	Characteristic
Horror Punk	Morbid Imagery
Anarcho-Punk	Anarchist Ideas
Speed Metal	Heavy Metal Played Fast
Doom Metal	Darkness, Despair, Doom
Goth Metal	Cross of Doom/Heavy Metal
Death Metal	Extreme Brutality, Speed, Mortality
Alternative Metal	Experimental Heavy Metal

Rap

In 1979, The Sugar Hill Gang released the single "Rapper's Delight" and, in doing so, introduced Rap music to the American public. Rap is characterized by the rhythmic speaking of rhyming lyrics over a musical background. Subgenres of Rap include the sociopolitically driven "Alternative" and the misogynistic and violence-laden "Gangsta Rap." More recently, "Rapcore" (a.k.a. rap-metal) has emerged as a fusion of Rap and Heavy Metal. In this hybrid subgenre, the artist raps lyrics to a Heavy Metal sound. Although Rap started on the streets of the South Bronx and was primarily embraced by the black community, Rap's appeal quickly crossed racial lines. By the mid-1990s, only a quarter of Rap fans were black (Bryson, 1996). Moreover, the fact that the top selling albums of 2002 (Eminem's *Eminem Show*) and 2003 (50 Cent's *Get Rich or Die Tryin'*) were Rap albums is a testament to the widespread popularity of Rap. In fact, recent statistics indicate that by far the most popular form of music for white, black, and Hispanic 7th- through 12th-grade adolescents is Rap/Hip Hop (Roberts et al., 2005). (See Figure 9.1.)

The Popularity of Music

The importance of music to adolescents cannot be overstated. By the time adolescents enter high school, the amount of time spent listening to music each day is comparable to, or exceeds, the amount of time watching television. In fact, in a typical week, the average adolescent will spend the equivalent of one full day listening to music (Gentile et al., 2004). When asked by Roberts and Henriksen (1990) what media they would take with them if stranded on a desert island, youth in middle school and high school

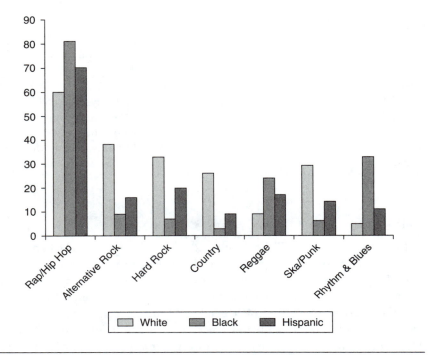

Figure 9.1   Proportion of Youth Who Listened to Each Genre the Previous Day

SOURCE: Data from Roberts, Foehr, & Rideout (2005)

consistently made music their first choice. Moreover, the percentage of adolescents choosing music first increased from 7th grade (40%), to 9th grade (44%), to 11th grade (52%). These findings are consistent with the results of Roberts, Foehr, and colleagues (1999) who demonstrated that as adolescents age, the amount of time spent every day listening to music increases. Such differences, however, are qualified by gender and race. Starting in adolescence and coinciding with the beginning of middle school, girls tend to listen to music more than boys do. Moreover, across adolescence, black youth listen to music for significantly more hours than white youth (Roberts et al., 2003).

    What is intriguing about this area of research is that it often fails to take into consideration exposure to background music and may therefore underestimate adolescents' total exposure to music (Roberts et al., 2003). Background listening refers to the passive exposure to music while attention is primarily focused on other tasks, such as doing homework, talking with friends, or reading for pleasure. Research on the effects of listening to background music while completing tests of cognitive performance has been contradictory, with some studies finding that background music enhances performance and other studies finding that it impedes performance (see Kallinen & Ravaja, 2004). The fact that performance was going up or down while listening to music, however, suggests that background music has the potential to impact individuals psychologically. Consequently, additional research on the impact of listening to Heavy Metal and Rap as background music warrants investigation.

The Lyrical Content of Heavy Metal and Rap

Many researchers believe that given the high level of consumption by adolescents, music is the most significant medium to which adolescents are exposed (Roberts & Christenson, 2001). However, it is not just the total amount of time spent listening to music that accounts for its significance. Instead, the importance of music may lie in the messages relayed to youth through the song's lyrical content.

Lyrics and Sexual Content

Rock 'n' roll music has been associated with sex and violence for nearly half a century. In fact, many of the controversies surrounding musical offerings center on their lascivious lyrics and the sexually explicit imagery that accompany them. When Elvis Presley appeared on *The Ed Sullivan Show* in 1956, he was televised from the waist up, for fear of exposing the American public to his trademark hip gyrations. The top grossing (adjusted for inflation) live-action movie musical of all time, *Grease,* is replete with sexually explicit lyrics. Consider the following: the lines from the song "Greased Lightning"—"You know that ain't no shit we'll be getting lots of tit" and "You know that I ain't bragging she's a real pussy wagon"—are not referring to Danny Zucko's fondness for udders and kittens. Justin Timberlake's "Rock Your Body" contains the lyrics "Cause I gotta have you naked by the end of this song." And when Janet Jackson (Ms. Jackson if you're nasty!) obliged during a duet with Mr. Timberlake during the 2004 Super Bowl halftime show, the FCC imposed a $550,000 fine for indecency. In the examples listed above, there was no sexual innuendo; the sexual references were explicit. It would surprise no one to learn that over the past half-century, music lyrics have become increasingly explicit and less reliant on innuendo (Christenson & Roberts, 1998).

Lyrics and Violent Content

Similar to the increasing sexual explicitness of modern-day lyrics, over the past half century the graphic nature of lyrical violence has increased as well. Currently, Heavy Metal and Rap lyrics repeatedly communicate themes of misogyny, racism, murder, drug use, violence, and Satanism (Roberts et al., 2003). For example, consider the following lyrics from the Limp Bizkit song "Break Stuff": "I pack a chainsaw, I'll skin your ass raw, and if my day keeps going this way, I just might break your fuckin' face tonite." Rap lyrics are notorious for their level of extreme lyrical violence, as well. In the top-selling album of 2003, *Get Rich or Die Tryin'* by 50 Cent, the lyrics to "Many Men" include the phrase "walk around gun on my waist, chip on my shoulder till I bust a clip in your face, pussy, this beef ain't over." These types of graphic lyrics give parents and legislators pause, causing them to worry about the impact of such words on youthful attitudes and behavior. In fact, in response to such worries, albums deemed to contain sexually explicit or violent lyrics currently receive parental advisory warning labels (see Chapter 14 for a more detailed explanation). Prior to evaluating the impact of lyrically violent content on youthful aggression, it is necessary to understand why lyrics could affect youth in the first place.

The Potential Effects of Lyrics

Anderson, Carnagey, and Eubanks (2003) posit several different routes through which lyrical content can promote aggressive behavior. First, lyrics are simply a string of words. And the words in many Heavy Metal and Rap songs have aggressive, violent, and hateful meanings. Research on priming has consistently shown that words related to aggression can prime aggression-related constructs such as thoughts and perceptions. Thus, in response to aggression-laden lyrics, a whole host of aggression-related thoughts, feelings, and so on are cognitively activated. Second, given that music is listened to repeatedly over time, the short-term priming effects mentioned above have the potential to become chronically activated. Whereas short-term priming leads to short-term effects on aggression, chronic activation has the potential to influence aggressive behavior over longer periods of time. Thus, aggression-laden thoughts, feelings, perceptions, and so on could become the norm. Finally, similar to comic books, music has the potential to engage the adolescent's imagination. However, unlike comic books, music has no visual imagery whatsoever. As such, when reading or singing lyrics, youth may become fully engaged in the music and create their own pictorial representation of the content. Thus, hearing violent lyrics can lead to an imagined reality in which the adolescent visualizes those violent acts being carried out.

Lyrics: Are They Really That Important?

At first glance, it would appear that lyrics are relatively unimportant to adolescents. After all, it is the vocals, music, and melody (i.e., "the sound") that are the primary reasons that youth report being attracted to music. In fact, the lyrical content of songs is reported to be the least important factor when determining how much a teenager likes a song (Prinsky & Rosenbaum, 1987). Along these same lines, studies have shown that between 60% and 70% of youth do not know the lyrics to their favorite song (Desmond, 1987). And even when teenagers do know the lyrics, they may not necessarily comprehend them correctly (Prinsky & Rosenbaum, 1987).

Lyrical Comprehension Across Development

Not surprisingly, the ability to understand lyrics improves with age. For instance, in an assessment of youth's lyrical comprehension of Bruce Springsteen's "Born in the USA," Greenfield and colleagues (1987) found that 20% of 4th graders, 60% of 8th graders, and 95% of 12th graders correctly understood that a "hometown jam" referred to a dilemma that an individual faced in the town in which he was raised. However, when asked to define the general meaning of that song, comprehension was very poor. None of the 4th graders correctly understood that "Born in the USA" deals with the abstract concepts of despair and disillusionment. Comprehension was not that much better for the older adolescents, as only 30% of 8th graders and 40% of 12th graders stated the correct meaning of the song.

Why Developmental Differences in Lyrical Comprehension Occur

Cognitive Development. In the Greenfield et al. (1987) study, the fact that the 4th graders did not understand the abstract nature of a "hometown jam" is not surprising, given their cognitive developmental status. Prior to adolescence, children's logical thinking tends to be limited to concrete information. Typically, the ability to understand abstract issues does not appear until late childhood or early adolescence (DeHart et al., 2004). For instance, it is not until age 9 that children understand that death is final, irreversible, and universal (Stambrook & Parker, 1987).

However, as the Greenfield et al. (1987) data indicates, the ability to think abstractly in no way guarantees that youth will understand the conceptual and metaphorical nature of song lyrics. Children and early adolescents tend to interpret lyrics in a literal fashion. Such differences may impair youth's ability to perceive underlying themes of sex and violence in music.

For instance, most children would have difficulty understanding that the AC/DC lyric "You shook me all night long" is a reference to sex. Overall, when comparing adult comprehension of lyrics with more youthful interpretations, adults are more likely to perceive themes of sex and Satanism than are teenagers (Prinsky & Rosenbaum, 1987).

Memory. One could argue that the reason adolescents do so poorly in song comprehension is that they are unable to remember all of the relevant information necessary to comprehend the underlying meaning of the song. However, even when the lyrics are given to youth to read, comprehension is often lacking (Greenfield et al., 1987).

Garbled Lyrics. Additionally, the fact that Heavy Metal lyrics (and to a lesser extent, Rap lyrics) are not clearly enunciated reduces lyrical comprehension and increases the likelihood that the garbled lyrics will be misinterpreted. One of the most famous examples of the misinterpretation of garbled lyrics involves the song "Louie Louie" by the Kingsmen (1963). In response to parental complaints of "filthy lyrics," the FBI attempted to discern the words in the "offending song" by listening to it on a 45 RPM record. J. Edgar Hoover's G-Men played the song at regular speed, but to no avail. So they slowed the song down in an attempt to identify the obscene lyrics. Once again, their efforts proved useless. In the end, the FBI concluded that they were "unable to interpret any of the wording in the record," and the case was dropped (The Smoking Gun, 2004). As it turns out, the Kingsmen's version of "Louie Louie" is just as muddled as the cover version done by the drunk boys of Delta House at Faber College (as seen in *Animal House*).

Lyrical Incomprehension:
A Double-Edged Sword

The finding that youth do not fully comprehend lyrics is a double-edged sword. On the one hand, a lack of comprehension mitigates the potential influence of antisocial lyrics. It is hard to be affected by what you cannot understand. On the other hand, the failure to comprehend the lyrical content of a song could result in a misinterpretation of the lyrics. Moreover, the ambiguity of lyrics allows individual differences in social information processing to affect the interpretation of the song. For instance, in the absence of meaning, youth with an already existing hostile attribution bias might ascribe hostile and aggressive interpretations to ambiguous lyrics.

The Best Comprehension Is Related
to the Perceived Importance of the Music

Although many teenagers do not know the lyrics or understand the underlying meaning of the songs they are singing, those who listen to Heavy Metal and Rap music are more knowledgeable of their genre's lyrical content. In general, the more important the music is to a teenager, the more important the lyrics become when evaluating a song. Moreover, the greatest amount of attention is paid to lyrics that are controversial or represent defiance of authority and teenage angst (Roberts & Christenson, 2001). What is more, it is just these types of rebellious songs that contain explicit violence and graphic lyrical content. To sum it all up, even though comprehension of lyrical content is generally poor, the greatest level of comprehension is associated with songs that are the most violent and offensive.

On Hearing Things
That Cannot Be Heard

No discussion of music lyrics would be complete without a mention of *backwards masking*. Backwards masking refers to the embedding of lyrical messages within a recording that can only be consciously heard when the music is played backwards. For instance, Begg, Needham, and Bookbinder (1993) heard the following "evil" message when they listened to a recording by the Heavy Metal group Adrenalin Overdose played backwards: "I like puppies; God is good."

Can Backwards-Masked
Messages Be Detected?

When music is played backwards, Vokey and Read (1985) found that participants can correctly identify backwards messages 85% of the time. Although at first this seems impressive, the participants in this part of the study were given specific lyrics to listen for. However, the ability to detect backwards messages dramatically decreased (less than 20%) when participants were not told the specific lyrics to identify. Thus, knowing what words and phrases are backwards masked helps individuals "hear" such phrases. These data indicate that messages can be detected when a recording is played backwards, but knowing what to listen for helps.

Can Backwards-Masked Messages Be Heard When a Song Is Played Forward?

The controversy surrounding backwards messages does not lie in the fact that messages can be detected when the music is played backwards. Instead, the controversy involves the belief that when a recording is played as it should be (i.e., forward), the meaning of the "backwards message" leaks through, due to *subliminal processing,* and subsequently affects behavior. Subliminal processing refers to situations in which stimuli are perceived without conscious awareness. Although words can be identified when music is played backwards, there is no research to support the belief that backwards-masked messages can be heard or even subliminally processed when the music is played *forwards* (Begg et al., 1993). Even if the presence of reverse speech could be subliminally processed during forwards play, to have an effect the individual would then be required to subliminally re-reverse the lyrics for comprehension (e.g., nataS becomes Satan). Quite a feat, and it has yet to be proven that it can be done.

Backwards-Masked Messages, Suicide, and the Law

Notwithstanding the findings of Begg and colleagues (1993), the claim that backwards messages can dramatically affect behavior has been forwarded for nearly 40 years. Backwards masking shot into prominence in the 1960s, when it was revealed that The Beatles' song "Rain" ended with the first line of the song vocalized backwards. With this new knowledge firmly in hand, teenagers around the country began spinning their records backwards in search of hidden messages. The Beatles were not actually trying to hide messages in their songs; they simply liked the way the backwards lyrics sounded on tape.

Although backwards masking may have started out as a musical effect, over the years fundamentalist groups around the country decried backwards masking as promoting Satanism and antisocial themes (Oates, 1996). For example, in the classic Led Zeppelin ballad "Stairway to Heaven," the following lyrics can be heard when the song is played backwards: "Oh, here's to my sweet Satan." Public concern over backwards masking was heightened in the late 1980s following a suicide and attempted suicide by two adolescent boys. The teenagers had listened to the Judas Priest song "Better by You Better than Me," in which the words "do it" were reportedly backwards masked. The parents of the boys believed that the subliminal message within the song had triggered the boys' suicidal behavior. In the summer of 1990, the Heavy Metal group was sued by the boys' parents for placing a subliminal message in their song that contributed to one of the boys' suicide. The plaintiffs were unsuccessful at trial. The presiding judge ruled that the "strongest evidence presented at the trial showed no behavioral effects other than anxiety, distress, or tension" (Vance/Roberson v. CBS Inc/Judas Priest, 1990).

Although the judge's decision rejected the idea that backwards masking affects suicidal behavior, the ruling left open the possibility that psychological processes and, in particular, emotions could be affected. Does the current body of literature support the judge's contention? Simply put, no. There is no empirical evidence to support the contention that when music is played forwards, backwards-masked lyrics can alter behavior or any other psychological process. Presumably, after listening to "Stairway to Heaven" a teenager would be just as likely to worship a Krispy Kreme hot glazed original donut as he would Satan.

Rockin' and a Rollin' and a Fightin'

When you look beyond the shocking nature of the lyrical content, the lyrics of Heavy Metal and Rap music connote defiance against authority, rebellion against those who would oppress, and the overwhelming angst of youth. The names of the many Heavy Metal bands, such as *All Out War, Terror, Megadeth, Slayer, Brutality,* and *Hatebreed,* also reflect rebelliousness and antisocial attitudes. Such themes are exceedingly popular with preteens and adolescents. Regardless of the reasons for listening to music wrought with violence, however, those who are exposed to lyrical violence tend to be affected by the words that they hear. At least, that is what parents and newspapers tend to suggest. For instance, according to one study, nearly 50% of mothers with school-aged children believe that lyrical violence in Rap music is a *significant* contributor to school violence (Kandakai, Price, Telljohann, & Wilson, 1999). A poll by CNN found that nearly two-thirds of teenagers believe that music violence bears some responsibility for adolescent violence, including school shootings (Senate Committee on the Judiciary, 1999). But what does the research suggest? Are aggressive behavior and aggression-related constructs impacted by music violence?

The Effects of Music Violence on Youth

Correlational Research

Surprisingly, little research has been conducted on the effects of music violence on youth. In fact, there is no research on the effects of music violence on children. Moreover, the research on adolescents has been limited to correlational designs. Atkin, Smith, Roberto, Fediuk, and Wagner (2002) found in an assessment of 2,300 13- to 15-year-olds that a preference for violence-oriented, Heavy Metal and Rap music was positively correlated with verbal aggression. Similarly, Took and Weiss (1994) were able to demonstrate a link between a preference for Heavy Metal and Rap music and school-related behavior problems (which may or may not involve aggression) throughout adolescence. Miranda and Claes (2004) found that for French-Canadian youth, a preference for Rap music (and, in particular, French Rap music) was associated with deviant behaviors such as violence and street gang involvement. Importantly, these findings held even after statistically controlling for the influence of peer-related deviancy. Additional correlational research has shown that clinically diagnosed antisocial youth preferred Heavy Metal music more so than youth from non-clinical populations (King, 1988).

Directionality and Third Variable Issues. Rather than violent music causing deviance and aggression, it is possible aggressive youth prefer to listen to music with aggressive themes. Carpentier, Knobloch, and Zillmann (2003) contend that some youth prefer Heavy Metal and Rap music because violence depicted in the lyrics mirrors the youth's hostile nature and aggressive lifestyle. In support of this contention, juvenile delinquents report that their choice of music is more a reflection of their delinquent lifestyle than a cause of it (Gardstrom, 1999).

Additionally, personality characteristics have been forwarded to explain the connection between aggressive youth and aggressively themed music. For instance, Arnett (1991) demonstrated that youth high in sensation seeking prefer Heavy Metal music. Drug use, casual sex, reckless driving, and other sensation-related behaviors were more prominent among Heavy Metal fans than among fans of other musical genres. Moreover, Carpentier et al. (2003) contend that adolescents high in trait rebelliousness are attracted to defiant, antisocial music (and more so than are other adolescents) in an attempt to define their social identity. For these individuals, a preference for Heavy Metal and Rap may not reflect an attempt to embrace a hostile and aggressive lifestyle. It just so happens that, in today's musical world, songs that are socially deviant and signify rebelliousness also tend to contain violent lyrics. Even if youth consume violent media in an effort to seek stimulation or mirror a particular lifestyle, those youth may not necessarily be immune to the effects of the exposure. To date, however, very little is known about what those effects might be.

Experimental Research

Currently, there are no experimental studies on the effects of violent music on children and adolescents. Thus, the purported short-term effects adolescents are risking by listening to violence-laden music have yet to be experimentally validated. Unfortunately, little guidance can be gleaned from research on adults, since experimental studies sampling college students have been equivocal. Whereas many studies fail to find that music violence influences aggressive behavior in response to hypothetical scenarios (e.g., Ballard & Coates, 1995), others have found that it impacts aggression-related constructs, such as aggressive thoughts and feelings (Anderson, Carnagey, & Eubanks, 2003). Clearly, given the importance that the public ascribes to music violence, and the theoretical models that predict that violent music should negatively impact youth, such research is necessary. It is better to base opinion on sound research than on anecdotal evidence and biased beliefs, even if the evidence goes against the hypothesis that violent music influences aggressive behavior and aggression-related constructs.

Linking Suicidal Lyrics and Suicidal Behavior

Prevalence and Risk

According to the American Academy of Child and Adolescent Psychiatry, suicide is the third leading cause of death for adolescents 15 and older (Ballard & Coates, 1995). Moreover, for every suicide death, there may be as many as 25 attempted suicides (Satcher, 1999). According to the Surgeon General, more teenagers and young adults died in 1996 as a result of suicide than from the combined deaths due to AIDS, birth defects, cancer, heart disease, lung disease, stroke, pneumonia, and influenza (Satcher, 1999). Given these statistics, the importance of identifying youth who are at risk of suicide (and providing them with treatment) cannot be overstated. To that end, a variety of risk factors for suicide have been identified. Included in this list are access to guns; presence of stressful events; alcohol and drug abuse; and psychological disorders involving psychosis, internalizing (e.g., depression), and externalizing behaviors (e.g., aggressiveness). For instance, adolescents attempting suicide tend to be significantly more aggressive than youth suffering from the same psychological disorder who do not attempt suicide (Mann, Waternaux, Haas, & Malone, 1999).

The lyrical content of certain Heavy Metal songs has been a source of concern for parents, politicians, and researchers alike. For instance, lyrics in the Metallica song "Nothing Else Matters" extol suicidal thoughts—"I have lost the will to live, simply nothing more to give, there is nothing more for me, need the end to set me free"—as do the more graphic lyrics to the Alice in Chains song "Dirt," which includes the lyrics "I want to taste dirty, a stinging pistol, in my mouth, on my tongue, I want you to scrape me from the walls and go crazy like you've made me."

Lyrics and Suicidal Ideation

A preference for musical themes of death and suicide, such as those just mentioned, are considered relevant to suicidal behavior because the liking of themes of death and self-destruction may indicate the presence of *suicidal ideation*. Suicidal ideation refers to both nonspecific thoughts of death and specific thoughts involving the intent to die accompanied by a plan of action. Thus, an adolescent's focus on the death/suicide-related lyrical content in Heavy Metal music could be thought of as suicidal ideation involving nonspecific death thoughts. However, it is important to remember that although suicidal ideation is predictive of suicidal behavior, its presence is not considered a threat of imminent suicidal attempts.

Heavy Metal Music and Suicide

As we have seen previously, backwards-masked music has been implicated and subsequently vindicated in the suicides of teenagers. Here, the focus is on Heavy Metal music played forwards as an additional risk factor for suicide. The link between Heavy Metal music and suicide is taken very seriously among those in the medical community. Preference for Heavy Metal music has been considered to be a potential indicator of psychological problems among adolescents for over 15 years (Brown & Hendee, 1989). The concern over Heavy Metal music is not without good reason. Research has consistently shown that in comparison to youth who listen to other forms of music, youth who prefer to listen to Heavy Metal have higher rates of suicidal risk factors, such as substance use, delinquency, reckless behavior, depression, family conflict, and school-related problems (Scheel & Westefeld, 1999). Scheel and Westefeld (1999) found that high school upper-classmen who were self-reported Heavy Metal fans offered fewer reasons to justify *not* wanting to kill themselves in comparison to fans of other music genres (e.g., pop, alternative, country).

Gender differences are apparent as well, with female fans of Heavy Metal being at greater risk levels of suicidal ideation than male fans. In fact, the American Academy of Child and Adolescent Psychiatry recommends that youth demonstrating a preoccupation with Heavy Metal music with destructive themes, such as death and suicide, undergo psychiatric evaluation (Alessi, Huang, James, Ying, & Chowhan, 1992). Moreover, the basis for a medical decision to hospitalize a suicidal adolescent often includes an evaluation of the adolescent's musical preferences (Rosenbaum & Prinsky, 1991).

Amplification Effects and Suicide

Some have suggested that a mood "amplification effect" occurs when listening to music. Thus, because Heavy Metal fans often report listening to music when they are angry or depressed, it has been hypothesized that they will become angrier or more depressed after listening to Heavy Metal (see Roberts et al., 2003). In direct contrast to this supposition, Scheel and Westefeld (1999) found that when adolescents listen to their preferred genre of music, their mood remains the same or improves, even if they prefer Heavy Metal. Additionally, when Heavy Metal fans report listening to music when they are angry, they become less angry (not more, as hypothesized) after listening to Heavy Metal music.

Of note, Scheel and Westefeld (1999) found that adolescents reporting the greatest amount of anger, in comparison to less angry teens, reported the fewest reasons for not killing themselves. Moreover, in contrast to other youth, the "angrier teens" became even angrier after listening to their preferred genre of music. This finding held across a variety of musical genres, including Pop, Alternative, Rap, and Heavy Metal. It may be that extremely angry youth experience a mood intensification following a session of listening to music because of non-music-related factors, such as poor coping skills.

Heavy Metal Music and Suicide: A Link That Is Broken

The factors that place youth at risk for attempting suicide are many and varied. The consensus among a variety of researchers, however, is that listening to Heavy Metal music is not typically among them (e.g., Scheel & Westefeld, 1999; Strasburger & Wilson, 2002). For instance, using a *multiple regression* analysis, Lacourse, Claes, and Villeneuve (2001) found that an initial significant relationship between Heavy Metal music and suicidal risk became non-significant as other factors (e.g., drug use, family relationships) were entered into the statistical analysis. Multiple regression is a statistical technique in which several independent variables (e.g., race, gender, age) are used to predict scores on a dependent variable (e.g., verbal aggression). This technique allows researchers to *statistically control* (i.e., remove the influence of) variables that could confound the results. Thus, when Lacourse statistically controlled for drug use (and other variables), listening to Heavy Metal music no longer predicted suicidal risk. However, even if the relationship remained significant, it is important to remember that although in multiple regressions independent variables are said to "predict" the dependent variable, causality should not be assumed, for multiple regressions are based on correlational relationships. Thus, the rationale used to explain why researchers cannot ascribe causality in correlations (e.g., third variable problem) applies to multiple regressions as well.

More recently, an experimental study of college students found that listening to rock music with suicidal themes primed suicidal-related themes during a projective story writing task, but failed to negatively influence variables associated with suicidal risk, such as attitudes towards suicide and increased hopelessness (Rustad, Small, Jobes, Safer, & Peterson, 2003). Instead of being a noteworthy contributor to suicidal tendencies, Heavy Metal music is thought to be an important factor in the identification of teenage suicidality, a "red flag" if you will.

Although the direct links between Heavy Metal and suicide are lacking, several indirect paths may remain. First, aggressiveness is associated with suicidal behavior, and there is evidence (equivocal though it may be) that the violent music influences aggressive thoughts and feelings (Anderson, Carnagey, & Eubanks, 2003). Second, for vulnerable youth, the subculture of Heavy Metal has the potential to "nurture" the already present suicidal ideation (Strasburger & Wilson, 2002). Thus, while the typical teen might not be influenced by Heavy Metal music, those teens at the greatest risk for suicide may be influenced by suicide-related lyrical content the most. However, to date, there are no scientific data directly linking Heavy Metal music to suicidal behavior, even among those at greatest risk.

Sex, Violence, and Video Tape

As the following lyrics reveal, there is noteworthy violent content in the song "Jeremy" by Pearl Jam: "And the dead lay in pools of maroon below"; "Gnashed his teeth and bit the recess lady's breast"; "he hit me with a surprise left"; and "Jeremy spoke in class today." The first three quotes above are concrete representations of violence, and as such, the aggressive content is easy to discern (even if the vocalizations in the song are not). The last quote, however, is a metaphor, and without additional information, it is impossible to understand its symbolic meaning. As it turns out, "Jeremy spoke in class today" refers to the suicidal act of an adolescent boy who, in front of his classmates, stuck a gun in his mouth and pulled the trigger. Although the lyrics of "Jeremy" provide little content that would lead to the correct interpretation of this line, the music video clearly, and more graphically, provides a context (e.g., blood on the shirts of classmates who look on with horrified stares). Such is the power of music video, for it can provide clear and powerful images to help clarify lyrics that at times can be incomprehensible.

The Buggles Were Wrong

In 1981, the first music video broadcast on the fledging cable channel MTV was The Buggles, "Video Killed the Radio Star." At that time, MTV was solely a music video station, and as such, it played music videos around the clock. By the mid 1980s, youth were watching music videos for an average of two hours per day (and more on weekends; Sun & Lull, 1986). Patterns of music video watching varied throughout development, as early adolescents tended to watch more music videos than older adolescents. Recent studies, however, suggest that by the 1990s, teenagers were watching music videos for only 15 to 30 minutes per day (Roberts et al., 2003). Thus, the halcyon days of the music video appear to be over.

Today, in response to the diminishing interest in music videos, reality-based television shows such as *MTV Cribs, The Real World, Made, Room Raiders, Punk'd, Pimp My Ride, Viva La Bam,* and *Laguna Beach* dominate the programming on MTV. During the time periods that children and adolescents are awake, MTV primarily broadcasts music videos from 5:00–6:00 P.M. during the "count-down" music video show *Total Request Live* (TRL). Of course, music videos can be seen on less frequented cable channels, such as MTV2, BET, VH-1 Classic, and VH-1 Mega Hits, but the days in which adolescents congregated around the television to watch the latest video are long gone. The Buggles were wrong. Video did not kill the radio star.

Why Music Videos May Still Be Important in the Study of Media Violence

Yearly Consumption

Although the average daily consumption of music videos is only 15 to 30 minutes, over the course of a year the typical adolescent will view music videos for a cumulative total of 90 to 182 hours. For the 5% to 15% of the teenage population that watch music videos for 1 to 2 hours per day (Roberts et al., 2003), the yearly accumulation increases to 365 to 730 hours. Thus, the content of music videos to which adolescents are exposed is not inconsequential. And a recent content analysis of music videos played on MTV, BET, and VH-1 revealed that nearly 20% of music videos aired feature violence.

Music Video Content

Not only that, but when violence is shown in music videos, it is done in ways that tend to have the greatest potential to harm the child and adolescent viewer. For instance, the majority of music videos with violent elements depict the violence in a realistic manner, in which the perpetrator goes without punishment, the consequences to the victim (e.g., harm and pain) are not portrayed, and violent acts are repeatedly shown (Smith & Boyson, 2002). As has been illustrated in previous chapters, repetitive acts of realistic aggression that go unpunished tend to increase aggressive behavior and aggression-related constructs in youthful viewers. Moreover, the failure to show the pain and suffering of the victim (often referred to as sanitizing) may decrease the likelihood that youth will associate real-life aggression with real-world injury and pain (Smith & Boyson, 2002). It is noteworthy that the failure to realize that victims of violence suffer is characteristic of bullies. The point here is *not* that watching music videos will turn youth into bullies. Instead, the point is that watching music videos with sanitized violence may help create the mindset of a bully in youth who do not engage in bullying behavior.

The Effects of Violent Music Videos on Adolescents

Although there is great concern over the effects of music videos on aggression, there is little research on the matter. To date, only two studies have been published in peer-reviewed journals, and both of these studies used adolescent participants. Additionally, there are no published empirical studies involving children. Moreover, the little research that has been conducted has focused on aggressive attitudes and perceptions. In fact, there is no research relating violent music videos and aggressive behavior in youth.

In one of the few studies conducted on the effects on violence in music videos on youth, Greeson and Williams (1986) found that after watching music videos replete with themes of sex, violence, and anti-establishment themes for 30 minutes, 10th graders (but not 7th graders) became less disapproving of violence. However, given that the videos contained sex, violence, and themes of rebelliousness, it is difficult to know which of these three impacted the older adolescents' aggressive attitudes.

Johnson, Jackson, and Gatto (1995) assessed the impact of violent Rap music on adolescents' responses to hypothetical scenarios involving violence or academic aspirations. To accomplish this, 46 inner-city black teenage males (aged 11 to 16) were assigned to one of three groups. The first group watched music videos featuring nonviolent Rap; the second group watched violent Rap music videos; and the third group did not watch any video.

Responses to hypothetical scenarios revealed that the adolescents watching the violent Rap music videos espoused a greater acceptance of the use of violence in comparison to adolescents in the other two experimental conditions. It is noteworthy that in the Johnson et al. (1995) study, demand characteristics were reduced by telling participants that they were participating in two separate studies: one involving memory for the content of Rap music videos and the other involving decision-making skills. However, as is the case in most research on media violence, there was no follow-up assessment to validate that the deception worked.

Research on college students has also demonstrated that music videos featuring violence can alter attitudes, perceptions, and emotions. In comparison to watching music videos with and without violent elements, the viewing of violent music videos has been shown to lead to favorable impressions of individuals engaging in antisocial acts (Hansen & Hansen, 1990b). Thus, after watching violent music videos, attitudinal changes occurred in that aggressive behavior became more socially sanctioned. With regard to emotions, Hansen and Hansen (1990a) demonstrated that when watching music videos with varying levels of sex and violence, only the level of violence predicted negative emotions (e.g., anger, anxiety, fear) and aggressiveness. Moreover, music videos replete with violence or a combination of sex and violence were rated to be the most unappealing of the music videos shown. Although rated as unappealing, violent music videos appear to increase negative emotions and promote favorable attitudes towards violence. Peterson and Pfost (1989) found that college students watching violent music videos reported more after-viewing anger and frustration than participants watching violent music videos with erotic elements and nonviolent music videos with and without erotica.

College Students Are Not Children

The research on college students is compelling. However, it is important to remember that the presence of negative effects associated with watching violent music videos in early adulthood does not guarantee that the same effects will be present in childhood or adolescence. Additionally, even if, in fact, effects are present for youth, they may not be of the same magnitude throughout development. If adult data reliably predicted child and adolescent data in a one-to-one fashion, there would be no need to conduct research on youth. However, this is not the case. And because scientific fact requires data and not assumption, research on adult participants cannot be used as a basis of fact when discussing the effects of violent music and music videos on children and adolescents. Show me the data!

Comparing Music Videos to Music Alone

The finding that anger increases following the viewing of a music video featuring violence contradicts the data on listening to music, in which feelings of anger lessen after listening to Heavy Metal music (Scheel & Westefeld, 1999). It may be that the realistic and graphic nature of the violence depicted in music videos produces an amplification effect for emotion. In contrast, when listening to music without visual accompaniment, the imagined content may not be graphic or realistic enough to amplify negative emotion. Moreover, the incomprehensibility of many Heavy Metal songs may reduce the likelihood that the listener will perceive the hostile messages within, unless there are visual images to accompany the lyrics (as is the case in music videos). Without lyrical comprehension, emotion is less likely to be affected. Perhaps the combination of lyrical violence and violent imagery is more detrimental to the psychological well-being of youth than lyrical violence alone. Clearly, more research is needed to investigate this issue.

It is also possible that demand characteristics may differ for research involving music and research investigating music videos. In support of this contention, Roberts et al. (2003) suggest that the studies involving violent music videos may not have properly disguised the intent of their studies. However, there is no current research quantifying the differences in demand characteristics between studies involving violent music and those involving violent music videos.

Summary

- With age, youth consume increasing amounts of music.
- There is no research on the effects of violent music on children. Research is also lacking regarding the effects of violent background music on children and adolescents.
- Heavy Metal and Rap lyrics are filled with violence, misogyny, racism, murder, and Satanism.
- Violent lyrics are thought to prime aggressive thoughts, lead to the chronic activation of aggression-related constructs, and lead to the imagination of violent imagery.
- Lyrical comprehension increases throughout development. But even late adolescents have difficulty interpreting the metaphorical lyrics in many songs.
- Factors that influence the comprehensibility of lyrics include the cognitive developmental status of the listener and the enunciation of the lyrics.
- Although the comprehension of lyrical content is generally poor, the greatest level of comprehension is associated with songs that are the most violent and offensive.

- Backwards-masked lyrics can be detected when the music is played backwards. When played forwards, however, comprehension of backwards-masked lyrics is lacking. There is no evidence that backwards-masked music causes suicidal behavior.
- Correlational studies have linked preferences for Heavy Metal and Rap with antisocial behavior and school problems. However, it is also possible that consumers of these genres prefer the rebellious and antisocial themes depicted in the music more so than the violent content.
- No experimental studies involving violent music have been conducted with child and adolescent participants.
- A preference for musical themes of death and suicide may indicate suicidal ideation. However, the use of/preference for Heavy Metal music is not considered a significant risk factor for suicidal behavior.
- The visual images of music videos can help clarify incomprehensible lyrics. The typical violent music video depicts repeated acts of unrealistic and unpunished violence. Additionally, there is little regard for the pain and suffering of the victim.
- There is no research relating violent music videos and aggressive behavior in youth. The watching of violent music videos, however, has been shown to increase adolescents' acceptance of the use of violence to solve problems.
- In college students, the viewing of violent music videos has been shown to increase feelings of anger and engender more positive attitudes towards the use of aggression. These data may or may not mirror the effects of violent music videos throughout childhood and adolescence.
- Whereas violent music has been shown to decrease feelings of aggression, violent music videos have been shown to increase such feelings. The graphic and visual presentation of violence in music videos may cause an amplification effect. Demand characteristics can also explain this difference.
- Researchers use deception to reduce demand characteristics. However, researchers rarely test to see if participants were, in fact, deceived.
- The statistical concepts of multiple regression and statistical control were introduced.

10

Watching the Beast

Live-Action Television and Movie Violence

In deference to Batman, riddle me this: I can be found in virtually every home in America (99%). In an average household, there are more of me than children or toilets. I have occasionally been referred to as a "babysitter." And like the babysitter who lets children stay up past their bedtime, I, too, can keep children awake at night. Children love to spend time with me. For decades, I have been the number one after-school activity for youth. I am not a pet, but children always want me. Twenty percent of children under age 7, 69% of 8- to 10-year-olds, and 68% of teenagers keep me in their bedrooms. The more time you spend with me, the more likely you are to be obese and do poorly in school, but I am not a doughnut (Annenberg Public Policy Center, 1999; Bushman & Huesmann, 2001; Gentile & Walsh, 2002; Roberts et al., 2005). What am I? A television set, of course.

Violence on Television

Television programs, in both animated and live-action forms, are replete with violent content. Even if children are limited to watching programs without violence, they still may be exposed to televised violence through the commercials aired during nonviolent children's programming. For instance, Larson (2003) found that over one-third of the nearly 900 commercials directed at children contained aggressive elements. Similarly, Tamburro,

Gordon, D'Apolito, and Howard (2004) found that commercials airing during major sporting events (e.g., Super Bowl, World Series) that attract a youthful audience highlight aggressive or unsafe behaviors nearly 50% of the time.

Bushman and Huesmann (2001) report that the amount of violent content televised in dramatic and comedic programming is far greater than the amount of violence occurring in real life. Based on viewing patterns and television content, Huston et al. (1992) report that children will view more than 8,000 murders and 100,000 total acts of violence by the time they head off to their first day in junior high school. But as the previous chapter on music violence revealed, the *presence* of violent content, no matter how brutal, does not necessarily equate to aggressive behavior in youthful media consumers. As such, the purpose of this chapter is to assess the impact of television and movie violence on aggression throughout childhood and adolescence.

Differences Between Movies and Television

Experimental research on movie violence often involves the screening of films on television sets. However, there are three noticeable differences between movies and television that are worth mentioning: First, theatrical films are viewed on much larger screens than are television programs. Recent research has demonstrated greater physiological responding and memory for the content of videos shown on larger screens (e.g., 56") than on smaller ones (e.g., 13"; Reeves, Lang, Kim, & Tatar, 1999; Heo, 2004). As such, the possibility exists that movies viewed in theaters (with screens measured in feet instead of inches) could produce larger effects than the same movies viewed on television screens. Second, films, more than television shows, are watched in the presence of others. Research on college students has revealed that in comparison to watching a movie alone, the presence of vocal and reactive co-spectators increased post-viewing aggression (Dunand, Berkowitz, & Leyens, 1984). Third, unique to television is the presence of commercial breaks. These two-minute-long interruptions disrupt the flow of televised content, potentially masking prosocial and anti-aggressive messages that may appear within. For instance, Collins (1973) found that the presence of commercials placed in between aggressive acts and the associated punishments made it difficult for 3rd-grade children to realize that aggressive acts were, in fact, punished. In turn, because the anti-aggressive message was missed, children's post-viewing aggressive responding increased. Taken together, these findings suggest that the effects of viewing violent movies in theaters may be greater than the effects of watching television at home. As of yet, however, this contention has not been researched in children, adolescents, or adults.

The Context of Aggression and Television Violence

Not all television violence is alike, for the manner in which it is presented differs greatly by program. For instance, the 1960s live-action television series *Batman* depicts violent crime and crime fighting in a humorous manner. In contrast, the recent drama *NYPD Blue* presents a more realistic version of criminal behavior and apprehension. In previous chapters, a variety of factors surrounding the ratings of media violence were presented, including graphicness, sanitization (i.e., not showing the pain and suffering of the victim), fantasy vs. reality, and the effect of humor in trivializing violence. In short, programs that sanitize violence, present it in a humorous context, or depict violence unrealistically (e.g., cartoons) are rated as less violent than shows that depict graphic, unsanitized, and realistic violence.

Moreover, the effects of media violence on aggression tend to vary as a function of the presentation of the violence. Violence that is punished or depicts the pain and suffering of the victim tends to decrease the likelihood that youth will act aggressively. In contrast, aggressive behavior in youth is encouraged after viewing sanitized, trivialized, and realistic violence (Wilson, Smith, et al., 2002). In this chapter, two more contextual factors and their influence on aggressive behavior in youth are addressed: glamorized and justified violence.

Glamorized Violence

The glorification of violence during children's television programming is rampant. On television, perpetrators of violence are rarely condemned or punished. In fact, nearly 70% of "good" perpetrators (e.g., the hero) go unpunished and 32% of them are rewarded for their violent actions. Moreover, immediately following an act of violence, "bad" perpetrators (i.e., the villain) go unpunished over 80% of the time. Adding to the glamorization of violent behavior is the fact that the perpetrators of such acts tend to be presented in an attractive manner, with charismatic and powerful personalities—characteristics to which many youthful viewers are drawn (Wilson, Smith, et al., 2002).

Glamorized Violence and Learning

The glamorization of televised violence is important, for children are more likely to imitate and learn from models to which they are attracted. Imitation and learning are especially likely to occur if the viewed action is vicariously reinforcing (i.e., fun to watch) *and* the model is attractive, characteristics which are hallmarks of children's television programming (Bandura, 1986). Moreover, violence performed by child and adolescent actors may have a greater negative impact on youth than similar behaviors performed by adults (Hoffner & Cantor, 1991). In support of this contention, consider the following findings: in laboratory experiments, children are more likely to imitate aggressive behaviors performed by same-aged peers than adults (Wilson, Colvin, & Smith, 2002). Children's favorite television characters are more likely to be under 18 years of age than over (Hoffner, 1996). When aggressive behavior is shown on television, youthful perpetrators are less likely to be punished, more likely to be attractive, and more likely to be portrayed as "good guys," in comparison to adult perpetrators. Additionally, the victims of the youthful perpetrators tend to suffer less than the victims of adult perpetrators (Wilson, Colvin, et al., 2002). Thus, the characteristics of violent television directed at children should theoretically produce large effects on youth.

Research on the Effects of Glamorization on Aggression in Youth

Currently, there is little research linking the glamorization of television characters to aggressive behavior in youth. There is research linking the consequences that aggressive models receive and the imitation of aggressive behavior in youth, with reinforcements increasing aggressive behavior and punishments decreasing it (Bandura, 1965; Bandura et al., 1963). However, the behaviors imitated in the studies by Bandura were directed at inanimate objects. Given that there are more social prohibitions against aggressing against people than toys, it remains to be seen if televised consequences to the perpetrator affect aggressive behavior involving real youth. Moreover, there is no research on youth linking the physical attractiveness of the televised perpetrator to real-life aggression. Clearly, given the theoretical importance of "glamorized violence," empirical findings involving children and adolescents are needed.

Moreover, there is little research on the factors that "glamorize" violence from the perspective of children and adolescents. Thus, a question in need of answering is "How does the perception of glamorized violence change throughout development?" In fact, there is no standard operational definition of "glamorized violence" in the media violence literature. Whereas in some studies, the consequences to a violent perpetrator are used to define glamorization (Anderson, Berkowitz, et al., 2003), in other studies, the attractiveness of the perpetrator is used as an index of glamorization (Hoffner & Cantor, 1985). Such differences are not unimportant. Hoffner and Cantor have found that as children age, the attractiveness of a perpetrator becomes less important when evaluating television characters, but their behavior and the outcomes associated with it become more important.

Justified Violence

When the use of violence is perceived as necessary to the solution of a problem, it is considered justified. Approximately 27% of child-oriented programming and 35% of adult-oriented programming involve the presentation of justified violence (Wilson, Smith, et al., 2002). Justified violence has been linked with aggressive behavior in youth. In an assessment of 2,100 adolescents, Hartnagel, Teevan, and McIntyre (1975) found correlational evidence that youth perceiving violence on television as justified report engaging in more violent acts than youth lacking this perception.

Justified Violence in the Context of Fantasy and Reality

Whether or not televised violence is perceived as justified may be related to the context in which the violence is presented, namely, fantasy or reality. Krcmar and Valkenburg (1999) found that among children and early adolescents, the greatest acceptance of justified violence comes from youth with a history of watching fantasy violence on television. Given that the vast majority of violence (87%; Wilson, Smith, et al., 2002) depicted in children's programming occurs in a fantasy context, youth are presented with ample opportunities to be socialized to believe that violence is acceptable. Krcmar and Valkenburg contend that when fantasy violence is televised, it is done in the context of "aggression for the greater good." Typically, a hero violently and justifiably defeats a villain. As Bandura (1986) states, when aggressive behavior is modeled by someone who is powerful and attractive to youth, learning is very likely to follow.

In contrast, youth with a history of watching realistically portrayed violence (such as that shown in the program *Cops*) are less likely to accept the use of justified violence (Krcmar & Valkenburg, 1999). During realistic shows, violent perpetrators are arrested and the message that violence should not be used to solve problems is relayed to the viewing audience. In other words, the perpetrators are punished, a fact that has been consistently shown to reduce the imitation of aggressive behavior in youth (Bandura, 1986).

Contrast Effects

An additional explanation for the above findings, and one that is untested in youth, centers on the concept of *contrast effects*. A contrast effect is the inverse relationship between a judgment and a related stimulus (Schwartz & Bess, 1992). According to King (2000), the viewing of sobering, realistic media violence (i.e., the related stimulus) may cause distress in viewers, thereby reducing their approval of real-life aggression (i.e., the judgment). Conversely, media violence that is not distressing (such as comedic or fantasy violence) may lead to greater approval of real-life aggression. The pattern of findings in the Krcmar and Valkenburg (1999) study, in which fantasy violence is associated with greater approval of aggression and realistic violence is associated with lesser approval of aggression, is consistent with that of a contrast effect.

Experimental research on college students supports the contention that contrast effects moderate the justified violence-aggression relationship. Specifically, participants viewing justified violence tend to act more aggressively than participants viewing unjustified violence (Berkowitz & Powers, 1979; Berkowitz & Rawlings, 1963).

However consistent the above findings tend to be, developmental issues should not be ignored. Krcmar and Cooke (2001) found that younger children (4 to 7 years old), but not older children (8- to 11-year-olds), tend to view unpunished violence as more justified than punished violence (Krcmar & Cooke, 2001). According to the authors, younger children's tendency to base the rightness or wrongness of an act on the observable consequences renders punished aggression as wrong and unpunished aggression as justifiable. In contrast, for older children (but not younger children), aggressive responses to provoked aggression (e.g., the child is attacked by a peer) are considered to be more justifiable than aggressive responses to unprovoked aggression (e.g., the child attacks a peer). These data are consistent with developmental research showing that, in middle childhood, aggressive responses to attack are considered appropriate (Shaffer, 2000). Thus, the impact of justifiable media violence on youth appears to vary as a function of age and the context of the televised aggression.

The Effects of Television Violence on Aggressive Behavior

Taking into consideration all forms of violent media, more research has been conducted on violent television/movies than on comic books, music, sports violence, and video games. In addition to the research using adult participants, numerous studies have been conducted on the effects of violent television on children and adolescents. Below are selected studies meant to illustrate important concepts or address inconsistent findings. Here, the focus is on describing and evaluating the empirical research. The overall magnitude of the effects will be discussed in a later chapter. Moreover, to help identify "holes" in the literature, the research on children and adolescents will be discussed separately. At times, longitudinal studies spanning over a decade will be presented. When this occurs, the research will be discussed in the child or adolescent section based on the age of the child at the beginning of the study. Public and political concerns tend to focus on the effects of violent television on aggressive behavior in youth. Theoretically, aggression-related constructs are just as important as aggressive behavior. As such, studies addressing aggression-related constructs will be discussed independent of the research on aggressive behavior.

Correlational Studies in Childhood

Although correlational studies cannot provide causal explanations regarding the effects of violent television exposure on aggressive behavior, the findings are still important. In particular, correlational studies can falsify the contention that media violence influences aggression. For instance, if the viewing of television violence did not positively correlate with aggressive behavior in youth, concern over the directionality of the supposed causal link (i.e., does media violence cause aggression or do aggressive people seek out violent media?) could be forsaken.

Preschool

In order to assess the impact of violent television watching on aggressive behavior, Singer and Singer (1981) observed preschool children over the period of one year. During the assessment period, parents reported that their children watched many adult-oriented shows containing violence, including *Kojak, Starsky and Hutch,* and *The Six Million Dollar Man.* It seems strange that preschoolers would want to watch adult-oriented action/adventure shows. In all likelihood, however, the parents were the ones who wanted to watch these programs (which aired between 8:00 and 11:00 P.M.) and did so with their young children present.

In the Singer and Singer study, the frequency of aggressive behavior such as hitting, pushing, seizing toys, and destroying property was assessed in the context of free play. For both boys and girls, higher levels of violent television viewing were associated with greater amounts of aggressive behavior during play. These correlations remained significant even after statistically removing the influence of potential confounds (e.g., IQ and social class). However, a third variable accounting for the aforementioned correlation is possible. Perhaps significant parenting differences occurred between those who let their 3- to 4-year-old children stay up too late to watch adult oriented programs like *The Bionic Woman* and those who did not.

The Singers (1981) provide some evidence to support this contention. Aggressive youth with high levels of television exposure of all kinds (e.g., game shows, cartoons, sports, dramas, action/adventure) were the least likely to have toys, books, musical instruments, and records. Moreover, these highly aggressive, high television-viewing preschoolers were less likely than other youth to be read to at night and have a stable bedtime routine. Aggressive preschoolers were also more likely to be spanked than nonaggressive preschoolers. Thus, the possibility exists that an unassessed third variable related to parenting accounted for the significant correlation between violent television viewing and peer-related aggression.

Middle Childhood

Viemero and Paajanen (1992) assessed the relationship between peer-nominated aggression and exposure to violent television in 8- and 10-year-old Finnish children. The authors found that the viewing of violent television was positively correlated with peer-nominated aggression for boys, girls, and 10-year-olds. The correlation for 8-year-olds, however, was not significant. Interestingly, 8-year-olds reported watching fewer violent television shows than 10-year-olds. Viemero and Paajanen suggest that parents may have more control over the television programs that 8-year-olds watch than those 10-year-olds watch. However, no data are offered to support this contention. An alternative explanation for the non-significant correlation is that a *floor effect* was present. A floor effect refers to situations in which most responses occur at the low end of a range in which high scores are also possible. With such a restricted range of responses, it becomes more difficult to find significant correlations.

Eron, Huesmann, Lefkowitz, and Walder (1972) followed over 850 youth from 3rd grade to age 19. Violent television exposure was related to peer-nominated levels of physical and verbal aggression. For boys, after factoring out a wide range of potential confounds (such as parenting style, SES, IQ, initial levels of aggression), violent television viewing at age 8 was significantly correlated with the adolescent indices of aggression. However, no significant effects were evident for girls.

In contrast, using a different sample, Huesmann et al. (1984) found evidence for the relationship between violent television consumption and peer-nominated aggression for girls. In this study, 1st- and 3rd-grade children were longitudinally followed for three years. Levels of peer-nominated aggression and violent television consumption during the first year of the study were used to predict violent television consumption and peer-nominated aggressive behavior in the third year of the study. After controlling for initial levels of aggression, the results indicated that for girls, but not boys, first-year violent television exposure significantly predicted third-year levels of aggressive behavior. For both boys and girls, first-year levels of peer-nominated aggression predicted third-year violent television consumption. Thus, while there was strong evidence that aggressive children seek out media violence, the contention that violent media increases levels of aggression was only partially supported. It may be that peer-related aggressive behavior is influenced by violent television in middle childhood more than at other times of development. Of course, additional research is necessary.

Huesmann followed up this research by re-contacting the participants some 15 years after the original assessment (Huesmann et al., 2003). Participants, now in their early 20s, filled out a variety of questionnaires and were interviewed about their use of physical, verbal, and indirect aggression. Based on their responses, a composite measure of adult aggression was created. After statistically controlling for a host of potentially confounding variables (e.g., early childhood aggression, parent education), violent television consumption in childhood significantly predicted aggressive behavior in young adults. When adult levels of physical aggression and indirect aggression (i.e., aggression without direct contact with the victim) were assessed separately, gender differences appeared. Whereas for boys, violent television consumption only predicted adult levels of physical aggression, for girls, both physical and indirect forms of aggression were significantly predicted by violent television viewing in childhood. This finding may reflect the fact that females are more likely to engage in indirect aggression than males. Interestingly, levels of childhood aggression did not significantly predict adult levels of violent television consumption. This finding contradicts the notion that violent youth will continually seek out violent media.

Summary of Correlational Research

Surprisingly, few correlational studies have assessed the impact of live-action television on preschool children. Most of the research using preschoolers has focused on the effects of cartoon violence on aggression. This makes sense given that preschool children are more likely to be exposed to cartoon violence than live-action shows containing violence. However, as the Singer and Singer (1981) study indicates, preschoolers are exposed to adult action/adventure television shows. Given that realistic violence may have a greater impact on youth than cartoon violence, additional research is necessary to determine the effects of live-action violence on preschoolers.

Across early and middle childhood, research has demonstrated significant associations between violent television consumption and aggressive behavior. However, during the preschool years, the television violence–aggression link could just as easily be accounted for by parenting variables. Moreover, research conducted during middle childhood has produced inconsistent findings, with some studies finding significant effects for boys but not girls and other studies finding the opposite. Additional research is necessary to clarify these contradictions.

Experimental Research in Childhood

In an attempt to measure the effects of violent television on children's behavior in a laboratory, and thereby establish causality, Liebert and Baron (1971) had 5- to 9-year-old children view either an aggressive or a nonaggressive television clip for 3 ½ minutes. After viewing the clip, children were told that another child was playing a game in a different room and that by pressing one of two buttons, they could either help the other child win the game or prevent the child from doing so. Behavior during a post-viewing free play session with aggressive and nonaggressive toys was also assessed. Regardless of age, the viewing of the violent television clip led to the greatest amount of interpersonal aggression (i.e., preventing the child from winning the game). Moreover, for all children, aggressive play was more likely to follow the viewing of the violent clip than the nonviolent clip.

Boyatsis, Matillo, and Nesbitt (1995) conducted a field experiment on the effects of violent television on aggression during play using one of the most popular and violent television shows ever directed at children, *The Mighty Morphin' Power Rangers*. In a typical episode of intergalactic crime fighting, over 200 acts of violence will occur between the heroic band of teenage "Power Rangers" and evil alien forces (Kiesewetter, 1993). In the Boyatsis et al. (1995) study, 52 children participating in an after-school program (ages ranging from 5 to 11 years) were randomly assigned to watch or not watch a complete 22-minute violence-laden episode. Prior to and following the experimental manipulation, levels of aggressive play were observed in the classroom for each child. Acts of verbal and physical aggression were tallied. The authors report that in comparison to the control group, youth watching the violent television program exhibited seven times as many acts of aggression.

However, as intriguing as these findings are, the authors failed to differentiate aggressive behavior occurring during play and aggressive play (i.e., rough-and-tumble play). Boyatsis et al. (1995) provide evidence that youth may have been playfully imitating televised behaviors. The authors state, "One manifestation of the boys' emulation of the Power Rangers' violence was their precise imitation of the characters' acts, such as flying karate kicks" (p. 50). Similarly, Ling and Thomas (1986) found that after viewing a video of youth engaging in acts of aggression such as hitting, name calling, and arguing, 8-year-old children closely imitated the behaviors that they had just observed. In the 1960s, Bandura conducted a series of experiments in which young children imitated acts of aggression modeled for them in a video (Bandura, 1965; Bandura et al., 1963). In fact, children are aware of their aping behavior. In one survey, 60% of young children report knowingly imitating behaviors seen on television (Liebert, Neale, & Davidson, 1973).

Summary of Experimental Research

Taken together, the aforementioned findings suggest that throughout childhood children imitate observed acts of violence. Although such behaviors are often imitated in the context of play, at times children may inappropriately imitate the behaviors. Consider the following anecdotal evidence reported to me by a parent: "The other day, as I was making weird faces at my 6-year-old son, he slapped me in the face. I yelled, 'Why'd you do that?' He responded, 'That's what they do on TV to get someone to stop freaking out.'" Although aggressive play can turn into aggression, rough-and-tumble play should not be construed as aggression. In the short term, the imitation of aggressive behavior during play may not be problematic. However, it has been theorized that repeated practice at using aggressive behavior, even in the context of play, could result in youth developing a pattern of behavior that is conducive to real acts of aggression.

Research on Adolescents

Correlational Studies

More often than not, higher levels of violent television consumption have been associated with higher levels of aggressive behavior (Anderson, Berkowitz, et al., 2003). For instance, in an assessment of nearly 500 7th and 10th graders, McLeod, Atkin, and Chaffee (1972) found significant positive correlations between viewing violent television and teenage self-reports of aggressive behavior. Similarly, Slater, Henry, Swaim, and Anderson (2003) found that among 6th- and 7th-grade adolescents, violent media use (TV, video games, Internet) predicted not only current levels of aggressive behavior but also levels of aggressive behavior two years later. Moreover, current levels of aggressive behavior predicted future levels of violent media consumption. These findings complement those of Vidal, Clemente, and Espinosa (2003), who found that the more youth watch violence, the more they tend to enjoy it. Thus, a reinforcing pattern of media violence and aggressive behavior may develop in which violent media increase aggressive behavior, aggressive youth become attracted to violent media, violent media consumption becomes more enjoyable, which leads to greater violent media consumption (see Figure 10.1).

Quasi-Experiments

In each of the studies reported below, experimental groups (e.g., high or low television exposure) were created based on self-reported levels of violent television consumption; random assignment to experimental and control groups did not occur. For instance, Belson (1978) found that youth reporting high levels of violent television consumption reported engaging in more acts of violence than youth reporting little violent television consumption. Hartnagel et al. (1975) found the highest levels of self-reported violent behavior (i.e., hurt someone badly, get in a serious fight at school, get in a gang-like fight) in teenagers who categorize their "favorite show" as violent. However, when additional factors such as gender and school performance were entered into the data analyses, violent television exposure no longer predicted violent behavior.

Figure 10.1   Cyclical Pattern of Violent Media and Aggressive Behavior

One reason for the conflicting results may be related to the measurement of violent behavior. For instance, Hartnagle et al. primarily assessed serious acts of violence. Belson (1978), on the other hand, assessed a much broader range of aggressive and violent behavior, including taunts, threats, attempted rape, assault, and attempted murder. Simply stated, *method variance* could explain the diverging results. Method variance refers to variance that is attributable to the measurement method rather than to the constructs the measures represent. In other words, although both studies were attempting to assess the construct of "violence," differences in the methods used to assess this construct (i.e., the questions asked) may be the reason that the findings conflicted.

Experimental Research

Although experimental designs have been used with adolescents, the subjects in these studies were delinquent youth, and therefore, the findings may not generalize to normal youth. Nonetheless, the findings are still important, for they suggest that violent media can impact aggressive youth. For instance, Leyens, Camino, Parke, and Berkowitz (1975) assigned delinquent Belgian boys to watch either a violent movie or a nonviolent movie for five consecutive nights. On each night, post-viewing aggressive behaviors, such as hitting, slapping, and kicking, were counted. As expected, boys watching the violent films were more aggressive than boys watching the nonviolent films. Similar findings have been demonstrated for delinquent youth in the United States (Parke, Berkowitz, Leyens, West, & Sebastian, 1977). Additional research on normative adolescents is needed to see if the effects of violent television exposure on delinquent teenagers generalize to normal adolescents.

Introduction of Television and Aggressive Behavior

Williams's (1986) classic study of three Canadian towns, each with a different level of television exposure, demonstrates the potential influence of television violence on aggressive behavior. Williams compared levels of physical and verbal aggression in children from three towns (listed by pseudonyms): Notel, a town that did not receive television; Unitel, which received one television channel; and Multitel, a town that received four television channels. Prior to the introduction of television to Notel, children in the three towns did not differ in either verbal or physical aggression. This is surprising given the contention that exposure to television violence increases aggression. Because children in Unitel and Multitel were already exposed to television prior to the start of the study, they should have been more aggressive than youth from Notel. The fact that they were not calls into question the results and implications of the study.

Following the introduction of television in Notel, levels of physical and verbal aggression in Notel youth increased significantly beyond the levels of children in the other two towns. Some have interpreted this finding to mean that the introduction of television violence caused Notel youth to become aggressive. However, there are several limitations to this study that mitigate the importance of the findings. First, Williams assessed television viewing in general and not violent television viewing. Perhaps factors related to general patterns of television viewing (e.g., less parental monitoring) rather than violent television viewing caused the results. Second, rates of verbal and physical aggression increased only in Notel. Given the contention that television exposure causes an increase in aggression, youth in Multitel and Unitel also should have experienced increases in aggressive behavior. The aforementioned difficulties may have occurred due to the fact that Williams had used data from a *natural experiment*.

Natural Experiments

In a natural experiment, "experimental" and "control" groups are created by some naturally occurring event, such as the introduction of television. The researcher then observes the effects of this naturally occurring change. The research does not, however, cause the change to occur. Unlike laboratory experiments, in natural experiments there is no random assignment to condition and there is no control over factors that could potentially confound the data. Thus, the ability to make causal inferences in natural experiments is weakened. In the Notel study, it is extremely plausible that the observed increases in aggressive behavior were the result of undocumented social changes (e.g., unemployment and divorce rates) occurring around the same time as the introduction of television.

Indirect Aggression

As the previous review revealed, exposure to television violence has been shown to affect aggressive behavior in childhood and adolescence. However, a closer inspection of the correlational and experimental studies conducted reveals an oversight in the literature. The research that has been conducted has been primarily limited to studies in which youth view televised portrayals of aggressive behavior during face-to-face encounters (i.e., direct aggression). In contrast, no study using children, and only one study using adolescents, has assessed the effects of televised depictions of violence on indirect aggression. In the lone adolescent study, Coyne, Archer, and Eslea (2004) found that the viewing of either direct or indirect televised violence increased 11- to 14-year-olds' use of indirect aggression (e.g., anonymously evaluating a rude confederate). Similarly, Huesmann et al. (2003) found that for females, childhood exposure to television violence predicted the use of indirect aggression in adulthood.

Moreover, Coyne et al.'s (2004) results complement those of Kirsh and Olczak (2002), who found that the reading of direct aggression in extremely violent comic books leads to increased use of indirect aggression when responding to hypothetical provocation situations involving both direct and indirect aggression. Together, these findings suggest that the viewing of television violence has the potential to influence multiple forms of aggression (direct and indirect), not just the type of aggression that was televised (direct or indirect). Moreover, the prevalence of direct and indirect aggression varies throughout development and by gender. Thus, it is imperative that when assessing the impact of televised violence on youth, both direct and indirect forms of aggression are assessed. In previous research, the failure to find evidence relating television violence with aggressive behavior may reflect the fact that only one form of aggression was being assessed rather than the lack of an experimental effect.

The Effect of Television Violence on Aggression-Related Constructs

Aggression-related constructs are factors internal to the individual that influence the likelihood that the individual will act aggressively. Prior to this chapter, a paucity of research existed with regard to the assessment of aggression-related constructs in youth. However, the 50-plus years of research on television violence have resulted in a wide range of research endeavors, many of which meet the criteria of an aggression-related construct. As the following review will reveal, however, little research has assessed the same aggression-related construct as a function of development. In fact, in order to establish a pattern of sound developmental research for each of the aggression-related constructs listed below, additional research is needed at some point in development. See if you can identify the holes in the literature.

Attitudes Towards the Use of Aggression

Does violent television exposure engender more positive attitudes toward the use of aggressive behavior? To address this issue, youth are often asked a series of questions about their beliefs regarding the use of aggression, and their responses are correlated with the amount of violent television consumed. For instance, Dominick and Greenberg (1972) found that 4th-through 6th-grade boys and girls with high levels of television violence were more likely than those not highly exposed to report more positive attitudes with regard to (1) their willingness to use violence and (2) the perceived effectiveness of the violent force. Level of television violence exposure, however, was unrelated to their approval of violence when solving problems. Using a sample of 9-, 12-, and 15-year-old British youth, Greenberg (1974) found that positive attitudes towards both the willingness to use violence and its perceived effectiveness were more likely to be expressed by youth with a history of watching a great deal of violent television.

In addition to simply asking children about their beliefs surrounding the use of aggression, children are frequently presented with hypothetical scenarios in which a provocation of some sort occurs; for example, a child gets bumped into while on the playground. Next, youth are asked a series of questions related to the course of action that should follow the provocation.

Leifer and Roberts (1971) assessed 4- to 16-year-olds' aggressive tendencies after viewing a violent television program. After hearing a hypothetical conflict situation (e.g., "You are walking down the street. Some kid is mad at you and comes up and hits you. What do you do?"), youth were required to choose from one of four possible solutions: "Hit him," "Call him stupid," "Leave him," and "Tell a grownup." As expected, youth who viewed the violent television show gave more aggressive responses than children and adolescents who viewed the nonviolent television show. However, these results were qualified by the presence of gender and developmental differences. Results indicated that boys gave consistently more aggressive responses than girls. Additionally, aggressive responding tended to increase with age.

Similarly, Wotring and Greenberg (1973) found, among 8th- and 9th-grade adolescents, youth seeing violent film clips (16 minutes in length) reported more post-viewing physically aggressive responses to hypothetical conflict scenarios than teenagers seeing a brief, nonviolent film clip. However, contrary to expectations, no differences were seen in verbally aggressive responses between youth in the experimental and control groups.

Emotional Expression

The expressions that children make while viewing violent television may indicate their propensity to use aggression. In general, children are more likely to express joy when watching nonviolent television than when watching violent television (Lagerspetz, Wahlroos, & Wendelin, 1978). Thus, a greater tendency to express happiness when watching live-action violence becomes noteworthy. For instance, in an additional assessment of the 5- to 6-year-old children used in the Liebert and Baron (1971) study (in which youth could help or hurt another child's chances to win a game by pressing a button), Ekman et al. (1971) assessed aggressive behavior in relation to their facial expressions while viewing the violent television clip. For boys only, displaying positive facial expression, such as pleasure or happiness, was associated with an increased likelihood of pushing the button used to hurt the other child's chances of winning the game. Moreover, during the subsequent free play session, facial expressions of happiness were positively correlated with aggressive play.

Fantasizing

Rehearsal of aggressive scripts is theorized to be an important contributing factor to aggressive behavior (Anderson & Bushman, 2001). Fantasy play and thinking involving aggression are thought to be mechanisms of rehearsal for youth. Viemero and Paajanen (1992) found that peer-nominated aggressive 8- and 10-year-old children were likely to engage in aggressive fantasies. Additionally, boys with higher levels of violent television exposure exhibited the greatest number of aggressive fantasies. Although the results are intriguing, Veimero and Paajanen did not remove the influence of preexisting differences in aggressive behavior when calculating the correlation between television violence exposure and aggressive fantasies. Consequently, because aggressive children are drawn to violent television, it is possible that the significant association was the result of behavioral differences in aggression and not violent television consumption. More doubt is cast on the relationship between television violence and aggressive fantasy in that Huesmann et al. (1984) failed to find a significant correlation between violent television exposure and aggressive fantasies in the United States or in Finland. These authors did find, however, that aggressive fantasizing correlated positively with peer-nominated aggression.

Identification With the Aggressor

Identification with the aggressor refers to the extent to which youth wish to be like the televised aggressor or believe in and value the similarities between the aggressor and the self. To assess identification, youth are asked if they have ever "acted like" or "did things like" the violent characters they watch on television. Huesmann et al. (2003) found that identification with same-sex aggressive television characters in childhood significantly predicted levels of physical and verbal aggression 15 years later. This finding occurred independent of the amount of violent television watched.

If replicated throughout development, the importance of this finding cannot be overstated. For some children and adolescents, the amount of violent television watched may be a relatively unimportant contributor to aggression; instead, all that is necessary to influence aggression is that youth identify with a violent character. This finding may help explain some of the low magnitude correlations between television violence exposure and aggressive behavior. For youth with little television violence exposure but high levels of aggressive behavior, identification with the aggressor may be influencing the higher rates of aggression. Thus, the overall correlation between television violence and aggressive behavior will be lower because youth with little television exposure are acting aggressively.

Moreover, the findings of Huesmann and colleagues (2003) suggest that violent television exposure and identification with the aggressor are factors independent of aggression. Thus, the presence of one or more of these factors may result in different levels of aggression. For instance, Huesmann and colleagues found that for boys, violent television consumption along with identification with a violent male character led to the greater levels of aggressive behavior in young adulthood. Here, the accumulation of risk produced the greatest amount of aggression.

Memory

In most theories of aggression, the easy activation and retrieval of aggression-related memories and the rehearsal of aggressive scripts are thought to be characteristic of aggressive youth. As such, televised imagery that would increase the likelihood that youth will recall aggression-related thoughts becomes a risk factor for increased aggressiveness. Although the aforementioned contentions are frequently stated, there is very little research on memory processes in youth in response to viewing violent television. In an assessment of 5th- and 6th-grade children, Maccoby, Levin, and Selya (1955) found that in comparison to just viewing a violent film, the combination of frustration (via a rigged spelling bee) *and* the viewing of violence led to better recollection for the central themes of the movie one week later. It is noteworthy that violence alone did not lead to better retention of the details of the films.

Perhaps for memory to be affected a certain threshold of aggressive feelings needs to be reached. Research on youth has shown that the viewing of violent action/adventure shows is associated with higher levels of anger

(Singer & Singer, 1981). Research on undergraduates has found that televised news images that induce anger are the most memorable (Newhagen, 1998). However, television-induced anger/hostility as a factor in enhancing memory in youth has yet to be established.

Interpretation of Ambiguous Stimuli

A *projective test* is designed to reveal information about the characteristics of an individual based on his or her responses to ambiguous objects or situations. Assessing children's responses to perceptually ambiguous stimuli following the viewing of televised violence, therefore, is meant to reveal aggressive characteristics induced by the violence exposure. In measuring the relationship between violent television and aggressivity (a composite variable that describes a person's overall level of aggressiveness) among 13-year-olds, Vetro, Csapo, Szilard, and Vargha (1998) relied on the Rosenzweig Picture-Frustration Test (PFT; Rosenzweig, Fleming, & Rosenzweig, 1948). The PFT is a projective technique used to assess patterns of aggressive responding to everyday stress. During PFT, youth are shown a series of cartoon-like pictures in which a mildly frustrating situation occurs. Participants are then asked to make a verbal response from the perspective of the person who had been frustrated. Vetro et al. (1998) found that early adolescents with a history of watching crime and adventure shows had a higher aggressivity level than youth watching little television violence.

Hess, Hess, and Hess (1999) assessed the effects of violent movies on aggressive responding in high school juniors, using a projective inkblot test developed by Swartz and Holtzman (1963). During this test, youth are presented with a series of inkblots and asked to give one response per inkblot. In the Hess et al. (1999) study, a pretest-posttest design was used, in which a series of inkblots were responded to prior to and following the viewing of a three-minute-long nonviolent or violent movie clip. Hess and colleagues found that adolescents who watched the violent movie clip interpreted the inkblots using more "violent responses" that youth viewing the nonviolent movie clip.

Desensitization

In the movie *Scream*, seven grisly murders take place. In the sequel, *Scream 2*, the body count creeps higher, as 10 gruesome killings occur (*The Diabolical Dominion*, 2004). Prior to being bludgeoned himself in *Scream 2*, Randy states the three simple rules of horror sequels: (1) the killings become more elaborate (i.e., ingenious and gorier); (2) the body count always goes up; and (3) never, ever assume that the killer is dead. The first two rules are relevant to the study of media violence on youthful aggression: they reflect the underlying belief that in order to create an emotional change in those who watch a sequel, the level of violence depicted needs to supersede the previous film (Sparks, 2001). In support of this contention, consider the following statistic: for the 10 movies comprising the *Friday the 13th* series, I calculated a very strong positive correlation ($r = .895$) between sequel numbers and the movie's body count.

Over the last few decades, concern has been raised over the fact that repeated exposure to increasing levels of violence in television and movies may make children and adolescents callous and indifferent to violence (Freedman, 2002). The term *desensitization* has been frequently used to describe this phenomenon. However, because the term desensitization has been defined differently by different researchers (Anderson, Berkowitz, et al., 2003), two distinctly different effects have been conflated: habituation to *media* violence and desensitization to *real-world* violence.

Habituation to Media Violence

The *habituation to media violence effect* refers to a decreased level of responsiveness to *media violence* as a result of repeated viewings of violent *media* images. Presumably, the first violent act on television that children see will produce greater effects than when children watch an act of televised violence for the 100th time. For instance, initially a fight televised during the *Power Rangers* might grasp the undivided attention of a child and create feelings of excitement and physiological arousal. After repeated viewings of similar *Power Ranger* battles, however, such acts of violence may become less interesting and exciting to the child and produce less pronounced heart rate and blood pressure elevation (or none at all).

Desensitization to Real-World Violence

In contrast, the *desensitization to real-world violence effect* refers to a decreased level of responsiveness to *real-world* violence as a result of repeated exposure to *media* violence. Thus, as a consequence of witnessing pretend violence on television, children are thought to become less affected by, and more indifferent and callous to, genuine violence. Consider the following illustration: after repeated exposure to battling aliens in the *Power Rangers,* children who were once upset at seeing two classmates argue and fight are now uncaring and unsympathetic to such real-world, aggression-related occurrences. Moreover, it has been suggested that youth who are desensitized to violence are more likely to engage in violent behavior themselves.

Importance of Discriminating Habituation and Desensitization

The difference between the habituation effect and the desensitization effect on children and adolescents is not unimportant. It is one thing to suggest that youth become less responsive to the depictions of media violence; it is quite another to suggest that repeated media violence exposure results in youth becoming less responsive to real-world violence and subsequently, more likely to engage in violent behavior themselves. In terms of immediacy, in comparison to the habituation effect, the desensitization effect is thought to put youth at greater risk for engaging in aggressive behavior. However, the habituation effect is still important to the understanding of childhood aggression. For instance, as youth become more habituated to violence, they may seek out more and more violent imagery to experience the same level of responsiveness (e.g., increased physiological arousal) that once occurred when watching less violent imagery. Thus, similar to drug addicts requiring larger doses to produce the desired effects, so, too, might youth who repeatedly watch violent television (i.e., the "plug-in" drug) require more brutal, shocking, and gruesome acts of violence to hold their attention and generate feelings of interest and excitement. In turn, this exposure to extreme levels of violence increases the risk that the child will act aggressively.

Research on Habituation

Relatively few studies have been conducted on habituation and desensitization effects in children and adolescents. Cline, Croft, and Courrier (1973) found evidence of habituation effects in children between the ages of 7 and 14. After viewing a violent movie, children with a history of high television exposure were less physiologically aroused (i.e., skin conductance, blood volume) than youth with little prior television exposure. To date, no other studies have assessed habituation to violence in children and adolescents.

Research on Desensitization

With regard to desensitization, four primary components can be assessed: *physiological, cognitive, emotional,* and *behavioral.* Physiological desensitization refers to lower levels of physiological arousal (e.g., heart rate) when viewing real-life aggression; cognitive desensitization reflects a change in

Table 10.1   Types of Desensitization

Type	Characteristic
Physiological	Lower levels of physiological arousal when viewing real-life aggression
Cognitive	More positive attitudes towards real-life aggression
Emotional	The blunting of emotional responses when viewing real-life acts of violence
Behavioral	Less likely to intervene in the face of real-world violence

attitudes towards real-life aggressive behavior, such as the development of pro-violence attitudes; emotional desensitization refers to the blunting of emotional responses when viewing real-life acts of violence (what was once shocking is now mundane); and behavioral desensitization refers to changes in behavior when faced with violence, such as a reduction in the amount intervention offered.

Behavioral Desensitization

Drabman and Thomas (1974) found evidence that the viewing of a violent film behaviorally desensitized 3rd- and 4th-grade children to real-life violence. After watching a film, children were required to observe the behavior of two preschool children in another room. To operationalize desensitization, Drabman and Thomas measured the amount of time it took children to seek out adult help when the initially calm play of the children became increasingly disruptive, destructive, and aggressive. Results indicated that in comparison to children viewing a nonviolent film, children viewing a violent film took longer to get aid once the preschooler's behavior began to decompensate. The tolerance for acceptable real-life aggression appeared to have been raised as a result of viewing media violence. This study and a successful replication using slightly older children (4th & 5th graders; Molitor & Hirsch, 1994) provide direct evidence of behavioral desensitization in youth.

Developmental Considerations. In contrast, when using a slightly younger sample of children (2nd & 3rd graders), Horton and Santogrossi (1978) failed to replicate the findings of Drabman and Thomas (1974). It is worth noting, however, that in Horton's study, participants heard anti-aggressive, non-aggressive, or neutral comments during the viewing of the violent film. It is possible that the comments acted as a form of mediation, thereby reducing the effect of the violence. However, it may be that age influences desensitization. In a replication of their earlier study, Thomas and Drabman (1975) found evidence of desensitization (i.e., slower to summon help) for 3rd graders but not for 1st graders (who were generally slow, regardless of condition). The authors suggest that the social immaturity of the 1st graders, and their general inexperience in being in positions of responsibility, may have contributed to their slow reaction times. Together, these studies suggest that in comparison to older children, younger children may be less likely to become behaviorally desensitized to televised violence. The reasons for such differences have yet to be firmly established and thus require additional investigation.

Physiological Desensitization

Thomas, Horton, Lippincott, and Drabman (1977) replicated and extended the study by Cline et al. (1973). However, instead of measuring habituation effects, physiological desensitization effects were assessed. In this study, the methodology used was identical to that of Drabman and Thomas (1974) with one major exception: the dependent variable in the new study was the children's overall level of physiological arousal, as indicated by *galvanic skin response* (GSR). GSR measures levels of physiological arousal by determining the resistance of the skin to a small electrical current. Higher skin resistance indicates lower levels of arousal, whereas low skin resistance indicates higher levels of arousal. Thomas et al. (1977) found that when viewing preschool petulance on a video monitor, children who had previously viewed the violent film clip were less aroused than youth who had viewed the nonviolent segment beforehand: physiological desensitization had occurred.

Cognitive and Emotional Desensitization

More recently, Funk, Bechtoldt-Baldacci, Pasold, and Baumgardner (2004) investigated cognitive and emotional desensitization to real-world violence as a function of previous media violence consumption. In this study, 4th and 5th graders' television and movie violence exposure, violent video game play, and witnessing of real-world violence were used to predict empathy (to assess emotional desensitization) and attitudes towards violence (to assess cognitive desensitization). Patterns of cognitive and emotional desensitization were found. Youth with a history of violent video game play or violent movie exposure reported greater pro-violence attitudes. Moreover, higher levels of violent video game consumption were associated with lower levels of empathy. Television violence consumption, however, did not predict either form of desensitization.

Limitations of the Desensitization Research

Research on desensitization has almost entirely been limited to children in grade school. In fact, not a single, television-based desensitization study has been conducted on adolescents. In the desensitization literature on children, effects have only been shown for older elementary school children. Thus, developmental issues may mediate the process of desensitization. Given the paucity of research, however, additional research is necessary to see whether desensitization effects vary as a function of age or the type of desensitization assessed (i.e., cognitive, behavioral, emotional, physiological).

Summary

- Even if children are prevented from watching violent television shows, they may be exposed to televised violence during commercials.
- Movie viewing differs from television viewing in the following ways: movies are viewed on much larger screens than television; there are more likely to be others present when watching a movie than when watching television; and movies are not interrupted by commercials. The effects of these differences on aggression in youth are unknown.
- Violence on children's television is often glamorized, with acts of violence being performed by attractive, charismatic, and young perpetrators. Although theoretically, glamorized violence should produce larger effects than unglamorized violence, there is little research on the topic. Additionally, developmental changes in the factors that youth consider to be glamorous have yet to be assessed.
- Significant amounts of televised violence depict justified violence. Youth who perceive violence on television as justified report engaging in more violence than others.
- The viewing of fantasy violence is associated with increases in the acceptance of justified violence. The viewing of realistic violence is linked with a decreased acceptance. Contrast effects may explain this difference.
- Young children view unpunished aggression as justifiable and punished aggression as unjustifiable. In older children, aggression in response to provocation is considered justifiable.
- Few correlational studies have assessed the impact of live-action television on preschoolers. One of the few studies conducted found that the viewing of violent adult-oriented violent television programs was associated with higher levels of peer-related aggression.
- Exposure to television violence in middle childhood has been shown to be related to current and subsequent levels of peer-nominated aggression. However, when gender is taken into consideration, the findings become less consistent across studies.

- Experimental research in early and middle childhood indicates that in the context of play, children imitate aggressive behaviors seen on television.
- Correlational and quasi-experimental research indicate that during adolescence, violent television consumption is associated with increased levels of self-reported aggressive behavior. Experimental research on delinquents indicates that violent television can increase aggression behavior.
- Research suggesting that the introduction of violent television in the town of "Notel" caused an increase in aggressive behavior is significantly flawed.
- Few studies have assessed the influence of violent television on indirect aggression.
- In general, viewing television violence tends to lead to more positive attitudes towards the use of violence.
- The expression of joy when watching violent media may indicate a greater willingness to act aggressively in young children.
- Violent television does not appear to increase children's aggressive fantasies.
- Independent of violent television viewing, identifying with aggressive characters is linked with aggressive behavior.
- Television violence may influence memory after a certain threshold of hostility or anger is reached.
- The viewing of television violence has been shown to lead to more aggressive responding on projective tests.
- Desensitization and habituation to media violence are different constructs. Youth can be desensitized behaviorally, cognitively, emotionally, and physiologically. Research on children indicates that repeated exposure to television violence can cause each of these. Additional research on adolescents is needed.
- The following methodological concepts were introduced: natural experiment, floor effects, and method variance.

11

Playing With the Beast

Violent Video Games

Click. Click. Boom! Blood splatters and the bodies hit the floor. During violent video game play, gun-related deaths are virtual. In real life, gun-related deaths are all too real. From Jonesboro, AR to Littleton, CO to Erfurt, Germany, youth have tragically taken the lives of their classmates—youth who had a penchant for violent video games. Erik Harris and Dylan Klebold, the teenagers who committed the atrocities at Columbine High School, preferred the violent video game *Doom*, and even designed additional levels for the game (i.e., "The Harris Levels"). But contrary to urban mythology, the levels were not based on the floor plan of Columbine High School (Snopes.com, 2004).

It is the association between real-life tragedy and violent video game play that has focused the attention of the world on the effects of violent video game play on youth. For instance, several of the leading researchers in the field recently testified at a U.S. Senate Commerce Committee hearing about the deleterious effects of violent video games on children and adolescents (e.g., Anderson, 2000; Funk, 2000). In Germany, virtualized human deaths violate decency standards. As such, when a humanoid figure is shot during a video game, springs spurt forth as an indication that a robot was deactivated, as opposed to a virtual human life being taken. In Australia, violent video games deemed unsuitable for public use are "refused classification," that is, banned; not even adults can buy them. For instance, in 2004

Manhunt was banned, in part because of "scenes of blood and gore that go beyond strong" (Office of Film and Literature Classification, 2004, p. 1). Although illegal, video games that are refused classification can still be purchased in classified ads, a black market of sorts (O'Brien, 2004).

The Popularity of Violent Video Games

For nearly 30 years, playing video games has been one of the preferred leisure activities of youth. Currently, video game sales gross over $10 billion annually (Richtel, 2005). The popularity of violent video games in particular cannot be overstated. In 1993, sales of the violent fighting video game *Street Fighter II* exceeded $1.5 billion. The historical preference for violence in video games is also revealed by the following statistic: the bloody version of *Mortal Kombat* sold seven times more units than the less violent version of the same game (Goldstein, 1999). Today, violent video games are still a driving force in the industry. During October, 2004, *Grand Theft Auto: San Andreas* sold over two million units in just five days. Shortly thereafter, *Halo 2* sold 2.4 million copies on its first day of release (Morris, 2004).

Teaching Kids to Kill

Lt. Col. Dave Grossman contends that violent video games, and in particular, violent video games involving light guns (i.e., guns that look like real guns and function by pulling a trigger), teach children how to kill, remove the natural hesitancy associated with killing, and provide youth with a will to kill (Grossman & DeGaetano, 1999). Is Lt. Col. Grossman correct? As the following review will reveal, there are noteworthy links between violent video game play and aggressive behavior in youth. However, the vast majority of research has focused on children or late adolescents (i.e., college students). In fact, no experimental studies have assessed the influence of violent video games on aggression during the age periods (i.e., early and middle adolescence) associated with school shootings (Kirsh, 2003). With regard to *killing*, there is no experimental or correlational data on youth to back Grossman and DeGaetano's (1999) sensationalistic claims. In this chapter, the research that has been conducted on children and adolescents will be evaluated. Moreover, the areas of research requiring additional investigation will be identified.

Video Game Eras and Video Game Violence

As Gentile and Anderson (2003) aptly point out, when assessing the impact of violent video games on youth, the technology involved in game play cannot be ignored. To that end, a brief overview of the technological advances in violent video game realism, associated graphic quality, and level of depicted violence is necessary. Gentile and Anderson divided the history of video games into three eras based on the dominant video game console of the time: Atari (1977–1985), Nintendo (1985–1995), and Sony (1995–present).

Atari Era: Abstract Violence

Video games of the Atari Era were simplistic by today's standards. At that time, "state of the art" meant abstract blips, stick figures, and crudely rendered space craft. Video games such as *Missile Command* and *Asteroids* were considered to be "violent" because they portrayed smaller blips destroying larger blips. With its chasing down and munching of dots and blue ghosts, *Pac Man* was considered to be a low-level violent video game (Cooper & Mackie, 1986; Dominick, 1984). During the Atari Era, stick-like representations of human beings rarely attacked other stick-like representations. That would soon change.

Nintendo Era: Increasing Realism

With the onset of the Nintendo Era came better graphics, better sound, an increase in the level of violence, and the frequent spilling of virtual blood. Moreover, the playing of video games in arcades, which dominated the Atari Era, began to be replaced with home-based play on dedicated consoles or personal computers (Buchman & Funk, 1996). It was during the Nintendo Era that abstract fighting and shooting was replaced by more realistic and graphic violence. Fighting games, such as the much-maligned *Street Fighter,* and shooting games, such as *Virtua Cop,* portrayed human characters killing other human characters. In the ultra-violent video game series *Mortal Kombat,* the words "Finish him" preceded extreme depictions of brutality and gore, including crimson blood spurting after a decapitation, a torso being ripped in half, and a spine being torn from the body in which it once resided.

Sony Era: Lifelike Violence

Ten years ago, Sony introduced the PlayStation video game console; the Sony Era was upon us. The original PlayStation quickly became the world's number one selling video game console, a ranking that its successor, PlayStation 2, currently holds today. The continuing widespread popularity of video games can be seen in the number of consoles sold by Sony. The original PlayStation console sold 20 million units worldwide. But its more powerful heir, PlayStation 2, has currently sold over 70 million units, with thousands of additional sales occurring daily (Becker, 2004). The more than tripling of Sony video game console sales can be attributed, in large part, to improvements in the game's processing speed, graphics, sound, and realistic representation of the human form. Consider the following statistic related to the computerized processing of polygons per second (pg/s; a measure of graphics quality). Whereas the original PlayStation console processed 350,000 pg/s, PlayStation 2 consoles can process 66 million pg/s. Such technological advances have allowed for more realistic representations of violent characters and their violent actions (Gentile & Anderson, 2003).

Types of Violent Video Games

Griffiths (1999) identified nine different types of video games: sport simulations (e.g., golf, baseball), racers (e.g., motor sports), adventures (e.g., fantasy rescue), puzzlers (e.g., brainteasers), platformers (e.g., jump to and from platforms), platform blasters (e.g., platformer with shooting), beat 'em ups (e.g., games with punching and kicking), shoot 'em ups (e.g., shooting and killing with weapons), and weird games (i.e., games that do not fit other categories). Violence can be found in virtually every video game genre mentioned above. Even puzzlers and weird games have the potential to be violent. For instance, in the video game *Typing of the Dead,* in order to kill bloodthirsty zombies and avoid being bitten, the gamer must correctly type a series of letters or words in a specified time period. With each correct letter typed, bullets tear into the flesh of a zombie, releasing copious amounts of blood and tissues. (See Table 11.1.)

First and Third Person Perspective Violent Video Games

In addition to video game genre, the manner in which the gamer controls the virtual character is worth noting. The two main orientations of character control are based on first person and third person perspectives. Each of these will be discussed in turn.

Table 11.1   Video Game Genres

Genre	Example
Racers	Grand Turismo 4, Ford Racing 2
Sport Simulations	MVP Baseball, Tiger Woods PGA Tour
Adventures	The Legend of Zelda, Starfox Adventures
Puzzlers	Snood, The Qube
Platformers	Sonic the Hedgehog, Super Mario Brothers
Platform Blasters	Prince of Persia, Gunstar Heroes
Beat 'em Ups	Mortal Kombat: Deception, WWE: SmackDown!
Shoot 'em Ups	Doom, Half-Life 2
Weird Games	The Sims, Zoo Tycoon

First Person Shooter: Multi-tiered Environment (FPS-MTE)

In FPS-MTE video games, the gamer "sees" the virtual environment from the perspective of the character. The primary character element that is visible to the gamer is the gun being held in the character's hand. In essence, the game is played as though you were looking down the barrel of a gun. Popular video games in this genre include *Wolfenstein, Quake,* and *Doom.* The object of most FPS-MTE videos games is to escape from a multi-tiered environment (often referred to as "levels"). As you attempt to complete each level, essentials such as deadlier weapons, food and health supplies, and extra lives can be obtained. Deadly monsters and enemies lurk around every corner, waiting to kill or be killed. With each completed level, a new layout appears, as do new monsters and bad guys.

First Person Shooter: Rail (FPS-R)

Unlike the free-ranging movements associated with FPS-MTE games, in FPS-R games, the character moves about the virtual environment as though it were tied to a rail. The game, rather than the gamer, dictates where the virtual character will go. The goal of FPS-R games is to shoot the enemy before the enemy shoots or bites or otherwise maims and kills the avatar (the video character controlled by the gamer). Popular rail games featuring extreme levels of violence include *Silent Scope, House of the Dead (I, II, III),* and the arcade version of *Area 51.* With their quick pace and rapid-fire shooting, the body count in FPS-R games quickly builds into the hundreds. Because the movement of the virtual character is controlled by the computer, FPS-R games are likely to involve the use of a light gun. When using a light gun, the shooter lines up the sights of the gun on the onscreen target, holds the gun as if it were a real gun, and assumes a shooting stance. Thus, the use of a replica gun adds an element of realism that is missing in controller and mouse-based shooting games.

In an effort to increase gun sales to youth, gun manufacturers such as Colt, Browning, and Remington began marketing name brand, first person shooter video games to youth. Ironically, the video games did not sell well because they were not violent enough (Hardy, 2002). Despite the contention that such activities train children and adolescents to use real weapons, as well as increase their desire to seek out weaponry (Grossman & DeGaetano, 1999), there is no empirical research on the topic. However, given the fact that gun safety programs featuring admonitions against gun use consistently fail (Hardy, 2002), it is possible that the use of virtual guns in video games may increase the lure of real guns. This area is in dire need of research.

Third Person Shooting and Fighting (TPSF)

In TPSF games, the gamer sees the entire video game character (or space-craft) and the virtual world from a vantage point above, behind, or to the side of the character. Games in this genre include *Hitman, Grand Theft Auto,* and *Max Payne.* For some video games, such as *Star Wars: Jedi Knight,* it is possible to toggle the video game between first and third person perspectives. An additional characteristic of TPSF video games is that gamers get to choose the avatars that they will be controlling. The gamer can choose the abilities, race, gender, and overall look of his or her character. Secret characters are often "hidden" within the game, characters who can only be "unlocked" for use after the gamer has reached a certain level of killing proficiency.

Subgenres of Violent Video Games

Within first and third person violent video games, distinct subgenres exist. What differentiates these games is the emphasized aspect of game play. The three most popular subgenres are *stealth, survival-horror,* and *tactical.* Stealth-based video games (e.g., *Tenchu*) focus on avoiding detection by opponents and silent killing. Here, the mantra is "kill before you are seen." Survival-horror games, such as *Resident Evil,* require the killing of a large number of demonic creatures in a virtual environment reminiscent of a horror film. In survival-horror games, you kill anything that moves, with the occasional exception of a "victim/hostage." Tactical video games emphasize team-based tactics and carrying out a variety of "missions." Unlike the survival-horror genre, killing alone is not enough to be successful in these types of video games; instead, missions need to be accomplished. The United States Army has developed its own tactical video game, *America's Army*. Other games include *Rainbow Six* and *Ghost Recon*. Tactical video games have become extremely popular to play online, either fighting alone or as a team against multiple players.

Online, Multiplayer Violent Video Games

Thousands of players can play together online in a forum known as a massively multiplayer online role-playing game (MMORPG). Research has yet to address the impact of multiplayer gaming on youthful aggression. Given that MMORPG is a growing trend, with several hundred thousand users paying monthly for this type of online video game experience (Gentile & Anderson, 2003), future research should investigate the influence of MMORPG on youth. Does cooperation during nonviolent and violent video games differentially affect aggressive behavior? Does the cooperative nature of MMORPG game play impact aggressive behavior to a greater or lesser extent than solo playing of the same violent video games? What role does development play in the impact of MMORPG on children's and adolescents' aggressiveness? These questions are in need of answering.

The Effects of Violent Video Games on Youth as a Function of Video Game Era and Game Type

Over the past 30 years, violent video games have become more violent and realistic in their representation of violence, a fact that has research implications. For instance, the "violent" video games of the Atari Era would be considered minimally violent or even nonviolent today. Starting in the Nintendo Era, however, the violence depicted in video games became increasingly realistic. Thus, differences in the comparative disparity between the level of violence depicted in violent and nonviolent video games became greater with each successive era (Gentile & Anderson, 2003). By today's standards, Atari Era "violent video game" research pitted mildly violent (or nonviolent) video games against nonviolent video games. In contrast, research conducted during the Sony Era assessed the effects of very violent video games versus nonviolent video games. Given such differences, it is important to evaluate the effects of violent video games on youth as a function of the era in which the research was conducted.

Correlational Research

Atari and Nintendo Eras

During the Atari Era, not a single study was conducted that directly assessed the association between *violent* video game play and aggression. Instead, the studies that were conducted investigated the association between *video game play* in general and aggressive behavior. In these studies, the total amount of video game play (i.e., regardless of the presence of violent content) was correlated with aggression. For instance, Dominick (1984) found that during early adolescence, time spent in video arcades was positively correlated with aggression and delinquency, but home video game play was not. Similarly, Kestenbaum and Weinstein (1985) found that the amount of time and money spent in arcades during early adolescence positively correlated with delinquency and negatively correlated with frustration tolerance.

Similar to Atari Era research, correlational research conducted during the Nintendo Era investigated the relationship between total video game play and aggression. Once again, associations between violent video game play and aggression were not assessed. Similar to the Atari Era, different effects were identified for home and arcade video game play. For instance, using a sample of 11- to 17-year-olds, Fling et al. (1992) found a positive association between video game play and aggressive behavior. In contrast, Lin and Lepper (1987) found that aggressive behavior among 4th- through 6th-grade boys was related to the frequent playing of video games in arcades, but not to playing at home.

Sony Era

The recognition that not all youth who play video games play violent video games led to research during the Sony Era that focused specifically on violent video game play and its subsequent effect on youth.

Research on Children. In one of the few studies conducted on children, Funk and colleagues (2004) found that for 150 4th- and 5th-grade students, both violent video game play and the viewing of violent movies were associated with more positive attitudes towards violence. However, Funk, Buchman, Jenks, and Bechtoldt (2003) found that long-term violent video game exposure was unrelated to children's ($N = 66$, ages 5–7 and 8–12) responses to hypothetical vignettes, in which a negative event happens and aggression is a probable next occurrence.

According to *cultivation theory* (Gerbner et al., 1994), heavy exposure to television violence causes youth to (1) perceive the real world to be more violent than in reality, and (2) believe that the likelihood that they will be victimized is greater than it really is. Both of these contentions have been supported by research (Shanahan & Morgan, 1999). Van Mierlo and Van den Bulck (2004) attempted to see if violent video game play also causes cultivation effects. To accomplish this, 322 3rd- through 6th-grade Flemish children's perceptions of real-world crime were correlated with the amount of violent television and violent video game play. Evidence of cultivation effects was found: violent video game play was positively correlated with children's perception of the prevalence of violent crime and the number of police in the workforce. Although cultivation effects were present for violent video games, they were considerably weaker than those observed for violent television.

Research on Adolescents: Aggressive Behavior. The relationship between violent video game play and aggressive behavior during adolescence has produced inconsistent findings, with nearly as many studies failing to find a significant association as those that do. For instance, Funk et al. (2002) failed to find a significant relationship between violent video game play and aggressive emotions and behaviors in 32 15- to 17-year-olds. In contrast, using a sample of over 600 8th- and 9th-grade students, Gentile et al. (2004) found significant positive associations between violent video game play and self-reported arguments with teachers, frequency of physical fights, and overall levels of hostility. Gentile and colleagues then subdivided the sample into the top and bottom quartiles of video game play and the top and bottom quartiles of trait hostility. And when high versus low levels of violent video game play were assessed as a function of high and low levels of trait hostility, some intriguing patterns emerged.

Whereas the greatest percentage of physical fights (63%) were reported by youth with high levels of trait hostility and high levels of violent video game play, the lowest percentage of physical fights (4%) were reported by youth low in trait hostility and low in violent video game play. And youth who were high in only one of these two areas reported fighting at levels in between the other two groups (28% and 38%). Thus, the accumulation of factors associated with aggression (e.g., hostility and video game play) appeared to have a bigger impact on aggressive behavior than either factor alone.

Research on Adolescents: Aggression-Related Constructs. Research on aggression-related constructs has also produced contradictory findings. In an assessment of 2,312 8th graders, Krahé and Möller (2004) found that as either the frequency of violent video game play or the preference for violent video games increased, so too did the acceptance of physical aggression. However, in the same study, the tendency to interpret ambiguous stimuli in terms of aggression and hostility (i.e., a hostile attribution bias) was related to violent video game preference and play in boys, but not girls.

Putting the "Inconsistent" Correlational Findings in Perspective

Atari and Nintendo Era Research. Atari and Nintendo Era research produced inconsistent findings for home- and arcade-based video game play. The fact that the results differed by location supports the contention that an unmeasured, third variable (such as lax parenting) may be accounting for the contradictory findings. Moreover, a potential fatal flaw of Atari and Nintendo Era "violent" video game research is that *violent* video game play was not independently assessed. Thus, it is impossible to determine whether video game play in general (regardless of content) or violent video games were responsible for the significant correlations. However, recent research suggests that the greatest amount of violent video game play occurs in youth who play video games the most. For instance, for Sony Era youth, Krahé and Möller (2004) found an incredible correlation of .98 between the frequency of total video game play and the frequency of violent video game play. As intriguing as this finding might be, there are no data available to confirm that a similar correlation exists for the Atari and Nintendo Eras.

Sony Era Research. There are some who would argue that the failure to consistently connect violent video game play with aggression indicates that violent video games have no effect on youth (Freedman, 2002; Jones, 2002). I disagree. First, statistical *power* is an important consideration. Power refers to the probability that a significant difference will be found when such a difference actually exists. Moreover, as power levels increase, so too does the likelihood of finding real statistical differences. Small samples tend to have low power, thereby reducing the likelihood of establishing statistical significance. In the violent video game literature, the correlational studies that failed to connect violent video game play with aggression more often than not had small sample sizes and relatively little power. Thus, even if an association between violent video game play and aggression was present, the samples lacked the power to detect it.

Second, developmental and gender issues may be influencing the results. To date, correlational studies involving 8th-grade boys have always produced significant correlations, but the findings for 8th-grade girls and either younger or older youth have been less consistent. The reason for this pattern is unclear. Perhaps 8th-grade boys are more vulnerable to the effects of violent video games than other youth.

Third, in the six descriptive studies reviewed above, six different dependent variables were assessed. The effects of violent video game play may not uniformly influence all aspects of aggressive behavior and aggression-related constructs in the same way.

Fourth, characteristics of violent video game play have been overlooked. For instance, the extant body of research has failed to assess the associations among first person perspective video game play, third person perspective video game play, and aggression. Additionally, the effects of video game sub-genres (e.g., tactical, horror, stealth) on aggression remain untested, as does the systematic assessment of differing amounts of violence and gore.

Finally, longitudinal studies assessing the impact of violent video game play on youth are lacking. Such studies could investigate the influence of varying lengths of violent video game play (e.g., one year, two years, five years) on aggression. An additional study of interest would be to assess the relationship between the age of children when they first start playing violent video games and subsequent aggressive behavior. Clearly, more research is needed to resolve these issues.

Experimental Research

The vast majority of experimental research on children and adolescents was conducted during the Atari Era. As you recall, with each successive video game era, violent video games became increasingly more violent and realistic. Thus, the effects of violent video games on children and adolescents were studied *the most* during the era in which violent video games contained *the least* amount of violence.

Atari Era

In total, five experiments involving aggression were conducted: four on children in elementary schools and one using adolescent participants. The violent video games used in these studies included *Missile Command, Pac Man, Space Invaders, Atari Boxing, Gangster Alley, Berzerk,* and games produced by The Arcade Machine (Cooper & Mackie, 1986; Graybill, Kirsch, & Esselman, 1985; Graybill, Strawniak, Hunter, & O'Leary, 1987; Silvern & Williamson, 1987; Winkel, Novak, & Hopson, 1987). Each of these studies involved abstract or blip-like aggression. For instance, in *Atari Boxing* the gamer looks down upon black and white depictions of two circles (the heads) connected to L-shaped arms and circular boxing gloves; bodies were missing.

Of the five studies conducted, only two studies found evidence of significant differences in aggression as a function of violent video game content.

Silvern and Williamson (1987) conducted an interesting field experiment involving the effects of cartoon violence and video game violence on aggressive and prosocial behavior in preschoolers. The experiment, which took place over a three-day period, involved the assessment of baseline aggression during dyadic play with a classmate, the viewing of the humorously violent *Road Runner* cartoon, and the playing of the violent video game *Space Invaders*. Following violent media consumption, children were observed in a free play session with the toys that were available during the baseline assessment of aggression. Dependent variables included the amount of aggressive and prosocial behavior and fantasy play. A total score of aggression was created by tallying incidents of peer-related physical and verbal aggression and the frequency of object-oriented aggression. Relative to baseline levels of response, after playing the violent video game, preschoolers demonstrated higher rates of aggressive behavior and lower rates of prosocial behavior during free play. Fantasy play was unrelated to video game play.

Cooper and Mackie (1986) assigned 4th- and 5th-grade youth to play one of two video games (1) the aggressive *Missile Command* or (2) the less aggressive *Pac Man*. Youth were assigned to a control condition in which they were required to solve pencil-and-paper maze problems. Following the experimental manipulation, children engaged in free play for eight minutes, during which aggressive and nonaggressive toys were made available. Then, youth were asked to assign one of three punishments (e.g., not allowed outside, restricted TV, or being sent to room) to a child who had misbehaved. The amount of punishment administered was indicated by the length of time that the children pushed a red buzzer. For girls, aggressive toys were played with the most following violent video game play. Violent video game play did not impact the boys' toy choice. For both genders, the type or amount of punishment and the length of time it was administered were unaffected by violent video game play.

Graybill and colleagues conducted two studies on the impact of violent video games on aggressive responding in 2nd-, 4th-, and 6th-grade children. In the first study, children were exposed to either a violent (*Atari Boxing*) or a nonviolent (*Atari Basketball*) video game. In the later study, children played one of six Atari video games (three violent and three nonviolent), which were equated for difficulty, excitement, and enjoyment. Both studies failed to show deleterious effects on youth from playing violent video games. In the first study, aggressive responses to the Rosenzweig Picture-Frustration Study (RPFS, which measures aggressive fantasizing in response to being frustrated) was unaffected by violent or nonviolent video game play (Graybill et al., 1985). Graybill and colleagues replicated the non-significant findings for the RPFS in a separate study published two years later. Additionally, the latter

Graybill study found that violent video game play did not impact children's willingness to help or hurt a child playing a game in a different room (Graybill et al., 1987).

Finally, in an assessment of 8th-grade boys and girls, heart rate and aggressive behavior (as measured by monetary deductions for mistakes in a "teacher-learner" situation) were unaffected by violent video game play (Winkel et al., 1987).

Nintendo Era

Only two experimental studies were conducted on youth during the Nintendo Era. Both involved third person perspective fighting games and both found that violent video games increased aggressive play in children. The first study assessed the impact of playing a violent video game (*Karateka*) and a nonviolent video game (*Jungle Hunt*) on the free play behavior of 30 children between the ages of 5 and 7. *Karateka* is a hitting and kicking fighting game. *Jungle Hunt* involves swinging a character from vine to vine in an attempt to avoid falling. Within gender, children were randomly placed into pairs. Both partners played a video game five minutes and watched their partner play a video game for five minutes. Next, participants were placed in a room with a Bobo doll dressed in a makeshift karate-gi, a toy jungle swing, and assorted stuffed animals and books. Results indicated that both groups of children imitated many of the behaviors portrayed in the game. Children playing *Karateka* displayed significantly more aggressive actions (i.e., hitting) towards the doll and the other child. Moreover, swinging behavior during play was more likely to occur for youth playing *Jungle Hunt* than *Karateka*.

In relation to violent or nonviolent video game exposure, Irwin and Gross (1995) assessed heart rate, toy choice (aggressive vs. nonaggressive), and physical and verbal aggression towards people and objects during free play. Moreover, following the experimental manipulation and subsequent free play period, the authors assessed aggressive behavior towards a confederate in response to being frustrated. In this study, 60 boys were randomly assessed to play the violent video game *Double Dragon* or the nonviolent video game *Excitebike*. Following solitary video game play, the child was escorted to a play room where a confederate 8-year-old boy was waiting. Ten minutes of dyadic free play ensued. Next, both boys participated in a coloring contest to win a dollar. The contest was rigged so that the confederate, who was boasting and bragging along the way, would win. Aggressive behavior was observed during the coloring contest. The results indicated that heart rate and toy choice (e.g., swords, action figures, yoyos) did not vary by video game condition. However, boys playing *Double Dragon* engaged in more acts of object-oriented, physical, and verbal aggression and more acts of verbal aggression towards the confederate during free play than boys playing *Excitebike*. Additionally, during the frustration task, boys who had previously played the violent video game were more likely to engage in physical aggression towards the confederate than boys who had played the nonviolent video game. The authors state that many of these actions appeared to be "direct imitations" of the aggressive actions enacted in the video game, and the verbal aggression that occurred primarily happened in the context of "fantasy play." Although the aggressive actions occurring during free play were more likely to be instances of aggressive play than aggressive behavior, the same cannot be said for the acts of aggression displayed during the frustration task. Here, the behavior seemed to be indicative of aggressive behavior and not aggressive play. However, a relatively small number of youth playing the violent video game (23%) acted aggressively during the frustration task. Clearly, some children were more affected by violent video game play than others.

Sony Era

Kirsh (1998) investigated the effects of playing violent versus nonviolent video games on the interpretation of ambiguous provocation situations. In such stories, a same-sex child is negatively provoked (e.g., a child returns from the bathroom to find his favorite toy broken), but the intent of the provocateur is unclear. Participants were 52 3rd- and 4th-grade children. Children played either a very violent video game, *Mortal Kombat II*, or a relatively nonviolent video game, *NBA JAM: TE,* for 13 minutes. *Mortal Kombat II* involves rounds of hand-to-hand combat between two martial artists with the winner proceeding to the next round. *NBA JAM: TE* is a two-on-two basketball game. Following video game play, children were read five ambiguous provocation stories. After each story, children were asked a series of questions about the peer's intent, subsequent actions, and whether the peer should be punished and how much. Responses were coded in terms of amount of negative and violent content. Results indicated that children playing the violent video game responded more negatively on three of the five ambiguous provocation story questions than children playing the nonviolent video game. For instance, when asked why the child in the story was provoked and what the child should do after being provoked, children playing the violent video game responded significantly more negatively than children playing the nonviolent video game. Additionally, children playing *Mortal Kombat II* were more likely than children playing *NBA JAM: TE* to state that the peer disliked the provoked child.

Funk et al. (2003) assessed aggressive responses to hypothetical vignettes following violent and nonviolent video game play. Thirty-one 5- to 7-year-old children played the violent video game *Earthworm Jim: New Junk City* or the nonviolent video game *Croc: Legend of the Gobbos*. Thirty-five 8- to 12-year-olds played either the violent video game *Terra Nova* or the non-violent video game *Marble Drop*. Aggressive responding did not differ for youth playing the violent and nonviolent video games. Funk et al. describe the video game violence in this research as "relatively benign."

In this study, the violent video game *Terra Nova* was rated T (13 years +) and *Earthworm Jim* was rated E (6 years +). In contrast, Kirsh (1998) used a video game rated M (17 years +). Moreover, as opposed to *Mortal Kombat II*, the violence in *Terra Nova* does not involve humanoid figures. Instead, a plane shoots weaponry at invading spacecraft. It may be that certain levels of violence, and certain types of violence (e.g., humanoid), are necessary to influence aggressive responding to hypothetical scenarios.

Important Issues Related to Experimental Research

In this next section, issues relevant to the interpretation of the aforementioned studies will be presented. Additionally, research questions in need of answering will be forwarded.

Graphics and Game Type. Experimental research using Atari Era games has produced mixed results, with more studies finding *no* effect of violent video game exposure than studies finding an effect, and those that reached significance may not have been assessing aggressive behavior. Considering the fact that significant differences only emerged during assessments of play and toy choice (and not other measures of aggression), the possibility exists that it was rough-and-tumble play that increased following violent video game play and not aggressive behavior. Thus, there is little experimental evidence that the violence in the first generation of violent video games influenced aggressive behavior.

Is it surprising that so few violent video game effects were evident during the Atari Era? Not really. The graphics were poor, there was no sense of realism to the characterization of the avatar, the violent video games were not very violent, and the difference between "aggressive" and "nonaggressive" games was small. For instance, Cooper and Mackie (1986) asked youth to evaluate the amount of "aggression towards people" in the "violent" video game *Missile Command* and the "less violent" video game *Pac Man*. Out of a possible high score of 8, youth responded with ratings of 4.3 and 3.3, respectively. Two things are noteworthy: first, both video games were rated in the middle of the scale, suggesting that neither was really very violent.

Second, and more important, there were no virtual people in either of those games, so an assessment of the "aggression towards people" is inappropriate. Thus, the fact that respondents identified moderate levels of aggression in those games calls into question the validity of the measure. Youth were also asked to rate the destruction of inanimate objects during the game. Here, the ratings for both video games were in the lower half of the scale. In other words, when measuring the type of violence purportedly occurring during game play, youth did not perceive a high degree of violence.

Of note, all research conducted on children in the Atari Era involved third person fighting and shooting video games. This was not a research oversight. First person video games were not commercially released until the middle of the Nintendo Era. However, not a single study conducted on youth, in either the Nintendo or Sony Eras, assessed the impact of first person shooter games on aggression. This is somewhat surprising given how detrimental to youth these games are thought to be (Grossman & DeGaetano, 1999).

Research on adults suggests that violent, first person video games can influence aggressive responding (e.g., Kirsh, Olczak, & Mounts, in press). However, additional research is necessary to validate the contention that first person video games increase aggression in youth. Moreover, similar to correlational studies, the influence of different subgenres of violent video game play and overall level of violence and gore on aggression has yet to be systematically addressed.

Developmental Issues. When considering violent video game play and aggressive behavior, it is striking how little developmental research has been conducted. During the Nintendo and Sony Eras, only four studies with child participants were conducted. Even more surprising, there were no experimental studies with adolescent participants. Additionally, over the last 20 years, not a single longitudinal study has been conducted and only one study (Funk et al., 2003) has employed a *cross-sectional design*. In a cross-sectional study, children of different ages are assessed at the same time. Differences between age groups are thought to reflect developmental differences.

With ethical reasons in mind, the violent video games used in the Funk and colleagues study differed for the older and younger children, thus making comparison across ages difficult. Ethical concerns are legitimate when conducting media violence research on youth. It is inappropriate to expose children to potential harm that they would not otherwise encounter. However, children over the age of 7 can readily buy M-rated video games (which should only be *sold* to youth 17 and older), and nearly 80% of 13-year-olds have played M-rated games. These data suggest that future research should consider investigating the effects of extremely violent video games on older children and adolescents (Walsh et al., 2003).

Gamer Issues. There are several issues related to the characteristics of the gamer that have yet to be addressed in youth and, therefore, should be investigated in future experimental research. First, how does violent video game play differentially influence those who frequently play such games, in comparison to those who do not? Second, do developmental issues interact with gaming experience to influence short-term experimental effects? Finally, how does youthful perception of video game violence, regardless of actual game violence, influence aggressive responding?

Role of Frustration. Players, especially those new to the game, "die" quickly or get "stuck" and are unable to proceed. The effects of game-related frustration should not be underestimated. There is both theory and research to support the contention that game-related frustration could significantly contribute to aggressive responding following video game play (Dollard et al., 1939). However, few studies involving children and adolescents report perceived level of frustration associated with video game play. It is possible, therefore, that violent and nonviolent games used in previous studies differed in game-related frustration.

Moreover, a completely overlooked area in the violent video game research is the impact of *game-stopping frustration* on participants' aggressive responding. Game-stopping frustration refers to the frustration felt by participants who have to stop playing video games shortly after starting them (see Table 11.2 for length of time participants played video games during experiments). In most instances, youth in experiments play video games for less than 15 minutes, and just when they are getting into the game, they are forced to stop play. The result of stopping game play before children would like to stop could result in frustration (and possible high levels of frustration for some children).

It is hoped that you are thinking to yourself, "Self, would not game-stopping frustration affect both violent and nonviolent games equally?" Yes, assuming that the video games involved are equally exciting and that youth are equally upset about stopping game play. Beyond excitement level, however, there is one thing that violent video games "have" that nonviolent ones do not: parental and governmental disdain. Such disdain creates a "forbidden fruit effect" in adolescents, thereby increasing the desire to consume the media. Youth may be forbidden to play violent video games at home and therefore relish the opportunity to play them in the laboratory. Given that frustration influences aggression, it may be that video game–related

Table 11.2   Length of Time Youth Played Video Games in Experimental
Studies

Study Authors	Length of Time Playing Video Games (in minutes)
Cooper & Mackie (1986)	8
Funk et al. (2003)	15
Graybill et al. (1985)	11
Graybill et al. (1987)	14
Irwin & Gross (1995)	20
Kirsh (1998)	13
Schutte et al. (1988)	5
Silvern & Williamson (1987)	6
Winkel et al. (1987)	10

frustration, as opposed to video game-related violence, is accounting for
increases in aggression.

The Color of Money and Blood. Holding a replica of a snub-nosed revolver
in my hand, I aimed at the monitor in my office, squeezed the trigger, and
watched as a zombie's head exploded in a splatter of green blood. Green
blood? Since when do zombies have green blood? I've seen just about every
zombie movie ever filmed (not that I'm proud of that), and they always spurt
crimson, not green. Fortunately, I was able to download a "blood patch"
from the Internet, and in doing so, became able to toggle the blood from
green to crimson. But why was the blood green in the first place? Is it that
green blood is less violent, gory, or realistic than red blood?

   Research on color suggests that the perceived realism and gore of a video
game might be affected by the color of blood being spilled. After all, whereas
the color red connotes aggression, anger, and rage, the color green evokes
feelings of comfort and relaxation (Boyatzis & Varghese, 1994). Moreover,
humans do not bleed green, so the killings may be perceived as less realistic
and gory. But less violent? Quantitatively, the number of violent acts is
unaffected by a color change. Green or red, the same number of decapitations, arms getting ripped off in a hail of bullets, holes appearing in the middle of torsos, and teeth gnashing into flesh will occur. Thus, the perception
of the level of violence should not change. However, the effect of the color
of virtual blood on gamers' perceptions of violence, realism, gore, and subsequent behavior is an empirical question, and one that has yet to be
assessed. Most likely, green blood is used to increase video game sales. For
instance, in Germany, in order for a video game to avoid violating "decency

standards," which would will limit purchases to those over 18 years of age, virtual blood needs to run green (Pham & Sandell, 2003). As mentioned above, green is a color that induces relaxation and comfort. But do we really want youth feeling comforted and relaxed when blowing things up?

Summary

- Violent video games have been a driving force in the video game industry for decades.
- There is no evidence to support the contentions that violent video games teach children how to kill, remove the natural hesitancy associated with killing, or provide youth with a desire to kill.
- An avatar can be controlled using a first or third person perspective. Within these perspectives, distinct subgenres of violent video games exist, including stealth, survival-horror, and tactical.
- Research has yet to address the impact of online, multiplayer violent video games on youthful aggression.
- There have been three eras of video game play: Atari, Nintendo, and Sony. Over time, violent video games have become increasingly more violent and realistic. Research during the Atari Era assessed the impact of violent video games containing little, if any, violence.
- The effects of violent video games on youth vary in relation to video game era.
- Correlational studies of Atari and Nintendo Eras are flawed because they assessed the relationship between total video game play and aggression and not violent video game play and aggression.
- During the Sony Era, significant correlations were found in children between violent video game play and positive attitudes towards violence. Violent video game play may also lead to cultivation effects in children. Research on adolescents of this era, however, has produced contradictory findings. Potential reasons for these inconsistencies include power, development, gender, and game-related characteristics.
- The effects of violent video games on youth were studied the most during the era in which video games contained the least amount of violence.
- Overall, very few experimental studies have been conducted with children and adolescents as participants: five experimental studies were conducted during the Atari Era, two were conducted during the Nintendo Era, and two were conducted during the Sony Era. Studies from the Nintendo and Sony Eras have demonstrated that violent video games can lead to increases in aggressive play, aggressive behavior, and aggressive thoughts.
- There is no research on the effects of first person shooter video games on children and adolescents. Additional areas in need of research include game-related and game-stopping frustration. It is surprising how little developmental research has been conducted in this area.

PART III

Media Violence and the Concept of Risk

12

Aggressive Behavior

Risk and Protective Factors

During my childhood, when I wasn't feeding tokens into arcade video games or watching grisly horror movies or reading the latest and scariest Stephen King novel, I liked to play games such as *Risk, Battleship,* and *Rock 'Em Sock 'Em Robots.* However, not all of the games that I owned were played with equally, as the games with little violence tended to be played less frequently. One such game, located on the bottom shelf of my bookcase, was the seldom-played Milton Bradley offering *Don't Spill the Beans.* For those not familiar with *Don't Spill the Beans,* the rules of the game are quite simple. Each player starts out with an equal number of plastic beans. One at a time, each player adds a bean to the lid of a covered pot that is precariously balancing on a pair of hands. At some point during the game, a bean will be placed onto the lid that causes the pot to tip over, spilling its contents onto the game's base. The goal of the game is to get rid of your stash of beans without upsetting the pot. I still own a copy of *Don't Spill the Beans,* but it is no longer relegated to a bottom shelf. Instead, the game is prominently displayed on the top shelf of a centrally located bookcase in my office. Although the game itself is far from violent entertainment fare, to me *Don't Spill the Beans* is, and always will be, a symbol of aggression.

Beans and Aggression

How is it possible that such an ostensibly benign game came to be associated with hitting, kicking, and other antisocial acts? When I played *Don't Spill the Beans* as a child, did controversial bean placements result in arguments, the throwing of beans, and the flailing of plastic hands? Did the game itself become a cue for aggression as the result of some bean-related childhood trauma? Were the beans bullet-shaped, thus warranting a need to shoot them out of straws? None of those things happened. Rather, the answer to the question requires an understanding of the related concepts of *risk factors* and *protective factors* for aggression.

Defining Risk and Protection

A risk factor for aggression is any experience or personal characteristic (e.g., temperament, hormonal makeup) that increases the likelihood that an individual will act aggressively in a given situation. For instance, after being insulted, adults are more likely to respond with aggression if they had been in a hot room prior to the altercation (Anderson & Anderson, 1998). In this situation, temperature becomes a risk factor for aggression. In contrast, protective factors are experiences and personal characteristics that decrease the likelihood that aggression will occur in a given situation. In the aforementioned study, a comfortable room temperature reduced the likelihood of aggression following provocation and, therefore, is considered a protective factor. In the game *Don't Spill the Beans,* I like to think of each bean being placed onto the lid as a risk factor for aggression. Any bean coming off the lid, in comparison, would be a protective factor for aggression. And the pot tipping over, well, that is equivalent to an act of aggression.

It is important to recognize that the final bean placed onto the pot that "causes" the pot to tip over actually is not the *cause* of the pot tipping. Instead, it is the *accumulation* of beans that causes the pot to tip. In fact, if all the other beans were removed from the lid, then the last bean added would be a lone bean and the pot would remain upright. Simply put, no one bean causes the pot to tip. And simply put, no one risk factor for aggression causes a child or adolescent to act aggressively. By itself, even the vilest, goriest, and most aggressive video game will not cause youth to aggress. Instead, it is the accumulation of risk factors that leads to an aggressive act. The previous chapters have demonstrated that entertainment violence is a risk factor for aggression. In the current chapter, non-media-related risk factors for and protective factors against aggression are presented.

Table 12.1   Risk Factors for Aggression

Child-Based Risk Factors	Environmental Risk Factors
Genetics	Parenting Styles and Discipline
HPA Axis	Parental Monitoring
HPG Axis	Home Environment
Temperament	Siblings
Attachment	Peers
Developmental Status	Neighborhood

Child Characteristics That Are Risk Factors for Aggression

Are children born "bad to the bone," that is, destined to hurt, maim, and kill others? Early theories of aggression focused on children's contribution to their own aggressive and antisocial behavior. Known as the *child effects model,* this paradigm held that innate characteristics of the child not only caused the child's aggressive behavior, but they engendered punitive reactions from others. In other words, children caused other people to be mean to them. According to this model, regardless of parenting, whether or not a child was aggressive, antisocial, or just plain mean was already determined at birth. Although innate characteristics of the child are no longer viewed as the sole reason for aggressive behavior, child characteristics do influence aggression. In the following section, five such child-based characteristics are addressed: genetics, hormones, temperament, attachment, and developmental status.

Genetics

The results of multiple studies have indicated that genes contribute to aggressive behavior in children and adolescents. For instance, research has shown that identical twins (i.e., monozygotic twins; two siblings with the same genetic material) show greater similarities in their aggressive tendencies than do fraternal twins (i.e., dyzogotic twins; two siblings with 50% of the same genetic material; see Moeller, 2001). However, research does not indicate that genes can cause a child to be "born bad." Instead, genes *predispose* children toward or away from acts of aggression. That is to say, given the same environmental situation, children with a predisposition toward aggression are more likely to act aggressively than children without a predisposition toward aggression. However, environmental experiences can alter the child's genetically predisposed aggressive tendencies, either by increasing them or by decreasing them. For instance, responsive parenting can reduce a child's likelihood of acting aggressively, even when a predisposition towards aggression is present. Thus, genetic predispositions are starting points for aggressive behavior; they are not end point causes for aggressive behavior. Ultimately, the children's level of aggression is determined by the accumulation of all risk factors, not just genetic ones.

Hypothalamic-Pituitary-Adrenal Axis (HPA)

The HPA axis is a network of tissues and glands in which the hypothalamus, pituitary gland, and adrenal gland are the central components (Jacobson & Sapolsky, 1991). In response to stressful situations, the HPA axis releases hormones into the bloodstream (Nelson, 2000). The HPA axis operates in a feedback loop whereby circulating hormones alter HPA activity, either by increasing it or decreasing it. Importantly, these types of feedback loops allow the HPA axis to vary hormone release based on the presence of either short-term or chronic stress.

Cortisol and dehydroepiandrosterone (DHEA) and its sulphated esther, dephydroepiandrosterone sulphate, collectively referred to as DHEA(s), are two of the central hormonal products of the HPA axis. Both cortisol and DHEA(s) are produced in response to similar stressors, such as aggressive confrontation (Parker, Levin, & Lifrak, 1985). However, cortisol and DHEA appear to have different functions within the HPA axis. For instance, whereas cortisol is a potential *neurotoxin*, DHEA has *neuroprotectant* properties. Neurotoxins are substances that damage and kill neurons, and neuroprotectants do the opposite; they prevent harm to important cells found within the central nervous system. In fact, DHEA may help directly ameliorate the neurotoxic properties of cortisol. For instance, DHEA is thought to mitigate the negative effects that cortisol has on memory (i.e., cortisol increases forgetting) and emotionality (i.e., cortisol is associated with increased feelings of anxiety; Majewska, 1995). Furthermore, during stressful encounters, DHEA release becomes dissociated from cortisol release, with cortisol levels increasing and DHEA levels decreasing (Schwartz, 2002).

Research on basal cortisol levels indicates that children without psychopathology produce higher levels of cortisol than individuals with oppositional deviant disorder (ODD) and conduct disorder (CD) (Flinn & England, 1995; Moss, Vanyukov, & Martin, 1995). Similarly, research on basal DHEA(s) suggests that individuals without psychopathology produce lower levels of basal DHEA(s) than individuals with CD and ODD (Dmitrieva,

Oades, Hauffa, & Eggers, 2001; van Goozen, Matthys, Cohen-Kettenis, Thijssen, & von Engeland, 1998). More recently, research suggests that *relative* differences between DHEA and cortisol release may play an important role in aggression. For instance, Granger, Booth, and Shirtcliff (under review) have shown that individuals with the greatest amount of cortisol relative to DHEA were the most antisocial. Thus, children and adolescents predisposed to produce lower levels of cortisol and higher levels of DHEA (i.e., a low cortisol to DHEA ratio) may be less likely to engage in aggression than youth without the beneficial cortisol to DHEA ratio.

In summary, normal youth and youth with disruptive behavior disorders (DBD) present with opposite patterns of HPA axis functioning. Normal youth show lower levels of DHEA and higher levels of cortisol than individuals with DBD. In direct opposition, youth with DBD show higher levels of DHEA and lower levels of cortisol than children and adolescents without psychopathology involving aggressive outbursts.

Throughout childhood and adolescence HPA axis activity changes. Convergent evidence from both cross-sectional and longitudinal studies indicates that basal levels of cortisol rise during adolescence (Lupie, King, Meaney, & McEwen, 2001; Walker et al., 2001). For instance, Walker et al. (2001) found that the cortisol levels (µg/dL) of 17-year-olds were greater than twice the level of 11- and 12-year-olds. Similarly, basal DHEA(s) sharply increases with the onset of adrenarche (i.e., increased production of adrenal androgens that generally occurs between ages 6 and 9), peaking between ages 25 and 30 (Granger, Schwartz, Booth, Curran, & Zakaria, 1999; Yen & Laughlin, 1998).

Hypothalamic-Pituitary-Gonadal Axis (HPG)

Similar to the HPA axis, the HPG axis involves the hypothalamus and the pituitary gland. However, in place of the adrenal glands, the gonads complete the HPG axis. Initially active during fetal and early infant development, the HPG axis reactivates with the onset of puberty (i.e., gonadarche). Gonadarche begins at approximately ages 10 and 11 for boys and between ages 8 and 10 for girls (with African American girls beginning gonadarche on average one year earlier than white girls; Herman-Giddens et al., 1997). One of the central hormones of the HPG axis is testosterone (T). Levels of T increase dramatically across puberty for males (i.e., approximately 18 times prepubertal levels) as well as increasing, albeit to a much lesser extent, for females (approximately two times prepubertal levels; Nottelmann et al., 1987).

Levels of circulating T have been associated with aggressive behavior. Although research involving animals consistently finds positive associations between T levels and aggressive behavior, research on humans is more controversial (Book, Starzyk, & Quinsey, 2001). For instance, research on adolescent boys and girls has failed to find significant differences in T between aggressive and nonaggressive prepubertal and early adolescent youth (Brooks-Gunn & Warren, 1989; Halpern, Udry, Campbell, & Suchindran, 1993). In contrast, Olweus (1986) found a significant positive correlation between T levels and aggressive responding to provocation in 15- to 17-year-old boys. Additional studies have shown negative relationships between T and behavior problems (Schaal, Tremblay, Soussignan, & Susman, 1996; Susman et al., 1987). In a recent meta-analysis, Book et al. (2001) identified a significant, albeit weak, positive relationship between T and aggression. The strongest relationship between T and aggression was found for individuals between the ages of 13 and 20.

Aggression and General Underarousal

In addition to HPA and HPG differences mentioned above, aggressive youth have lower resting heart rates, lower skin conductance (indicating lower arousal), and lower levels of neurotransmitters associated with the inhibition of emotional behavior (i.e., serotonin). Simply put, aggressive children tend to be physiologically underaroused. In fact, it has been hypothesized that physiologically underaroused youth seek out environmentally arousing experiences and act impulsively in an attempt to stimulate the central nervous system. Thus, underarousal may be associated with increased levels of aggressive behavior because acts of aggression stimulate the central nervous system (Moeller, 2001).

It is important to note that although physiological indicators of underarousal are biological in nature, they are not biological determinations of behavior; instead, they are biological predispositions for behavior. In fact, long-term exposure to stress has been shown to alter physiological functioning. Consider the following: for normal children, stress increases the release of cortisol (a neurotoxin). In response to chronically high levels of cortisol in the blood, a defense mechanism against the effects of long-term stress is activated. Specifically, the HPA axis becomes chronically underaroused, thus reducing daily levels of stress-related hormones (and their potential negative effects). Although underarousal may be a significant contributor to aggression, it reduces day-to-day feelings of anxiety. Thus, underarousal may be "beneficial" to chronically stressed youth because it reduces the negative physiological and psychological effects of being in a state of constant anxiety (e.g., having neurotoxins constantly circulating in the bloodstream). However, as a result of a basal change in HPA axis functioning, these children become hyper-aggressive. Additional research has shown that underarousal is associated with a lack of an empathetic understanding of the emotional states of others. Thus, an underaroused HPA axis results in aggressive children who are unable to consider the emotional consequences of their actions for others.

Temperament

The characteristic manner in which children approach new situations or respond to environmental stimuli is referred to as *temperament.* Thought of as a biological predisposition, temperament is believed to be stable across development, yet modifiable by environmental experience. For instance, temperamentally shy children raised with social, outgoing parents may become less shy over time than would have been predicted based on temperamental predispositions alone. Furthermore, temperament is viewed as a core component of childhood and adolescent personality. In fact, Connor (2002) aptly describes personality as the interaction between life experience and temperamental characteristics. For instance, adolescents with shy personalities start out life as *behaviorally inhibited* infants and toddlers. Behavioral inhibition is a temperamental attribute characterized by fearful reactions to, and a tendency to withdraw from, new situations (Kagan, 1992; Schwartz, Snidman, & Kagan, 1999).

Although numerous subtypes of temperament have been identified, temperament is frequently characterized by six key components: ease of adaptation to new situations, overall level of irritability and fussiness, ease of positive emotional expression, overall activity level, attention span and task persistence, and regularity of sleeping and eating (Rothbart & Bates, 1998). However, with regard to aggression, most researchers have relied on three broad temperamental profiles based on the aforementioned temperamental components (Thomas & Chess, 1977): *easy temperament, difficult temperament,* and *slow-to-warm-up temperament.* Children with an easy temperament show lots of positive affect, transition to new situations easily, and have regular eating and sleeping patterns. In contrast, a difficult temperament is exemplified by high levels of activity, difficulty in transitioning and adapting to new situations, pervasive negative mood with intense responding (e.g., kicking and screaming), and irregular sleep and eating habits. Finally, children with a slow-to-warm-up temperament demonstrate low levels of activity, and slowly adapt to new situations and experiences while expressing low levels of negative affect.

Although not every child can be categorized into one of Thomas and Chess's three profiles of temperament (about 35%–40% cannot), those children who can be characterized as having a difficult temperament are at risk for aggressive behavior across development. Multiple longitudinal

studies have shown that childhood and adolescent aggression and delinquency are strongly linked with a difficult temperament in infancy and
childhood (Olweus, 1980). Furthermore, children with difficult temperaments are at risk not only for increased levels of aggression but also for
psychopathology. For instance, several studies have found that children
with difficult temperaments are at risk for developing conduct disorder
(Connor, 2002).

Attachment

Children's *attachment* to their primary caregiver has been shown to be a
significant predictor of childhood aggression. Attachment refers to a child's
emotional connection to an attachment figure (i.e., a caregiver) that is characterized by a desire to be near the caregiver and a need to seek out the caregiver during times of stress (e.g., when frightened; Bowlby, 1969/1982). In
general, two overarching qualities of attachment relationships have been
identified (Ainsworth, Blehar, Waters, & Wall, 1978): *secure* and *insecure*.
Children with a secure attachment to a caregiver wholeheartedly believe that
their emotional needs will be met by that caregiver. For instance, secure
children know that when they are scared, their mothers will respond to their
cries for help and effectively soothe them. In contrast, children with an
insecure attachment believe that their emotional needs will not be met by the
caregiver; instead, their emotional needs will be ignored, rejected, or some
combination of the two.

Three subtypes of insecure attachments have been identified: *insecure-
avoidant, insecure-ambivalent* and *insecure-disorganized*. Based on a history
of experiencing caregiver rejection of their emotional needs, insecure-avoidant
children minimize their emotional expressions (e.g., suppress the expression of
anger) and minimize the use of their mother for comfort and support. In contrast, after having their emotional needs responded to, inconsistently insecure-
ambivalent children maximize their emotional expressions (e.g., they are quick
to tantrum) and maximize the use of their mother for comfort and support.
Finally, because they have been abused as infants and toddlers, insecure-
disorganized children fail to develop a clear strategy for interacting with their
mothers (Ainsworth et al., 1978; Main & Solomon, 1990).

With regard to aggression, research has consistently shown that in
comparison to secure children, insecure children show the greatest levels of
aggression. For instance, Marcus and Kramer (2001) found that a group of
"insecure" 3- to 8-year-olds (sub-classifications of insecurity were not used
in this study) displayed more acts of reactive (i.e., retaliation) and proactive
(i.e., unprovoked aggression used to dominate) aggression than similarly

aged secure children. However, additional research has shown that insecure-avoidant or insecure-disorganized children are more likely to become aggressive or develop aggression-laden forms of psychopathology than either secure or insecure-ambivalent children (Cassidy & Kobak, 1988; McElwain, Cox, Burchinal, & Macfie, 2003). In fact, insecure-ambivalent children do not typically act aggressively (Cassidy & Berlin, 1994).

Developmental Status

Children's and adolescents' vulnerability to the effects of environmental and child-based risk factors may vary as a function of developmental status. Specifically, early adolescence appears to be a time of increased vulnerability (Kirsh, 2003). In comparison to late childhood and late adolescence, early adolescence is a time of heightened aggressive thoughts, feelings, and behavior (Lindeman, Harakka, & Keltikangas-Jaervinen, 1997; Loeber & Stouthamer-Loeber, 1998; Steinberg, 2001). The increase in aggressive behavior and conflicts accompanying early adolescence appears to be related to the variety of new physical, social, and emotional challenges that arise during early adolescence. For instance, early adolescents must adjust to rapid physical growth and maturation and to increasing sexual feelings. In addition, early adolescents are faced with increasing cognitive and socio-emotional challenges at school and changes in the emotional, social, and psychological relationships with their parents and peers (Steinberg, 2001). Apart from psychosocial factors, changes in HPA and HPG axis activity during early adolescence may also influence the aforementioned increase in aggressive behavior.

Additional research has indicated that structural changes occur in the brain during adolescence. According to Spear (2000), between 7 and 16 years of age, adolescents lose one-half of their prepubertal neocortical synapses (at a rate of 30,000 synapses per second). Although the resulting impact of synaptic pruning on adolescent functioning is not well known, Brownlee (1999) suggests that pruning enhances the efficiency of prefrontal cortical processing. In early adolescence, prior to pruning, excessive synapse connections may limit the prefrontal cortex's ability to efficiently process and evaluate situations, in turn reducing early adolescents' ability to make sound judgments (Brownlee, 1999). Thus, it is possible that higher levels of conflict during early adolescence are in part due to biologically driven limitations in rational thought and evaluation of consequences.

Functional magnetic resonance imaging (fMRI) suggests that the brains of early and late adolescents may work differently. FMRI is a form of brain imaging that detects blood flow to functioning areas of the brain. Using fMRI technology, Yurgelun-Todd (1998) observed the brains of 10- to 18-year-olds while they were viewing emotionally laden pictures. Yurgelun-Todd found that during picture viewing, both the limbic system (emotional responses) and the prefrontal cortex (center for higher thinking) of late adolescents became activated (i.e., increased blood flow). In contrast, for early adolescents, emotionally laden drawings were processed primarily with the limbic system. It may be that early adolescents are responding to emotionally laden situations with less prefrontal cortical activity, and thus are proportionally more emotion driven than older individuals.

Environmental Risk Factors

In direct contrast to the child effects model, the *parent effects model* posits the idea that parents are the cause of their child's behavior, both good and bad. Thus, according to this environmentally based model, children *become* aggressive because of bad parenting. Take, for example, the following situation, which exemplifies a hard-nosed belief in the parent effects model. Terry Hunt was sentenced to 179 days in the county jail because her 15-year-old son was excessively truant from school (Johnson, 2003). Her son's incredibly poor school attendance was viewed as her responsibility. Furthermore, the parent effects model assumes that children do not influence their own behavior. Thus, the child is like clay being molded by the parent. Today, we know that a wide range of environmental factors beyond parenting influence aggressive behavior. In the following section, both familial and extrafamilial influences on aggressive behavior are presented. In particular, special attention will be paid to the influence of families, peers, and neighborhoods on childhood aggression.

Parenting and the Parent-Child Relationship

Parenting Styles

Before there were "soccer moms" and "NASCAR dads," that is, before parenting was portrayed as the ability to drive children to sporting events or watch professional drivers turn left for four hours, parenting was described based on two major dimensions: *warmth/hostility* and *permissiveness/control*. The warmth/hostility dimension refers to the degree to which parents interact with their children in a warm or hostile manner. Parents high in warmth are typically caring, responsive, and affectionate toward their children. In contrast, hostile parents criticize, belittle, and act harshly toward their children, while rarely displaying any warmth. The permissiveness/ control dimension refers to the level of behavioral control exerted over their children. Parents high in permissiveness have few rules, and the rules they do have are inconsistently enforced. Furthermore, permissiveness is associated with limited supervision of children and the implicit transference of decision-making control to their children. Finally, parents high in control have lots of rules and enforce them consistently. Additionally, controlling parents supervise their children regularly and make most of the decisions for them.

By crossing the warmth/hostility dimension with the permissiveness/ control dimension of parenting, four unique parenting styles are formed: *Authoritative, Authoritarian, Permissive,* and *Uninvolved* (Baumrind, 1971, 1991). Authoritative parenting is characterized by high levels of warmth and flexible control. These parents are responsive to their children's needs, while at the same time are consistently enforcing rules and providing justification for those rules. Consider the following as an example of authoritative parenting: In the classic 1970s TV series *The Brady Bunch,* Greg, Peter, and Bobby refuse to share their newly built clubhouse with Marcia, Jan, and Cindy. In retaliation against being discriminated against, the girls destroy the boys' clubhouse. To resolve this conflict and prevent further escalation, the patriarch of the family, Mike Brady, warmly and moralistically talks to his three children and three stepchildren about the importance of sharing and respecting the rights of others.

Authoritarian parents tend to display little warmth, affection, and responsiveness. Also, these parents exert tremendous control over their children by rigidly enforcing strict obedience to parental commands. To authoritarian parents, rules are meant to be followed, not explained. In J. K. Rowling's popular *Harry Potter* series, Petunia and Vernon Dursley make use of an authoritarian parenting style when interacting with their nephew, Harry Potter. As evidence, consider the following: the Dursleys show no positive affect towards Harry, they force him live in a tiny closet under the stairs, and they require that Harry receive permission to speak. Furthermore, when Harry is perceived to be disobedient, he is sent to his room without dinner.

Permissive parenting is typified by a great deal of warmth and affection along with an equally impressive lack of control of, and supervision over, their children. Consider once again the Dursleys, who when interacting with their son, Dudley, utilize a permissive parenting style. For instance, after finding out that he had received the same number of presents for his current birthday as he did the year before, Dudley began to have a tantrum. In response to the tantrum, Petunia told Dudley that he would receive more gifts. Giving in to excessive demands from children, especially to stop or avoid temper tantrums, is characteristic of permissive parenting.

Finally, the absence of control, supervision, affection, and warmth along with the presence of hostility and insensitivity comprise the uninvolved parenting style. Examples of uninvolved parenting occur on the TV series *Judging Amy*. For instance, while presiding over a case involving under-aged shoplifting, Amy discovers that the children are left unsupervised for extended periods and that they have to fend for themselves to meet their basic living needs. As the following section reveals, delinquency is a common occurrence for children experiencing uninvolved parenting.

Over the past 30 years, a great deal of research has investigated the impact of the various parenting styles on child and adolescent development. In general, authoritative parenting produces the best social, emotional, and cognitive outcomes for youth. For instance, children of authoritative parents are more sociable, outgoing, and emotionally expressive, and they display higher levels of self-esteem and academic achievement than children of authoritarian, permissive, or uninvolved parents (Maccoby & Martin, 1983). With regard to aggression, children experiencing permissive and uninvolved parenting show the greatest levels of aggressive behavior across development. However, acts of violence, delinquency, and antisocial behavior are more likely to be committed by children raised by uninvolved parents than by children reared under any other parenting style.

Punishment and Monitoring

Beyond the four parenting styles mentioned above, additional parenting characteristics have been identified as risk factors for aggressive behavior in youth. Of particular importance are *spanking* and *parental monitoring*. Spanking is a form of discipline in which an open hand is used to hit a child on the buttocks or extremities without leaving bruises (Kazdin & Benjet, 2003). Parental monitoring refers to the degree to which a parent knows the child's whereabouts, day-to-day activities, and activity partners. Research on spanking and other forms of corporal punishment suggests a link between corporal punishment and heightened levels of aggressive behavior in children and a greater frequency of antisocial behavior in adolescence and adulthood (Gershoff, 2002). With regard to parental monitoring, research has consistently found that a lack of adequate parental monitoring is associated with high levels of delinquency and antisocial behavior (Farrington, 1995). For instance, the parents of Eric Harris, one of the Columbine killers, failed to notice that their son had stored guns, ammunition, and bombs in his bedroom in preparation for his murderous rampage (Bartels, 2004).

Siblings

As the previous review on parenting has revealed, the training ground for youthful aggression often takes place within the confines of the home. However, parents are not the only family members to influence children's aggressive behavior; siblings play a significant role, as well. Siblings fight with words and with deeds; with physical aggression and with relational aggression; and with deceit, trickery, and humiliation (DeHart et al., 2004). Although conflicts can occur at any point during development, quarrels between siblings occur with the greatest frequency during early adolescence (Steinberg, 2001). Throughout development, sibling arguments have a tendency to escalate when confrontations are frequent (Patterson, 1982). That is to say, when siblings engage in repeated altercations, successive conflicts have a tendency to become more and more aggressive: teasing becomes pushing, pushing becomes shoving, and shoving becomes hitting. Some sibling relationships are so tumultuous that they meet the criteria for abuse. *Sibling abuse* is characterized by a prolonged pattern of frequent victimization in which one sibling, typically an older one, dominates, humiliates, and assaults another sibling (Wiehe, 1997).

Methodological Issues in Sibling Research

Given that there is no set limit to the number of siblings found in any one family, conducting research with siblings presents some unique methodological challenges. Consider the following difficulties associated with conducting research in a two-sibling dyad, the simplest of sibling compositions to investigate. In a two-sibling family, there are four gender-by-age compositions to consider: older brother/younger brother, older brother/younger sister, older sister/younger brother, and older sister/younger sister. With each additional sibling studied, the number of potential gender-by-age compositions increases. For instance, in a three-sibling family there are eight possible gender-by-age combinations.

The abovementioned difficulties in conducting sibling research have resulted in equivocal findings. For instance, whereas several studies have found that the older brother/younger brother dyad produces the most conflictual relationships, other studies have shown that older brothers and younger sisters engage in the most conflict (Aguilar, O'Brien, August, Aoun, & Hektner, 2001). In addition to the issues surrounding the number of siblings and their gender composition, within each gender-by-age composition the age gap between the siblings needs to be considered as well. In general, siblings who are closer in age (three years or less) have greater levels of conflict than siblings with a larger age gap (four years or more; Aguilar et al., 2001). However, additional research is needed to verify that these conflict levels are consistent across the various age-by-gender-by-age-gap combinations.

Home Environment

One of the major tenets of Gestalt theory is the belief that "the whole is greater than the sum of its parts." With regard to the impact of the family on childhood aggression, the aforementioned Gestalt contention seems to be appropriate. As the previous sections revealed, research has consistently shown that parenting and sibling variables uniquely contribute to childhood aggression. However, above and beyond the individual contribution of parents and siblings to childhood aggression, the family unit itself (composed of parents and children) influences youthful aggression.

Patterson's (1982) concept of the *coercive home environment* exemplifies this point. A coercive home environment is rife with bickering and aggression between family members, adults and children alike. The house is in a whir of constant conflict, punctuated with irritating behavior and threats of aggressive retaliation. Beyond threat making, when one family member annoys another, aggression is the typical method used to stop the bothersome behavior. Patterson has found that many children from coercive home environments are highly aggressive and perceived by others as "out of control." Children from such homes are defiant of authority, and they frequently engage in acts of aggression in a variety of contexts, including at school and on the playgrounds.

Peers

As children age, peers play an increasingly important role in the socializing of behavior. In part, this change is a result of the doubling of time children spend with other children that occurs by age 7 and the concomitant 40% reduction in time that children spend with adults (Ellis, Rogoff, & Cromer, 1981). Peers significantly influence children's overall level of happiness, self-esteem, feelings of loneliness, and a wide range of attitudes, such as those related to sex, drug use, clothing style, and music (DeHart et al., 2004). Additionally, peers pose a significant risk to the development and maintenance of aggressive behavior (Bandura, 1986). Of paramount importance in this regard is the frequently researched area known as *peer acceptance*.

Peer Acceptance

Peer acceptance refers to the degree to which children and adolescents are accepted, rejected, or ignored by their peer group. Peer acceptance is most often assessed by asking children to identify those peers who they like and dislike or by asking children to rate the desirability of other children as play-mates and companions. The use of the above-mentioned procedures, collectively referred to as *sociometric techniques,* has resulted in the creation of five general categories for peer acceptance: *popular, rejected, neglected, controversial,* and *average.* Popular children receive many positive peer nominations and few negative ones. In contrast, rejected children receive many negative peer nominations while receiving few positive ones. Neglected children receive few votes of any kind, either positive or negative. Controversial children are the "Howard Sterns" of the primary and secondary school set, in that they are both liked and disliked by many. Finally, average children receive the average number of positive nominations and negative nominations doled out (Coie, Dodge, & Coppotelli, 1982).

Although many factors influence a child's sociometric standing (e.g., physical attractiveness, impulsivity, intelligence), the use of physical and relational aggression is an important determinant as well. For instance, a subclass of peer-rejected youth, known as *aggressive-rejected children,* engage in high levels of physical and relational aggression in an effort to socially dominate other children (Coie, Dodge, Terry, & Wright, 1991). However, recent research has shown that being highly aggressive is not limited to rejected children. In fact, popular elementary school–aged boys and girls frequently act physically and relationally aggressive to control the behavior of others (Lease, Kennedy, & Axelrod, 2002; Rodkin, Farmer, Pearl, & van Acker, 2000;). Finally, it is worth noting that not only does aggressive behavior influence peer status, but peer status influences the use of aggression. For instance, being aggressive may help a boy become popular, but in order to maintain his current level of popularity, the boy engages in more aggressive behavior. Thus, because of the cyclical nature of the peer aggression and popularity (aggression influences popularity and popularity influences aggression), peer status is a risk factor for continuing aggressive behavior.

Peer Relationships

In the classic 1970s TV series *Happy Days,* Richie Cunningham and Arthur Fonzarelli (a.k.a. Fonzie) were the best of friends—mismatched friends, that is. Richie was a kind, intelligent, and clean-cut teenager. On the other hand, Fonzie was tough, "cool," and intimidating. And unlike Richie, Fonzie had an established reputation as a street fighter. In fact, as a juvenile delinquent, Fonzie had dropped out of school and had been a member of "The Falcons," a motorcycle gang. In real life, could Fonzie and Richie really have been friends? The answer to this question can be found by examining the empirical literature on the nature of peer relationships of aggressive and nonaggressive youth.

Similar to nonaggressive children, aggressive youth have "best friends" and participate as members of larger social clusters of children. However, unlike nonaggressive youth, the friendships and social clusters of aggressive children and adolescents are almost uniformly composed of aggressive children (Cairns & Cairns, 1994). Thus, if Fonzie and Richie had met while Fonzie was a delinquent, it is doubtful that they would have been able to maintain a long-term relationship. But why do peer groups and friendships differ along aggressive lines in the first place? In part, such differences occur because children hang out with and befriend other children who have similar values with regard to the use of aggression to dominate others and solve problems. Thus, aggressive children create and maintain friendships with children who approve of and value aggressive behavior. Furthermore, while nonaggressive children punish others for the use of aggression (e.g., quitting play), aggressive children tend to reinforce one another for engaging in aggressive acts (Poulin & Boivin, 2000). Over time, aggressive social clusters can transform into *deviant social networks*. In a deviant social network, prosocial values and activities (e.g., sharing and helping) are shirked, while antisocial activities, such as drug use and criminal behavior, are promoted. Although deviant social networks are portrayed in the movies as an adolescent phenomenon (e.g., *The Outsider* and *Rumblefish*), such antisocial networks are often in place by age 10 (Cairns, Cadwallader, Estell, & Neckerman, 1997).

Neighborhood Violence

Beyond the confines of the family, the neighborhood in which children and adolescents live also has the potential to influence the likelihood that children and adolescents will engage in acts of aggression and violence. Consider, for example, the very violent neighborhood of Cabrini-Green. Located on the north side of Chicago, Cabrini-Green was one of the most notorious public housing projects in the United States. Residents of this poverty-stricken environment lived in high-rise apartment buildings that were designed with motel-like exterior hallways (picture an elongated balcony). Adding to the infamy of Cabrini-Green was the fact that the external hallways were encased in steel mesh to prevent children from falling over the railings. Gangs controlled individual buildings, and the flash of gunfire was frequently seen. Drug sales and use were rampant. Children living at Cabrini-Green were afraid to play on the grounds of the complex, for fear of getting caught in the crossfire or being victimized in some other way (e.g., assaulted, mugged, or raped).

Across the United States, children living in violent neighborhoods like Cabrini-Green experience high levels of victimization. Moreover, not only are youth in these impoverished neighborhoods victims of violence, but they frequently witness violence perpetrated against others as well. Take, for example, these shocking statistics: in violence-prone neighborhoods, between 40% and 60% of children report witnessing a shooting, stabbing, or killing (Jenkins & Bell, 1994). Such horrific visual experiences appear to impact youthful aggression. For instance, research has shown that children witnessing real-world violence firsthand are more likely to endorse the use of aggression in their personal lives are than children who have not witnessed violence first hand (Schwab-Stone et al., 1999). Additional research has shown that in comparison to nonviolent neighborhoods, higher levels of aggression and delinquency are found in violent neighborhoods, even after statistically controlling for family and economic variables (Peeples & Loeber, 1994).

Summary of Risk Factors

As the previous sections have illustrated, aggressive behavior is the result of a multitude of child and environmental characteristics. As such, neither the child effects model nor the parent effects model adequately explains the genesis of aggressive behavior during childhood. Today, the risk factors associated with aggressive behavior are understood using a *transactional model of development*. According to the transactional model, both the child and the environment reciprocally influence one another across time. In other words, throughout development, the child's behavior affects the behavior of parents, siblings, peers, and so on, and the behavior of parents, siblings, peers affects the child's behavior. For instance, temperamental, hormonal, and genetic characteristics may predispose a child to act aggressively, and because her parents use an authoritarian style of parenting, the child's aggressive tendencies are met with hostile and controlling behavior. In response to this pattern of parenting, the child acts more aggressively. Furthermore, the presence of high levels of conflict within the sibling relationship results in escalating sibling aggression and the development of a coercive family home. In turn, the child begins to hang out around aggressive children, who are easy to find because the neighborhood is filled with aggressive youth. As a result of all of these factors and transactional influences, the child becomes hyper-aggressive. Under this model, the child is both the artist and the clay.

Protective Factors From Aggression

Superman possesses amazing powers: he can fly faster than a speeding bullet; he can leap the tallest building in a single bound; and he is stronger than a locomotive. The source of Superman's powers is none other than the yellow sun found in our solar system. The sun shields Superman from the dangers of bullets, knives, and bombs. The sun gives Superman great strength and superior hearing and vision. Yet, in the presence of green kryptonite, Superman weakens. And prolonged exposure to this green source of alien radiation will prove fatal to the "Man of Steel." However, when kryptonite is encased in lead, its deadly radiation cannot reach Superman to do him harm. Thus, to Superman, a small lead box can be an important protective factor. Protective factors, that is, characteristics of the child or the environment that lessen the impact of environmental perils (Rutter, 1985), also exist in relation to childhood aggression.

Protective Characteristics of the Child

In many ways, protective factors are the opposite of the risk factors mentioned above. For instance, the following child characteristics have been associated with lower levels of aggressive and antisocial behavior in childhood and adolescence: easy temperament, genetic predisposition towards nonaggressive behavior, low sensation-seeking behavior, and an HPA axis functioning characterized by high levels of cortisol and low levels of DHEA. In the face of environmental stressors, children possessing the aforementioned characteristics are more likely to become *resilient youth*. Resilient youth are able to function well under environmental stress, recuperate fully from trauma, and eschew the negative outcomes typically associated with harrowing and painful life events (Werner & Smith, 1982). In addition to child characteristics, child and adolescent resiliency is promoted by characteristics found in the environment.

Protective Characteristics in the Environment

Within the family, authoritative parenting, secure attachments, and parental monitoring/supervision of youthful behavior are associated with positive developmental outcomes and low levels of aggression and antisocial behavior. Positive sibling relationships and harmonious family dynamics also function as protective factors. Additionally, high levels of religious involvement are associated with low levels of aggression and delinquency. Extra-familial protective factors include positive friendships, involvement with prosocial activities and peers, and a neighborhood characterized by *collective efficacy*. Collective efficacy refers to an interconnected group of neighbors that monitor, and if necessary, intervene, with the activities of local and non-local residents in a neighborhood (Sampson, Raudenbush, & Earls, 1997; Tolan, Gorman-Smith, & Henry, 2003).

On the Importance of Risk and Protective Factors in Media Violence Research

Garbarino (1999) contends that the number of risk factors that children and adolescents are exposed to is an important determinant of aggression. Most children are thought to be able to cope with one or two risk factors (e.g., impoverished family, exposure to violence) without increasing their levels of aggression. When three or more risk factors are present, Garbarino contends that aggressive behavior is more likely to occur than not. However, buffering against the deleterious effects of risk factors are the protective factors mentioned above. It may be that violent entertainment has its most deleterious effects on youth possessing two or more risk factors and few protective factors. However, it is also possible that for violent media to negatively impact youth, it is the quality (or type) of risk factors that is of paramount importance more so than the quantity of risk factors present. Determining the additional risk that violent entertainment consumption poses to aggressive behavior in relation to the quantity and quality of those risk factors is a much needed area for future research.

According to Borum (2000), the construct of "risk of violence" is determined by "contextual," "dynamic," and "continuous" influences. Risk of violence is "contextual" in that violent acts occur in particular settings (e.g., school) and under certain circumstances (e.g., peer rejection). The potential for violence changes from day to day, and therefore the risk of violence is "dynamic." Finally, risk of violence is "continuous" in that the probability of violent acts varies along a continuum. Risk approaches to violence determine the likelihood of youth acting violently and the nature of that violence (e.g., physical or verbal assault) given certain circumstances (e.g., bumped into) and contexts (e.g., surrounded by aggressive peers). To better understand the impact of exposure to violent video games on aggressive behavior, research needs to move beyond two- and three-factor assessments (e.g., video game violence, trait hostility, gender) and employ a risk factor approach. Aggressive behavior in its various forms (e.g., physical or verbal assault) is the result of the cumulative influence of a variety of factors involving a multitude of contexts. Thus, entertainment violence research needs to reflect the fact that the risk of violent behavior is contextual, dynamic, and continuous.

Furthermore, it is imperative that developmental issues be considered when assessing the influence of violent video games on aggressive behavior. As previously reviewed, research has demonstrated that biological (e.g., adrenarche, gonadarche, synaptic pruning) and psychosocial (e.g., peers, parents, siblings, school) components of aggression differentially impact the adolescent across development: early adolescents appear to be more vulnerable than late adolescents. Thus, it may be that the risks associated with violent video games are the greatest during early adolescence (the developmental period during which adolescents play violent video games the most) because, overall, there are more risk factors for aggression during early adolescence than during later periods of adolescent development.

Summary

- Risk factors increase the likelihood that youth will act aggressively. Protective factors reduce that risk.
- No one risk factor for aggression can cause a child or adolescent to act aggressively.
- Risk factors for aggression that are characteristic to the child include genetics, temperament, and hormones. Genetic predispositions, difficult temperaments, high levels of DHEA, and low levels of cortisol are associated with high levels of aggressive behavior. In addition, aggressive children tend to be physiologically underaroused.
- Risk factors for aggression that are characteristic to the environment include parenting style, attachment, sibling relationship, peers, and neighborhoods. Children and adolescents are at risk for aggression if they experience permissive or uninvolved parenting, spanking, certain insecure-avoidant or insecure-disorganized attachments, high rates of sibling conflict, poor parental monitoring, a coercive home environment, peer rejection, or they live in a violent neighborhood.
- The vulnerability of youth to the effects of environmental and child-based risk factors for aggression may vary as a function of developmental status, with early adolescence as a period of increased risk.
- The risk factors associated with aggressive behavior are best conceptualized using a transactional model of development, in which both the child and the environment reciprocally influence one another across time.
- The following child characteristics have been associated with lower levels of aggressive behavior in childhood and adolescence: easy temperament, genetic predisposition towards nonaggressive behavior, low sensation-seeking behavior, and HPA axis functioning characterized by high levels of cortisol and low levels of DHEA.
- Environmental protective factors include authoritative parenting, secure attachments, parental monitoring, positive sibling relationships, harmonious family dynamics, high levels of religious involvement, positive friendships, involvement with prosocial activities and peers, and a neighborhood characterized by collective efficacy.

- Children may only be able to withstand two or three risk factors before succumbing to their effects. It may be that violent entertainment affects aggression the most in youth possessing two or more risk factors and few protective factors.
- Entertainment violence research needs to conceptualize the risks for aggressive and violent behavior as contextual, dynamic, and continuous.

13

The Threat of Media Violence

Assessing Its Magnitude and Reducing Its Effects

To what extent should parents, teachers, and policy makers worry about the effects of media violence on the behavior of youth? How much of aggressive behavior can be attributed to media violence consumption? Should parents gather together and throw their PlayStation 2 video game consoles, aggression-laden comics, lyrically violent music, and violent videos into a large bonfire? Would such actions provide a sense of communal catharsis? Research has provided an answer to the last question, for Bushman (2002) has shown that aggressive actions do not afford individuals a cathartic release. But, what about the issue surrounding the magnitude of media violence effects? Just how big is the threat of media violence to youth?

Individual research studies addressing the impact of violent entertainment on children's and adolescents' aggressive behavior and aggression-related constructs were presented in previous chapters. The cumulative body of evidence suggests that violent media, in and of itself, can influence aggression and aggression-related constructs. However, much of the research reviewed was conducted without consideration of the many and varied risk and protective factors that influence aggression. In this chapter, research specific to media violence in the context of multiple risk and protective factors is examined. Additionally, the specific ways to ameliorate the negative effects of media violence exposure are discussed. However, before media violence is placed in the context of other variables, it is important to grasp an initial understanding of the magnitude of media violence effects on youthful aggression.

Sizing It All Up

Narrative literature reviews involve the critical evaluation of previously published material in narrative form. When writing a narrative literature review, the goal is to organize, evaluate, and integrate the findings of numerous empirical studies. Moreover, such reviews often raise new issues that future research should consider. However, narrative literature reviews have been widely critiqued as being biased toward the viewpoint of the author (Freedman, 2002). Although narrative literature reviews identify key points in each study and identify strengths or weaknesses of theory and methodology, the process of selecting and reporting findings is still relatively subjective. In contrast, systematic reviews offer a means of examining the scientific literature in a way that minimizes the threat of preconceived notions and reviewer bias. One of the most widely used types of systematic reviews is the statistical procedure known as the *meta-analysis*.

Meta-Analysis

Meta-analysis is a statistical technique for combining the numerical findings from independent research projects in order to *objectively* appraise the research literature. Thus, in contrast to narrative reviews, meta-analyses are quantitative in nature, that is, they use numbers. And unlike subjective narrative reviews, the results from various studies are combined in a standardized, systematic way. Given that the method, independent variables, dependent variables, and the age and gender of participants frequently differ between studies, such differences are noted and are incorporated into the meta-analysis. In fact, Comstock and Scharrer (2003) argue that by combining individual studies into a single large study, the individual weaknesses of specific studies (such as poor procedures) become less important. However, the inclusion of multiple studies with similar flaws or questionable methodology can render the findings from the meta-analysis meaningless. In other words, a meta-analysis is only as good as the studies upon which it is based. Thus, it is imperative that each individual study be reviewed for methodological soundness, prior to inclusion in the meta-analysis.

Limitations of Meta-Analysis

As the previous point illustrated, meta-analysis is not without limitations. The goal of a meta-analysis is to combine all *well-conducted relevant studies* that are *combinable*. Poorly conducted studies and studies that tangentially assess the issue under investigation are justifiably omitted from inclusion in a meta-analysis. Furthermore, only studies that address similar aspects of the reviewed construct are included. For instance, when using a meta-analysis to investigate aggressive behavior (e.g., hitting and kicking), studies on aggressive thoughts would be excluded. Thus, in terms of the choice of articles to include in a meta-analysis, researchers are required to make subjective decisions. Additionally, it may be difficult to find all of the relevant research articles that warrant inclusion in a meta-analysis. In particular, journals that publish empirical papers are more likely to publish research findings involving statistically significant differences between groups than research that fails to find such differences. Thus, because finding unpublished research is difficult, the data included in meta-analyses are often biased towards the presence of an effect.

Strengths of Meta-Analysis

Meta-analysis is most often used when the research literature is replete with studies made up of small and medium-sized samples. Unlike studies with large sample sizes, studies with smaller samples are low in power. That is, smaller studies often lack the ability to detect real differences between the experimental and control groups when such differences are present. Thus, the results of the meta-analysis are more reliable and valid than those produced by any one study. Furthermore, meta-analysis is employed to clarify the presence of an effect (or lack thereof) when the literature has provided inconclusive or contradictory evidence. In essence, meta-analysis combines the findings from smaller samples in order to create one large sample. In doing so, the aggregated findings are meant to provide a clearer picture of the effect(s) under study (Comstock & Scharrer, 2003).

Meta-Analysis and the Magnitude of Effects

Not only do meta-analyses establish the presence of effects, but through the *effect size correlation* they also measure the magnitude of the effects. Effect size correlation (r_+) refers to the average strength of the relationship between an independent variable and a dependent variable. Effect size correlation coefficients are considered *small* when around .10, *medium* in the region of .30, and *large* when in the vicinity of .50 (Rosnow, Rosenthal, & Rubin, 2000). To place effect sizes in their proper perspective, the concept of *variance* needs to be introduced.

Variance

Variance can be defined as the percentage of a dependent variable that is accounted for by an independent variable. For our purposes, aggressive behavior and aggression-related constructs represent the dependent variables under study, and the various forms of media violence correspond to relevant independent variables. Thus, research on media violence attempts to reveal the percentage of aggressive behavior that can be attributed to the consumption of violent media. In general, small effects account for around 1% of the variance, medium effects account for approximately 10% of the variance, and large effects account for at least 25% of the variance. It is important to recognize that even when effect sizes are large, as much as 75% of the variance is left unaccounted for, thus leaving unexplained the vast majority of the concept under study.

Accountable Variance in the Social Sciences

In social science research, the general lack of conclusive, explanatory findings is not a reflection of bad research. Instead, it is a reflection of the fact that human behavior is an incredibly complex phenomenon. With that in mind, it becomes clear that deriving accurate explanations for normative aggressive behavior and individual differences in aggression becomes a very difficult task. Rarely does a single variable have a large enough effect size to be considered the primary *cause* of aggressive behavior. Remember, a primary goal of science is understanding. Thus, the identification of variables with significant effect sizes, both large and small, brings us closer to understanding the genesis of aggression.

Meta-Analysis and Research on Media Violence

One of the most widely cited meta-analytic studies on media violence is Paik and Comstock's (1994) systematic review of over 215 empirical studies. Each of the individual studies included in this meta-analysis assessed the negative effects of violent imagery seen in movies and on television on aggressive behavior. Paik and Comstock's meta-analysis proved to be an important piece of work, as the impact of violent television and movies on aggressive behavior produced medium-sized effect sizes ($r_+ = .31$), far larger than many critics had suspected. More recently, Anderson and Bushman (2001) conducted a systematic review of the impact of violent video games on aggression and aggression-related constructs using 35 independent research projects. The results of this meta-analysis provided empirical support for the contention that violent video games influence aggressive behavior ($r_+ = .19$), aggressive cognitions ($r_+ = .27$), hostile affects ($r_+ = .18$), and increased physiological arousal ($r_+ = .22$).

However, because the violent video game literature is relatively small, Anderson and Bushman reviewed the extant video game literature, including studies that were methodologically flawed. Anderson (2004) points out the possibility that poorly conducted studies included in his previously published meta-analysis could have artificially inflated or decreased the magnitude of the aforementioned effects sizes. However, due to a limited number of studies in the 2001 meta-analysis, Anderson was unable to statistically test the impact of study quality on effect size. To address this issue, Anderson (2004) reanalyzed the now larger video game literature and identified studies that contained few methodological flaws.

In order to identify methodologically sound studies, Anderson made use of a nine-item coding scheme. Included within this scheme were the following weaknesses: a nonviolent video game condition that involved the playing of a game that actually contained violence (and, therefore, was not nonviolent); a violent video game condition that contained little violence; differences between the violent and nonviolent conditions in terms of difficulty, frustration level, or generated interest, and so on. Each of these coding criteria was selected because it represents confounds that could call into question the validity of the findings. Studies coded as having few weaknesses were labeled as "best practice" studies. When Anderson limited the revised meta-analysis to "best practice" studies, the effects sizes for aggressive behavior, aggressive cognitions, and hostile affects and physiological arousal all increased. For instance, the effect size for aggressive behavior went from $r_+ = .19$ to $r_+ = .26$. This finding suggests that far from increasing the magnitude of video game–related effect sizes, poorly conducted research actually decreased the effect sizes.

Video Games: The Baddest of the Bad?

Are violent video games the most pernicious form of media currently on the market? If parents had to choose, would they be better off letting their children play the violent video game *Resident Evil* or watching the Milla Jovovich motion picture adaptation of that video game? First, let us place this question in its proper historical context. As you recall from Chapter 1, Starker (1989) contends that as the popularity of a particular form of media grows, the perceived negative influence on youth grows with it. And currently, video games are reaching incredible heights of popularity, garnering over $10 billion in sales worldwide. However, are there data to support the contention that video games are, in fact, the baddest of the bad? Gentile and Anderson (2003) suggest that this may be the case, for they posit the notion that violent video games are more harmful to child and adolescent functioning than violent television. Gentile and Anderson forward multiple reasons to support their contention. Each will be addressed in turn.

Identification With the Aggressor and the Rewarding of Violent Behavior

Children and adolescents are more likely to imitate the aggressive behavior of television characters with which they identify (Bandura, 1986). However, given that television shows have multiple characters, there is no guarantee that youth will identify with the aggressor. In fact, when watching violent television, the opposite may happen, resulting in the child identifying with the victim. Although identification with an aggressor may increase the likelihood of aggressive behavior, identification with the victim may actually decrease it (Moeller, 2001). In contrast, when playing video games, Gentile and Anderson (2003) contend that youth are required to identify with the character they are playing. This may be especially true if the video game is a first person shooter game, in which the view screen shows the virtual environment from the eyes of the virtual character. Furthermore, given that extra lives, points, weaponry, and so on accompany successful violent video game play, children learn that the aggressive behavior is reinforced.

To summarize, violent video games may be more harmful to youth than television because, in contrast to television, only violent video games force identification with the aggressor and consistently reinforce acts of violence. Unfortunately, there is little, if any, research on youth to support these intriguing contentions. Thus, future research should address whether the guiding of a virtual character through a virtual universe is tantamount to identification with that character and whether rewarding video game experience is more detrimental to youth than video games offering fewer rewards.

Active Learning

Based on their review of educational research, Gentile and Anderson (2003) conclude that youth *learn* more through active learning than through passive learning. Given that television is a passive medium but video game play is an active one, it follows, then, that children should learn more from video games than television. In support of this contention, Lt. Col. David Grossman reports that the U.S. Army uses video games to help soldiers learn how to fire weapons and overcome a natural hesitancy to shoot at and kill human beings. However, research has yet to provide data supporting the contention that children learn more about *aggression* from violent video games than from television. If such differences are present, then the following question should also be addressed: Does long-term exposure to violent television and violent video games lead to the same level of aggressive knowledge, despite initial differences in the speed of learning? It may be that video games foster the learning of aggression knowledge faster than television, but that constant exposure to television violence produces the same level of knowledge as long-term exposure to violent video games. The answer to these questions may help parents, teachers, and policy makers evaluate the relative short-term and long-term influences of television and video game violence.

Practice Effects and Murder

Practice makes perfect . . . perfect killers that is. According to Gentile and Anderson (2003), violent video games give youth practice at planning and carrying out virtual murder. Furthermore, because of the repetitive nature of games, gamers can learn from their mistakes to improve their game performance (e.g., number of skills, success of plan). With time and practice, they become better aggressors. In support of this contention, Gentile and Anderson report that the U.S. Army uses violent video games, such as Tom Clancy's *Rainbow Six,* to train their special operation forces in the art of implementing Special Forces operations (Ubi Soft, 2001). In contrast, television and movies rarely show the steps necessary to carry out premeditated homicide.

However, violent video games alone are not able to directly cause aggressive behavior (Anderson, Berkowitz, et al., 2003), let alone murder. Furthermore, even though video games are played repeatedly, there is no evidence that children and adolescents actually learn how to commit murder from violent video games. It should be noted that learning and doing are quite different. Even if children do learn the art of skullduggery from violent video games, there is little evidence that violent video game play alone will lead to actual skullduggery in the real world.

Continuous Exposure to Violence

Paik and Comstock's (1994) meta-analysis of movie and television violence revealed that continuous displays of violent imagery have larger effects on aggression than presentations of violent imagery that are periodically interrupted with nonviolent imagery (e.g., commercials and scenes of nonviolence). In comparison to television and movies, violent video games allow for youthful consumption of violent imagery that is consistent and unrelenting. As such, Gentile and Anderson (2003) suggest that violent video games place youth at a greater risk for aggression than violent television. However, as interesting as this hypothesis is, it remains untested. Moreover, it may be that for heavier consumers of violent television, the overall level of violence consumed overrides the aggression-reducing effects of viewing non-violent commercial imagery.

Does Size Matter When It Comes to Different Types of Violent Media?

Although Gentile and Anderson (2003) make the intriguing suggestion that video games may be a greater health hazard than violent television, additional research is necessary to support their contention. In fact, in the current body of research on media violence there is evidence in the opposite direction of what Gentile and Anderson suggest. Specifically, meta-analytic studies have shown that the effect sizes associated with television and aggression are slightly higher than the effect sizes associated with violent video game play and aggressive behavior. Furthermore, no study has assessed the meta-analytic effect sizes associated with other forms of media violence, such as violent music, books, and comic books. Music lyrics can be visualized; book content can paint a picture in one's mind; and reading comic books requires that the reader visualize the action from panel to panel. Given that these forms of media violence actively engage the imagination, it is possible that the impact of their consumption is just as great as the impact associated with television or video games. Until more research is done, the baddest of the bad cannot be identified.

Placing the Effect Sizes for Violent Media in the Context of Other Risk Factors for Aggression

Media Violence Effect Sizes in Comparison to Health-Related Effect Sizes

In an effort to help the American public understand the strength of the effect sizes for media violence and aggression, Anderson and Bushman (2001) compared the findings from Paik and Comstock's (1994) meta-analysis with other health-related effect sizes. It is worth noting that the effect sizes for media violence and aggression are *stronger* than the effect sizes for condom use and sexually transmitted HIV, passive smoking and lung cancer at work, exposure to lead and IQ scores in children, nicotine patch and smoking cessation, and calcium intake and bone mass. Only the effect size for smoking and lung cancer was greater than the effect size for media violence and aggression, but that difference was less than .10.

Although the risk associated with violent media is consistent with other health hazards that concern the American public, the popular press has consistently failed to identify violent media exposure as a potential risk to health (Bushman & Anderson, 2001). It may be that because aggression is viewed as a social phenomenon and not a biological one, less merit is given to the factors that influence it. After all, biological influences create physical changes in the body, whereas social phenomena are thought to only introduce psychological changes. Unlike viruses, such as HIV, and chemical compounds like nicotine and calcium, media violence exposure is not consistently, nor directly, linked with death or body malformations, and as such, may be viewed less seriously. Biological processes *appear* to be more directly connected to biological outcomes than psychological processes are connected to social outcomes, at least by the public. Even when people learn that the influence of media violence on aggressive behavior is larger than any biological influences on health and well-being, the impact of that statement is often miniscule. Even though psychological processes are rooted in biology, most fail to recognize the connection.

Media Violence Effect Sizes in Comparison to Other Risk Factors for Aggression

Although the effect sizes for media violence and aggression have been compared with the effect sizes of other health hazards, the effects sizes for media violence and aggression have yet to be placed in the context of other risk factors for aggression. Such an assessment is important, for it provides a framework from which to evaluate the risk associated with media violence consumption, relative to other factors that influence aggression. As such, I have created a figure that compares the effects sizes of various factors that influence aggression in youth. As the data in Figure 13.1 indicate, the effects sizes for television and video game violence are in line with other risk factors for aggression. In several instances they are larger than a number of personality, familial, environmental, and biological effect sizes associated with aggressive behavior. Thus, media violence is one of many important factors that can influence aggression.

Critique of Effect Size Revelations

Although the findings from the aforementioned meta-analyses are impressive and make a strong case that violent media is a significant risk factor for aggression, such meta-analytic studies are not universally lauded. The

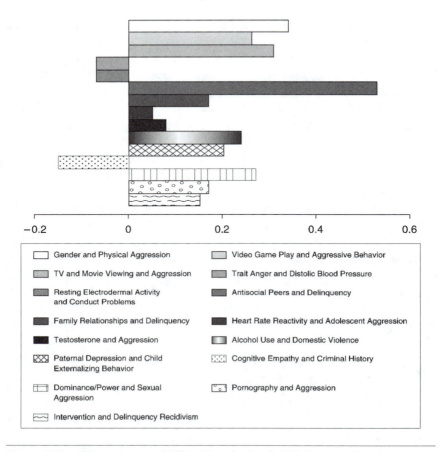

Figure 13.1   Comparison of Effect Sizes for Media Violence With Other
Aggression-Related Factors.

statistical phenomenon known as GIGO (garbage in-garbage out) has been
cited as a reason for devaluing media violence–related meta-analyses. In
particular, Freedman (2002) has been one of the most vocal critics of media
violence research. Freedman states that if the findings from studies are consistent, then "fancy statistics," such as meta-analyses, are not needed to
determine if an effect is present.

Remember, media violence research is incredibly complex and there is no
standardized procedure from which to work. For instance, aggression and
aggression-related constructs vary from study to study, thus making direct
comparisons difficult; a lack of governmental funding has made it difficult

281 The Threat of Media Violence

to conduct large-scale longitudinal studies, in which a wide range of risk factors are assessed; the amount and intensity of media violence displayed varies from study to study; additional factors, such as humor, realism, and amount of exposure vary as well. Furthermore, people vary greatly in the amount of media violence they consume and accurately report. Meta-analytic procedures are necessary to help ferret out the presence and magnitude of effects. Freedman also disagrees with many of the "legitimate articles" included in the meta-analysis and the coding of variables within those studies. This is a valid criticism, because choosing articles for inclusion in meta-analyses is subjective. However, Freedman fails to conduct his own meta-analysis with his recoded and newly included studies. Given that Anderson's (2004) recent video game meta-analysis showed that poorly conducted research resulted in a decrease in the magnitude of aggression-related effect sizes, Freedman's concern may be moot.

Media Violence Exposure and Moderators

Regardless of age, those who consume violent media appear to be influenced by it. However, not all consumers of media violence are affected to the same degree. For instance, children with disruptive behavior disorders are more negatively affected by violent media than are children without psychopathology (Grimes et al., 2004). Beyond mental illness, there are characteristics of youth and their environments that alter the impact of violent media, either by exacerbating or mitigating its effects. Such characteristics have been referred to as *moderators*. In the following section, research on moderators that are characteristic of youth will be discussed. In particular, the moderating effects of age, gender, and trait aggressiveness will come under scrutiny. Subsequent to that, research on the moderating effects of the environment, such as SES and parenting, will be presented.

Child and Adolescent Moderators

Age

The primary focus of this book has been on the influence of violent media on children and adolescents. It would follow, then, that the effect sizes for media violence should vary as a function of age. In fact, in the previous chapter I made the argument that entertainment violence should have the greatest impact during early adolescence, more so than during other developmental periods. Somewhat surprisingly, meta-analytic studies have failed to find consistent support for this age-based contention. The findings of Paik and Comstock (1994) actually contradict the hypothesis that early adolescents are affected by media violence to a greater extent than other youth. Instead, an inverse relationship was seen, with the largest effects sizes linked with watching violent television occurring for preschoolers (5 years of age or less; $r = .46$), followed by primary school children (6 to 11 years of age; $r = .22$) and adolescents (12 to 17 years of age, $r = .22$). In direct contradiction to the Paik and Comstock findings, Anderson and Bushman's (2001) recent meta-analysis of violent video games failed to find *any* evidence that effect sizes varied as a function of the participant's age. Thus, based on this new meta-analysis, one possible conclusion is that violent media similarly impact the aggressive behavior of children, adolescents, and adults. However, before the contention that media violence effects vary by age is ruled out, it is important to recognize the fact that meta-analytic studies have not adequately tested the influence of media violence using developmentally appropriate age breakdowns. Let me explain.

A One-Minute Course on Development. A father once said to his children, "Hey kids, I've been working out. What do you think of my new muscles?" Without missing a beat, his 10-year-old daughter retorted, sarcasm dripping, "Oh, yes, Dad, they're SOOO impressive." To which the father replied, "Nice sarcasm." "I know," she gleefully answered. This exchange was followed by a query from the father's 6-year-old son, "What's sarcasm?"

Under the age breakdowns used in past meta-analyses, the 6-year-old and the 10-year-old would have been placed in the same "primary school" category. But as the previous example illustrates, the cognitive ability of my children differed, a difference directly attributed to their developmental status. In fact, a great number of psychological changes occur between 6 and 11 years of age, and across adolescence, for that matter—changes that could influence the relative impact of violent media.

Consider, for example, developmental changes occurring during the primary school years: from 6 to 12 years of age, the ability to regulate one's emotional state increases. Thus, 11-year-olds are better able to stay calm in the face of conflict or stress than 8-year-olds, who in turn are more skillful at self-regulation than 6-year-olds. Similarly, emotions such as shame and guilt are more likely to be incorporated into a child's internalized sense of right and wrong with increasing age (Shaffer, 2000). Additionally, whereas children 8 years of age and older understand that the same situation (e.g., watching a movie) can elicit diverse reactions from different children (e.g., joy or fear), children younger than 8 do not grasp this distinction (Gnepp & Klayman, 1992). From 7 to 11 years of age, the ability to display an emotional state that is incongruous with the emotion being felt increases yearly (e.g., the ability to display positive affect while feeling emotionally disappointed; Saarni, 1984). The nature of companionship also changes across the primary school years, with younger children spending proportionally more time with adults than older children and older children spending proportionally more time with peers than younger children (Ellis et al., 1981). Thus, peer influences and experiences with peers (think video game play, watching movies, etc.) become increasingly more common. *Role taking,* which is the ability to take another person's perspective and understand his or her behaviors, feelings, intentions, and thoughts, qualitatively changes from 6 to 12 years of age (Selman, 1980). For instance, whereas 6- to 8-year-olds understand that two individuals viewing the same behavior may perceive it differently, it is not until they are 10 years of age that children are able to anticipate how different people react to the same situation, based on these conflicting perspectives.

Of course, developmental differences are not limited to primary school children, for youths differ across early, middle, and late adolescence. In addition to the changes mentioned in the previous chapter, the following differences emerge across adolescence. The overall level of positive mood decreases yearly from 5th grade until 10th grade (Larson, Moneta, Richards, & Wilson, 2002). The nature of peer relationships changes as well. In early adolescence, youth tend to hang in small groups of same-sex friends (i.e., *cliques*). By middle adolescence, boy cliques and girl cliques start interacting together, eventually creating a larger, mixed-gender clique (Dunphy, 1963). In early adolescence, self-esteem begins to incorporate successes and failures in interpersonal relationships, such as with boys, girls, teachers, and so on (Harter, Waters, & Whitesell, 1998). By late adolescence, success or failure in romance or romantic competence becomes a significant contributor to boys' overall levels of self-esteem (Thorne & Michaelieu, 1996). At the same time, self-esteem is less stable in early adolescence than in late adolescence (Trzsniewski, Donnellan, & Robins, 2003).

The abovementioned developmental changes are but a sampling of the many and varied transformations that occur across childhood and through adolescence. No self-respecting baseball coach would create a team with players whose ages vary by five or six years, as the older children are much more skilled, powerful, and coordinated than the younger children. IQ tests do not assign scores solely based on the number of test questions answered correctly, as older children know more information than younger children. Eighteen-year-olds do not typically date 12-year-olds, and those who do can be arrested.

In fact, a good rule of thumb for determining whether or not children of different ages should have been combined into a single group for statistical analysis is the *Dating Rule of Development*. Essentially, if you feel comfortable allowing youth of different ages to go out on a date, then it would be acceptable to combine their data. For instance, although most people would feel uncomfortable having 16-year-olds date 12- and 13-year-olds, they would be more comfortable with 16-year-olds dating 15-year-olds. Thus, researchers should avoid creating a single group of participants ranging in age from 12 to 16, but a combined group of 15- to 16-year-olds would be considered appropriate. So, why, then, have meta-analytic studies used the rather large and sweeping age-based categories of preschool, primary school, and secondary school?

On the Importance of Being Earnest About Age. The creation of large age-based categories in media violence–related meta-analyses occurs out of statistical necessity. Even though a wide range of ages is assessed within individual media violence studies (e.g., ages 10, 11, and 12), most of these studies do not report findings by individual ages. Instead, the participants are combined to form a larger sample, the average age of the participants is reported (e.g., 11 years), and age is omitted as a factor in subsequent analyses. For instance, Atkin (1983) assessed 98 5th and 6th graders but only reported results for the combined sample.

Compounding the difficulty for researchers wanting to conduct a meta-analysis is that there are no set rules that establish which ages are deemed developmentally appropriate for combining. Because of the lack of consistency among studies, media violence research is replete with partially overlapping age-based combinations. For instance, whereas Gentile et al. (2004) use a combined sample of 8th and 9th graders, Funk and Buchman (1996) use a combined sample of 7th and 8th graders. Similarly, whereas Josephson (1987) used a combined sample of 2nd and 3rd graders, Kirsh (1998) used a combined sample of 3rd and 4th graders. In each of these studies, the results for the individual age group were not reported separately. As such, the meta-analytic researcher cannot separate the published findings by age. Thus, in order to include these studies in the meta-analytic studies, researchers have no choice but to use larger age-based categories created along broader developmental lines.

Although preschool, primary school, and secondary school provide a framework for classifying children by age, such classifications are made without theoretical backing. Given that theoretical justification is a necessary component of science, researchers have utilized Piaget's stages of development to create large age-based categories. In particular, participants are classified as belonging to one of the following Piagetian stages: *preoperational, concrete operational,* or *formal operational.* The preoperational stage (2 to 7 years of age) is characterized by the use of mental representations and illogical thought. Children in the concrete operational stage (7 to 11 years of age) can think logically about concrete objects, but lack abstract thought. The formal operational stage (age 11 and older) is distinguished by logical thought and the ability to think abstractly and hypothetically about situations (Piaget, 1970). However, the problem with using such classifications is the assumption that children within the same stage have the same abilities. As it turns out, children display nascent abilities at the beginning of each stage, but by the time the stage has ended, their abilities have fully blossomed. Thus, classification into the same Piagetian stage is not equivalent to having the same cognitive abilities.

In order to adequately test the influence of media violence on children and adolescents across development, a standardized means of combining children close in age (i.e., within a year) into larger age groups needs to be created. For instance, children could be combined along the following age-based guidelines: 5–6, 7–8, 9–10, 11–12, 13–14, 15–16, 17–18. If such guidelines were universally followed, then meta-analytic studies would be able to more accurately assess the effect sizes associated with age.

Gender

Although males tend to be more physically aggressive than girls, and girls tend to be more relationally aggressive than boys (Leschied et al., 2000), the few meta-analytic studies that have assessed gender differences have failed to find that media violence differentially impacts the relational and physical aggression of boys and girls (e.g., Paik & Comstock, 1994). It should be pointed out, however, that the difficulties associated with age mentioned above also influence the findings related to gender. Because the number of boys and girls used in meta-analysis is reported in the context of large age-based categories, it is possible to have an uneven distribution of boys and girls within the age of any one group. For instance, in the Paik and Comstock (1994) study, it is possible that there were more 11-year-old boys than girls and more 6-year-old girls than boys. If such an uneven distribution of males and females occurred, the ability to statistically identify actual differences between genders would be impaired.

Recent evidence points to the fact that the aggressive behavior of boys and girls may be differentially impacted by media violence consumption. For instance, Huesmann et al.'s (2003) 18-year longitudinal study found that childhood violent media consumption was associated with physical aggression for adult males and indirect aggression for adult females. Thus, when assessing the impact of violent media on youth, researchers may need to more carefully consider the nature of the dependent variable (e.g., physical vs. relational aggression), along with the gender of the participants. Furthermore, future research should assess gender differences as a function of age, using developmentally appropriate age breakdowns. It may be that media violence influences relational aggression for girls during certain developmental periods and physical aggression for boys during other periods of development.

Trait Aggression

Trait aggression refers to an individual's characteristic pattern of aggressive behavior across development. Youth high in trait aggression tend to act more aggressively on a consistent basis than youth low in trait aggression. The research assessing the moderation of media violence effects in terms of trait aggression has been equivocal. Several studies have shown that youth high in trait aggression are influenced by violent media to a greater extent than youth low in trait aggression. For instance, in a longitudinal study, Dorr and Kovaric (1980) found that highly aggressive children who watched a significant amount of violent television programming displayed the greatest levels of aggression in adulthood. Similarly, in a randomized experiment, Josephson (1987) found that individuals high in characteristic aggressiveness became more aggressive after watching violent television than individuals low in characteristic aggression. In contrast, additional studies have failed to find that trait aggressiveness moderated the effects of violent media, while others found that those low in trait aggressiveness were affected to a greater extent than individuals high in trait aggressiveness (Anderson, Berkowitz, et al., 2003). Recently, Gentile et al. (2004) found evidence supporting the importance of using a risk factor approach in the assessment of media violence effects. Specifically, Gentile and colleagues found that for adolescents, high levels of trait hostility and frequent violent video game play appeared to have an additive effect, in that the combination of the two was associated with higher levels of aggression than either variable alone.

The Reverse Hypothesis. As we have seen, violent media influence aggression in children and adolescents, but what about the argument that aggressive youth seek out violent entertainment? Such a conjecture has been referred to as *the reverse hypothesis,* because aggressive behavior is being used to predict media violence consumption instead of the other way around. Could not the reverse hypothesis explain the significant effect sizes evident between media violence exposure and aggressive outcomes? The reverse hypothesis is a legitimate conjecture because correlations do not provide a causal explanation in terms of the direction of an effect. In other words, a significant correlation between media violence and aggressive behavior could occur because media violence influences aggressive behavior, or it could occur because aggressive children seek out violent media.

Recent evidence suggests that trait aggressiveness may, in fact, influence the choice of media consumed by youth. However, the consumption of that violent media, in turn, influences the likelihood that youth will engage in aggressive behavior. In short, trait aggression influences media violence via a process known as a *downward spiral model*. A downward spiral model posits that aggressive youth seek out media violence, while at the same time being influenced by the violent media that they consume. In turn, a negative feedback loop develops, in which media violence reinforces and exacerbates aggressive behavior, and aggressive behavior increases the appetite for media violence (Slater et al., 2003).

In a study of more than 1800 middle school 6th and 7th graders, Slater and colleagues (2003) found evidence that aggressive behavior predicted violent media use across a two-year period and that violent media consumption predicted current and future levels of aggression. There are several important implications from this research. First, as many critics of media violence research point out, aggressive and violent youth do seek out violent entertainment. However, in contrast to those suggesting that media violence effects are the result of the reverse hypothesis, aggressive and violent youth are still affected by the violent media that they consume. Thus, youth are not just passive recipients of media violence; they, in fact, actively seek out violent media, selectively exposing themselves to it. Furthermore, Slater and colleagues contend that relative to nonviolent children and adolescents, youth prone to antisocial behavior are at the greatest risk from the cumulative and negative effects of a downward spiral model. The reinforcing nature of media violence, the tendency to associate with violent peers, and the general disinhibition towards violence associated with antisocial youth are cited as reasons for this concern. Although research on the downward spiral model has received limited attention, the implication that some youth may be more at risk than others is an important contention that requires additional empirical investigation.

Environmental Moderators

Socioeconomic Status (SES)

SES refers to a standardized way of dividing the population based on parental occupation, income, power, prestige, and education. The terms low, middle, and high SES refer to the lower, middle, and upper quartiles of the SES composite index distribution. SES categories are often viewed as being synonymous with the social class categories of working class, middle class, and upper class. Research on media violence consumption indicates that low SES youth watch more violent television than other children (Comstock & Paik, 1999). It would follow, then, that because of the positive correlation between violent television consumption and aggressive behavior, youth from low SES would show a greater increase in aggressive behavior following media violence consumption relative to children from the other SES categories. However, there is little evidence to suggest that violent media influence low SES youth any differently than they do middle and high SES youth (Anderson, Berkowitz, et al., 2003; Simonson, 1992). The lack of evidence in the predicted direction suggests that there are risk factors for aggression that may supersede the effects of media violence. For instance, it is possible that exposure to community violence (to which low SES children are generally exposed the most) affects aggression in such a way that the traditional effects of consuming violent media do not appear. It is also possible that the cumulative risk from low SES status, media violence consumption, and other factors compound to negatively affect aggressive behavior in a way that does not affect middle and high SES status youth. This is an intriguing area that requires additional investigation.

Parenting

"It's 8 o'clock; do you know where your children are?" Growing up in the late 1970s and early 1980s, this question was aired on television in the form of a brief public service announcement. At the time, and as an egocentric youngster, I thought that it was a silly question to ask. Of course parents knew where there children were; they were watching television, just like me! The above question, however, was meant to give parents pause and have them think about the lives of their children beyond the veil of parental control. The psychological term used to describe the degree to which parents monitor the daily activities and friends of their children is called *parental monitoring*. Parental monitoring is an important variable in the assessment of youthful aggression, for a lack of parental monitoring has been associated with childhood delinquency and antisocial behavior (McCord, 1979; Patterson & Dishion, 1985; Singer et al., 1999). Similarly, research on media violence has found that parental monitoring of media exposure is related to aggressive behavior. In particular, parents who limit their child's overall level of media consumption or limit the amount violent media consumed produce the least aggressive children and adolescents (Gentile et al., 2004; Strasburger & Donnerstein, 1999).

While parental monitoring appears to moderate the effects of violent media consumption, the variable itself may be confounded with other parenting practices. For instance, Singer and Singer (1981) found that children with high amounts of unrestricted television viewing were also likely to be disciplined by corporal punishment and experience little in the way of positive regard or intimacy from their parents. It is possible, therefore, that the "third variable" issue of correlation is at play here. Specifically, it may be that the reason that parental monitoring of media violence is correlated with aggressive behavior is parents who do not monitor their children's media habits tend to be poor parents (e.g., withdraw love, engage in lax or excessive discipline, lack intimacy). Thus, it is the poor parenting that is causing the child's aggressive behavior and not the lack of parental monitoring of media violence. Additional research is necessary to tease apart the particular parenting practices (e.g., authoritative vs. authoritarian parenting styles) that moderate the effects of violent media consumption. However, parents can play an important moderating role in the media lives of their children, for experimental research has shown that when parents talk to their children about the content of violent media, the effects of violent media exposure can be significantly reduced (Nathanson & Cantor, 2000).

Multiple Moderators and Future Research

To date, few studies have assessed media violence effects in the context of multiple moderators. Moreover, just as important as understanding how specific forms of violent media interact with specific moderators is discovering the relative risk associated with the *overall* level of violent media consumption (e.g., television + video games + music) in the context of multiple moderators. Thus, a question in need of answering is: How do the moderators that are characteristic of youth and the environment interact with total violent media consumption to affect aggression and aggression-related constructs?

Reducing the Effects of Media Violence Consumption Through Mediation

Media violence–related *mediation* refers to an intervention strategy in which the normal process of child and adolescent media consumption is disrupted. More often than not, the parent is the source of the intervention; however, siblings, peers, and teachers can be mediators as well.

Types of Mediation

Although the choices of violent media to be consumed in childhood are varied (e.g., violent video games, comic books, music), mediation research has almost uniformly focused on reducing the harmful effects of television viewing. To that end, Nathanson and Cantor (2000) have identified three different types of television mediation: *co-viewing, restrictive,* and *active.*

Co-viewing mediation is a passive process in which a parent participates in the consumption of media along with the child. During co-viewing mediation, the parent watches television sitting quietly alongside the child. Given that children consume violent images from media other than television, the term *co-consuming* will be used to describe the restriction of all forms of media violence, including video games and music.

Restrictive mediation refers to limitations placed on the quantity of media consumed or the type of media consumed. Examples of restrictive mediation include limiting the amount of television that children can watch during the day and preventing children from watching television shows replete with violent content.

Active mediation refers to the process of talking to youth about the content of violent media. For instance, telling a child who is watching hand-to-hand combat in the violent cartoon *Dragon Ball Z* that getting kicked in the head can cause serious injury or even death is an example of active mediation. Such discussions can take place before, during, or after violent media consumption.

Mediation Research

Research on Co-viewing Mediation

Parents often offer the following admonition to their children: "If you can't say anything nice, don't say anything at all." This phrase may help train children in the art of social interaction. However, with regard to adults watching media violence alongside their children, the failure to say "anything at all" about violent content is tantamount to making positive comments about it. Far from reducing aggressive tendencies, recent research has shown that co-viewing mediation is associated with *higher* levels of aggressive behavior in youth (Nathanson, 1999). To date, research on co-consuming mediation has been limited to the consumption of television violence (i.e., co-viewing mediation). Future research should investigate whether an adult's silent presence near youth while they play violent video games, listen to violence-laden music, or read graphically violent comic books also leads to higher levels of aggressive behavior.

Research on Restrictive Mediation

At first glance, restrictive mediation seems as though it is the perfect mediation strategy. Children cannot be influenced by images that they do not see or hear. Thus, children who do not watch violent television shows or listen to violent music lyrics cannot be influenced by the violent content of those media. As such, restrictive mediation is a one-step intervention strategy that requires little cognitive effort on the part of the parent or the child. Additionally, the age of the child appears to be irrelevant to the effectiveness of the strategy since there is no information to be processed (e.g., violent images) that could be influenced by developmental status. Moreover, with vigilant parental monitoring, children's viewing of violent television, playing of violent video games, reading of violent comic books, and listening to violent lyrics can be restricted within the home. In support of such efforts, several companies have made available for purchase remote controls for TVs that limit the number of channels that children can watch to "child friendly" channels such as Nickelodeon and PBS. Furthermore, children can be prevented from watching violent television shows by activating the V-chip found in modern television sets that prevents the viewing of shows laden with violence. However, first glances are not always what they seem.

Restricting the consumption of media in general (both violent and nonviolent) is quite simple. All a parent needs to do is turn off the TV, shut down the computer, turn off the radio, sell the comic books, and force the kids go outside and play. In contrast, effectively restricting the consumption of violent media when nonviolent media consumption is allowed is a bit more difficult. As Forest Gump says, "Life is like a box of chocolates. You never know what you're going to get." And with any form of media, you never know when violent content may appear. For instance, Wilson et al. (2002) found that 70% of television shows aimed at children contain violent imagery. Similarly, Thompson and Haninger (2001) found that for video games rated E (meaning appropriate for children 6 and older), an average of 30% of game play involved aggressive encounters, with some E-rated games involving violence as much as 90% of the time.

And when children are out of sight of their parents, the odds of obtaining violent material meant for adults are surprisingly high. According to a recent Federal Trade Commission Report (FTC; 2004), 25% of 13-year-olds, 29% of 14-year-olds, 35% of 15-year-olds, and 62% of 16-year-olds were able to buy tickets to an R-rated movie without parental consent. For teens attempting to buy R-rated DVDs from merchants, the odds get better, with 79% of 13-year-olds, 82% of 14-year-olds, 79% of 15-year-olds, and 92% of 16-year-olds being able to purchase an R-rated DVD by themselves. Unaccompanied teens, ranging in age from 13 to 16, were able to buy recordings with explicit content labels an average of 83% of the time (range 69% to 96%). For M-rated video games (i.e., games with intense violence or strong sexual content and require that the buyer be 17 years of age),

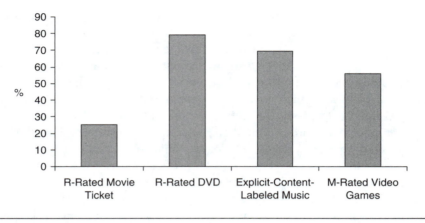

Figure 13.2   Percentage of 13-Year-Olds Buying Adult Media

underage teens were able to make purchases an average of 69% of the time (range 56% to 85%). It is worth noting that the music, video game, and movie industries all actively market content meant for legal adults to teens. For instance, M-rated video games were frequently advertised during MTV's late afternoon program *Total Request Live,* a show geared towards teens under 18 years of age (Federal Trade Commission, 2004). Thus, the best efforts of parents to restrict access to violent media are threatened by children's and adolescents' desires to see such media, the steps that youth will take to do so, and the advertising of violent material during the nonviolent shows that parents allow their children to watch.

Despite the challenges associated with imposing restrictive mediation, both experimental and correlational studies have demonstrated that restricting violent media consumption is associated with a reduction in aggressive behavior. However, such reductions are most likely to occur when *moderate* restrictions are put in place (Cantor & Wilson, 2003). In contrast, youth experiencing either low or high levels of restrictive mediation tend to be more aggressive than other children (Nathanson, 1997, 1999). Furthermore, teens experiencing high levels of restrictive mediation report more negative attitudes towards their parents and a greater desire to see such media in comparison to teens experiencing moderate levels of restrictive mediation. And because these highly restricted youth cannot view/play/read violent media at home, these teens are more likely to consume violent media with their friends and without their parent's knowledge (Nathanson, 2002). In essence, high levels of restrictive mediation function in a manner similar to that of explicit content warning labels used in the music industry and create a forbidden fruit effect. Thus, parents may wish to reduce exposure to media violence rather than eliminate it all together. Given that it is an inevitability that during childhood and adolescence, youth will come into contact with entertainment violence, instilling youth with appropriate coping strategies during such times becomes of paramount importance. Active mediation provides children with such strategies.

Research on Active Mediation

Since the late 1960s, research has investigated the impact of active mediation on the effects of television violence (e.g., Hicks, 1968). Many of these studies have relied on negative comments about media-portrayed aggression made by teachers, unfamiliar adults, and parents to affect children's perceptions of the outcomes associated with aggression (Cantor & Wilson, 2003). Negative comments regarding aggressive behavior include anti-aggression statements such as "how awful," "hitting is wrong," and "shooting someone is terrible." More often than not, aggressive behavior enacted on television shows geared toward children is met with positive consequences. For instance, the Powerpuff Girls are lauded by the people of Townsville for pummeling the evil villain Mojo Jojo.

According to social learning theory (Bandura, 1986), the observation that the aggressive actions of others are positively received should increase the likelihood that the viewer will act aggressively. With this in mind, the goal of active mediation has been to have youth perceive the putative positive consequences of using aggression negatively, thereby reducing the likelihood that such behavior will be imitated. In general, such criticisms do appear to reduce the amount of aggression imitated by children. However, the effects tend to be stronger in older children than in preschool-aged children (Grusec, 1973). Active mediation is a means for communicating to youth what behavior is and is not acceptable. Even if youth are feeling more aggressive after watching violent television content, they are also learning that they will need to control their own behavior to avoid punishment. Thus, the finding that older children imitate aggression to a lesser extent than younger children should not be too surprising, given that older children have better impulse control than younger children.

Additional research on active mediation has focused on whether youthful attitudes towards aggression can be impacted by negative comments. Once again, teachers, unfamiliar adults, parents, and even "commercial messages" (commercial-like, anti-aggression statements) have been implemented to relay anti-aggression statements to youth. Similar to the findings for imitative aggression, the research on aggressive attitudes has shown that active mediation can make aggressive behavior less normal and less acceptable to youth (Corder-Botz, 1980). However, in contrast to the research on imitative aggression, mediation statements appear to have a bigger impact on attitudes towards aggression for younger children than for preteens. Nathanson and Yang (2003) suggest that (1) older children may find statements such as "kicking someone in the head is wrong" as condescending, resulting in a "backlash" towards antiviolence attitudes, or (2) older children may tune out anti-aggressive statements to avoid hearing a lecture. The parent of any preteen will tell you that both possibilities are likely, given the negative attitude toward authority figures espoused by preteens with regard to lectures and pedantic statements. Furthermore, the issue of social desirability is critical in this type of research. The bigger impact of active mediation on aggressive attitudes for younger children may simply reflect their desire to please the experimenter, rather than a true change in attitude. Given that preteens and teens need to rebel, social desirability may play less of a role for these youth.

Finally, as opposed to research on inundating children with negative comments about the perpetrators of aggression, recent research has focused on the victim's feelings. For instance, Nathanson and Cantor (2000) assessed the impact of actively mediated cartoon violence on the acceptance of aggression to solve problems in elementary school students (e.g., pushing another child to get a toy). The 7- to 11-year-old children in this study were instructed to focus on the victim's feelings *prior* to watching a violent *Woody Woodpecker* cartoon. A control group of same-aged children was given no such instructions. This study involved a pretest-posttest design, in which aggressive tendencies were measured prior to and following the experimental manipulation. For boys, but not girls, active mediation reduced aggressive acceptance. Furthermore, for both boys and girls, those experiencing mediation found the cartoon less funny and less likeable.

Mediation Questions in Need of Answers

The current review of the mediation literature reveals questions that need further investigation. First, research on mediation has focused on either attitudes towards aggression or aggressive play. As such, future research should investigate measured aggression in an applied setting. Second, the long-term effectiveness of mediation has yet to be tested. It may be that mediation needs to be repeated a certain number of times before it becomes internalized and effective. However, overuse of mediation techniques by parents could lead to ignoring behavior or a backlash against parents. Third, mediation has been almost universally limited to studies on television. As such, future research should investigate the impact of active mediation while listening to music, playing video games, and so on. Finally, in order to get a better grasp of the effectiveness of mediation as a function of age, future research should assess a broader developmental spectrum, ranging from preschool to late adolescence.

Summary

- Narrative literature reviews organize, evaluate, and integrate the findings of empirical studies. However, the process of selecting and reporting findings is still relatively subjective.
- Meta-analysis combines the findings from individual studies in an attempt to objectively appraise the research literature. Meta-analysis is employed to clarify the presence of an effect when the literature has provided inconclusive or contradictory findings.
- When individual studies are combined into a single large study, the individual weaknesses of each study become less important.
- Single variables rarely have a large enough effect size to be considered the primary *cause* of aggressive behavior. However, the identification of variables with significant effect sizes, both large and small, helps clarify the causes of aggression.
- Meta-analytic studies conducted on television, movies, and video games have produced effect sizes in the low-medium to medium range. When the research is limited to the most soundly conducted studies, effect sizes tend to increase.
- In comparison to violent television, violent video games may impact aggression to a larger extent because violent video games increase the likelihood of identifying with the aggressor, reinforce acts of violence, involve active learning, provide opportunities to practice violence, and expose youth to continuous violence. However, these contentions remain untested.
- The effects sizes for television and video game violence are in line with other risk factors for aggression.
- Moderators of media violence effects that are characteristic of the child include age, gender, and trait aggressiveness.
- The lack of age effects in meta-analytic studies may be due to the inappropriate combining of youth of different ages into a single group.
- Gender effects may vary as a function of the type of aggression assessed and age.
- A downward spiral model explains how trait hostility, media violence preferences, and media violence effects reciprocally influence one another over time.
- Environmental moderators of media violence effects include SES and parenting.
- Few studies have assessed how multiple moderators and total media violence consumption interact to influence aggression.
- Active mediation and moderate levels of restriction can reduce the effects of violent media consumption on aggression. However, co-viewing mediation is ineffective.
- The following methodological concepts were introduced: narrative literature review, meta-analysis, effect size correlation, and variance.

14

Policy, Violent Entertainment, and Youth

Streaking, which can be defined as running around naked in public, is against the law. Although running around your house naked may be strange and uncomfortable for guests to watch, it would not be considered streaking and it is not illegal. Individuals found guilty of streaking are subject to fines, jail time, and frequent requests to "work out" more. During the half-time festivities of the 2004 Superbowl, Janet Jackson exposed her right breast and Mark Roberts pranced around Houston's Reliant Stadium wearing nothing but a smile. Streaking is not limited to football, as streakers have made recent appearances at the French Open tennis tournament and the U.S. Open golf tournament. Although there was little evidence that Janet Jackson's "wardrobe malfunction" adversely affected the youth who were watching, the fallout of Ms. Jackson's fall out has been a crackdown by the FCC on indecency. For instance, The Howard Stern Show was fined over $1.5 million for broadcasting sexually crude humor (Crawford, 2004). Although the definition of indecency is subjective, current FCC policy defines indecent material as containing content with sexual or excretory elements. Depictions of fist fights, murder, shootings, and other forms of violent behavior, however, are not considered to be indecent (Kunkel & Wilcox, 2001). Regardless of whether media violence should or should not be considered indecent, exposure to violent media has consistently been demonstrated as a risk factor for aggression.

As a risk factor for aggression, violent media can be viewed as a health threat, and when viewed as a health threat, violent entertainment becomes a legitimate target of policy makers. As Starker (1989) contends, as the consumption of a particular medium increases, the presumed threat of that medium to individual health and the social fabric also increases. And when the fabric of society is threatened, in comes the needle and thread of policy. In this chapter, the need for media-related public policy and the effectiveness of those policies will be addressed. Finally, recommendations for future policies on media violence will be proposed.

Legislating Media Violence: Is There Really a Need?

To date, the totality of research conducted points to media violence as a risk factor for aggression during childhood and adolescence. What has yet to be determined, however, is the relative size of that risk in comparison to other risk factors, such as peers and parents. If the effects of media violence on behavior are large, then the implication for policy relating to media violence is clear: legislate it. But what if the risk to aggression through violent media consumption is relatively small in comparison to the other risk factors? Is public policy still needed?

If the goal of public policy is to protect the welfare of children and adolescents, then there can be no doubt that public policy related to media violence is necessary even if the effects are small. For as Bushman and Anderson (2001) point out, even small effects on behavior can have big impacts on society. For instance, if after watching a violent television show that has a viewership of 1 million youth a mere 0.5% of those youth become increasingly prone to aggression, then 5,000 children and adolescents could be adversely affected. In support of the contention that "small is big" where public health is concerned, Gentile and Sesma (2003) report that the medical profession values public health decisions (e.g., take aspirin to reduce heart attacks) based on research accounting for less than 1% of the variance.

Under a risk factor approach, the removal of even one risk factor may be enough to reduce the likelihood of future acts of aggression. Thus, it becomes important to intervene in areas that can respond to intervention and can be subject to intervention. As it turns out, there are limited areas that can be legislated with regard to aggressive behavior in youth. Congress cannot legislate prohibitions against playground teasing; the president cannot create policy to make sure that one sibling is nice to another; Senate subcommittees cannot require that parents use rational explanations when putting their children to bed; and it is unethical to legislate the use of eugenics to ameliorate aggressive tendencies. However, policy can be created to educate parents about the effects of violent media. Furthermore, policy can be created that mandates that the content of media be made available to parents so that they can make informed judgments regarding their children's consumption of media. Determining the need for a policy is difficult; determining the exact nature of that policy is even harder.

A Brief Look at Policy Making

Prior to the general discussion of past and current attempts at governmental or self-regulatory processes in relation to media violence, it is necessary to discuss the process of policy making. Public policy typically occurs in a series of five stages: *agenda setting, policy deliberation, policy enactment, policy implementation,* and *policy evaluation* (Rochester, personal communication). Using the national alcohol prohibition of the 1920s as a reference point, the stages involved in creating public policy will be considered in turn.

During the initial stage of policy development, agenda setting, the primary focus is to get the relevant issue on the political radar screen. In other words, before a policy can be legislated, it is necessary to make the government aware that a *need* for such public policy exists in the first place. Although national alcohol prohibition did not take effect until 1920, by 1913 nearly 50% of the American public was subject to local prohibition laws. However, with the advent of World War I, prohibition would be added to the national agenda as liquor was portrayed as antipatriotic; beer drinking was viewed as an aspect of our enemy's (i.e., German) culture. Additionally, consuming alcohol was thought to divert resources from the war effort and weaken the efficiency of the American worker. Temperance had become a national issue; the agenda was set.

During the second stage of the public policy cycle, policy deliberation, various proposals are forwarded and considered for national adoption. With regard to prohibition, such deliberations resulted in a congressional resolution to prohibit the manufacture, importation, sale, and transportation of alcoholic beverages in the United States.

Policy enactment refers to the passage of a law or adoption of some decision. In 1917, Congress successfully passed the resolution for prohibition. All that remained was for individual states to ratify the resolution, resulting in the 18th Amendment to the Constitution. Approximately two years later, with the passage of the Volstead Act, national prohibition had been established.

Policy implementation consists of organized governmental activities directed towards the achievement of goals and objectives articulated in the policy. With regard to prohibition, punishment was the primary means of achieving the goals and objectives of the temperance-based policy. Individuals caught transporting, importing, selling, or drinking alcohol were now engaging in illegal activities, punishable by fines or imprisonment.

In the final stage of public policy, policy evaluation, reflection upon the efficacy of the policies takes place. Additionally, information useful in the creation of new policy is considered. The Volstead Act, which was repealed 13 years after it was enacted, is an example of a failed public policy. The national ban on alcohol transportation and sales, which resulted in the creation of a new illegal drug, is credited for the rise of organized crime and the creation of nefarious icons that soon followed, Al Capone being one of the most famous of these icons. Furthermore, the act was weakly enforced by law officials, many of whom were bribed to "look the other way." Additionally, due to the ease of transporting alcohol on one's person and the magnitude of the effect of imbibing it, drinking of hard liquor increased during the 13 years that the 18th Amendment was in place. Thus, the policy was viewed as ineffective (e.g., it did not reduce drinking), poorly implemented (e.g., many officials failed to enforce it), and poorly formulated (e.g., the impact on crime was not considered in advance).

Violent Entertainment and Current Policy

With regard to entertainment violence, most of the policies that will be reviewed have resulted in the implementation of a rating system. As such, a brief overview of the different types of rating systems currently in use is required. In general, there are three types of rating systems: *evaluative, descriptive,* and *hybrid.* Evaluative rating systems provide age-based recommendations regarding the appropriateness of a particular medium for consumption, as well as cautionary warnings such as "may not be suitable for young children" or "parental advisory warning." Descriptive rating systems detail the content of the medium offering. Also referred to as content-based ratings, descriptive rating systems *do not* make age-based recommendations regarding the appropriateness of the material for children and adolescents. Examples of content-based ratings typically listed for violent media include "intense violence," "explicit lyrics," or "blood and gore." Finally, hybrid rating systems combine elements of both descriptive and evaluative rating systems. For instance, the descriptions "not appropriate for young children; contains intense violence" exemplify a typical hybrid rating offering.

Legislating Comic Books . . . Almost

In 1954, Frederick Wertham published *Seduction of the Innocent,* a scathing indictment of the content found in the vaunted comic books of youth. Wertham claimed that the murder and mayhem illustrated in crime comics and the grisly depictions of death in horror comics were sure to promote deceit and increase antisocial behavior in children. Wertham's book was widely quoted in newspapers and magazines, and it eventually struck a chord with the American people. Congress took notice. In 1954, the Senate Subcommittee on Juvenile Delinquency initiated public hearings on the causes of juvenile delinquency and focused part of that hearing on the potential health threat associated with reading violent, gory, and ghastly comic books. The key witness during the proceedings was none other than Frederick Wertham. Public policy was never actually legislated for comic books. In fact, the interim Senate report on the impact of comic books on youth concluded that Wertham's claims were exaggerated and unfounded, an appropriate claim given that the methodology used to collect Wertham's data was suspect. However, in an effort to abate the chorus of public disapproval and, at the same time, avoid the potential of future legislation, the comic book industry formed the Comics Magazine Association of America (CMAA), which soon after adopted their own regulatory standards, the *Comics Code Authority* (CCA) (Savage, 1990).

Guidelines of the CCA

The CCA code is not a rating system. It is, in fact, a system of censorship, detailing what can and cannot be illustrated or written in comic books. The CCA code covers a wide range of comic book genres, including the publicly vilified areas of crime and horror. There were 41 standards of conduct presented in the CCA code. Included in the CCA code were the following directives.

Crime Comics:

- No comics shall explicitly present the unique details and methods of a crime.
- If a crime is depicted it shall be as a sordid and unpleasant activity.
- In every instance good shall triumph over evil and the criminal punished for his misdeeds.
- The word "crime" shall never appear alone on a cover.

Horror Comics:

- No comic magazine shall use the word "horror" or "terror" in its title.
- All lurid, unsavory, gruesome illustrations shall be eliminated.
- Scenes dealing with, or instruments associated with walking dead, torture, vampires and vampirism, ghouls, cannibalism, and werewolfism are prohibited. (Daniels, 1971)

Additionally, marriage, sex, nudity, and even paid advertising in the comic books came under the purview of the CCA. The following codes were included to help promote "good taste and decency":

- Suggestive and salacious illustration or suggestive posture is unacceptable.
- Females shall be drawn realistically without exaggeration of any physical qualities.
- The treatment of love-romance stories shall emphasize the value of the home and the sanctity of marriage. (Daniels, 1971)

Comic books failing to meet the standards set forth in the code were sent back to the publisher to be reworked. The CCA code was initially backed with economic power, as comic books would not typically be bought by magazine wholesalers or sold on newspaper stands unless they had received the actual CCA stamp of approval. The seal of the CCA is a graphic representation of a stamp with the words "Approved by the Comics Code Authority" emblazoned in bold capital letters (see Figure 14.1).

In an effort to reflect changes in societal values, the CCA code was refined in 1971 and once again in 1989. However, even with these societal-based changes, the CCA code was still a tool for censorship. For instance, in 1971 the CCA code was altered to allow the illustration of vampires, ghouls, and werewolves, as long as they were presented in a manner consistent with horror classics, such as Frankenstein and Dracula. However, brain-eating and flesh-oozing zombies remained banned. Apparently feasting on human remains is only considered to be an element of classic horror when it involves blood. By the mid-1980s, comic book publishers began selling their publications directly to stores specializing in the sale of comic books. As there was no longer a need for publishers to belong to the association in order to sell their comic books, the economic power of the CMAA eroded. With the economic power of the CMAA gone, comic book authors' general adherence to the code quickly dissipated. Today, the code is still "used" as a regulatory instrument for the few association members who remain (e.g., DC and Archie Comics). However, the stamp of the CCA does not guarantee that inappropriate material will not be depicted in the comic book.

Figure 14.1   Comics Code Authority Seal

In 2001, Marvel Comics, publisher of popular comic books such as *Spiderman, The X-Men, Daredevil,* and *The Hulk,* abandoned the CCA in favor of its own self-administered rating system. In an improvement over the CCA, comic book authors were now free to create their illustrated stories without fear of censorship. The following are excerpts from the rating system published on the Marvel.com Web site:

- ALL AGES: Appropriate for readers of all ages.
- MARVEL PG: Parents "may want to read them" with younger children.
- MARVEL PG+: Violence and language are "turned up a notch." Recommended for teen readers.
- PARENTAL ADVISORY/EXPLICIT CONTENT: Similar to the content of R-rated movies. Comic books may contain harsh language, intense violence, and "perhaps some partial nudity."

Evaluation of the Comic Book Industry's Attempt at Self-Regulation

Imagine a world without 500 television channels from which to choose; instead, there is only one, Nickelodeon. Imagine a world without Top 40, Punk Rock, Heavy Metal, and Rap; instead, there is only one musical format, Elevator. Imagine a world where movies lack swearing, vulgarity, nudity, and gratuitous violence; instead, there is only one format available to view, musicals in the tradition of *Mary Poppins*. You have just entered the world of comic books in the 1950s. Not a pretty sight, is it? In the 1950s, and for decades afterward, comic book choices were limited and storylines appealed to only the youngest of readers. The comic book industry's attempt at self-regulation turned into self-censorship.

Content inappropriate for children is appropriate for adults; content appropriate for older children may be inappropriate for younger children. Marvel's new rating system was an attempt to reflect the fact that the appropriateness of comic book content is age related. Unfortunately, Marvel's new rating system provides very little in the way of *useful* information. For instance, comics with a rating of Marvel PG+ contain content with violence and language that is "turned up a notch." OK, what does "turned up a notch" actually mean? I have no idea. Maybe it's the equivalent of "11" on Nigel's amplifier in the movie *This is Spinal Tap:*

Nigel: "All the numbers go to 11 . . ."

Director
Marty Dibergi: "I see, and most amps go up to 10. Does that mean it's louder?"

Nigel: "Well, it's one louder, isn't it? You see, most blokes will be playing at 10 . . . you're on 10 on your guitar. Where can you go from there? . . . Nowhere, exactly. So when we need that extra push over the cliff, you know what we do?"

Marty: "Put it to 11."

Apparently, when comic books get that extra push of violence, they go from Marvel PG to Marvel PG+; it's one louder, violently louder.

Rating comic books on content is a better alternative to censorship. Ratings allow for freedom of speech; they have the potential to prevent children from consuming inappropriate material; and they identify content that may be satisfying to adult tastes. However, to be effective, a rating system needs to provide useful information. That is, information that parents and other adults can use to determine whether the content of the media they are thinking about exposing to a child is appropriate for that child. Currently, an informative rating system is lacking in the comic book industry. Similar problems are apparent in the music industry as well.

Legislating Music

In an effort to protect children and adolescents from sexually explicit or violent lyrics, like those sung by the inimitable Marilyn Manson, the

Figure 14.2   Advisory Label

Recording Industry Association of American (RIAA) voluntarily labels music with an adolescent-attracting warning sticker: "Parental Advisory: Explicit Content" (Bushman & Cantor, 2003) (see Figure 14.2). However, the voluntary labeling came only after the recording industry came face-to-face with the Parents Music Resource Center (PMRC).

The PMRC, founded in 1985, comprised parents concerned about the lyrical content of the music to which their children were listening. Included as founding members of the PMRC were "Washington insiders" Tipper Gore (wife of then-Senator Al Gore), Susan Baker (wife of White House Chief of Staff James Baker), and Ethelynn Stuckley (wife of Congressman Williamson Stuckley). The PMRC publicly stated that they did not advocate censorship but, instead, simply wanted to inform parents about the lyrical content of music and to have the recording industry show "self restraint." In the fall of 1985, the Senate Subcommittee on Commerce, Science, and Transportation held hearings on the issue of record labeling (Nuzum, 2001). Testifying at the hearings on behalf of the recording industry and First Amendment rights were Frank Zappa, John Denver, and the lead singer of Twisted Sister, Dee Snider. Conspiracy theorists have noted that since testifying before the Senate subcommittee, both Frank Zappa and John Denver have died, as has the musical career of Dee Snider. Although legislation was never enacted following the highly publicized Senate hearings, the RIAA agreed to institute a self-regulated practice of labeling albums containing explicit content.

Evaluation of the Labeling System

The *parental advisory label* does not determine the appropriateness of the lyrics for children and adolescents. Rather, the label simply informs the buyer that parental discretion is advised. Although the label is meant to be "a notice to consumers that recordings identified by this logo may contain strong language or depictions of violence, sex, or substance abuse" (Recording Industry Association of America, 2004), the label itself provides little useful information as to the nature of the lyrical content. Thus, explicit lyrics may refer to strong language or they may refer to sex, but you'll have to listen to find out. In fact, Bushman and Cantor (2003) have demonstrated that warning labels tend to attract the attention and purchasing dollars of adolescents and children over the age of 8. Additionally, the labeling system provides no guidelines as to the appropriateness of the lyrics for children of varying ages. It is worth noting that in their original negotiations with the RIAA, the PMRC had requested a rating system (similar to the one used in movies). Such a system, problematic though it may be (see below), would have provided more information than the warning labels currently in use.

Legislating Movies

For over 100 years, the content of movies has been criticized as promoting immoral and criminal behavior to its youthful audience. Given that the planning and implementation of crimes were often portrayed in movies, the movie theaters themselves were thought to be training grounds for juvenile delinquency. As a result of public outcry, the National Board of Censorship of Motion Pictures was created to oversee movie content. By the early 1920s, 34 states had laws restricting what could be portrayed in movies. With the threat of continuing legislative intervention, William Hays developed a code of production in an effort to self-regulate the movie industry. In fact, The Hays Production Code resulted in the *censoring* of inappropriate content from movies. For instance, the Hays Production Code included prohibitions against swearing, vulgarity, the use of guns, revealing undergarments, and sympathy for criminals. Only movies that met the standards of the code were shown to the public. By the late 1960s, the rebelliousness and insurrection displayed in the streets of America were mirrored in the content of movies; the Hays Production Code had all but been abandoned. Instead of censorship, an "age-based" rating system was developed by the Motion Picture Association of America (MPAA) in order to provide "cautionary warnings" to parents (Valenti, 2001).

MPAA Rating System

The current version of the MPAA rating system has five categories, G, PG, PG-13, R, and NC-17. The general descriptions of the various ratings are listed below.

- G: General Audiences: All Ages Admitted
  The content of the movie contains nothing offensive.

- PG: Parental Guidance Suggested. Some Material May Not Be Suitable for Children.
  Some material unsuitable for their children, but the parent must make the decision.

- PG-13: Parents Strongly Cautioned. Some Material May Be Inappropriate for Children Under 13.
  May contain some violence, nudity, sensuality, or language but does not quite fit within the restricted R category.

- R: Restricted. Under 17 Requires Accompanying Parent or Adult Guardian.

  Definitely contains some adult material. Parents are strongly urged to find out more about this film before they allow their children to accompany them.

- NC-17: No One 17 and Under Admitted.
  Too adult for youngsters under 17. (MPAA, 2004a)

In addition to providing a general description of its "age-based" system, the MPAA also offers some clarification as to how ratings are assigned. For instance, single use of "harsher sexually-derived words" mandates a rating of PG-13, whereas using the same word twice would mandate an R rating. Furthermore, although sexually oriented nudity requires a rating of R, less explicit sexual content may result in the lower age–based rating of PG-13. Such was the case in the recent movie *Anchorman,* which received a rating of PG-13 even though the main character, Ron Burgandy, drops the F-Bomb and demonstrates a keen ability to show his affections towards a female

Figure 14.3   Voluntary Movie Rating System

coworker by sporting a huge, but cloth-covered, erection. The gang fight between competing news stations in which a newsman has his arm chopped off (and later ripped off by a bear), while another man is set on fire and a third newscaster is speared with a trident, falls into the MPAA category of "comic violence" and, therefore, does "not quite fit within the restricted R category."

Ratings Creep. Anecdotal evidence suggests that some parents were surprised to see that *Anchorman* was PG-13 instead of R. However, a recent study has found that the criteria for movie ratings have become less stringent over time, a phenomenon known as *ratings creep* (Thompson & Yokota, 2004). For instance, movies that used to receive a rating of R at times now receive a rating of PG-13; movies that were once rated as PG-13 are occasionally rated as PG; and many movies that used to garner a PG rating may now receive a rating of G. As evidence of ratings creep, Thompson and colleagues have empirically demonstrated that G-rated movies contain depictions of alcohol use, tobacco use, and violence, which clearly go against the MPAA contention that G movies contain "nothing that is offensive to the parents of younger viewers" (Yokota & Thompson, 2000).

Is money a motive behind ratings creep? It's hard to say for sure, but the evidence points towards the possibility. By far the most lucrative movies are rated G, averaging a gross profit margin of 66%. In contrast, movies rated PG, PG-13, and R make an average profit of 52%, 50%, and 37% respectively (Sirico, 1999). With each age-based increase in movie ratings, the average profitability decreases. Thus, ratings creep may help ensure that a movie remains in the most profitable money-making category, given its level of offensive content. Consider the following example: A sibling kills his older brother to gain power. A young child is chased by someone with murderous intent. The young boy flees his home but later returns to seek retribution against his uncle. Near the end of the movie, a gang fight ensues and a woman is hit and thrown to the ground. The movie ends when the young man destroys his enemy. What rating do you think a movie with the aforementioned plot developments should receive? Does this movie seem as though it contains nothing that would be offensive to parents of younger children who view the film? The movie described above received a G rating and is none other than the mega-blockbuster *The Lion King,* a movie for which parental guidance may have been warranted.

In fact, G-rated movies are replete with violence, alcohol, and tobacco use, content that many parents may find objectionable for young children (Yokota & Thompson, 2000). Furthermore, the evidence suggests that ratings creep is more pronounced in animated films than live-action films. Thompson and Yokota (2004) found that animated films with a rating of

G depict more onscreen violence than non-animated, G-rated films. However, as previous research has shown, the negative effects of violent media on fear and aggression occur for both animated and live-action movies and television shows; thus, the same criteria for ratings should apply to both live-action and animated movies.

Because the least profitable movies are rated R, it is in the movie industry's best interest to have movies rated in lower age categories, such as PG-13. Ratings creep helps accomplish this goal. Who knows? Maybe if the Ben Affleck and Jennifer Lopez movie *Gigli* was rated PG-13 instead of R, it might not have *lost* $67 million for its producers (Box Office Mojo, 2004). In reality, nothing would have saved *Gigli* from being universally trashed as a waste of celluloid, but the lower rating may have resulted in an increase in ticket sales from Bennifer-loving teenagers (Bennifer was the nickname given to the coupling of Ben Affleck and Jennifer Lopez, who were dating at the time *Gigli* was released). Teenagers, who comprise 26% of the movie-going market (Rauzi, 1998), were unable to attend *Gigli* because of the R rating. However, with a less restrictive rating, these same teenagers could have attended the movie—and then regretted it later, of course. Incidentally, in line with the movie, the Bennifer relationship also bombed.

Evaluating the MPAA Rating System

One of the major problems with the MPAA rating system is that the "age-based" system provides too few age-based categories. Young children and preteens differ in their ability to handle violent and fearful content, but the MPAA rating system suggests that both age groups may be taken to the same PG-rated movie. Take, for example, the recent movie *Harry Potter and the Prisoner of Azkaban*. This movie was rated PG for "frightening moments, creature violence and mild language." In fact, many young children found this movie to be scary. The warning of "may not be suitable for children under 6" would have provided an additional notice to parents about the suitability of the movie content for their young children. Thus, the MPAA's "age-based" system, given its overall lack of age-based categories, does not provide enough guidance for parents on the age-based appropriateness of the movie. Providing more ratings categories would result in a more complete but simple guide for parents on the appropriateness of a movie for their children. For instance, movies could be rated as "suitable for preschoolers" or "appropriate for children over the age of 6" or "best suited for teens 15 and older."

For those parents wishing to make a more informed choice, detailed information of the content of the movies should also be provided. Currently, the MPAA offers some additional facts to explain the movie's rating (e.g., contains sexual situations and comic book violence). However, the level of information presented is limited. The current system would benefit from reporting both the general content that parents might find objectionable (e.g., high levels of animated violence) as well as more specific information, such as the *intensity* and *graphicness* of that content (e.g., numerous fight scenes involving knives and guns with bloody depictions of murder).

Furthermore, movies should be advertised with all of the relevant information displayed. Currently, the content rating for a movie is often omitted during the advertising of that film. For instance, *Anchorman* is frequently listed in newspapers with just the assigned MPAA rating, PG-13, while omitting the MPAA rating descriptors, "Rated PG-13 for sexual humor, language, and comic violence." However, as previously mentioned, even when published, the current MPAA rating descriptors are lacking in detail. How violent is comic violence? What is the nature of the sexual humor? What exactly is the offensive language? The answers to these questions would help parents make viewing decisions for their children.

Finally, over the past decade, the phenomenon of ratings creep has resulted in children being exposed to higher levels of violence, smoking and alcohol use, and sexual situations than in previous decades. Moreover, parents often disagree with the assigned ratings for movies (Walsh & Gentile, 2001). In order to prevent ratings creep from continuing and to provide a more universally accepted system, a more standardized set of criteria for rating films needs to be developed. Additionally, checks need to be put in place to make sure that the MPAA is consistently applying the ratings as written.

Legislating Television

Around the same time that Frederick Wertham's treatise against the evils of horror and crime comics was published, 40 million viewers were tuning in to watch shows on black-and-white television sets, with a lucky few watching in color. Western dramas such as *Gunsmoke* and *Rifleman,* crime shows like *Dragnet,* and adventure shows along the lines of *Superman* dominated the airwaves of the late 1950s (Starker, 1989). In fact, the same 1954 Senate Subcommittee on Juvenile Delinquency that heard Wertham's anecdotal evidence on the harmful effects of reading comic books also heard testimony regarding violence in the newest form of mass media, television. Although the potential ills of comic books fell off the congressional map, the impact of violent television on youth has not.

In the decades following the Senate Subcommittee on Juvenile Delinquency, numerous congressional hearings on the impact of violent television have been held and the Surgeon General of the United States has even conducted a major scientific investigation into the topic. As a result of the continuing public pressure to reduce violence on television, several acts of legislation went to Congress, with only moderate success. For instance, during the mid-1970s, a "family hour" (8:00 P.M. to 9:00 P.M.) policy was established during which only content appropriate for the entire family was to be televised; violent content was to be broadcast after the family hour. The policy was soon ruled unconstitutional and was subsequently abandoned. Currently, indecent television content is prohibited until 10:00 P.M. (Kunkel & Wilcox, 2001). However, as Potter (2003) points out, such "safe-harbor" policies are doomed for failure, for throughout the evening, even as late as 11:00 P.M., children and adolescents are watching television in large numbers. As evidence, Potter provides the following information. Immediately following the "family hour," the number of children who continue to watch television drops by only 12%, leaving around 10.8 million youthful viewers. And by 11 P.M., nearly 3.2 million children and 3 million adolescents are still watching television. Following unsuccessful attempts to legislate parental advisory warnings and a rating system for violent content, as part of the Telecommunications Competition and Deregulation Act of 1996, the violence-blocking *V-Chip* was successfully passed into national law. Specifically, the law mandates that V-chip hardware be installed in all television sets sold in the United States.

Television Rating Systems and the V-Chip

When activated, the V-chip will thwart the viewing of violent material, but in order to do so, the chip first needs to identify violent content. The V-chip uses a rating system as a guide to identify prohibited subject matter. The television rating system, which is an adaptation of the MPAA movie rating system, currently contains six age-based categories and five content-based ratings:

- TVY: All Children.
  Appropriate for all children. No frightening content. Designed for children between 2 and 6 years of age.

- TVY7: Directed to Older Children.
  Geared at children age 7 and over. Elements in programs may include mild fantasy violence or comedic violence. May frighten children under the age of 7. Programs with intense, combative fantasy violence are designated TV-Y7-FV.

- TVG: General Audience.
  Contains little or no violence, no strong language and little or no sexual dialogue or situations.

- TVPG: Parental Guidance Suggested.
  Contents may be unsuitable for younger children. Many parents may want to watch it with their younger children. Programs may contain moderate

violence, some sexual situations, infrequent coarse language, or some suggestive dialogue (D).

- TV14: Parents Strongly Cautioned.
  Contents are only suitable for children 14 years of age and older. Parents are cautioned against letting younger children watch unattended. Program contains intense violence, intense sexual situations, strong coarse language, or intensely suggestive dialogue.

- TVMA: Mature Audience Only.
  Designed to be viewed by adults. Contents may be unsuitable for youth under 17. Program contains graphic violence, explicit sexual activity, or crude indecent language. (MPAA, 2004b)

Evaluating the Television Rating System and the V-Chip

When assessing the usefulness of the V-Chip, the hardware and software aspects of this violence prevention technology can be discussed separately. First, let us turn to the industry *developed* and *assigned* rating system. In comparison to the MPAA movie rating system, the current television rating system is an improvement in that there are more age-based categories and content descriptors for TV programs than for movies. However, as Potter (2003) illustrates, the current rating system provides very little in the way of useful information. The level of violence depicted in shows is not specified, nor is the context surrounding the use of violence. Programs with two acts of violence will receive the same rating (V) as programs with 100 acts of violence. As previous research has shown, glamorized violence impacts children negatively, whereas violence causing pain to the victim may reduce children's use of aggression. Yet, the current content descriptors fail to identify this important difference surrounding the context of displayed violence (Potter, 2003).

In terms of assigning ratings, the industry has been lax. Kunkel and colleagues (1998) found that nearly 80% of programs that should have received a content descriptor of V (violence) failed to receive such a rating. Even more astonishing is the fact that when television shows aimed at children were considered separately, slightly over 80% of the programs containing fantasy violence were missing the content descriptor of FV (fantasy violence). What is unclear is whether the failure to correctly assign the appropriate rating was

Figure 14.4   TV Rating Symbols

an act of omission (i.e., an error) or commission (i.e., on purpose). The fact that the ratings are assigned by the industry creates the possibility that the ratings are doled out with the potential effects of such ratings on audience size in mind. For instance, ratings and content descriptors that might lead to a smaller audience, and thus negatively influence future revenue from advertisers, would be absent. In contrast, ratings and content descriptors that might create a forbidden fruit effect, and thus attract youth, would be present (Potter, 2003). Additional problems exist with the inconsistent application of the rating system to all televised content. Notably absent from types of programs that require ratings are news and sports shows. The failure to rate news shows is a critical oversight, given the impact that viewing graphic and violent news images has on youth. For instance, the repeated viewing of graphic images associated with the events of September 11, 2001 has caused fear and anxiety in many youthful viewers (Saylor, Cowart, Lipovsky, Jackson, & Finch, 2003).

As an age-based system, the ratings provide many parents with a simple means of identifying the appropriateness of the program for their child. However, a disadvantage of any age-based system is that it assumes that all children are at the same developmental level, with identical abilities in handling violent content. Most experts agree that age-based categories underestimate the impact of individual differences in determining the appropriateness of television programs for children (Potter, 2003). Furthermore, most parents surveyed prefer a content-based system over an age-based system (Cantor, 1998b). Although parents *say* they prefer a content-based system over an age-based one, the evidence suggests that regardless of the system employed, parents tend to ignore it. In 2001, less than 30% of parents stated that they use the current television rating system regularly when making viewing decisions for their children (Johnson, 2001). Potter (2003) contends that a lack of understanding of what the ratings actually mean is the primary reason parents fail to use the current rating system. In support of his contention, Kunkel and colleagues (1998) have demonstrated that most parents incorrectly believe that shows rated TVY contain no violence.

Now that the nature of the application, misapplication, and lack of usage of the television rating system has been addressed, the hardware issue associated with the V-chip can be discussed. When turned on, the V-chip works. The problem with the V-chip is that the vast majority of parents (83%) are not turning it on (Johnson, 2001). Many parents (nearly 40%) do not even realize that their brand new television sets contain a V-chip, and the ones who do typically do not know how to turn it on (Potter, 2003). What has yet to be established, however, is whether parents want to turn on the

V-chip. For instance, when activated, the V-chip will prevent the viewing of popular nighttime dramas such as *NYPD Blue*. Thus, in order to watch the show, parents will have to program the V-chip to turn itself on and off based on time, date, or channel. The following are excerpts from the general instructions given on NBC.com to program the V-chip.

> The V-Chip will not operate unless the option is activated. All V-Chip TV sets require a personal identification number. This number—called a parental lock code—will act as the password allowing access to change settings, activate and de-activate the V-Chip. Once the parental lock code number is entered, select the ratings to block and then activate the V-Chip. The information is stored in the TV's "memory," and the V-Chip will continue to block programs with the selected ratings even when the television is turned off and back on. In addition to blocking based on ratings, many TV sets allow parents to block programs based on date, time or channel.

It is not surprising that most parents avoid using the V-chip, given the effort needed to program it correctly. When programmed with both children and parental viewing choices in mind, the V-chip prevents children from watching violence-laden television shows while at the same time allowing the adult viewing of television programs with violent content. Many parents may feel the inconvenience associated with programming and reprogramming the V-chip is not worth the effort.

Legislating Video Games

In 1993, Senator Joe Lieberman spoke out against the evils of violent video games during an investigation into the impact of violent video games on youth. However, the first public outcry surrounding violence in video games occurred some 17 years earlier, with the release of the Exidy produced arcade game, *Death Race*. This much-maligned video game was an adaptation of the ultra-violent Sylvester Stallone and David Carradine movie *Death Race 2000*. In the movie, the object of the cross-country automobile race was much more nefarious than the object of the video game, as humans were the target of choice. In fact, the movie started with the race participants driving through scores of wheelchair-bound octogenarians in order to start the race on the right foot. The movie was marketed with the following tag line, "In the year 2000, hit and run driving is no longer a felony. It's the national sport!" In contrast, the object of the video game was to run over "gremlins" to earn points. The gremlins in the video game were far from realistic representations of people; in fact, they looked more like tiny stick figures.

Adding to the furor over the game was the fact that when one of the stick-figure characters was run over, it screamed and turned into a cross. The public outcry against the video game was so great that the video game was quickly pulled off the market, resulting in the sale of only 500 units. Although the outrage surrounding *Death Race* did not lead to any regulatory action, the Senate hearings of 1993 led to the development of a video game rating system. The current version of this industry-wide voluntary rating system is overseen by the Entertainment Software Ratings Board (ESRB).

ESRB Rating System

On the front cover of any video game sold in the United States is the ESRB-assigned rating symbol. The ESRB symbol represents the age group for which the content of the video game would be considered appropriate. The five age groups and their general descriptors are as follows:

- EARLY CHILDHOOD (EC) - Content suitable for ages 3 and older. Contains no inappropriate material.
- EVERYONE (E) - Content suitable for children ages 6 and older. May contain minimal violence, comic mischief and/or mild language.
- TEEN (T) - Content suitable for teens ages 13 and older. May contain elements of violence, mild or strong language, and/or sexually suggestive themes.
- MATURE (M) - Content suitable for persons 17 years of age and older. Content contains mature sexual themes, intense violence, and/or strong language.
- ADULTS ONLY (AO) - Content meant only for adults. Contains graphic depictions of sex and/or violence. Not intended for minors. (ESRB, 2004)

Although the ESRB rating symbol is listed on the front cover of every video game, the general description of what the ESRB rating actually means can only be found on the ESRB Web site. The content responsible for the

Figure 14.5   ESRB Rating Symbols

Table 14.1   Some ESRB Content Descriptors Relevant to Violence

- **Animated Blood** - Discolored and/or unrealistic depictions of blood

- **Blood and Gore** - Depictions of blood and mutilated body parts

- **Cartoon Violence** - Violent actions involving cartoon-like situations and characters. May include violence where a character is unharmed after the action has been inflicted

- **Comic Mischief** - Depictions or dialogue involving slapstick or suggestive humor

- **Fantasy Violence** - Violent actions of a fantasy nature, involving human or non-human characters in situations easily distinguishable from real life

- **Intense Violence** - Graphic and realistic-looking depictions of physical conflict. May involve extreme and/or realistic blood, gore, weapons, and depictions of human injury and death

- **Language** - Mild to moderate use of profanity

- **Lyrics** - Mild references to profanity, sexuality, violence, alcohol, or drug use in music

- **Mild Violence** - Mild scenes depicting characters in unsafe and/or violent situations

- **Sexual Violence** - Depictions of rape or other violent sexual acts

- **Strong Language** - Explicit and/or frequent use of profanity

- **Strong Lyrics** - Explicit and/or frequent references to profanity, sex, violence, alcohol, or drug use in music

- **Violence** - Scenes involving aggressive conflict

assigned rating is listed on the back cover, along with a reprinting of the ESRB rating symbol. There are over 25 different descriptors that can be used to describe the content of a video game. The general categories include "sensitive" subject matter, such as violence, sex, language, substance abuse, and gambling. Examples of the descriptors related to violence are presented in Table 14.1.

According to the ESRB Web site (ESRB, 2004), three trained raters assign age-based ratings and content descriptors. Ratings are assigned based on the viewing of videotaped footage of the game supplied by the game's producer, along with additional game descriptors. Furthermore, ESRB raters are not allowed to have "any ties to the computer and video game industry."

Evaluating the ESRB Rating System

The ESRB rating system is the best of the various rating systems currently in use, in that both the age-based appropriateness and a large variety of content descriptors can be listed for each game. As with previous rating systems, however, there are several significant flaws that limit the usefulness of the system. First, there is ambiguity with regard to the E (Everyone) rating. A rating of E, as described by the ESRB, reflects a determination that the video game is appropriate for children ages 6 and up, yet the title suggests that the game is appropriate for children of all ages, that is, *everyone*. Thus, without the presence of reference material defining the ESRB rating, parents are required to remember or make assumptions regarding the appropriateness of the game based on age. Second, there is ambiguity surrounding the definition of the word "minimal." Along the lines of Bill Clinton's infamous quote, "it depends what your definition of *is* is," the categorization of "minimal" violence is publicly undefined by the ESRB. Although the ESRB contends that E-rated games contain "minimal" violence, a study by Thompson and Haninger (2001) found that a significant amount of violence may be present in E-rated games (ranging from 1.5% to 91.2% of game play; average of 30.7%).

Furthermore, for both E- and T-rated games, the absence of a content descriptor of *violence* does not necessarily mean that violence is absent from the game. Thompson and colleagues have found that approximately 44% of video games rated E and 48% of video games rated T contain content (e.g., hitting) not listed on the video game cover (e.g., *violence;* Haninger & Thompson, 2004; Thompson & Haninger, 2001). There are two primary reasons for missing content. First, the producers of video games (e.g., EA Sports) submit video footage of their game for the purpose of evaluation; the raters do not actually play the game. Thus, content descriptors may be lacking because the footage containing such material was not forwarded to the ESRB. Second, it is possible that a "threshold" for violence needs to be surpassed before the ESRB raters assign a violence rating. In other words, the presence of one or two acts of violence may not be enough to garner a rating descriptor of "violence." However, additional information is needed to determine why violent game content is omitted from the content description of video games.

Over 25 different descriptors are available to describe the content of video games. With regard to violence, a video game may be rated in a number of different ways. For instance, video games can be described as containing "mild violence," "violence," "intense violence," "sexual violence," "fantasy violence," "blood," and "blood and gore." Although the ESRB should be commended for providing multiple descriptors, the definition for the aforementioned violence ratings can be found only on the ESRB Web site, not on the games themselves. Once again, it is up to the parent to remember or assume what the descriptors actually are. However, research suggests that only half of parents who buy video games actually understand the rating system (Walsh et al., 2003). Furthermore, when a descriptor of violent content is listed, it only refers to the presence of said violence. What is unclear, however, is the frequency of the listed content. As Thompson and Haninger (2001) have illustrated, video games rated as violent may contain as little as 1% or as high as 90% violent content. Yet, under the current system, video games significantly differing in the amount of violent content would receive the same content descriptor. Future rating systems should provide a general estimation of the frequency of violence that occurs during game play.

Media Violence Policy: A Look to the Future

Agenda setting, policy deliberation, policy enactment, policy implementation, and policy evaluation represent the five stages surrounding the making of public policy. However, as the previous sections have revealed, very little public policy has been enacted by Congress with regard to the consumption of violent media. Groups such as the National Institute on Media and the Family (www.mediafamily.org) keep the public informed on the violent content of media through press releases and by providing information on their Web sites. Newspapers are quick to report associations between violent media and tragic events such as those that took place at Columbine. Violent media are frequently on the national radar. Additionally, formal agenda setting frequently takes place in the guise of Senate hearings, with occasional policy deliberation actually taking place. In general, however, such deliberations result in the *threat* of future legislation if the industry does not comply with requests to create and implement some sort of rating system, rather than the creation of new legislation to accomplish the same goals. The self-regulated policies have been implanted and occasionally revised to assuage continuing public outcry (e.g., the modification of the TV rating system). However, a media-wide public policy evaluation of the various current rating systems has yet to be addressed by Congress. In all likelihood, such an evaluation would result in the leading researchers in the field suggesting that a *singular* rating system be created to be used for all media and that such a system be governed by an agency outside of the media industry (see Bushman & Cantor, 2003). Let me explain why such recommendations would be forwarded.

The current situation utilizing multiple rating systems has proven to be ineffective. Although nearly 80% of parents surveyed state they use ratings to help guide their movie choices, such decisions are most likely done in an effort to prevent their children from being exposed to nudity and profanity, rather than violence. Furthermore, far fewer parents, averaging between 40% and 60%, state that they use ratings to guide television choices and purchases for music and video games. Moreover, parents who do use the various media rating systems frequently do not fully comprehend the ratings. In fact, they frequently misremember or misunderstand what the ratings actually mean. Reducing the number of rating systems to one would reduce the confusion associated with multiple rating systems and increase parents' ability to remember the meanings of the ratings. In turn, such changes could potentially increase parental usage of media ratings when making media consumption decisions for their children. Importantly, news and sports programs should be rated so that parents are aware of the images and messages to which their children may be exposed.

Although there is no direct evidence of a conspiracy to manipulate ratings in an attempt to increase revenue, the possibility does exist. At the very least, the presence of ratings creep, which has the potential to influence all rating systems, warrants that checks and balances be put in place to standardize the application of ratings to media content. Having a centralized agency responsible for assigning ratings that is independent of the media industry would remove any appearance of impropriety, as well as reduce the possibility of direct manipulation from industry sources.

Regardless of the rating system employed, there are currently too few age-based categories. With the help of experts in child development who have an understanding of children's cognitive, social, and emotional development, a greater number of age-based categories could be proposed. Such a development would help parents make quick and relatively accurate decisions regarding the appropriateness of a media offering for their child. For those parents desiring more information, the content used to determine the age-based rating needs to be presented in an easily accessible location. For instance, currently, many movie theaters display the definition of the ratings near the ticket booth. Similar signs could be posted in stores where music, video games, and comic books are purchased. In addition to describing the presence of objectionable content in a media offering, the frequency and intensity of that content should also be displayed. For instance, rather than simply stating that a movie contains violence, the movie could be rated as having frequent displays of mutilation involving zombies.

Reporting the intensity, context, rewards, and punishments associated with violent acts would provide parents with informative information on which to base their children's media consumption. For instance, a rating describing the presence of glamorized, trivialized, and rewarded violence may result in different parental decisions regarding the appropriateness of a media offering for their child than a less informative rating of "violence." Moreover, as Bushman and Cantor (2003) suggest, the potential risks associated with the content of a media offering should be presented, taking into consideration the child's developmental level. As an example, the warning, "This film contains imagery that is inappropriate for preschool children. Viewing this movie puts a child at risk of short-term fright and the development of enduring fears" provides detailed information as to the deleterious effects that may be associated with the viewing of this movie. Finally, some effort will need to be expended on the part of merchants to make sure that they follow the intent of the ratings by only selling media offerings (e.g., music, video games) to individuals at or above the required age.

The development of an effective rating system that can be applied to all media will not be without challenges. The new rating system will not only need to provide detailed information as to the content of the media offering, but it will also have to present information in such a way that parents will understand and use the system. Research and testing will be an important tool in the development of any new rating system. Equally important, however, will be government funding of these large-scale studies.

Summary

- Small risk factors can influence a significant number of people in the population.
- The five stages of public policy making are agenda setting, policy deliberation, policy enactment, policy implementation, and policy evaluation.
- Rating systems for violent media can either be evaluative (age-based recommendations), descriptive (content information), or a hybrid of the two.
- In 1954, as a result of public outcry and Wertham's Senate Subcommittee testimony on the evils of crime and horror comics, the comic book industry created the CCA and adopted its own regulatory standards.
- Included in the CCA code were strong prohibitions against violence and sex. Comic books that violated the CCA code could not be sold on magazine or newspaper stands. Over time, the code changed to allow more sex and violence. Today, the CCA code has been abandoned by most comic book manufacturers, and the CCA stamp of approval no longer guarantees the absence of violence or sexual imagery.
- Marvel Comics has created its own rating system. However, the system as currently constructed is lacking in useful information.
- As a result of public and political pressure generated by the PRMC, the RIAA voluntarily labels music with "Parental Advisory: Explicit Content"

warning labels. However, the *parental advisory labels* do not determine the appropriateness of the lyrics for children and adolescents.

- Public outcry against indecent movie content led to the Hays Production Code, which censored inappropriate material. The Hays code was eventually replaced by the age-based rating system developed by the MPAA. In addition to the age-based ratings (G, PG, PG-13, R, NC-17) system, the MPAA rating system also provides content descriptors.

- As a result of ratings creep, movies are often rated one category lower than they used to be (e.g., PG-13 instead of R). Maximizing profit may be the motive behind ratings creep. A more standardized set of criteria for rating films needs to be developed and enforced.

- There are too few age-based categories in the MPAA system. Content descriptors need to be more readily available to consumers.

- Safe-harbor policies to protect children from exposure to adult content do not work. The V-chip was legislated to protect children from such content. Although all newer television sets contain V-chips, they are infrequently turned on by parents.

- The rating system that the V-chip operates on contains six age-based categories: TVY, TVY7, TVG, TVPG, TV14, and TVMA. However, the level of violence depicted in rated programs is not specified, nor is the context surrounding the use of violence. In addition, programs are often incorrectly categorized or, in the case of news and sport programs, not categorized at all.

- Video games are currently rated on an age-based system developed by the ESRB. The box of each video game available for purchase displays one of five ratings, EC, E, T, M, or AO. There is confusion surrounding the rating of EC and E and the presence of offensive content. Although content descriptors are provided for each video game, the meaning of the content descriptor is not provided. In addition, the lack of a content descriptor (e.g., blood) does not guarantee the absence of that content (e.g., blood).

- Multiple ratings systems for media violence are ineffective and confusing. It is recommended that a singular rating system for all media, and one that is governed by an agency outside of the media industry, be developed.

PART IV
Nonviolent Media and Youth

15

The Good, the Bad, and the Ugly

Effects of Nonviolent Media on Children and Adolescents

S ea monkeys! Ever since I was a little boy, I was enthralled with the idea of having these "exotic animals" as pets. The advertisements I read in comic books heightened both my desire and *need* for these playful aquatic creatures. Just by adding water, smiling, pink, and crowned families of sea monkeys would spring forth, bringing laughter, joy, and fulfillment to all who were lucky enough to be present. Unfortunately, I was never able to convince my parents to buy me these vaunted creatures of the sea. I guess the lack of enthusiasm I displayed for my Chia Pet and the quick destruction of my Popeil Pocket Fisherman dissuaded them from any additional infomercial purchases. Some 30 years later, after encountering a picture of a happy sea monkey family in a toy store, I excitedly bought some for my daughter. Much to my surprise, the sea monkeys did not look or act like miniature monkeys. In fact, a magnifying glass was needed to see them. It is not that the sea monkeys are uninteresting; after all, they can reproduce both sexually and asexually (which is an interesting concept to try to explain to an 8-year-old). It is just that they were not what I expected. As it turns out, my high expectations had been forged by the advertisements I had seen in my youth. As this example illustrates, the effects of media consumption are not limited to violent content. To further address the wide-ranging influence of media on youth, this chapter will explore both the positive and negative influences of *nonviolent* media consumption. Borrowing from the classic Clint Eastwood Western, the current chapter will focus on the good, the bad, and the ugly effects associated with nonviolent media exposure.

Defining the Good, the Bad, and the Ugly

In the previous chapters of this book, the negative consequences associated with violent media consumption were presented. Such a review might lead the reader to the impression that *all* forms of media are "bad" and that "bad things" happen to the consumers of media. However, as the following sections reveals, nonviolent media *can* promote both healthful attitudes and behaviors among children and adolescents. Thus, the positive impact of non-violent media consumption is referred to as *The Good*.

In the next section, fondly referred to as *The Bad,* many of the varied negative effects associated with nonviolent media use are presented. In particular, special attention is paid to the influence of media on gender role stereotypes and attitudes and behavior surrounding drug use and sexuality. Furthermore, this "bad" section discusses a pernicious genre of media that appears in many different forms, including in print, on the radio, in video games, and on television. And unlike video games, television shows, and the like, the primary purpose of this genre of media is not to entertain but to influence the spending behavior of youth. Of course, I'm referring to advertising.

In the final section of this chapter, *The Ugly,* the influence of mass media on children's and adolescents' perceptions of their bodies and the role of such images in the development and maintenance of eating disorders are explored. Although mass media consumption is associated with obesity (Robinson, 1998), the heading for this section does not refer to the fact that images on television, in movies, and in magazines can make youth unattractive to others. Instead, the title for this section refers to the fact that such images can make youth unattractive to themselves. See Table 15.1 for a summary of the effects of nonviolent media consumption.

The Good

Educational and Information Programs

In 1990, the Children's Television Act established national policy requiring that television broadcasters provide educational and informational (E/I)

Table 15.1   The Good, the Bad, and the Ugly of Nonviolent Media
Consumption

The Good
  Prosocial Actions
  Academic Learning
  Prejudice and Stereotype Reduction

The Bad
  Prejudice and Stereotype Formation
  Effects of Advertising
  Drug Use
  Sexual Attitudes and Behavior

The Ugly
  Body Image
  Eating Disorders
  Muscle Dysmorphia

programs for youth. Because many broadcasters were airing E/I programming when children were asleep, whereas others were categorizing *The Power Rangers* and *Jetsons* as E/I programs, stricter guidelines were required (Jordan, 2000). Thus, in 1996, the Federal Communications Commission established the so-called three-hour rule, which mandated at least three hours of E/I programming per week (Federal Communications Commission [FCC], 1996). Furthermore, the new FCC guidelines specified the types of programs that could be classified as E/I programming, the minimum length of E/I programs (i.e., 30 minutes), and times during the week that such programming would be offered (i.e., between 7:00 A.M. and 10:00 P.M.).

E/I programming can be divided into two major categories: academic and prosocial. Academic E/I programs focus on traditional academic fare, such as scientific facts, animal behavior, social studies, and history. Prosocial E/I programming provides content that is social or emotional in nature. Sharing, self-respect, and the acceptance of diversity are common social and emotional themes. Not only does this type of programming reflect the day-to-day difficulties, dilemmas, and problems that children face, but it can also provide guidance through these complicated social issues.

Consider, for example, the episode "Phoebe Cheats" from the animated children's television show *Hey Arnold,* a show that depicts the trials and tribulations of 5th-grade children in a city neighborhood. Phoebe, driven by a need to maintain her high academic standing, uncharacteristically plagiarizes a poem from a book in order to win a poetry contest. Phoebe wins the contest and receives a trophy as a prize. Thereafter, Phoebe is troubled by a guilty conscience, the imagined voice of her trophy, and reappearance of the trophy after repeatedly attempting to throw it away. In the end, Phoebe publicly admits her wrongdoing and learns that victory at all costs is not a victory at all. This episode accurately reproduces the pressure that many middle school children feel regarding the need to achieve academic success. It also addresses the pitfalls associated with placing achievement over effort and cheating to accomplish goals. At the same time, "Phoebe Cheats" models a potential solution to this difficult situation.

Prosocial Media and Prosocial Actions

Just as theory can be used to explain the negative consequences of media violence for youth, so too can theory be used to explain the positive aspects of nonviolent media consumption. In particular, the tenets of Bandura's (1986) social learning theory predict not only that children and adolescents can learn antisocial actions by observing others but also that through prosocial media consumption, youth can counter ethnic and gender stereotypes and increase prosocial behavior. *Prosocial behavior* refers to any action that benefits another person. Comforting, sharing, and helping are all examples of prosocial actions.

Research on the effects of prosocial media on youth has been conducted using a variety of methodologies, including experimental (e.g., one-time exposure, repeated exposure) and correlational designs. More often than not, these studies have assessed the influence of prosocial television viewing on youth. Television shows used in these studies include *Lassie, Sesame Street, Barney, Mister Rogers' Neighborhood, Gilligan's Island,* and *Freestyle.* The results of such studies suggest that the viewing of prosocial television content can increase positive interactions among youth during play (e.g., friendliness) and increase altruism (Mares, 1996). For instance, in a study of preschool children, Friedrich and Stein (1973) found that the repeated viewing of *Mister Rogers' Neighborhood* led to increases in cooperative and friendly behavior for lower SES youth.

It is worth noting, however, that in the Friedrich and Stein (1973) study, the aforementioned prosocial effects were not found for children from higher SES groups. Thus, just as there are moderators for aggressive behavior, so too are there moderators for prosocial behavior. For example, the effect of viewing prosocial content is the strongest when paired with discussions of that content, such as those led by a teacher (Johnston & Ettema, 1987). Additionally, the influence of prosocial media consumption appears to be slightly stronger in girls than in boys (Hearold, 1986; Mares, 1996). This finding may reflect socialization pressures placed on girls to be nurturing, cooperative, and kind to others (Parsons, 1955). Furthermore, girls, more so than boys, tend to prefer shows with social and emotional themes (Calvert et al., 2002), thereby potentially increasing the saliency of the show's content and its subsequent influence.

The age of the media viewer appears to moderate the effects of prosocial content, as well. In fact, it is also possible that the prosocial benefits of television viewing are strongest during periods of development in which children are the most likely to act in such a way as to please others. Under this contention, it would be expected that younger children would be influenced the most by prosocial media and that adolescents would be influenced the least by it. In general, research has supported this contention, in that the effect sizes associated with prosocial television watching and prosocial behavior increase across the preschool years, peaking around age 7, and then decline from that point forward (Mares & Woodward, 2001). It is worth noting that the quality of prosocial television programming cannot be used to explain the trend. Woodard (1999) found that 73% of prosocial programs aimed at preschoolers could be deemed as high quality, but that less than 30% of programming aimed at elementary- and secondary-aged children was classified as high quality. Thus, although 7-year-olds watch less high quality prosocial television than preschoolers, they are impacted by prosocial television to a greater extent than are preschoolers.

Developmental considerations may be able to explain these findings. With regard to prosocial behavior, there is a general trend toward increasing altruism from the preschool years forward (Green & Schneider, 1974; Underwood & Moore, 1982). However, the pattern for the effects of prosocial media on prosocial behavior and developmental trajectories of prosocial behavior do not parallel one another. Media influences on prosocial behavior peak in early childhood and then decline. In contrast, throughout development prosocial behavior continues to increase. It may be that across childhood the process of shifting from external control of prosocial behavior (e.g., parents force you to share) to internalized standards of conduct and self-control of prosocial behavior (e.g., share on own accord) mitigates the influence of televised prosocial actions. In other words, the power of prosocial media may be lessened as youth take on more responsibility to determine the situations in which they will or will not act prosocially. Furthermore, the rebelliousness of adolescence may lead to a backlash against prosocial messages targeted at youth (Rubinstein & Sprafkin, 1982), thus continuing the declining influence of televised prosocial messages.

Effect Sizes of Prosocial Media

Given that prosocial actions promote societal norms, it has been postulated that the prosocial benefits of media consumption could be stronger
than the antisocial effects concomitant with violent media consumption. In
fact, the first meta-analysis on this topic provided clear support for this contention. Hearold (1986) found that the effect size for watching prosocial
television on prosocial behavior was twice as big as the effect size associated
with watching violent television on antisocial behavior (Hearold, 1986).
However, the definition of prosocial behavior in this study was too broad
(Mares & Woodard, 2001). For instance, Hearold included borrowing
books from the library as prosocial acts. More recent meta-analytic studies
have tried to limit the studies included in the meta-analysis to those studies
that link prosocial television content with social interactions such as friendly
and cooperative behavior. The results of these newer studies actually contradict those found by Hearold (1986), for the effect sizes for prosocial
media tend to be slightly less than the effect sizes for violent media (Mares
& Woodard, 2001; Paik & Comstock, 1994).

However, not all media portrayals of prosocial actions promote prosocial
behavior in youth. In particular, the observation of prosocial behavior accomplished through the use of aggressive actions (e.g., pummeling a villain to
protect the townsfolk), commonly referred to as *prosocial-aggressive acts,*
promote aggressive behavior more so than nonviolent, prosocial actions (e.g.,
helping behavior; Mares & Woodard, 2001). For instance, Silverman and
Sprafkin (1980) found that the viewing of conflictual behavior on *Sesame
Street* led to a decrease in cooperative behavior among young children during
a post-viewing marble game, even though the televised conflicts were resolved
through nonviolent prosocial means. Similarly, Liss et al. (1983) found after
watching an episode of *Superfriends,* during which prosocial-aggressive acts
were committed by superheroes, kindergarten children displayed a greater
number of aggressive actions and fewer prosocial actions relative to children
watching prosocial content on TV.

Although nearly 40 studies have assessed the influence of prosocial
television on youth (Mares, 1996), few studies have assessed the effects of
prosocial content disseminated through media other than television, such as
video games and comic books. And the few studies that have been conducted
have produced findings contrary to the contention that prosocial content
can positively influence prosocial behavior in youth. For instance, in a study
of elementary and middle school youth, Chambers and Ascione (1987)
found that the playing of prosocial video games (e.g., *Smurfs*) did not affect
participants' prosocial actions, such as donating money to charity and

sharpening pencils for another. As it turns out, the findings for this study are in line with those found for studies on televised altruism involving the generalization of a modeled behavior. Specifically, following the viewing of prosocial content on television, when children were given the opportunity to engage in an altruistic behavior that was not explicitly modeled during the broadcast, prosocial behavior did not increase (Friedrich & Stein, 1975). It is worth noting, however, that beyond television, additional forms of media may provide benefits to youth. For instance, video game play has been found to aid hand-eye coordination, improve children's attention to detail, and aid the recovery of oncology patients (Funk, 1993). Similarly, comic books have been shown to increase children's understanding of physical disabilities (Kokaska, 1984) and have been used to promote sex and AIDS education (Gillmore et al., 1997; Gordon & Conant 1974).

Media and Academic Learning

One of the major critiques levied at television is that it is a passive medium, requiring little in the way of physical and cognitive activity from its viewers (Singer & Singer, 1979). As research has shown, the lack of physical movement concomitant with television viewing can be physically unhealthy for children and adolescents in the long run. However, the same cannot necessarily be said of television and cognitive activity. For although it is commonly believed that the fixed stares, "vegging out," and "couch potato" behavior associated with television viewing give the appearance of cognitive inactivity, research on E/I programming suggests that a great deal of cognitive activity can take place, especially when youth are processing academic content.

"Sunny Day. Sweepin' the clouds away. On my way to where the air is sweet. Can you tell me how to get, how to get to Sesame Street?" Over the past 30 years, shows such as *Sesame Street, Teletubbies, Barney,* and *Blue's Clues* have provided academic learning opportunities for toddlers and preschool-aged children. For older children, programs such as *Zoom, Cyberchase,* and *Zoboomafoo* are replete with informative, scientific facts. For pre-teens and teenagers, cable channels such as *Animal Planet, The Discovery Channel,* and *The Learning Channel* offer a wide range of educational fare. For instance, on *Animal Planet,* the program *Petsburgh USA* airs E/I content about animal breeds, pet training, and even cooking for pets. Thus, there are ample chances for youth to view academic content. However, recent research suggests that such opportunities are not equally taken advantage of by children and adolescents across development.

Toddlers, preschoolers, and young children of both genders tend to enjoy watching academic and social/emotional E/I programming. However, by middle childhood, girls prefer to watch social/emotional programs over academic programs and boys prefer *not* to watch E/I programming of any type (Calvert & Kotler, 2003). Thus, for both boys and girls, there is an age-related decrease in the viewing of academic programming.

Although the viewing of academic programming decreases across development, the influence of viewing during the preschool years has been shown to reap positive rewards beyond those immediately seen post viewing. As an illustration, consider the findings from a longitudinal study by Anderson and colleagues on the association between watching *Sesame Street* and other educational shows at age five on academic success some 10 to 14 years later (Anderson, Huston, Schmitt, Linebarger, & Wright, 2001). Anderson et al. found a positive correlation between *Sesame Street* watching at age five and overall high school GPA. Incidentally, the correlation remained significant even after removing the influence of important demographic variables that could influence high school GPA, such as parental education, birth order, and school location.

Given that research has consistently shown that the viewing of academic television in early childhood produces educational benefits post viewing and years later (Bickham, Wright, & Huston, 2001), is it possible that the above-mentioned decrease in the viewing of academic programming across development actually impedes academic learning during later grade school years? To answer this important question, it will be necessary to take a closer look at the empirical evidence.

Research on word acquisition during the toddler and preschool years has shown that academic television can teach children new words or enrich their understanding of previously learned words. However, young children do not appear to learn words from programs that are not E/I in nature (Naigles & Mayeux, 2001). Given that children often view programming geared for older children and adults, the fact that they are less likely to learn new words from the viewing of these shows may actually be a good thing. For instance, after watching the musical *Grease,* my 10-year-old daughter did not understand many of the lyrics to a song in which Betty Rizzo mockingly sings, "Look at me I'm Sandra Dee, lousy with virginity . . ." Unfortunately, her lack of understanding has not prevented her from constantly singing this song around the house!

Furthermore, there are limitations to what children can learn from academic programming. As an example, the empirical evidence indicates that the viewing of shows such as *Barney* and *Sesame Street* does not positively influence the viewer's grammar (Naigles & Mayeux, 2001). And more recent research has shown that first graders and children deemed at great risk for literacy problems in kindergarten do not benefit from academic programming focusing on emergent literacy, such as that shown in the PBS offering *Between the Lions* (Linebarger, Kosanic, Greenwood, & Doku, 2004). Similarly, research on *computer-assisted instruction* (CAI), in which computers are used in the classroom to augment traditional learning techniques, has found both enhancements and declines in mathematical understanding following CAI. In both 4th and 8th grade, the drilling of mathematical concepts through CAI has been associated with lower test scores for math achievement. In contrast, when CAI was used to simulate and apply concepts or used in concert with games, math achievement scores were higher (Wenglinsky, 1998).

As the previous review illustrates, E/I is not beneficial to all youth at all ages. In part, the child's level of understanding *prior* to E/I exposure can moderate its effects. For instance, in the Anderson et al. (2001) study, the correlation between *Sesame Street* watching and high school GPA was stronger for boys than girls. Anderson conjectured that this difference occurred because 5-year-old girls are better prepared for school than 5-year-old boys, thus reducing the potential impact of E/I television viewing on GPA for girls. Secondly, whereas academic programming on TV can positively influence certain domains of academic achievement (e.g., vocabulary growth), other domains appear to be less impacted (e.g., grammar).

In order for children to learn from media, the content needs to be presented within their *zone of proximal development*. The zone of proximal development (ZPD) refers to a range of tasks that children can complete *only* with the guided assistance of a more skilled partner (Vygotsky, 1978). Tasks that are beyond children's ZPD are too complex for children to figure out (even with outside help). In contrast, tasks beneath the ZPD can be accomplished by children alone but receive little attention from children due to their ease (Anderson & Lorch, 1983). Thus, the inability of television to affect grammar (as well as other concepts) may occur because the type of guidance needed to learn certain tasks cannot be experienced over the television. In contrast, CAI (involving simulations and activities) is better suited for teaching within children's ZPD, as the computer program automatically adjusts to the user's level of understanding. Currently, there is little research on CAI across development. Given that CAI is designed to operate within the ZPD of the user, additional research is warranted. It may be that the individualized instruction provided by CAI can positively influence academic achievement in a way that television cannot.

Prejudice and Stereotype Reduction

In an effort to reduce prejudicial behavior among children, as well as to promote cross-race relationships, the producers of *Mister Rogers' Neighborhood* embarked on an ambitious, class-based intervention program involving nine videos for children along with guides and training for teachers. The series, titled *Different and the Same: A Prejudice Reduction Video Series,* used racially diverse puppets to model a variety of behaviors such as resisting peer pressure, looking beyond stereotypes, including others, reaching out to helpful adults, and honoring differences and similarities. Furthermore, each video had a race-related theme that ran throughout the program. Included as themes were name calling, being excluded from a group, stereotyping, speaking a different language, cultural identity, and standing against prejudice. Finally, each video relayed a specific way to solve a race-related issue/problem, such as being called a "Mophead" or "Pumpkinhead" (see Graves, 1999).

To investigate the effectiveness of the *Different and the Same* video series, the racial knowledge, attitudes, and behavior of 3rd-grade children of African, Asian, European, and Latino decent were assessed. In comparison to a control group of children who did not participate in the classroom video series, those children exposed to *Different and the Same* were less likely to offer prejudiced attitudes and beliefs, more likely to report knowing how to effectively handle interracial conflict, more likely to make cross-race friendships, and more likely to offer help to a child of a different race. Graves (1999) attributes the effectiveness of this video series to the practical and positive ideas portrayed in the videos, along with the engagement of the teachers to facilitate the child's understanding of the depicted messages.

Few studies have addressed the use of television to promote positive attitudes and behavior toward children of different races. Clearly, more work needs to be done in this important area. Additional research is needed to assess the effectiveness of such programs across development. It may be that this type of stereotype reduction works better at certain ages than others. Moreover, in addition to television, the relative influence of familial and peer factors in reducing prejudice and stereotypes needs to be assessed. For instance, *Sesame Street* modified the content of its shows during the 1990s to address race/ethnic cultural relations, the appreciation of cultural differences, and the inclusion of friends regardless of physical or cultural differences. Although children liked the shows addressing these important topics, the preschool-aged viewers stated that their *mothers* would not support cross-race friendships and that they would become angry or sad if the child attempted to develop one (Lovelace, Scheiner, Dollberg, Segui, & Black, 1994). From these data, it becomes clear that beyond developmental status and television viewing, additional factors (such as parental attitudes) play a critical role in the development and maintenance of stereotypes and prejudice.

The Bad

Prejudice and Stereotype Formation

Just as mass media images can reduce prejudice, so too can they negatively influence the attitudes of youth. Such is the case with *gender role attitudes*. Gender role attitudes refer to the beliefs that individuals hold with regard to appropriate jobs, appearance, and behavior specific to each gender. Since the early 1970s, correlational research has consistently shown that across childhood and adolescence, higher levels of television watching are associated with more stereotyped gender role attitudes (Signorelli, 2001). Stereotyped gender role attitudes reflect rigid beliefs about the work, appearance, and behaviors of males and females. For instance, under such belief systems, males are expected to engage in traditionally male-oriented jobs (e.g., doctor, firefighter, police officer), be the "bread winner" for the family, and rarely show emotions. In contrast, under this stereotyped viewpoint, females are thought to engage in traditionally female-oriented professions (e.g., nurse, teacher) or homemaking, wear "feminine" clothing, and be emotionally expressive.

Experimental research has confirmed the correlational findings that television can influence gender role attitudes (Signorelli, 2001). In particular, Williams's (1986) classic study of three Canadian towns, each with a different level of television exposure, demonstrates the potential influence of mass media on gender role attitudes. The gender role attitudes of children from a town without television (referred to by Williams as Notel) were compared with the gender role attitudes of children from towns with one (Unitel) or greater than four (Multitel) television channels. The results of this first wave of data collection revealed that girls (but not boys) from Notel possessed significantly fewer gender stereotypes than children from Unitel or Multitel. However, following the introduction of television into Notel, both boys and girls espoused stronger stereotyped views.

Advertising and Youth

The following quote was said to me by my then 5-year-old son one Saturday afternoon: "I want that, I want that! Dad come quick, you GOTTA see this . . . you can jump on the bed and the wine glass won't move!" In 2002, youth between the ages of 4 and 12 spent nearly $40 billion dollars on goods and services. Not to be outdone by their younger counterparts, adolescents between the ages of 14 and 19 spent an amazing $155 billion of their own money. In total, nearly $500 billion of family spending is thought to be influenced by youth (National Institute on Media and the Family, 2004). In an effort to direct this rather large sum of money into the hands of specific businesses, retailers rely on advertisements. In a typical year, youth will view upwards of 40,000 commercials on TV and countless other advertisements in magazines, on the Internet, and on the radio (Kunkel & Gantz, 1992). So, just what are advertisements getting youth to spend a half a trillion dollars on? The four main categories of advertising directed at youth, which account for nearly 80% of the total number of advertisements, are toys, cereal, candy, and fast food (Kunkel, 2001).

Advertisements directed at youth are meant to make the products appear fun and the user happy. Providing factual information regarding the product is not typically a goal of advertisements directed at children and adolescents (Kunkel & Gantz, 1992). For instance, in a recent commercial for the Yu-Gi-Oh duel disk launcher, several boys are seen engaging in a boisterous but highly enjoyable card game. The take-home message from the commercial is that if you play with this product you will have lots of fun. Nowhere in the advertisement does it state that you need to have an understanding of this rather complicated card game in order to use this product. Furthermore, the purchase of the 40-card playing deck that is required to play the card game is "sold separately," a concept that young children have difficulty understanding.

To children under 7 or 8 years of age, commercials are perceived as entertainment or as a source of information for new and better products, rather than as an attempt to *persuade* them to buy certain goods. For preschool-aged children, commercials are often interpreted as short, funny programs, or a continuation of the television show that they were viewing (Kunkel, 2001). The cognitive ability of the child explains this developmental pattern. Children less than 7 years of age tend to have difficulty recognizing the perspective of another person, and as such, they are unable to take the perspective of the advertiser. Thus, because of their egocentric perspective, young children perceive advertisements as being consistent with their own use of the advertised products: a source of entertainment and happiness. In contrast, because older children can take the perspective of the advertiser, they are better able to recognize the fact that advertisements are simply attempts to persuade the viewer to buy their products (Ward & Wackman, 1973). Furthermore, the limited cognitive ability of younger children prevents them from understanding disclaimers that accompany ads, such as "batteries not included," "some assembly required," or "each part sold separately" (Liebert, Sprafkin, Liebert, & Rubenstein, 1977).

Should advertisers care that older children recognize their attempts at persuasion and adjust their advertisements accordingly? Simply put, no. Consistently, research suggests that regardless of age and understanding of persuasive intent, advertisements work. Exposure to commercials increases the youth's desire for that product, and repeated exposure to the same commercial increases the desire even more (Gorn & Goldberg, 1977). Additionally, across development, heavy viewers of commercials request advertised products from parents more often than those who watch commercials less frequently (Buijzen & Valkenburg, 2003). And when children want a product, more often than not they will get it (Ward & Wackman, 1972).

To further enhance the desire for products among youth, advertisers use celebrities to pitch products, or they promote the product by including a premium prize (e.g., a toy) with every purchase. With regard to the former, research has shown that products, advertised by celebrities receive more favorable evaluations than the same product advertised without celebrity endorsement (Ross et al., 1984). Furthermore, older children and adolescents appear to be influenced by celebrity endorsements to a greater extent than younger children (Atkin & Block, 1983). With regard to the latter, premium prizes increase children's and adolescents' desire and requests for products (Atkin, 1978; Miller & Busch, 1979). Strasburger and Wilson (2002) reported that McDonald's repeatedly sold out of Teenie Beenie Babies when they were included in Happy Meals. Recently, my son requested that we go to Burger King *every night*, so that he could get all of the different Yu-Gi-Oh toys that were included in each Kid's Meal.

Drug Use and the Media

Because children watch television throughout the day, and because they are often watching shows geared towards adults, youth will be exposed to advertisements ostensibly aimed at adult consumers. However, many of the "adult-oriented" commercials (and advertisements in other media, such as magazines) include content that is entertaining to youth and therefore captures their attention. Talking lizards, frogs that comically attach themselves to trucks with their tongues, and majestic horses playing football are just a few of the commercials for alcoholic products that grab the attention of the youngest of viewers. Lieber's (1996) finding that 9- to 11-year-old children are better able to recognize the Budweiser frogs (73%) than Tony the Tiger (57%) supports the contention that youth are indeed attending to ads for products that can only legally be used by adults. In fact, many of these "adult-oriented" advertisements are purposefully designed to be attractive to youth (Gerbner, 1990).

Consider, for instance, the advertising strategy of the tobacco industry. With their base of consumers dying off daily by the thousands, the profitability of these companies relies on the recruitment of new smokers. Although it is illegal to directly market cigarettes to youth, the goal of cigarette advertising has been to attract young smokers. Why else would Old Joe the Camel, a cartoonish rendering of a camel, be used to advertise cigarettes? In fact, nearly 50% of cigarette advertising takes place in magazines popular with adolescents, such as *People, Sports Illustrated,* and *TV Guide* (King, Siegel, Celebucki, & Connolly, 1998). Not only do teens view these ads, but younger children do as well, and they are having an impact. Fischer, Schwart, Richards, Goldstein, and Rojas (1991) found that 6-year-olds were just as likely to recognize Old Joe the Camel as they were to recognize the logo for *The Disney Channel.* Furthermore, by showing physically fit and attractive young men and women smoking on billboards and in magazines, teenagers are associating smoking with fame, physical attractiveness, and being cool. Moreover, just like going out for ice cream after a baseball game or going bowling on a rainy day, such advertisements make smoking and drinking appear as a normative behavior of youth (Strasburger & Donnerstein, 1999).

Beyond the targeting of youth through indirect advertising, cigarette smoking, alcohol consumption, and drug use are frequently portrayed in television shows, movies, and music videos that *are* directly targeted at children and adolescents. For instance, a recent study found that 60% of G-rated films depict smoking or alcoholic beverage consumption (Thompson & Yokota, 2004). For films rated PG-13 the numbers increase, with the overwhelming majority of films (>80%) showing characters smoking and drinking. Moreover, nearly 20% of movies rated PG-13 portray illegal drug use (Roberts, Henriksen, & Christenson, 1999). Substance use on television is no better. In a review of the 20 most popular television shows among 12- to 17-year-olds, tobacco use occurred around 10% of the time. Alcohol use, however, was depicted or mentioned more than 70% of the time. Even more surprising, in over half of those episodes, alcoholic beverages were consumed by a character in a leading role (Christenson, Henriksen, & Roberts, 2000).

Just as the likelihood of engaging in acts of aggression is impacted by a multitude of risk factors, so too is adolescent drug use. Peers, personality, parenting, and school performance have been linked with the initiation and maintenance of smoking, alcohol consumption, and illicit drug use (Strasburger, 2001). However, media images also appear to influence drug use. For instance, Pechmann and Knight (2002) found that a combination of peer factors and exposure to advertising influenced adolescents' intentions to smoke. In particular, adolescents seeing videos of peers smoking in addition to viewing cigarette advertising expressed a greater intent to smoke than those teens reading cigarette advertisements without seeing a peer smoke. Moreover, adolescents were more likely to view peer smokers in a more positive light (e.g., cool) if they had been exposed to cigarette advertising than if they had no such exposure. Similar to the findings for smoking, the number of advertisements for alcohol adolescents view has been associated with drinking among teenagers, with higher exposure to advertisements associated with higher levels of alcohol consumption (Unger, Schuster, Zogg, Dent, & Stacy, 2003).

Beyond the influence of advertising, the viewing of media with and without smoking and alcohol appears to influence adolescent attitudes and behaviors towards these substances. For instance, Pechmann and Shih (1999) used a professional editor to create two versions of the film *Reality Bites,* one version with and one version without scenes depicting smoking. Nonsmoking 9th graders viewing the movie with the smoking scenes included were more likely to indicate that they intended to smoke and were more likely to convey more positive attitudes towards the smoker than those 9th graders viewing the movie with the smoking scenes deleted. Not only is the intent to smoke, drink, and use drugs associated with media exposure, but so, too, is use of these substances. Wingood et al. (2003) found that adolescent black females watching Rap music videos were more likely to use drugs and alcohol than those females with less Rap music video consumption. These findings remained even after taking into consideration additional factors, such as parental monitoring and religiosity.

Sexual Attitudes and Behavior

Across adolescence, youth begin to explore their burgeoning sexuality. During this time, decisions are made with regard to the moral, behavioral, and health-related aspects of sexual intercourse and non-coital sexual activity (collectively referred to as *sexual behavior*). Additionally, the reasons for and against engaging in sexual behavior (e.g., pregnancy, sexually transmitted diseases [STDs], feeling loved) are explored. Part of this exploratory process involves watching sexual content on television. Finding such content on television is not very difficult, as nearly 65% of all television programs involve sexual behavior (e.g., kissing, implied intercourse) or sexual dialogue (e.g., references to sex or innuendo; Kunkel et al., 2003). It has been estimated that in an average year, youth will view around 14,000 scenes involving some form of sexual content (Harris & Associates, 1988) with less than 15% of these scenes discussing contraception or STDs (Kunkel et al., 2003).

Although all teens typically rank mass media (e.g., TV, magazines, movies) behind parents and friends as a source of sexual information, during late adolescence the informative ability of mass media is ranked higher than that of schools (Yankelovich Partners, 1993). It is worth noting that while teens state that they would prefer to learn sexual information from their parents, on important issues such as contraception and pregnancy more than half of all teens report learning about these topics from television and movies (Sutton, Brown, Wilson, & Klein, 2002). Given that over 50% of high school students have had sexual intercourse (Centers for Disease Control and Prevention, 1999), the rate of teen pregnancies in the United States is higher than in all other industrialized countries (Singh & Darroch, 1999), 25% of teens engaging in sexual behavior contract a sexually transmitted disease (Institute of Medicine, 1997), and most teens wish they had waited to engage in sexual intercourse (National Campaign to Prevent Teen Pregnancy, 2001), the influence of mass media on sexual behavior is a legitimate health concern.

According to Delameter (1981), one of the strongest influences on teenage sexual behavior is culture. Given that television, movies, music, and other forms of mass media are integral parts of the adolescent culture, the messages relayed through these media have the potential to significantly affect sexual behavior (Collins et al., 2004). Theoretical support for this contention comes from Gerbner's *cultivation theory* (Gerbner et al., 1994). Essentially, cultivation theory contends that heavy exposure to television (and, to a lesser extent, related forms of mass media) results in attitudes and belief systems that are more consistent with the media's version of reality than with the way the world actually is. Thus, through the portrayals of an imaginary world, television socializes and educates viewers about the real world. With regard to sexual behavior among adolescents, cultivation theory predicts that the depiction of sexual behavior on TV will create attitudes and behaviors consistent with televised reality. Unfortunately, this prediction has been widely supported.

Teens watching high levels of sexual content on television tend to feel dissatisfied with being a virgin (Courtright & Baran, 1980), endorse casual sex (Bryant & Rockwell, 1994), and normalize unusual sexual behavior (e.g., group sex; Greenberg & Smith, 2002). Beyond attitudes, the heavy viewing of sexual content has been linked with increases in the onset of intercourse and the amount and type of noncoital sexual activity (e.g., breast and genital touching). Recently, Collins and colleagues (2004) found that after controlling for a wide range of social factors, teens who were heavy viewers of sexual content were twice as likely to engage in intercourse the following year in comparison to light viewers of sexual content. Furthermore, heavy television viewing was associated with more sexually advanced, non-coital sexual activity. To help make these findings concrete, Collins and colleagues state that after heavy viewing of sexual content, a 12-year-old will engage in sexual behavior consistent with that of a 14- or 15-year-old. Finally, whether sexual content was directly viewed or inferred from dialogue, Collins and associates' findings remained the same. Thus, exposure to sexual content appears to increase sexual activity, regardless of whether it is explicitly shown or simply talked about.

The Ugly

Affective body image is defined as the positive and negative feelings that youth hold regarding the appearance of their bodies (Cash & Green, 1986). Similar to other developmental outcomes, there are many contributing factors that influence affective body image, including biological predispositions and socializing agents such as peers (Banfield & McCabe, 2002). Of course, mass media play a role as well; unfortunately, the role that mass media frequently play is to help foster negative affective body images among youth. For instance, Mundell (2002) found that after watching a music video featuring Britney Spears, 10-year-old girls became dissatisfied with their bodies. Such dissatisfactions appear to be directly related to the fact that females on television are more beautiful and thinner than is typically found in the real world. In fact, women on television frequently meet the criteria of anorexia (Brown & Witherspoon, 2002).

Across adolescence, greater exposure to mainstream television programming is associated with poorer body image among white females. It is worth noting, however, that among black females, the viewing of television programs and, in particular, the viewing of programming with predominantly black casts, is associated with positive body images (Schooler, Ward, Merriwether, & Caruthers, 2004). To explain these findings, Schooler and colleagues rely on the nature of the message portrayed on television and *social comparison theory* (Festinger, 1954).

According to social comparison theory, youth make comparisons between themselves and others who are perceived to be like themselves. When such comparisons result in a positive view of the self, the individual's mood is elevated. In contrast, when comparisons lead to dissatisfaction with the self, the individual's mood is depressed. Recent content analyses have shown that the physical attractiveness and body size of black casts is more varied than in predominately white casts (Tirodkar & Jain, 2003). Thus, black women appear to be making comparisons with black women on television, who are perceived to be more like themselves than white cast members. As such, for black women, the broader range of body types and physical attractiveness of black casts result in a more positive view of the self. In contrast, white women appear to compare themselves to white cast members who are perceived to be more like themselves than black cast members. And because these televised women are unrealistically thin and uncharacteristically beautiful, a negative body image results for white female viewers. Essentially, Schooler et al.'s (2004) research demonstrates that the unrealistic images of women depicted on television do not simply affect the viewer in a passive manner. Instead, the viewers' predispositions regarding body image and the nature of their social comparisons work together to actively influence the *interpretation* and subsequent power of the messages viewed.

Given that models, television stars, and movie stars are significantly thinner than the average woman and that the images of women deemed sexy and attractive by society often meet the body mass index criteria for anorexia, the dissatisfaction that girls face with regard to their bodies places them at risk for eating disorders, such as anorexia nervosa and bulimia nervosa (Polivy & Herman, 2004). Whereas anorexia nervosa is characterized by self-starvation and the maintenance of unhealthy weight, bulimia nervosa is typified by binge eating, followed by the elimination of the food through self-induced vomiting or laxatives. For each of these disorders, among the varied familial and experiential risk factors is the presence of a distorted body image. And as the empirical literature has found, mass media help engender a distorted body image in females of all ages.

One of the most intriguing studies demonstrating the power of televised images on eating disorders was conducted using a naturalistic experiment on Fijian teens (Becker, Burwell, Gilman, Herzog, & Hamburg, 2002). As you recall, a naturalistic experiment involves the introduction of significant change to the environment that occurs without manipulation from the researcher. In this case, Becker and colleagues assessed the impact of the "natural" introduction of television on the purging behavior of Fijian adolescent girls. In comparison to girls who had less than one month of exposure to television, girls with three years of television exposure showed dramatic increases in purging behavior. Additionally, nearly 70% of these girls reported going on a diet in order to lose weight. This finding alone is profound, given that prior to the introduction of television, dieting among Fijian girls was unheard of. In part, the perceived need for dieting occurred as a result of the vast majority of Fijian girls' *new* belief that they were "too big or fat"—a belief that was uncommon prior to the introduction of television. More disturbing, however, was the finding that among girls with three years of television exposure, 11% reported self-induced vomiting to lose weight. In comparison, there was no such behavior (i.e., 0%) among girls with relatively little exposure to television programming.

It should be pointed out that dissatisfaction with one's body is not limited to girls, adolescents, and young women. Recent research has found that the body image of adolescent males also appears to be negatively affected by mass media. However, whereas media images of females in print and on television promote an unrealistic ideal for thinness that encourages dieting, for males the media portray an unrealistic ideal for muscularity (Agliata & Tantleff-Dunn, 2004). For instance, Pope, Olivarida, Gruber, and Borowiecki (1999) found that the rippling pecs and bulging biceps of toy action figures surpass the proportions of world-class body builders. Moreover, the depictions of the male physique in magazines and the muscularity of heroic action movie stars such as Brad Pitt and Hugh Jackman provide youth with the impression that the ideal male, in terms of societal expectations, is Adonis-like in stature (Pope, Phillips, & Olivardia, 2000). Recent research has shown that for late adolescent men, exposure to hyper-mesomorphic images results in increased dissatisfaction with one's muscularity and a greater likelihood of becoming depressed (Agliata & Tantleff-Dunn, 2004).

Just as images of thin and attractive women place females at risk for eating disorders, so, too, do images of muscular men place males at risk. However, instead of focusing on losing weight, males focus on gaining weight—muscle weight, that is. In fact, exposure to hyper-mesomorphic images is a significant risk factor for developing the psychological disorder known as *muscle dysmorphia*. Muscle dysmorphia is a pathological preoccupation with increasing muscularity. For these individuals, the presence of muscle mass is more important than the loss of fat. In fact, males with this disorder pursue "bigness" with the same vigilance that women with anorexia pursue "thinness." Whereas anorexia and bulimia tend to be strongly influenced by familial influences and childhood experiences, these factors do not appear to influence muscle dysmorphia (Olivardia, Pope, & Hudson, 2000). However, the results of Olivardia and colleagues were based on case studies, thereby limiting their generalizability. Moreover, given the fact that the extant body of literature on muscle dysmorphia is relatively small, more research is necessary before the risk factors associated with muscle dysmorphia and their relative importance across development can be established.

Summary

- The "three-hour rule" mandates at least three hours of E/I programming per week.
- There are two main types of E/I programming: academic and prosocial.

- The viewing of prosocial television content can increase positive interactions among youth during play and increase altruism.
- The effect sizes associated with prosocial television watching and prosocial behavior peak around age 7 and then decline. In contrast to older research, newer research estimates that effect sizes for prosocial television and prosocial behavior are less than the effects sizes for television violence and aggression.
- Viewing prosocial behavior accomplished through the use of aggression promotes aggressive behavior more so than nonviolent prosocial action.
- Toddlers, preschoolers, and young children of both genders and older girls tend to enjoy watching academic and social/emotional E/I programming.
- There are limitations to what children can learn from academic programming. Certain forms of academic E/I programming work better than others. Whereas programming that focuses on the application of skills tends to help youth academically, academic E/I programming geared towards the drilling of concepts does not.
- Computer aided instruction has the potential to help youth academically, as it works within the child's zone of proximal development.
- Prosocial programming can reduce prejudice. However, beyond developmental television viewing, additional factors play a critical role in the development and maintenance of stereotypes and prejudice.
- The viewing of stereotyped television contributes to the development of stereotyped beliefs.
- Television commercials are perceived differently depending upon the child's age. Regardless of whether commercials are viewed as entertainment or information, exposure to commercials increases children's and adolescents' desires for the advertised product. Premium prizes increase youth's desire and requests for products.
- Many "adult-oriented" advertisements for alcohol and tobacco are purposefully designed to be attractive to youth. Cigarette smoking, alcohol consumption, and drug use are frequently portrayed in television shows, movies, and music videos that *are* directly targeted at children and adolescents. Such media depictions can influence youth's decisions to drink and smoke.
- Adolescence is a time of burgeoning sexuality. Teens learn about contraception, pregnancy, and "normal" sexual behavior from television and movies. Positive attitudes towards early sexual activity and the early onset of intercourse are associated with heavy viewing of sexual content.
- White females become dissatisfied with their bodies after viewing television programs featuring white casts. In contrast, for black females, the viewing of television programs with predominantly black casts is associated with a positive body image.
- The body image of adolescent males is negatively affected by mass media. In men, an increased dissatisfaction with a lack of muscularity is associated with exposure to hypermesomorphic media images.

References

Agliata, D., & Tantleff-Dunn, S. (2004). The impact of media exposure on males' body image. *Journal of Social and Clinical Psychology, 23,* 7–22.

Aguilar, B., O'Brien, K. M., August, G. J., Aoun, S. L., & Hektner, J. M. (2001). Relationship quality of aggressive children and their siblings: A multiinformant, multimeasure investigation. *Journal of Abnormal Child Psychology, 29,* 479–489.

Ainsworth, M. D. S., Blehar, M. C., Waters, E., & Wall, S. (1978). *Patterns of attachment: A psychological study of the strange situation.* Hillsdale, NJ: Erlbaum.

Alessi, N., Huang, M., James, P., Ying, J., & Chowhan, N. (1992). The influence of music and rock videos. Facts for families (No. 40). *Psychiatry Star, American Academy of Child and Adolescent Psychiatry, Facts for Families Index.*

Aluja-Fabregat, A. (2000). Personality and curiosity about TV and films violence in adolescents. *Personality and Individual Differences, 29,* 379–392.

Aluja-Fabregat, A., & Torrubia-Beltri, R. (1998).Viewing of mass media violence, perception of violence, personality, and academic achievement. *Personality and Individual Differences, 25,* 973–989.

Alvarez, M. M., Huston, A. C., Wright, J. C., & Kerkman, D. D. (1988). Gender differences in visual attention to television form and content. *Journal of Applied Developmental Psychology, 9,* 459–475.

American Library Association. (2003). Retrieved September 29, 2004, from http://ala.org

American Psychiatric Association. (1994). *Diagnostic and statistical manual of mental disorders* (4th ed.). Washington, DC: Author.

American Psychological Association. (2001). *Publication manual of the American Psychological Association* (5th ed.). Washington, DC: Author.

Anderson, C. A. (2000). *Violent video games increase aggression and violence.* U. S. Senate Committee on Commerce, Science, and Transportation hearing on "The Impact of Interactive Violence on Children." Retrieved March 1, 2004, from http://psych-server.iastate.edu/faculty/caa/abstracts/2000–2004/00Senate.html

Anderson, C. A. (2004). An update on the effects of violent video games. *Journal of Adolescence, 27,* 113–122.

Anderson, C. A., & Anderson, K. B. (1998). Temperature and aggression: Paradox, controversy, and a (fairly) clear picture. In R. Geen & E. Donnerstein (Eds.),

Human aggression: Theories, research and implications for policy (pp. 247–298). San Diego, CA: Academic Press.

Anderson, C. A., Berkowitz, L., Donnerstein, E., Huesmann, R. L., Johnson, J., Linz, D., et al. (2003). The influence of media violence on youth. *Psychological Science in the Public Interest, 4,* 81–110.

Anderson, C. A., & Bushman, B. J. (1997). External validity of "trivial" experiments: The case of laboratory aggression. *Review of General Psychology, 1,* 19–41.

Anderson, C. A., & Bushman, B. J. (2001). Effects of violent video games on aggressive behavior, aggressive cognition, aggressive affect, physiological arousal, and prosocial behavior: A metaanalytic review of the scientific literature. *Psychological Science, 12,* 353–359.

Anderson, C. A., & Bushman, B. J. (2002). Human aggression. *Annual Review of Psychology, 53,* 27–51.

Anderson, C. A., Carnagey, N. L., & Eubanks, J. (2003). Exposure to violent media: The effects of songs with violent lyrics on aggressive thoughts and feelings. *Journal of Personality and Social Psychology, 84,* 960–971.

Anderson, C. A., & Dill, K. E. (2000). Video games and aggressive thoughts, feelings, and behavior in the laboratory and in life. *Journal of Personality and Social Psychology, 78,* 772–790.

Anderson, C. A., & Ford, M. E. (1986). Affect of game player: Short-term effects of highly and mildly aggressive video games. *Personality and Social Psychology Bulletin, 12,* 390–402.

Anderson, D. R., Huston, A. C., Schmitt, K. L., Linebarger, D. L., & Wright, J. C. (2001). Early childhood television viewing and adolescent behavior: The recontact study. *Monographs of the Society for Research in Child Development, 66*(1), vii–147.

Anderson, D. R., & Lorch, E. P. (1983). Looking at television: Action or reaction? In J. Bryant & D. R. Anderson (Eds.), *Children's understanding of television: Research on attention and comprehension* (pp. 1–34). New York: Academic Press.

Anderson, R. C., Wilson, P., & Fielding, L. (1988). Growth in reading and how children spend their time outside of school. *Reading Research Quarterly, 23,* 285–303.

Annenberg Public Policy Center. (1999). *Media in the home.* Retrieved March 29, 2002, from www.appcpenn.org/mediainhome/conference/

Antonucci, M. (1998). Holy sales slump! Comic-book industry hit with a slowdown. *Knight-Ridder Tribune Business News* [Online]. Available from DIALOG File 20: World Reporter.

Arnett, J. J. (1991). Heavy metal music and reckless behavior among adolescents. *Journal of Youth and Adolescence, 20,* 573–592.

Arnett, J. J. (1995). Adolescents' uses of media for socialization. *Journal of Youth and Adolescence, 24,* 519–531.

Atkin, C. (1983). Effects of realistic TV violence vs. fictional violence on aggression. *Journalism Quarterly, 60,* 615–621.

Atkin, C. K. (1978). Observation of parent-child interaction in supermarket decision-making. *Journal of Marketing, 42*(4), 41–45.

Atkin, C. K., & Block, M. (1983). Effectiveness of celebrity endorsers. *Journal of Advertising Research, 23,* 57–61.

Atkin, C. K., Smith, S. W., Roberto, A. J., Fediuk, T., & Wagner, T. (2002). Correlates of verbally aggressive communication in adolescents. *Journal of Applied Communication Research, 30,* 251–266.

Ausbrooks, E., Thomas, S. P., & Williams, R. (1995). Relationships among self-efficacy, optimism, trait anger, and anger expression. *Health Values, 19*(4), 46–53.

Ballard, M. E., & Coates, S. (1995). The immediate effects of homicidal, suicidal, and nonviolent heavy metal and rap songs on the moods of college students. *Youth and Society, 27,* 148–168.

Bandura, A. (1965). Influence of models' reinforcement contingencies on the acquisition of imitative responses. *Journal of Personality and Social Psychology, 1,* 589–595.

Bandura, A. (1973). *Aggression: A social learning analysis.* Englewood Cliffs, NJ: Prentice Hall.

Bandura, A. (1986). *Social foundations of thought and action: A social cognitive theory.* Englewood Cliffs, NJ: Prentice Hall.

Bandura, A., Caprara, G. V., Barbaranelli, C., Gerbino, M., & Pastorelli, C. (2003). Role of affective self-regulatory efficacy in diverse spheres of psychosocial functioning. *Child Development, 74,* 769–782.

Bandura, A., Ross, D., & Ross, S. A. (1961). Transmission of aggression through imitation of aggressive models. *Journal of Abnormal and Social Psychology, 63*(3), 575–582.

Bandura, A., Ross, D., & Ross, S. A. (1963). Imitation of film-mediated aggressive models. *Journal of Abnormal Social Psychology, 66*(1), 3–11.

Banfield, S., & McCabe, M. (2002). An evaluation of the construct of body image. *Adolescence, 37,* 373–393.

Bartels, L. (2004). Harris home up for sale. *RockyMountainNews.com.* Retrieved December 27, 2004, from http://www.rockymountainnews.com

Bartholow, B. D., & Anderson, C. A. (2002). Effects of violent video games on aggressive behavior: Potential sex differences. *Journal of Experimental Social Psychology, 38,* 283–290.

Barton, J. (2004). Fla. teen pleads guilty in wrestling death. *Newsday.com.* Retrieved January 13, 2005, from http://www.newsday.com/news/nationworld

Baumrind, D. (1971). Current patterns of parental authority. *Developmental Psychology Monographs, Part 2, 4*(1), 1–103.

Baumrind, D. (1991). Parenting styles and adolescent development. In J. Brooks-Gunn, R. Lerner, & A. Petersen (Eds.), *The encyclopedia of adolescence* (pp. 746–758). New York: Garland.

Becker, A. E., Burwell, R. A., Gilman, S. E., Herzog, D. B., & Hamburg, P. (2002). Eating behaviours and attitudes following prolonged exposure to television among ethnic Fijian adolescent girls. *British Journal of Psychiatry, 180,* 509–514.

Becker, D. (2004). Playstation 2 passes sales milestone. *C/Net News.com*. Retrieved February 1, 2005, from http://news.com.com

Begg, I. M., Needham, D. R., & Bookbinder, M. (1993). Do backward messages unconsciously affect listeners? No. *Canadian Journal of Experimental Psychology, 47*, 1–14.

Belson, W. A. (1978). *Television violence and the adolescent boy*. Farnborough, UK: Saxon House.

Berenbaum, S. A., & Snyder, E. (1995). Early hormonal influences on childhood sex-typed activity and playmate preferences: Implications for the development of sexual orientation. *Developmental Psychology, 31*, 31–42.

Berkowitz, L. (1965). The concept of aggressive drive: Some additional considerations. In L. Berkowitz (Ed.), *Advances in experimental social psychology* (Vol. 2, pp. 301–329). Orlando, FL: Academic Press.

Berkowitz, L. (1993). *Aggression: Its causes, consequences, and control*. New York: McGraw-Hill.

Berkowitz, L., & Powers, P. C. (1979). Effects of timing and justification of witnessed aggression on the observers' punitiveness. *Journal of Research in Personality, 13*, 71–80.

Berkowitz, L., & Rawlings, E. (1963). Effects of film violence on inhibitions against subsequent aggression. *Journal of Abnormal and Social Psychology, 1*(3), 405–412.

Bernstein, D. A., Penner, L. A., Clarke-Stewart, A., & Roy, E. J. (2003). *Psychology* (6th ed.). New York: Houghton Mifflin.

Bernthal, M. J. (2003). The effects of professional wrestling viewership on children. *The Sport Journal*. Retrieved June 5, 2004, from http://thesportjournal.org

Bettelheim, B. (1967). *The uses of enchantment: The meaning and importance of fairy tales*. New York: Random House.

Bickham, D. S., Wright, J. C., & Huston, A. C. (2001). Attention, comprehension, and the inducational influence of television. In D. G. Singer & J. L. Singer (Eds.), *Handbook of children and the media* (pp.101–199). Thousand Oaks, CA: Sage.

Blackburn, R. (1993). *The psychology of criminal conduct*. Chichester, UK: Wiley.

Blakely, W. P. (1958). A study of seventh grade children's reading of comic books as related to certain other variables. *The Journal of Genetic Psychology, 93*, 291–301.

Bonte, E., & Musgrove, M. (1943). Influence of war as evidenced in children's play. *Child Development, 14*, 179–200.

Book, A. S., Starzyk, K. B., & Quinsey, V. L. (2001). The relationship between testosterone and aggression: A meta-analysis. *Aggression and Violent Behavior, 6*, 579–599.

Borum, R. (2000). Assessing violence risk among youth. *Journal of Clinical Psychology, 56*(10), 1263–1288.

Bowlby, J. (1969/1982). *Attachment and loss* (2nd ed.). New York: Basic Books.

Box Office Mojo. (2004). Retrieved December 27, 2004, from http://www.box officemojo.com

Boyatzis, C. J., Matillo, G. M., & Nesbitt, K. M. (1995). Effects of "The Mighty Morphin Power Rangers" on children's aggression with peers. *Child Study Journal, 25,* 45–55.

Boyatzis, C. J., & Varghese, R. (1994). Children's emotional associations with colors. *Journal of Genetic Psychology, 155,* 77–85.

Brame, B., Nagin, D. S., & Tremblay, R. E. (2001). Developmental trajectories of physical aggression from school entry to late adolescence. *Journal of Child Psychology and Psychiatry, 42*(4), 503–512.

Brand, J. (1969). The effect of highly aggressive content in comic books on seventh grade children. *Graduate Research in Education and Related Disciplines, 5,* 46–61.

Brooks-Gunn, J., & Warren, M. P. (1989). Biological and social contributions to negative affect in young adolescent girls. *Child Development, 60,* 40–55.

Brown, E. F., & Hendee, W. R. (1989). Adolescents and their music: Insights into the health of adolescents. *Journal of the American Medical Association, 262,* 1659–1663.

Brown, J., & Witherspoon, E. (2002). The mass media and American adolescents' health. *Journal of Adolescent Health, 31,* 153–170.

Brownlee, S. (1999). Inside the teen brain. *US News Online.* Retrieved February 22, 2003, from http://www.usnews.com/usnews/issue/990809/nycu/teenbrain.htm

Bruce, L. (1995). *At the intersection of real-live and television violence: Emotional effects, cognitive effects and interpretive activities of children.* Unpublished doctoral dissertation, University of Wisconsin, Madison.

Bryant, J., & Rockwell, S. C. (1994). Effects of massive exposure to sexually oriented prime-time television programming on adolescents' moral judgment. In D. Zillmann, J. Bryant, & A. C. Huston (Eds.), *Media, children, and the family: Social scientific, psychodynamic, and clinical perspectives* (pp. 183–196). Hillsdale, NJ: Erlbaum.

Bryson, B. (1996). "Anything but heavy metal": Symbolic exclusion and musical dislikes. *American Sociological Review, 61,* 844–899.

Buchman, D. D., & Funk, J. B. (1996). Video and computer games in the '90s: Children's time commitment and game preference. *Children Today, 24*(1), 12–15.

Buijzen, M., & Valkenburg, P. M. (2003). The unintended effects of television advertising: A parent-child survey. *Communication Research, 30,* 483–503.

Bushman, B. J. (1998). Priming effects of media violence on the accessibility of aggressive constructs in memory. *Personality and Social Psychology Bulletin, 24*(5), 537–545.

Bushman, B. J. (2002). Does venting anger feed or extinguish the flame? Catharsis, rumination, distraction, anger and aggressive responding. *Journal of Personality and Social Psychology, 28,* 724–731.

Bushman, B. J., & Anderson, C. A. (2001). Media violence and the American public: Scientific facts versus misinformation. *American Psychologist, 56,* 477–489.

Bushman, B. J., & Cantor, J. (2003). Media ratings for violence and sex. *American Psychologist, 58,* 130–141.

Bushman, B. J., & Huesmann, L. R. (2001). Effects of televised violence on aggression. In D. Singer & J. Singer (Eds.), *Handbook of children and the media* (pp. 223–254). Thousand Oaks, CA: Sage.

Bushman, B. J., & Stack, A. D. (1996). Forbidden fruit versus tainted fruit: Effects of warning labels on attraction to television violence. *Journal of Experimental Psychology: Applied, 2*, 207–226.

Buss, A. H. (1961). *The psychology of aggression*. New York: Wiley.

Cairns, R. B., Cadwallader, T. W., Estell, D., & Neckerman, H. J. (1997). Groups to gangs: Developmental and criminological perspective and relevance for prevention. In D. M. Stoff, J. Breiling, & J. D. Maser (Eds.), *Handbook of antisocial behavior* (pp. 194–204). New York: Wiley.

Cairns, R. B., & Cairns, B. D. (1994). *Lifelines and risks: Pathways of youth in our time*. Cambridge, UK: Cambridge University Press.

Caldera, Y. M., Huston, A. C., & O'Brien M. (1989). Social interactions and play patterns of parents and toddlers with feminine, masculine, and neutral toys. *Child Development, 60*, 70–76.

Calvert, S. L., & Kotler, J. A. (2003). Lessons from children's television: The impact of the Children's Television Act on children's learning. *Applied Developmental Psychology, 24*, 275–235.

Calvert, S. L., Kotler, J., Murray, W., Gonzales, E., Savoye, K., Hammack, P., et al. (2002). Children's online reports about educational and informational television programs. In S. L. Calvert, A. B. Jordan, & R. R. Cocking (Eds.), *Children in the digital age: Influences of electronic media on development* (pp. 165–182). Westport, CT: Praeger.

Cantor, J. (1998a). Children's attraction to violent television programming. In J. H. Goldstein (Ed.), *Why we watch: The attractions of violent entertainment* (pp. 88–115). New York: Oxford University Press.

Cantor, J. (1998b). Ratings for program content: The role of research findings. *Annals of the American Academy of Political Social Science, 557*, 54–69.

Cantor, J. (2002). Fright reactions to mass media. In J. Bryant & D. Zillmann (Eds.), *Media effects* (2nd ed., pp. 287–306). Mahwah, NJ: Erlbaum.

Cantor, J., Harrison, K., & Nathanson, A. (1997). *National television violence study, Vol. 2*. Thousand Oaks, CA: Sage.

Cantor, J., & Sparks, G. G. (1984). Children's fear responses to mass media: Testing some Piagetian predictions. *Journal of Communication, 34*, 90–103.

Cantor, J., & Wilson, B. J. (2003). Media and violence: Intervention strategies for reducing aggression. *Media Psychology, 5*, 363–403.

Caplan, M., Vespo, J., Pedersen, J., & Hay, D. F. (1991). Conflict and its resolution in small groups of one- and two-year-olds. *Child Development, 62*, 1513–1524.

Caprara, G. V., Regalia, C., & Bandura, A. (2002). Longitudinal impact of perceived self-regulatory efficacy on violent conduct. *European Psychologist, 7*, 63–69.

Carnagey, N. L., & Anderson, C. A. (2003). Theory in the study of media violence: The general aggression model. In D. Gentile (Ed.), *Media violence and children* (pp. 87–106). Westport, CT: Praeger.

Carpentier, F. D., Knobloch, S., & Zillmann, D. (2003). Rock, rap, and rebellion: Comparisons of traits predicting selective exposure to defiant music. *Personality and Individual Differences, 35*, 1643–1655.

Cash, T. F., & Green, G. K. (1986). Body weight and body image among college women: Perception, cognition, and affect. *Journal of Personality Assessment, 50*, 290–301.

Cassidy, J., & Berlin, L. (1994). The insecure/ambivalent pattern of attachment: Theory and research. *Child Development, 65*, 971–981.

Cassidy, J., & Kobak, R. R. (1988). Avoidance and its relation to other defensive processes. In J. Belsky and T. Nezworski (Eds.), *Clinical implications of attachment* (pp. 300–323). Hillsdale, NJ: Erlbaum.

Celozzi, M. J., Kazelskis, R., & Gutsch, K. U. (1981). The relationship between viewing televised violence in hockey and subsequent levels of personal aggression. *Journal of Sport Behavior, 4*(4), 157–162.

Centers for Disease Control and Prevention. (1999). *1996 youth risk behavior surveillance systems (YRBSS)*. Retrieved July 12, 2002, from http://www.cdc.gov

Cervone, D. (2000). Thinking about self-efficacy. *Behavior Modification, 24*, 30–56.

Chambers, J. H., & Ascione, F. R. (1987). The effects of prosocial and aggressive videogames on children's donating and helping. *Journal of Genetic Psychology 148*, 499–505.

Children's Television Act of 1990. (1990). Publ. L. No. 101–437, 104 Stat. 996–1000, codified at 47 USC Sections 303a, 303b, 394.

Christenson, P., & Roberts, D. (1998). *It's not only rock and roll: Popular music in the lives of adolescents.* Cresskill, NJ: Hampton Press.

Christenson, P. G., Henriksen, L., & Roberts, D. F. (2000). *Substance use in popular prime-time television.* Washington, DC: Office of National Drug Control Policy.

Cline, V. B., Croft, R. G., & Courrier, S. (1973). Desensitization of children to television violence. *Journal of Personality and Social Psychology, 27*, 360–365.

Coie, J., & Dodge, K. (1998). Aggression and antisocial behavior. In W. Damon (Series Ed.) & N. Eisenberg (Vol. Ed.), *Handbook of child psychology: Vol. 3. Social, emotional and personality development* (5th ed., pp. 779–862). New York: Wiley.

Coie, J., & Dodge, K., & Coppotelli, H. (1982). Dimensions and types of social status: A cross-age perspective. *Developmental Psychology, 18*, 557–570.

Coie, J., Dodge, K., Terry, R., & Wright, V. (1991). The role of aggression in peer relations: An analysis of aggression episodes in boys' play groups. *Child Development, 62*, 812–826.

Collins, R. L., Elliott, M. N., Berry, S. H., Kanouse, D. E., Kunkel, D. Hunter, S. B., et al. (2004). Watching sex on television predicts adolescent initiation of sexual behavior. *Pediatrics, 114*, 280–289.

Collins, W. A. (1973). Effect of temporal separation between motivation, aggression, and consequences: A developmental study. *Developmental Psychology, 8*, 215–221.

Collins-Standley, T., Gan, S., Yu, H. J., & Zillman, D. (1996). Choice of romantic, violent, and scary fairy-tale books by preschool boys and girls. *Child Study Journal, 26*(4), 279–302.

Comstock, G., & Paik, H. (1999). *Television and the American child.* San Diego, CA: Academic Press.

Comstock, G., & Scharrer, E. (2003). Meta-analyzing the controversy over television violence and aggression. In D. Gentile (Ed.), *Media violence and children* (pp. 205–226). Westport, CT: Praeger.

Connor, D. F. (2002). *Aggression and antisocial behavior in children and adolescents.* New York: Guilford Press.

Cooper, J., & Mackie, D. (1986). Video games and aggression in children. *Journal of Applied Social Psychology, 16,* 726–744.

Corder-Botz, C. R. (1980). Mediation: The role of significant others. *Journal of Communication, 30*(3), 106–118.

Courtright, J., & Baran, S. (1980). The acquisition of sexual information by young people. *Journalism Quarterly, 57,* 107–114.

Coyne, S. M., Archer, J., & Eslea, M. (2004). Cruel intentions on television and in real life: Can viewing indirect aggression increase viewers' subsequent indirection aggression? *Journal of Experimental Child Psychology, 88,* 234–253.

Crawford, K. (2004). Pricing Howard Stern. *CNNMoney.com.* Retrieved March 3, 2005, from http://www.cnnmoney.com

Crick, N. R., & Dodge, D. A. (1994). A review and reformulation of social information processing mechanisms in children's social adjustment. *Psychological Bulletin, 115,* 74–101.

Crick, N. R., Grotpeter, J. K., & Bigbee, M. A. (2002). Relationally and physically aggressive children's intent attributions and feelings of distress for relational and instrumental peer provocations. *Child Development, 73,* 1134–1142.

Crick, N. R., Werner, N. E., Casas, J. F., O'Brien, K. M., Nelson, D. A., Grotpeter, J. K., et al. (1999). Childhood aggression and gender: A new look at an old problem. In D. Bernstein (Vol. Ed.) & R. A. Dienstbier (Series Ed.), *Gender and motivation: The Nebraska symposium on motivation* (Vol. 45, pp. 75–141). Lincoln: University of Nebraska Press.

Cunningham, A. E., & Stanovich, K. E. (1991). Tracking the unique effects of print exposure in children: Associations with vocabulary, general knowledge, and spelling. *Journal of Educational Psychology, 83*(2), 264–274.

Daniels, L. (1971). *Comix: A history of comic books in America.* New York: Outerbridge & Dienstfrey.

DeHart, G. B., Sroufe, L. A., & Cooper, R. G. (2004). *Child development: Its nature and course* (5th ed.). New York: McGraw-Hill.

Delameter, J. (1981). The social control of sexuality. *Annual Review of Sociology, 7,* 263–290.

De La Paz, D. (2004). Advisory labels stimulate sales. *Fort Wayne Gazette.* Retrieved January 13, 2005, from http://fortwayne.com

Designboom. (2004). The history of video games: From "pong" to "pac-man." Retrieved November 12, 2004, from http://www.designboom.com/eng/education/pong.html

Desmond, R. J. (1987). Adolescents and music lyrics: Implications of a cognitive perspective. *Communication Quarterly, 35,* 276–284.

The Diabolical Dominion. (2004). Retrieved December 10, 2004, from http://diabolical-dominion.com

Diamond Comics. (1999). Retrieved August 20, 2002, from http://www.diamond comic.com

Dietz, T. L. (1998). An examination of violence and gender role portrayals in video games: Implications for gender socialization and aggressive behavior. *Sex Roles, 38,* 425–442.

Dill, K. E., & Dill, J. C. (1998). Video game violence: A review of the empirical literature. *Aggression and Violent Behavior, 3*(4), 407–428.

Dmitrieva, T. N., Oades, R. D., Hauffa, B. P., & Eggers, C. (2001). Dehydroepiandrosterone sulphate and corticotrophin levels are high in young male patients with conduct disorder: Comparisons for growth factors, thyroid and gonadal hormones. *Neuropsychobiology, 43,* 134–140.

Dodge, K. A. (1980). Social cognition and children's aggressive behavior. *Child Development, 51,* 162–170.

Dodge, K. A. (1986). A social information processing model of social competence in children. In M. Perlmutter (Ed.), *Minnesota symposium on child psychology* (Vol. 18, pp. 77–125). Hillside, NJ: Erlbaum.

Dodge, K. A., & Crick, N. R. (1990). Social information-processing bases of aggressive behavior in children. *Personality and Social Psychology Bulletin, 16*(1), 8–22.

Dodge, K. A., & Frame, C. L. (1982). Social cognitive biases and deficits in aggressive boys. *Child Development, 53,* 620–625.

Dollard, J., Doob, L., Miller, N., Mowrer, O. H., & Sears, R. R. (1939). *Frustration and aggression.* New Haven, CT: Yale University Press.

Dominick, J. R. (1984). Video games, television violence and aggression in teenagers. *Journal of Communication, 34,* 136–147.

Dominick, J. R., & Greenberg, B. S. (1972). Attitudes toward violence: The interaction of television, family attitudes and social class. In G. A. Comstock and E. A. Rubinstein (Eds.), *Television and social behavior. Vol. 3: Television and adolescent aggressiveness* (pp. 314–335). Washington, DC: Government Printing Office.

Dorr, A., & Kovaric, P. (1980). Some of the people some of the time—But which people? Televised violence and its effects. In E. L. Palmer & A. Dorr (Eds.), *Children and the faces of television: Teaching, violence, selling* (pp. 183–190). New York: Academic Press.

Drabman, R. S., & Thomas, M. H. (1974). Does media violence increase children's tolerance for real-life aggression? *Developmental Psychology, 10*(3), 418–421.

Dunand, M., Berkowitz, L., & Leyens, J. (1984). Audience effects when viewing aggressive movies. *British Journal of Social Psychology, 23*(1), 69–76.

Dunn, J. (1993). *Young children's close relationships: Beyond attachment.* Thousand Oaks, CA: Sage.

Dunphy, D. C. (1963). The social structure of urban adolescent peer groups. *Sociometry, 26,* 230–246.

Eisenberg, N., Tryon, K., & Cameron, E. (1984). The relation of preschoolers' peer interaction to their sex-typed toy choices. *Child Development, 55,* 1044–1050.

Eisenberger, N. I., Lieberman, M. D., & Williams, K. D. (2003). Does rejection hurt? An fMRI study of social exclusion. *Science, 302,* 290–292.

Ekman, P., Liebert, R. M., Friesen, W., Harrison, R., Zlatchin, C., Malmstrom, E. J., et al. (1972). Facial expressions of emotion while watching televised violence as predictors of subsequent aggression. In G. A. Comstock, E. A. Rubinstein, and J. P. Murray (Eds.), *Television and social behavior, Vol. I. Television's effects: Further explorations* (pp. 22–58). Washington, DC: U.S. Government Printing Office.

Ellis, G. T., & Sekyra, F. (1972). The effect of aggressive cartoons on behavior of first grade children. *Journal of Psychology, 81,* 37–43.

Ellis, S., Rogoff, B., & Cromer, C. C. (1981). Age segregation in children's social interactions. *Developmental Psychology, 17,* 399–407.

Entertainment Software Rating Board. (2004). *ESRB game ratings.* Retrieved October 30, 2004, from http://www.esrb.org/esrbratings.asp

Epkins, C. C. (1993). A preliminary comparison of teacher ratings and child self-report of depression, anxiety and aggression in inpatient and elementary school samples. *Journal of Abnormal Child Psychology, 21,* 649–661.

Epps, J., & Kendall, P. C. (1995). Hostile attributional bias in adults. *Cognitive Therapy and Research, 19*(2), 159–178.

Eron, L. D., Huesmann, L. R., Lefkowitz, M. M., & Walder, L. O. (1972). Does television violence cause aggression? *American Psychologist, 27,* 253–263.

EyeWitness to History. (2003). *The suicide of Socrates, 399 BC.* Retrieved September 5, 2004, from http://www.eyewitnesstohistory.com

Farrington, D. P. (1978). The family background of aggressive youths. In L. A. Hersov, M. Berger, & D. Schaffer (Eds.), *Aggression and antisocial behavior in childhood and adolescence* (pp. 73–93). Oxford: Pergamon.

Farrington, D. P. (1995). The development of offending and antisocial behaviour from childhood: Key findings from the Cambridge Study in Delinquent Development. *Journal of Child Psychology and Psychiatry, 360,* 929–964.

Federal Communications Commission. (1996). *Policies and rules concerning children's television programming: Revision of programming policies for television broadcast stations.* Washington, DC: Author.

Federal Trade Commission (2004). *Marketing violent entertainment to children: A fourth follow-up review of industry practices in the motion picture, music recording & electronic game industries.* Washington, DC: Author.

Feingold, A. (1994). Gender differences in personality: A meta-analysis. *Psychological Bulletin, 116,* 429–456.

FelixTheCat.Com (2005). *History of Felix*. Retrieved February 22, 2004, from http://felixthecat.com/history.htm

Feshbach, S. (1956). The catharsis hypothesis and some consequences of interaction with aggressive and neutral play objects. *Journal of Personality, 24*, 449–462.

Festinger, L. (1954). A theory of social comparison processes. *Human Relations, 7*, 117–140.

Fischer, P. M., Schwart, M. P., Richards, J. W., Goldstein, A. O., & Rojas, J. T. (1991). Brand logo recognition by children aged 3 to 6 years: Mickey Mouse and Old Joe the Camel. *Journal of the American Medical Association, 266*, 3145–3153.

Fiske, S. T., & Taylor, S. F. (1991). *Social cognition* (2nd ed.). New York: McGraw-Hill.

Flavell, J. H., Flavell, E. R., Green, F. L., & Korfmacher, J. E. (1990). Do young children think of television images as pictures or real objects? *Journal of Broadcasting and Electronic Media, 34*, 399–419.

Fling, S., Smith, L., Rodriguez, T., Thornton, D., Atkins, E., & Nixon, K. (1992). Video games, aggression, and self-esteem: A survey. *Social Behavior and Personality, 20*, 39–46.

Flinn, M. V., & England, B. G. (1995). Childhood stress and family environment. *Current Anthropology, 36*, 854–866.

Freedman, J. L. (2002). *Media violence and its effect on aggression*. Toronto: University of Toronto Press.

Friedrich, K. L., & Stein, A. H. (1973). Aggressive and prosocial television programs and the natural behavior of preschool children. *Monographs of the Society for Research in Child Development, 38*, 1–110.

Friedrich, K. L. & Stein, A. H. (1975). Prosocial television and young children: The effects of verbal labeling and role playing on learning and behavior. *Child Development, 46*, 27–38.

Funk, J. B. (1993). Reevaluating the impact of violent video games. *Clinical Pediatrics, 32*, 86–90.

Funk, J. B. (2000). *The impact of interactive violence on children*. U. S. Senate Committee on Commerce, Science, and Transportation hearing of "The Impact of Interactive Violence on Children." Retrieved March 21, 2000, from http://www.utoledo.edu/psychology/funktestimony.html

Funk, J. B., Bechtoldt-Baldacci, H., Pasold, T., & Baumgardner, J. (2004). Violence exposure in real-life, video games, television, movies, and the internet: Is there desensitization? *Journal of Adolescence, 27*, 23–39.

Funk, J. B., & Buchman, D. D. (1996). Playing violent video and computer games and adolescent self-concept. *Journal of Communication, 46*(2), 19–32.

Funk, J. B., Buchman, D. D., Jenks., J., & Bechtoldt, H. (2003). Playing violent video games, desensitization, and moral evaluations in children. *Applied Developmental Psychology, 24*, 413–426.

Funk, J. B., Hagan, J., Schimming, J., Bullock., W. A., Buchman, D. D., & Myers, M. (2002). Aggression and psychopathology in adolescents with a preference for violent electronic games. *Aggressive Behavior, 28*, 134–144.

Furtado, R. (2005). Moonsaults on mattresses: The wild world of backyard wrestling. *The Athens News*. Retrieved March 10, 2005, from http://www.athensnews.com

Garbarino, J. (1999). *Lost boys: Why our sons turn violent and how we can save them*. New York: Free Press.

Gardstrom, S. C. (1999). Music exposure and criminal behavior: Perceptions of juvenile behavior. *Journal of Music Therapy, 36*, 207–221.

Geen, R. G., & Thomas, S. L. (1986). The immediate effects of media violence on behavior. *Journal of Social Issues, 42*, 7–27.

Gentile, D. A. (2003). *Media violence and children*. Westport, CT: Praeger.

Gentile, D. A., & Anderson, C. A. (2003). Violent video games: The newest media violence hazard. In D. Gentile (Ed.), *Media violence and children* (pp. 131–152). Westport, CT: Praeger.

Gentile, D. A., Lynch, P. J., Linder, J. R., & Walsh, D. A. (2004). The effects of violent video game habits on adolescent hostility, aggressive behaviors, and school performance. *Journal of Adolescence, 27*, 5–22.

Gentile, D. A., & Sesma, A. (2003). Developmental approaches to understanding media effects on individuals. In D. A. Gentile (Ed.), *Media violence and children* (pp. 19–38). Westport, CT: Praeger.

Gentile, D. A., & Walsh, D. A. (2002). A normative study of family media habits. *Applied Developmental Psychology, 23*,157–178.

Gerbner, G. (1972). Violence in television drama: Trends and symbolic function. In G. A. Comstock & E. A. Rubenstein (Eds.), *Television and social behavior, Vol 1. Media Content and Control* (pp. 28–187). Washington, DC: U.S. Government Printing Office.

Gerbner, G. (1990). Stories that hurt: Tobacco, alcohol, and other drugs in the mass media. In H. Resnik (Ed.), *Youth and drugs: Society's mixed messages* (OSAP Prevention Monograph, 6, pp. 53–129). Rockville, MD: Office for Substance Abuse Prevention.

Gerbner, G., Gross, M., Morgan, L., & Signorielli, N. (1994). Growing up with television: The cultivation perspective. In J. Bryant & D. Zillmann (Eds.), *Media effects* (pp. 17–41). Hillsdale, NJ: Erlbaum.

Gershoff, E. T. (2002). Parental corporal punishment and associated child behaviors and experiences: A meta-analytic and theoretical review. *Psychological Bulletin, 128*, 539–579.

Gillmore, M. R., Morrison, D. M., Richey, C. A., Balassone, M. L., Gutierrez, L., & Farris, M. (1997). Effects of a skill-based intervention to encourage condom use among high risk heterosexually active adolescents. *AIDS Education and Prevention, 9*, 22-43.

Gnepp, J., & Klayman, J. (1992). Recognition of uncertainty in emotional inferences: Reasoning about emotionally equivocal situations. *Developmental Psychology, 28*, 145–148.

Goldstein, J. (1995). Aggressive toy play. In A. D. Pellegrini (Ed.), *The future of play theory* (pp. 127–147). Albany: State University of New York Press.

Goldstein, J. (1998). *Why we watch: The attractions of violent entertainment.* New York: Oxford University Press.

Goldstein, J. (1999). The attractions of violent entertainment. *Media Psychology, 1,* 271–282.

Gordon, S., & Conant, R. (1974). Why use comic books to teach about sex? In G. J. Williams & S. Gordon (Eds.), *Clinical child psychology: Current practices and future perspectives* (pp. 351–362). New York: Behavioral Publications.

Gorn, G., & Goldberg, M. (1977). The impact of television advertising on children from low income families. *Journal of Communication Research, 4,* 86–88.

Gottfredson, M. R., & Hirschi, T. (1990). *A general theory of crime.* Stanford, CA: Stanford University Press.

Graña, J. L., Cruzado, J. A., Andreu, J. M., Muñoz-Rivas, M. J., Peña, M. E., & Brain, P. F. (2004). Effects of viewing videos of bullfights on Spanish children. *Aggressive Behavior, 30,* 16–28.

Granger, D. A., Booth, A., & Shirtcliff, A. (2003). *Cortisol/ Dehydroepiandrosterone(s) ratio and psychiatric symptoms in men.* Unpublished manuscript.

Granger, D. A., Schwartz, E. B., Booth, A., Curran, M., & Zakaria, D. (1999). Assessing dehydroepiandrosterone in saliva. A simple RIA for use in studies of children, adolescents, and adults. *Psychoneuroendocrinology, 24,* 567–579.

Graves, S. B. (1999). Television and prejudice reduction: When does television as a vicarious experience make a difference? *Journal of Social Issues, 55,* 707–727.

Graybill, D., Kirsch, J. R., & Esselman, E. D. (1985). Effects of playing violent versus non-violent video games on the aggressive ideation of children. *Child Study Journal, 15,* 199–205.

Graybill, D., Strawniak, M., Hunter, T., & O'Leary, M. (1987). Effects of playing versus observing violent versus non-violent video games on children's aggression. *Psychology: A Quarterly Journal of Human Behavior, 24,* 1–7.

Green F., & Schneider, F. (1974). Age differences in behavior of boys on three measures of altruism. *Child Development, 45,* 248–251.

Greenberg, B. S. (1974). British children and televised violence. *Public Opinion Quarterly, 38,* 531–547.

Greenberg, B. S., & Smith, S. W. (2002). Daytime talk shows: Up close and in your face. In J. D. Brown, J. R. Steele, & K. Walsh-Childers (Eds.), *Sexual teens, sexual media* (pp. 79–93). Mahwah, NJ: Erlbaum.

Greenfield, P. M., Bruzzone, L., Koyamatsu, K., Satuloff, W., Nixon, K., Brodie, M., et al. (1987). What is rock music doing to the minds of our youth? A first experimental look at the effects of rock music lyrics and music videos. *Journal of Early Adolescence, 7,* 315–329.

Greeson, L. E., & Williams, R. A. (1986). Social implications of music videos for youth: An analysis of the content and effects of MTV. *Youth and Society, 18,* 177–198.

Griffin, R. S., & Gross, A. M. (in press). Childhood bullying: Current empirical findings and future directions for research. *Aggression and Violent Behavior.*

Griffiths, M. (1999). Violent video games and aggression: A review of the literature. *Aggression and Violent Behavior, 4*(2), 203–212.

Grimes, T., Bergen, L., Nichols, K., Bernberg, E., & Fonagy, P. (2004). Is psychopathology the key to understanding why some children become aggressive when they are exposed to violent television programming? *Human Communication Research, 30*(2), 153–181.

Grimes, T., Vernberg, E., & Cathers, T. (1997). Emotionally disturbed children's reactions to violent media segments. *Journal of Health Communication, 2,* 157–168.

Grossman, D., & DeGaetano, G. (1999). *Stop teaching our kids to kill.* New York: Crown.

Grusec, J. E. (1973). Effects of co-observer evaluations of imitation: A developmental study. *Developmental Psychology, 8,* 141.

Guilford, J. P. (1956). *Fundamental statistics in psychology and education* (3rd ed.). New York: McGraw-Hill.

Gunn, H. (2004). Web-based surveys: Changing the survey process. *First Monday, 7*(12). Retrieved June 26, 2004, from http://www.firstmonday.dk/issues/issue7_12/gunn/

Gunter, B. (1985). *Dimensions of television violence.* Aldershot, UK: Gower.

Gunter, B., & Furnham, A. (1984). Perceptions of television violence: Effects of programme genre and type of violence on viewers' judgements of violent portrayals. *British Journal of Social Psychology, 23,* 155–164.

Gustines, G. G. (2005, May 9). Even superheroes can use some buffing of the brand. *The New York Times,* p. C8.

Guttmann, A. (1998). The appeal of violent sports. In J. Goldstein (Ed.), *Why we watch: The attractions of violent entertainment* (pp. 7–27). New York: Oxford University Press.

Hakanen, E. (1995). Emotional use of music by African-American adolescents. *Howard Journal of Communications, 5,* 214–222.

Halloran, E. C., Doumas, D. M., John, R. S., & Margolin, G. (1999). The relationship between aggression in children and locus of control beliefs. *Journal of Genetic Psychology, 160,* 5–21.

Halpern, C. T., Udry, J. R., Campbell, B., & Suchindran, C. (1993). Relationships between aggression and pubertal increases in testosterone: A panel analysis of adolescent males. *Social Biology, 40*(1–2), 8–24.

Haninger, K., & Thompson, K. M. (2004). Content and ratings of teen-rated video games. *Journal of the American Medical Association, 291,* 856–865.

Hansen, C. H., & Hansen, R. D. (1990a). The influence of sex and violence on the appeal of rock music videos. *Communication Research, 17,* 212–234.

Hansen C. H., & Hansen R. D. (1990b). Rock music videos and antisocial behavior. *Basic & Applied Social Psychology, 11,* 357–369.

Hapkiewicz, W. G. (1979). Children's reactions to cartoon violence. *Journal of Clinical Child Psychology, 8,* 30–34.

Hapkiewicz, W. G., & Roden, A. H. (1971). The effect of aggressive cartoons on children's interpersonal play. *Child Development, 42,* 1583–1585.

Hapkiewicz, W. G., & Stone, R. D. (1974). The effect of realistic versus imaginary aggressive models on children's interpersonal play. *Child Study Journal, 4,* 37–44.

Hardy, M. S. (2002). Teaching firearm safety to children: Failure of a program. *Journal of Development and Behavioral Pediatrics, 23,* 71–76.

Hargreaves, D. A., & Tiggemann, M. (2003). Female "thin ideal" media images and boys' attitudes toward girls. *Sex Roles, 49,* 539–544.

Harris, L., & Associates. (1988). *Sexual material on American network television during the 1987–1988 season.* New York: Planned Parenthood Federation of America.

Harrison, K., & Cantor, J. (1999). Tales from the screen: Enduring fright reactions to scary media. *Media Psychology, 1,* 97–116.

Harter, S. (1986). Processes underlying the construction, maintenance, and enhancement of self-concept in children. In J. Suls & A. G. Greenwald (Eds.), *Psychological perspectives on the self* (Vol. 3, pp. 137–181). Hillsdale, NJ: Erlbaum.

Harter, S. (1987). Developmental and dynamic changes in the nature of self-concept: Implications for child psychotherapy. In S. R. Shirk (Ed.), *Cognitive development and child psychotherapy* (pp. 119–160). New York: Plenum.

Harter, S., Waters, P. I., & Whitesell, N. R. (1998). Relational self-worth: Differences in perceived worth as a person across interpersonal contexts among adolescents. *Child Development, 69,* 756–766.

Hartnagel, T., Teevan, J. J., & McIntyre, J. (1975). Television violence and violent behavior. *Social Forces, 54,* 341–351.

Hartup, W. W. (1974). Aggression in childhood: Developmental perspectives. *American Psychologist, 29,* 336–341.

Harwood, J. (1999). Age identification, social identity gratifications, and television viewing. *Journal of Broadcasting and Electronic Media, 43,* 123–146.

Haynes, R. B. (1978). Children's perceptions of "comic" and "authentic" cartoon violence. *Journal of Broadcasting, 22,* 63–70.

Hearold, S. (1986). A synthesis of 1043 effects of television on social behavior. In G. Comstock (Ed.), *Public communication and behavior* (Vol. 1, pp. 65–133). New York: Academic Press.

Hellendoorn, J., & Harinck, F. J. H. (1997). War toy play and aggression in Dutch kindergarten children. *Social Development, 6,* 340–354.

Heo, N. (2004). The effects of screen size and content type of viewers' attention, arousal, memory and content evaluations. *Dissertation Abstracts International, 64,* 9-A. (UMI No. AAI3106253)

Herman-Giddens, M. E., Slora, E. J., Wasserman, R. C., Bourdony, C. J., Bhapkar, M. V., Koch, G. G., et al. (1997). Secondary sexual characteristics and menses in young girls seen in office practice: A study from the Pediatric Research in Office Settings network. *Pediatrics, 99*(4), 505–512.

Hess, T. H., Hess, K. D., & Hess, A. K. (1999). The effects of violent media on adolescent inkblot responses: Implications for clinical and forensic assessments. *Journal of Clinical Psychology, 55,* 439–445.

Hicks, D. J. (1968). Effects of co-observer's sanctions and adult presence on imitative aggression. *Child Development, 39,* 303–309.

Hirschi, T., (1969). *Causes of delinquency.* Berkeley: University of California Press.

Hirschi, T., & Gottfredson, M. R. (1994). *The generality of deviance*. New Brunswick, NJ: Transaction Publishers.

Hofer, T., Przyrembel, H., & Verleger, S. (2004). New evidence for the theory of the stork. *Paediatric and Perinatal Epidemiology, 18*, 88–92.

Hoffner, C. (1996). Children's wishful identification and parasocial interaction with favorite television characters. *Journal of Broadcasting and Electronic Media, 40*, 389–402.

Hoffner, C., & Cantor, J. (1985). Developmental differences in responses to a television character's appearance and behavior. *Developmental Psychology, 21*, 1065–1074.

Hoffner, C., & Cantor, J. (1991). Factors influencing children's enjoyment of suspense. *Communication Monographs, 58*, 41–62.

Horton, R. W., & Santogrossi, D. A. (1978). The effect of adult commentary on reducing the influence of televised violence. *Personality and Social Psychology Bulletin, 4*, 37–40.

Hoult, T. F. (1949). Comic books and juvenile delinquency. *Sociology and Social Research, 33*, 279–284.

Howitt, D., & Cumberbatch, G. (1975). *Mass media violence and society*. New York: Halstead.

Huesmann, L. R. (1986). Psychological processes promoting the relation between exposure to media violence and aggressive behavior by the view. *Journal of Social Issues, 42*, 125–139.

Huesmann, L. R. (1998). The role of social information processing and cognitive scheme in the acquisition and maintenance of habitual aggressive behavior. In R. Geen & E. Donnerstein (Eds.), *Human aggression: Theories, research and implications for policy* (pp. 73–109). New York: Academic Press.

Huesmann, L. R., Lagerspetz, K., & Eron, L. D. (1984). Intervening variables in the TV violence-aggression relation: Evidence from two countries. *Developmental Psychology, 20*(5), 746–777.

Huesmann, L. R., Moise-Titus, J., Podolski, C. L., & Eron, L. D. (2003). Longitudinal relations between children's exposure to TV violence and their aggressive and violent behavior in young adulthood: 1977–1992. *Developmental Psychology Special Issue: Violent Children, 39*, 201–221.

Humphreys, A. P., & Smith, P. K. (1984). Rough-and-tumble in preschool and playground. In P. K. Smith (Ed.), *Play in animals and humans* (pp. 241–270). Oxford, UK: Basil Blackwell.

Huntemann, N., & Morgan, M. (2001). Mass media and identity formation. In D. G. Singer & J. L. Singer (Eds.), *Handbook of children and the media* (pp.309–322). Thousand Oaks, CA: Sage.

Huston, A. C., Donnerstein, E., Fairchild, H., Feshbach, N. D., Katz, P. A., Murray, J. P., et al. (1992). *Big world, small screen: The role of television in American society*. Lincoln: University of Nebraska Press.

Huston, A. C., & Wright, J. C. (1998). Mass media and children's development. In I. E. Sigel and K. A. Renninger (Eds.), *Handbook of Child Psychology* (Vol. 4, pp. 999-1058). New York: Wiley.

Institute of Medicine. (1997). *The hidden epidemic: Confronting sexually transmitted diseases.* Washington, DC: National Academy Press.

Irwin, A. R., & Gross, A. M. (1995). Cognitive tempo, violent video games, and aggressive behavior in young boys. *Journal of Family Violence, 10,* 337–350.

Jacobson, L., & Sapolsky, R. (1991). The role of the hippocampus in feedback regulation of the hypothalamic-pituitary-adrenocortical axis. *Endocrine Reviews, 12*(2), 118–134.

Jaglom, L. M., & Gardner, H. (1981). Decoding the worlds of television. *Studies in Visual Communication, 7*(1), 33–47.

Jenkins, E. J., & Bell, C. C. (1994). Violence exposure, psychological distress, and high risk behaviors among inner-city high school students. In S. Friedman (Ed.), *Anxiety disorders in African Americans* (pp. 76–88). New York: Springer.

Jenvey, V. (1992). *Toys, play, and aggression.* Paper presented at the ICCP/TASP conference, Paris, France.

Johnson, C. (2003). Kid's truancy gets parent jailed. *International Child and Youth Care Network.* Retrieved April 16, 2004, from http://cyc-net.org

Johnson, J. D., Jackson, L. A., & Gatto, L. (1995). Violent attitudes and deferred academic aspirations: Deleterious effects of exposure to rap music. *Basic and Applied Social Psychology, 16,* 27–41.

Johnson, S. (2001, August 7). Parents ignore the TV ratings safety net. *Los Angeles Times,* p. F10.

Johnston, C. (1996). Parent characteristics and parent-child interactions in families of nonproblem children and ADHD children with higher and lower levels of oppositional-defiant behavior. *Journal of Abnormal Child Psychology, 24,* 85–104.

Johnston, D. D. (1995). Adolescents' motivations for viewing graphic horror. *Human Communication Research, 21,* 522–552.

Johnston, J., & Ettema, J. (1987). *Positive images: Breaking stereotypes with children's television.* Beverly Hills, CA: Sage.

Jones, G. (2002). *Killing monsters: Why children need fantasy, super heroes, and make-believe violence.* New York: Basic Books.

Jonstone, M. (1999). *The history news in space.* Cambridge, MA: Candlewick Press.

Jordan, A. (2000). *Is the three-hour rule living up to its potential? An analysis of educational television for children in the 1999/2000 broadcast season.* Philadelphia, PA: Annenberg Public Policy Center.

Josephson, W. L. (1987). Television violence and children's aggression: Testing the priming, social script, and disinhibition predictions. *Journal of Personality and Social Psychology, 53,* 882–890.

Jowett, G. S., Jarvie, I. C., & Fuller, K. H. (1996). *Children and the movies: Media influences and the Payne Fund controversy.* New York: Cambridge University Press.

Jukes, J. (1991). *Children and aggressive toys: Empirical studies of toy preference.* Unpublished doctoral dissertation, University College, London, UK.

Kagan, J. (1992). Behavior, biology, and the meaning of temperamental constructs. *Pediatrics, 90,* 510–513.

Kallinen, K., & Ravaja, N. (2004). Emotion-related effects of speech rate and rising vs. falling background music melody during audio news: The moderating influence of personality. *Personality and Individual Differences, 37,* 275–288.

Kandakai, T. L., Price, J. H., Telljohann, S. K., & Wilson, C. A. (1999). Mothers' perceptions of factors influencing violence in school. *Journal of School Health, 69*(5), 189–195.

Kane, T. R., Suls, J. M., & Tedeschi, J. (1977). Humour as a tool of social interaction. In A. J. Chapman & H. C. Foot (Eds.), *It's a funny thing, humour* (pp. 13–16). Oxford, UK: Pergamon Press.

Kappes, B. M., & Thompson, D. L. (1985). Biofeedback vs. video games: Effects on impulsivity, locus of control and self-concept with incarcerated juveniles. *Journal of Clinical Psychology, 41,* 698–706.

Kazdin, A. E., & Benjet, C. (2003). Spanking children: Evidence and issues. *Current Directions in Psychological Science, 12,* 100–103.

Kestenbaum, G. I., & Weinstein, L. (1985). Personality, psychopathology, and developmental issues in male adolescent video game use. *Journal of the American Academy of Child Psychiatry, 24,* 325–337.

Kiesewetter, J. (1993, December 17). Top kids show also ranks as most violent. *The Cincinnati Enquirer,* p. A1.

King, C. (2000). Effects of humorous heroes and villains in violent action films. *Journal of Communication, 48,* 40–57.

King, C., III, Siegel, M., Celebucki, C., & Connolly, G. N. (1998). Adolescent exposure to cigarette advertising in magazines. *Journal of the American Medical Association, 279,* 516–520.

King, P. (1988). Heavy metal music and drug abuse in adolescents. *Postgraduate Medicine, 83,* 295–304.

Kirchengast, S., & Hartmann, B. (2003). Nicotine consumption before and during pregnancy affects not only newborn size but also mother modus. *Journal of Biosocial Science, 35*(2), 175–188.

Kirsh, S. J. (1998). Seeing the world through Mortal Kombat-colored glasses: Violent video games and the development of a short-term hostile attribution bias. *Childhood: A Global Journal of Child Research, 5,* 177–184.

Kirsh, S. J. (2003). The effects of violent video game play on adolescents: The overlooked influence of development. *Aggression and Violent Behavior: A Review Journal, 8*(4), 377–389.

Kirsh, S. J., & Olczak, P. V. (2000). Violent comic books and perceptions of ambiguous provocation situations. *Media Psychology, 2,* 47–62.

Kirsh, S. J., & Olczak, P. V. (2002). The effects of extremely violent comic books on social information processing. *Journal of Interpersonal Violence, 17*(11), 1830–1848.

Kirsh, S. J., Olczak, P. V., & Mounts, J. R. W. (in press). Violent video games induce an affect processing bias. *Media Psychology.*

Kochanska, G., Coy, K., Tjebkes, T. L., & Husarek, S. J. (1998). Individual differences in emotionality in infancy. *Child Development, 69,* 375–390.

Kokaska, C. J. (1984). Disabled superheroes in comic books. *Rehabilitation Literature, 45,* 286–288.

Krahé, B., & Möller, I. (2004). Playing violent electronic games, hostile attributional style, and aggression-related norms in German adolescents. *Journal of Adolescence, 27,* 53–59.

Krcmar, M., & Cooke, M. C. (2001). Children's moral reasoning and their perceptions of television violence. *Journal of Communication, 51,* 300–317.

Krcmar, M., & Valkenburg, P. (1999). A scale to assess children's interpretations of justified and unjustified television violence and its relationship to television viewing. *Communication Research, 26*(5), 608–634.

Kubey, R., & Csikszentmihalyi, M. (2002). Television addiction is no mere metaphor. *Scientific American.* Retrieved December 27, 2002, from http://www.scientificamerican.com

Kunkel, D. (2001). Children and television advertising. In D. G. Singer & J. L. Singer (Eds.), *Handbook of children and the media* (pp. 375–393). Thousand Oaks, CA: Sage.

Kunkel, D., Biely, E., Eyal, K., Cope-Farrar, K., Donnerstein, E., & Fandrich, R. (2003). *Sex on TV 3.* Menlo Park, CA: Kaiser Family Foundation.

Kunkel, D., Farinola, W. J. M., Cope, K. M., Donnerstein, E., Biely, E., & Zwaren, L. (1998). *Rating the TV ratings: One year out.* Menlo Park, CA: Kaiser Family Foundation.

Kunkel, D., & Gantz, W. (1992). Children's television advertising in the multichannel environment. *Journal of Communication, 42,* 134–152.

Kunkel, D., & Wilcox, B. (2001). Children and media policy. In D. G. Singer & J. L. Singer (Eds.), *Handbook of children and the media* (pp. 589–604). Thousand Oaks, CA: Sage.

Lacity, M., & Jansen, M. A. (1994). Understanding qualitative data: A framework of text analysis methods. *Journal of Management Information Systems, 11,* 137–166.

Lacourse, E., Claes, M., & Villeneuve, M. (2001). Heavy metal music and adolescent suicidal risk. *Journal of Youth and Adolescence, 30,* 321–332.

Lagerspetz, K. M., Wahlroos, C., & Wendelin, C. (1978). Facial expressions of pre-school children while watching televised violence. *Scandinavian Journal of Psychology, 19,* 213–222.

Larson, M. S. (2003). Gender, race, and aggression in television commercials that feature children. *Sex Roles, 48,* 67–75.

Larson, R. W., Moneta, G., Richards, M. H., & Wilson, S. (2002). Continuity, stability, and change in daily emotional experience across adolescence. *Child Development, 73,* 1151–1165.

Lease, A. M., Kennedy, C. A., & Axelrod, J. L. (2002). Children's social constructions of popularity. *Social Development, 11,* 87–109.

Lefkowitz, M. M., Walder, L. O., Eron, L. D., & Huesmann, L. R. (1973). Preference for televised contact sports as related to sex difference in aggression. *Developmental Psychology, 9,* 417–420.

Leifer, A. D., & Roberts, D. F. (1971). Children's response to television violence. In J. P. Murray, E. A. Rubinstein, & G. Comstock, (Eds.), *Television and social behavior, Vol. 2. Television and social learning* (pp. 43–180). Washington, DC: U.S. Government Printing Office.

Lemerise, E. A., & Arsenio, W. F. (2000). An integrated model of emotion processes and cognition in social information processing. *Child Development, 71,* 101–118.

Lemish, D. (1998). "Girls can wrestle too": Gender differences in the consumption of a television wrestling series. *Sex Roles, 38,* 833–849.

Leschied, A. W., Cummings, A., Van Brunschot, M., Cunningham, A., & Saunders, A. (2000). Female adolescent aggression: A review of the literature and the correlates of aggression. *Report for the Solicitor General of Canada.* Retrieved February 12, 2003, from http://www.sgc.gc.ca

Leyens, J. P., Camino, L., Parke, R. D., & Berkowitz, L. (1975). Effects of movie violence on aggression in a field setting as a function of group dominance and cohesion. *Journal of Personality and Social Psychology, 32,* 346–360.

Liben, L., & Signorella, L. (1993). Gender-schematic processing in children: The role of initial interpretations of stimuli. *Developmental Psychology, 29,* 141–149.

Lieber, L. (1996). *Commercial and character slogan recall by children aged 9 to 11 years: Budweiser frogs versus Bugs Bunny.* Berkeley, CA: Center on Alcohol Advertising.

Liebert, D., Sprafkin, J., Liebert, R., & Rubinstein, E. (1977). Effects of television commercial disclaimers on the product expectations of children. *Journal of Communication, 27,* 118–124.

Liebert, R. M., & Baron, R. A. (1971). Short-term effects of televised aggression on children's aggressive behavior. In J. P. Murray, E. A. Rubinstein, & G. A. Comstock (Eds.), *Television and social behavior. Vol. 2. Television and Social Learning* (pp. 181–201). Washington, DC: U.S. Government Printing Office.

Liebert, R. M., Neale, J. M., & Davidson, E. A. (1973). *The early window: Effects of television on children and youth.* Elmsford, NY: Pergamon.

Lin, S., & Lepper, M. R. (1987). Correlates of children's usage of video games and computers. *Journal of Applied Social Psychology, 17,* 72–93.

Lindeman, M., Harakka, T., & Keltikangas-Jaervinen, L. (1997). Age and gender differences in adolescents' reactions to conflict situations: Aggression, prosociality, and withdrawal. *Journal of Youth and Adolescence, 26*(3), 339–351.

Linebarger, D. L., Kosanic, A. Z., Greenwood, C. R., & Doku, N. S. (2004). Effects of viewing the television program Between the Lions on the emergent literacy skills of young children. *Journal of Educational Psychology, 96,* 297–308.

Ling, P. A., & Thomas, D. R. (1986). Imitation of television aggression among Maori and European boys and girls. *Journal of Psychology, 15*(2), 47–53.

Liss, M. B., Reinhardt, L. C., & Fredriksen, S. (1983). TV heroes: The impact of rhetoric and deeds. *Journal of Applied Developmental Psychology, 4,* 175–187.

Loeber, R., & Hay, D. (1997). Key issues in the development of aggression and violence from childhood to early adulthood. *Annual Review of Psychology, 48,* 371–410.

Loeber, R., & Stouthamer-Loeber, M. (1998). Development of juvenile aggression and violence: Some common misconceptions and controversies. *American Psychologist, 53,* 242–259.

Lovaas, O. I. (1961). Effect of exposure to symbolic aggression on aggressive behavior. *Child Development, 32,* 37–44.

Lovelace, V., Scheiner, S., Dollberg, S., Segui, I., & Black, T. (1994). Making a neighborhood the Sesame Street way: Developing a methodology to evaluate children's understanding of race. *Journal of Educational Television, 20,* 60–77.

Lowery, D. T., & Shidler, J. A. (1993). Prime time TV portrayals of sex, "safe sex" and AIDS: A longitudinal analysis. *Journalism Quarterly, 70,* 628–637.

Lupie, S. J., King, S., Meaney, M. J., & McEwen, B. S. (2001). Can poverty get under your skin? Basal cortisol levels and cognitive function in children from low and high socioeconomic status. *Development and Psychopathology, 13*(3), 653–676.

Lynch, P. J. (1999). Hostility, Type A behavior, and stress hormones at rest and after playing violent video games in teenagers. *Psychosomatic Medicine, 61,* 113.

Lynch, P. J., Gentile, D. A., Olson, A. A., & van Brederode, T. M. (2001, April). *The effects of violent video game habits on adolescent aggressive attitudes and behaviors.* Paper presented at the biennial conference of the Society for Research in Child Development, Minneapolis, MN.

Maccoby, E. E., Levin, H., & Selya, B. M. (1955). The effects of emotional arousal on the retention of film content. *American Psychologist, 10*(8), 359.

Maccoby, E. E., & Martin, J. A. (1983). Socialization in the context of the family: Parent-child interaction. In E. M. Hetherington (Ed.) & P. H. Mussen (Gen Ed.), *Handbook of child psychology: Vol. 4. Socialization, personality, and social development* (4th ed, pp. 1–102). New York: Wiley.

Main, M., & Solomon, J. (1990). Procedures for identifying infants as disorganized/disoriented during the Ainsworth Strange Situation. In M. T. Greenberg, D. Cicchetti, & E. M. Cummings (Eds.), *Attachment in the preschool years: Theory, research, and intervention* (pp. 121–160). Chicago: University of Chicago Press.

Majewska, M. D. (1995). Neuronal actions of dehydroepiandrosterone. Possible roles in brain development, aging, memory, and affect. *Annals of the New York Academy of Sciences, 774,* 111–120.

Mann, J. J., Waternaux, C., Haas, G. L., & Malone, K. M. (1999). Toward a clinical model of suicidal behavior in psychiatric patients. *American Journal of Psychiatry, 156,* 181–189.

Marcus, R. F., & Kramer, C. (2001). Reactive and proactive aggression: Attachment and social competence predictors. *The Journal of Genetic Psychology, 162*(3), 260–275.

Mares, M. L. (1996). *Positive effects of television on social behavior: A meta-analysis.* Philadelphia: University of Pennsylvania, Annenberg Public Policy Center.

Mares, M. L., & Woodard, E. H. (2001). Prosocial effects on children's social interactions. In D. G. Singer & J. L. Singer (Eds.), *Handbook of children and the media* (pp. 183–206). Thousand Oaks, CA: Sage.

Matthews, K. A. (1997). Hostility. *John D. and Catherine T. MacArthur Research Network on Socioeconomic Status and Health.* Retrieved July 9, 2004, from http://www. macses.ucsf.edu/Research/Psychosocial/notebook/hostility.html

McCauley, C. (1998).When screen violence is not attractive. In J. H. Goldstein (Ed.), *Why we watch: The attractions of violent entertainment* (pp. 144–162). New York: Oxford University Press.

McCloud, S. (1993). *Understanding comics.* Northampton, MA: Kitchen Sink Press.

McCord, J. (1979). Some child-rearing antecedents of criminal behavior in adult men. *Journal of Personality and Social Psychology, 9,* 1447–1486.

McCord, J. (1983). A longitudinal study of aggression and antisocial behavior. In K. T. Van Dusen & S. A. Mednick (Eds.), *Prospective studies of crime and delinquency* (pp. 269–275). Boston: Kluwer-Nijhoff.

McElwain, N. L., Cox, M. J., Burchinal, M. R., & Macfie, J. (2003). Differentiating among insecure mother–infant attachment classifications: A focus on child–friend interaction and exploration during solitary play at 36 months. *Attachment and Human Development, 5,* 136–164.

McEvoy, M. A., Estrem, T. L., Rodriguez, M. C., & Olson, M. L. (2003). Assessing relational and physical aggression among preschool children: Intermethod agreement. *Topics in Early Childhood Special Education, 23,* 53–63.

McLeod, J. M., Atkin, C. K., & Chaffee, S. H. (1972). Adolescents, parents, and television use: Adolescent self-report measures from Maryland and Wisconsin samples. In G. A. Comstock & E. A. Rubinstein (Eds.), *Television and social behavior: A technical report to the Surgeon General's Scientific Advisory Committee on Television and Social Behavior. Vol. 3. Television and adolescent aggressiveness* (DHEW Publication No. HSM 72–9058) (pp. 173–238). Washington, DC: U.S. Government Printing Office.

Meaney, M. J., Stewart, J., & Beatty, W. W. (1985). Sex differences in social play. In J. Rosenblatt, C. Beer, M. C. Bushnel, & P. Slater (Eds.), *Advances in the study of behavior* (Vol. 15, pp. 2–58). New York: Academic Press.

Meyer-Bahlburg, H. F., Feldman, J. F., Cohen, P., & Ehrhardt, A. A. (1988). Perinatal factors in the development of gender-related play behavior: Sex hormones versus pregnancy complications. *Psychiatry, 51,* 260–271.

Miller, J. H., & Busch, P. (1979). Host selling vs. premium TV commercials: An experimental evaluation of their influence on children. *Journal of Marketing Research, 16*(3), 323–332.

Miller, P. M. (1989). *Theories of developmental psychology.* New York: Freeman.

Miranda, D., & Claes, M. (2004). Rap music genres and deviant behaviors in French-Canadian adolescents. *Journal of Youth and Adolescence, 33,* 113–122.

Moeller, T. G. (2001). *Youth aggression and violence: A psychological approach.* Mahwah, NJ: Erlbaum.

Moise, J. F., & Huesmann, L. R. (1996). Television violence viewing and aggression in females. *Annual New York Academy of Sciences, 794,* 380–383.

Molitor, F., & Hirsch, K. (1994). Children's toleration of real-life aggression after exposure to media violence: A replication of the Drabman and Thomas studies. *Child Study Journal, 24,* 191–202.

Morris, C. (2004). Halo 2 sales top Grand Theft Auto. *CnnMoney.com.* Retrieved December 1, 2004, from http://money.cnn.com/2004/11/11/technology/halosales/index.htm

Moss, H. B., Vanyukov, M. M., & Martin, C. S. (1995). Salivary cortisol responses and the risk for substance abuse in prepubertal boys. *Biological Psychiatry, 38,* 547–555.

Motion Picture Association of America. (2004a). *Movie ratings.* Retrieved February 22, 2004, from http://www.mpaa.org/movieratings

Motion Picture Association of America. (2004b). *TV parental guidelines.* Retrieved February 22, 2004, from http://www.mpaa.org/tv/

Mundell, E. J. (2002). Sitcoms, videos make even fifth-graders feel fat. *Reuters Health.* Retrieved March 31, 2003, from http://story.news.yahoo.com

Murray, J. P. (2001). TV violence and brainmapping in children. *Psychiatric Times, 18.* Retrieved August 3, 2003, from http://www.psychiatrictimes.com/

Mussen, P., & Rutherford, E. (1961). Effects of aggressive cartoons on children's aggressive play. *Journal of Abnormal and Social Psychology, 62,* 461–464.

Naigles, L. R., & Mayeux, L. (2001). Television as incidental language teacher. In D. G. Singer & J. L. Singer (Eds.), *Handbook of children and the media* (pp. 135–152). Thousand Oaks, CA: Sage.

Nathanson, A. I. (1997, May). *The relationship between parental mediation and children's anti- and pro-social motivations.* Paper presented at the annual meeting of the International Communication Association, Montreal, Quebec, Canada.

Nathanson, A. I. (1999). Identifying and explaining the relationship between parental mediation and children's aggression. *Communication Research, 26,* 124–143.

Nathanson, A. I. (2002). The unintended effects of parental mediation of television on adolescents. *Media Psychology, 4,* 207–230.

Nathanson, A. I., & Cantor, J. (2000). Reducing the aggression-promoting effects of violent cartoons by increasing the fictional involvement with the victim: A study of active mediation. *Journal of Broadcasting and Electronic Media, 44,* 125–142.

Nathanson, A. I., & Yang, M. (2003). The effects of mediation content and form on children's responses to violent television. *Human Communication Research, 29,* 111–124.

National Campaign to Prevent Teen Pregnancy. (2001). *Halfway there: A prescription for continued progress in preventing teen pregnancy.* Washington, DC: The Campaign.

National Institute on Media and the Family. (2004). *Fact sheet: Children and advertising.* Retrieved May 4, 2004, from http://www.mediafamily.org/facts/facts_childadv.shtml

Nelson, R. J. (2000). *An introduction to behavioral endocrinology.* New York: Sinaur.

Newhagen, J. E. (1998). TV images that induce anger, fear, and disgust: Effects on approach-avoidance responses and memory. *Journal of Broadcasting and Electronic Media, 42*(2), 265–276.

Noble, G. (1975). *Children in front of the small screen.* Beverly Hills, CA: Sage.

Nottelmann, E. D., Susman, E. J., Blue, J. H., Inoff-Germain, G., Dorn, L., Loriaux, D. L., et al. (1987). Gonadal and adrenal hormone correlates of adjustment in early adolescence. In R. M. Lerner & T. T. Foch (Eds.), *Biological–psychological interactions in early adolescence* (pp. 246–260). Hillsdale, NJ: Erlbaum.

Nuzum, E. D. (2001). *Parental advisory. Music censorship in America.* New York: Perennial Currents.

Oates, D. J. (1996). *Reverse speech: Voices from the unconscious.* San Diego, CA: ProMotion Publishing.

O'Brien, S. (2004). Kids buying gore, sex. *News Interactive.* Retrieved December 23, 2004, from http://news.com.au/common

Office of Film and Literature Classification (2004). *Manhunt refused classification under review.* Retrieved December 13, 2004, from http://www.oflc.gov.au

Olivardia, R., Pope, H. G., & Hudson, R. I. (2000). Muscle dysmorphia in male weightlifters: A case-control study. *American Journal of Psychiatry, 157,* 1291–1296.

Olweus, D. (1979). Stability of aggressive reaction patterns in males. *Psychological Bulletin, 86,* 852–857.

Olweus, D. (1980). Family and temperamental determinants of aggressive behavior in adolescent boys: A causal analysis. *Developmental Psychology, 16,* 644–660.

Olweus, D. (1986). Aggression and hormones: Behavioral relationship with testosterone and adrenaline. In D. Olweus, J. Block, & M. Radke-Yarrow (Eds.), *Development of antisocial behavior* (pp. 51–72). Orlando, FL: Academic Press.

Orbach, I., Vinkler, E., & Har-Even, D. (1993). The emotional impact of frightening stories on children. *Journal of Child Psychology and Psychiatry, 34,* 379–389.

Paik, H., & Comstock, G. (1994). The effects of television violence on anti-social behavior: A meta-analysis. *Communication Research, 21,* 516–546.

Palmgreen, P., Wenner, L. A., & Rayburn, J. D. (1980). Relations between gratifications sought and obtained: A study of television news. *Communication Research, 7,* 161–192.

Pareles, J., & Romanowski, P. (1983). *The Rolling Stone encyclopedia of rock and roll.* New York: Rolling Stone Press.

Parke, R. D., Berkowitz, L., Leyens, J. P., West, S. G., & Sebastian, R. J. (1977). Some effects of violent and nonviolent movies on the behavior of juvenile delinquents.

In L. Berkowitz (Ed.), *Advances in experimental social psychology* (Vol. 10, pp. 135–172). New York: Academic Press.

Parke, R. D., & Slaby, R. G. (1983). The development of aggression. In P. H. Mussen (Series Ed.) & M. Hetherington (Vol. Ed.), *Handbook of child psychology: Vol. 4. Socialization, personality, and social development* (4th ed., pp. 547–642). New York: Wiley.

Parker, L. N., Levin, E. R., Lifrak, E. T. (1985). Evidence for adrenocortical adaptation to severe illness. *Journal of Clinical Endocrinology and Metabolism, 60,* 947–952.

Parsons, T. (1955). Family structure and the socialization of the child. In T. Parsons & R. G. Bales (Eds.), *Family socialization and interaction processes.* New York: Free Press.

Patterson, G. R. (1982). *Coercive family process.* Eugene, OR: Castelia.

Patterson, G. R., & Dishion, T. (1985). Contributions of families and peers to delinquency. *Criminology, 23,* 63–69.

Pechmann, C., & Knight, S. J. (2002). An experimental investigation of the joint effects of advertising and peers on adolescents' beliefs and intentions about cigarette consumption. *Journal of Consumer Research, 29,* 5–19.

Pechmann, C., & Shih, C. F. (1999). Smoking scenes in movies and antismoking advertisements before movies: Effects on youth. *Journal of Marketing, 63,* 1–13.

Peeples, F., & Loeber, R. (1994). Do individual factors and neighborhood context explain ethnic differences in juvenile delinquency? *Journal of Quantitative Criminology, 10,* 141–157.

Pelligrini, A. D. (1988). Elementary school children's rough-and-tumble play and social competence. *Developmental Psychology, 24,* 802–806.

Pelligrini, A. D. (1989). Elementary school children's rough-and-tumble play. *Early Childhood Research Quarterly, 4,* 245–260.

Pelligrini, A. D. (1995). A longitudinal study of boys' rough-and-tumble play and dominance during early adolescence. *Journal of Applied Developmental Psychology, 16,* 77–93.

Pelligrini, A. D. (2002). Rough and tumble play from childhood through adolescence: Development and possible function. *Handbook of childhood social development* (pp. 428–453). Oxford, UK: Blackwell.

Pelligrini, A. D. (2003). Perceptions and functions of play and real fighting in early adolescence. *Child Development, 74,* 1522–1533.

Peterson, D. L., & Pfost, K. S. (1989). Influence of rock videos on attitudes of violence against women. *Psychological Reports, 64,* 319–322.

Peterson, R. A., & Kahn, J. R. (1984, August). *Media preferences of sexually active teens.* Paper presented at the meeting of the American Psychological Association, Toronto, Canada.

Pham, A., & Sandell, S. (2003). Nudity in games OK, but blood verboten in Germany. *Los Angeles Times.* Retreived October 31, 2004, from http://www.chicagotribune.com/technology/reviews

Piaget, J. (1970). Piaget's theory. In P. H. Mussen (Ed.), *Carmichael's manual of child psychology,* Vol 1. New York: Wiley.

Plomin, R., DeFries, J. C., McClearn, G. E., & Rutter, M. (1997). *Behavioral genetics* (3rd ed.). New York: Freeman.

Polivy, J., & Herman, C. P. (2004). Sociocultural idealization of thin female body shapes: An introduction to the special issue on body image and eating disorders. *Journal of Social and Clinical Psychology, 23,* 1–6.

Pope, H. G., Olivardia, R., Gruber, A., & Borowiecki, J. (1999). Evolving ideas of male body image as seen through action toys. *International Journal of Eating Disorders, 26,* 65–72.

Pope, H. G., Phillips, K. A., & Olivardia, R. (2000). *The Adonis complex: The secret crisis of male body obsession.* New York: Free Press.

Potenza, M., Verhoeff, P., & Weiss, E. (1996). Comic books and development. *Journal of the American Academy of Child and Adolescent Psychiatry, 35*(12), 1573–1574.

Potter, W. J. (2003). *The 11 myths of media violence.* Thousand Oaks, CA: Sage.

Potter, W. J., & Berry, M. (1998, May). *Constructions of judgments of violence.* Paper presented at the Annual Meeting of the International Communication Association, San Francisco, CA.

Potter, W. J., & Warren, R. (1998). Humor as a camouflage of televised violence. *Journal of Communication, 48,* 40–57.

Potts, R., Huston, A. C., & Wright, J. C. (1986). The effects of television form and violent content on boys' attention and social behavior. *Journal of Experimental Child Psychology, 41,* 1–17.

Poulin, F., & Boivin, M. (2000). The role of proactive and reactive aggression in the formation and development of boys' friendships. *Developmental Psychology, 36,* 233–240.

Prinsky, L. E., & Rosenbaum, J. L. (1987). "Leer-ics" or lyrics: Teenage impression of rock 'n roll. *Youth and Society, 18,* 384–397.

Pryor, J. B., & Kriss, B. (1977). The cognitive dynamics of salience in the attribution process. *Journal of Personality and Social Psychology, 35,* 49–55.

Rauzi, R. (1998, June 9). The teen factor: Today's media-savvy youths influence what others are seeing and hearing. *Los Angeles Times,* p. F1.

Recording Industry Association of America. (2004). *Parental advisory.* Retrieved May 12, 2004, from http://www.riaa.com/issues/parents/advisory.asp

Reeves, B., Lang, A., Kim, E., & Tatar, D. (1999). The effects of screen size and message content on attention and arousal. *Media Psychology, 1,* 49–67.

Regan, P. M. (1994). War toys, war movies, and the militarization of the United States, 1900–1985. *Journal of Peace Research, 31,* 45–58.

Reid, C. (2005, April 18). U. S. Graphic novel market hits $200M. *Publishers Weekly.* Retrieved May 5, 2005, from http://www.PublishersWeekly.com

Richtel, M. (2005). Video game industry sales reach record pace in 2004. *The New York Times.* Retrieved January 27, 2005, from http://www.nytimes.com/2005/01/19/technology/19games.htm

Rideout, V. J., Vandewater, E. A., & Wartella, E. A. (2003). *Zero to six: Electronic media in the lives of infants, toddlers, and preschoolers.* Menlo Park, CA: Kaiser Family Foundation.

Roberts, D. F. (2000). Media and youth: Access, exposure, and privatization. *Journal of Adolescent Health, 27*(Supplement), 8–14.

Roberts, D. F., & Christenson, P. G. (2001). Popular music in childhood and adolescence. In D. G. Singer & J. L. Singer (Eds.), *Handbook of children and the media* (pp. 395–414). Thousand Oaks, CA: Sage.

Roberts, D. F., Christenson, P. G., & Gentile, D. A. (2003). The effects of violent music on children and adolescents. In D. A. Gentile (Ed.), *Media violence and children: A complete guide for parents and professionals* (pp. 153–170). Westport, CT: Praeger Publishers.

Roberts, D. F., Foehr, U. G., & Rideout, V. G. (2005). *Generation M: Media in the lives of 8–18 year-olds.* Menlo Park, CA: Kaiser Family Foundation.

Roberts, D. F., Foehr, U. G., Rideout, V. G., & Brodie, M. (1999). *Kids & media @ the new millennium.* Menlo Park, CA: Kaiser Family Foundation.

Roberts, D. F., & Henriksen, L. (1990, June). *Music listening vs. television viewing among older adolescents.* Paper presented at the annual meeting of the International Communication Association, Dublin, Ireland.

Roberts, D. F., Henriksen, L., & Christenson, P. G. (1999). *Substance use in popular movies and music.* Washington, DC: Office of National Drug Control Policy.

Robins, L. N. (1978). Sturdy childhood predictors of adult antisocial behavior: Replication from longitudinal studies. *Psychological Medicine, 8*, 611–622.

Robinson, T. N. (1998). Does television cause childhood obesity? *Journal of the American Medical Association, 279*, 959–960.

Rodkin, P. C., Farmer, T. W., Pearl, R., & van Acker, R. (2000). Heterogeneity of popular boys: Antisocial and prosocial configurations. *Developmental Psychology, 36*, 14–24.

Rosenbaum, J. L., & Prinsky, L. (1991). The presumption of influence: Recent responses to popular music subcultures. *Crime and Delinquency, 37*, 528–535.

Rosenzweig, S., Fleming, E. E., & Rosenzweig, L. (1948). The children's form of the Rosenzweig Picture-Frustration Study. *Journal of Psychology, 26*, 141–191.

Rosnow, R. L., Rosenthal, R. & Rubin, D. B. (2000). Contrasts and correlations in effect size estimation. *Psychological Science, 1*, 446–453.

Ross, R. P., Campbell, T. A., Wright, J. C., Huston, A. C., Rice, M. K., & Turk, P. (1984). When celebrities talk, children listen: An experimental analysis of children's responses to TV ads with celebrity endorsement. *Journal of Applied Developmental Psychology, 5*, 185–202.

Rothbart, M. K., & Bates, J. E. (1998). Temperament. In W. Damon (Series Ed.) & N. Eisenberg (Vol. Ed.), *Handbook of child psychology: Vol. 3. Social, emotional, and personality development* (5th ed., pp. 105–176). New York: Wiley.

Rotter, J. B. (1966). Generalizing expectancies for internal versus external control of reinforcement. *Psychological Monographs, 80*(1, Whole No. 609).

Rubinstein, E. A., & Sprafkin, J. N. (1982). Television and persons in institutions. In D. Pearl, L. Bouthilet, & J. Lazar (Eds.), *Television and behavior: Ten years of scientific progress and implications for the eighties: Vol. II* (pp. 322–330). Bethesda, Maryland: NIMH.

Rustad, R. A., Small, J. E., Jobes, D. A., Safer, M. A., & Peterson, R. J. (2003). The impact of rock videos and music with suicidal content on thoughts and attitudes about suicide. *Suicide and Life-Threatening Behavior, 33,* 120–131.

Rutter, M. (1985). Family and school influences on cognitive development. *Journal of Child Psychology and Psychiatry, 26,* 683–704.

Saarni, C. (1984). An observational study of children's attempts to monitor their expressive behavior. *Child Development, 55,* 1504–1513.

Salguero, R. A. T., & Moran, R. M. B. (2002). Measuring problem video game playing in adolescents. *Addiction, 97,* 1601–1606.

Sampson, R. J., Raudenbush, S. W., & Earls, F. (1997). Neighborhoods and violent crime: A multilevel study of collective efficacy. *Science, 27,* 918–924.

Sanson, A., & DiMuccio, C. D. (1993). The influence of aggressive and neutral cartoons and toys on the behaviour of preschool children. *Australian Psychologist, 28,* 93–99.

Sargent, J. D., Heatherton, T. F., Ahrens, M. B., Dalton, M. A., Tickle, J. J., & Beach, M. T. (2002). Adolescent exposure to extremely violent movies. *Journal of Adolescent Health, 31,* 449–454.

Satcher, D. (1999). *Message from the Surgeon General on child mental health month.* Retrieved September 22, 2003, from http://www.aboutourkids.org/aboutour/articles/surgeongeneral.html

Savage, W. W. (1990). *Comic books and America, 1945–1954.* Norman: University of Oklahoma Press.

Saylor, C. F., Cowart, B. L., Lipovsky, J. A., Jackson, C., & Finch, A. J. (2003). Media exposure to September 11. *The American Behavioral Scientist, 46,* 1622–1642.

Schaal, B., Tremblay, R., Soussignan, R., & Susman, E. (1996). Male testosterone linked to high social dominance but low physical aggression in early adolescence. *Journal of the American Academy of Child and Adolescent Psychiatry, 34,* 1322–1330.

Scheel, K. R., & Westefeld, J. S. (1999). Heavy metal music and adolescent suicidality: An empirical investigation. *Adolescence, 34,* 253–259.

Schooler, B., Ward, L. M., Merriwether, A., & Caruthers, A. (2004). Who's that girl: Television's role in the body image development of young White and Black women. *Psychology of Women Quarterly, 28,* 38–47.

Schwab-Stone, M., Chen, C., Greenberger, E., Silver, D., Lichtman, J., & Voyce, C. (1999). No safe haven II: The effects of violence exposure on urban youth. *Journal of the American Academy of Child and Adolescent Psychiatry, 38,* 359–367.

Schwartz, C. E., Snidman, N., & Kagan, J. (1999). Adolescent social anxiety as an outcome of inhibited temperament in childhood. *Journal of the Academy of Child and Adolescent Psychiatry, 38,* 1008–1015.

Schwartz, K. (2002). Autoimmunity, dehydroepiandrosterone (DHEA), and stress. *Journal of Adolescent Health, 30S,* 37–43.

Schwartz, N., & Bess, H. (1992). Construction reality and its alternatives: An inclusion/exclusion model of assimilation and contrast effects in social judgment. In L. Marti & A. Tesser (Eds.), *The construction of social judgments* (pp. 217–245). Hillsdale, NJ: Erlbaum.

Selman, R. L. (1980). *The growth of interpersonal understanding.* Orlando, FL: Academic Press.

Senate Committee on the Judiciary. (1999, September 14). *Children, violence, and the media: A report for parents and policy makers.* Washington, DC: U.S. Government Printing Office.

Shaffer, D. R. (2000). *Social and personality development* (4th ed). Belmont, CA: Wadsworth.

Shanahan, J., & Morgan, M. (1999). *Television and its viewers.* Cambridge, UK: Cambridge University Press.

Shermer, M. (1997). *Why people believe weird things: Pseudoscience, superstitions, and other confusions of our time.* New York: Freeman.

Siegel, A. E. (1956). Film mediated fantasy aggression and strength of aggressive drive. *Child Development, 27,* 442–447.

Signorelli, N. (2001). Television's gender role images and contribution to stereotyping. In D. G. Singer & J. L. Singer (Eds.), *Handbook of children and the media* (pp. 341–358). Thousand Oaks, CA: Sage.

Silverman, L. T., & Sprafkin, J. N. (1980). The effects of "Sesame Street's" prosocial spots on cooperative play between young children. *Journal of Broadcasting, 24,* 135–147.

Silvern, S. B., & Williamson, P. A. (1987). The effects of video game play on young children's aggression, fantasy, and prosocial behavior. *Journal of Applied Developmental Psychology, 8,* 453–462.

Simonson, H. (1992). Interaction effects of television and socioeconomic status on teenage aggression. *International Journal of Adolescence & Youth, 3*(3–4), 333–343.

Singer, D. G., & Singer, J. L. (1990). *The house of make-believe: Children's play and the developing imagination.* Cambridge, MA: Harvard University Press.

Singer, J. L., & Singer, D. G. (1979). Come back, Mister Rogers, come back. *Psychology Today,* 56–60.

Singer, J. L., & Singer, D. G. (1981). *Television, imagination, and aggression: A study of preschoolers.* Hillsdale, NJ: Erlbaum.

Singer, M. I., Miller, D. B., Guo, S., Flannery, D. J., Frierson, T., & Slovak, K. (1999). Contributions to violent behavior among elementary and middle school children. *Pediatrics, 104,* 878–884.

Singh, S., & Darroch, J. E. (1999). Trends in sexual activity among adolescent American women: 1982–1995. *Family Planning Perspectives, 31,* 212–219.

Sirico, R. A. (1999). *Watch your bottom line, Hollywood.* Retrieved April 17, 2004, from http://www.forbes.com

Slater, M. D. (2003). Alienation, aggression, and sensation seeking as predictors of adolescent use of violent film, computer, and website content. *Journal of Communication, 53,* 105–121.

Slater, M. D., Henry, K. L., Swaim, R. C., & Anderson, L. L. (2003). Violent media content and aggressiveness in adolescents: A downward spiral model. *Communication Research, 30*(6), 713–736.

Smith, R. (1986). Television addiction. In J. Bryant & D. Zillmann (Eds.), *Perspectives on media effects* (pp. 109–128). Hillsdale, NJ: Erlbaum.

Smith, S., & Boyson, A. (2002). Violence in music videos: Examining the prevalence and context of physical aggression. *Journal of Communication, 52,* 61–83.

The Smoking Gun. (2004). Retrieved November 11, 2004, from http://www.thesmokinggun.com

Sneegas, J. E., & Plank, T. A. (1998). Gender differences in pre-adolescent reactance to age-categorized television advisory labels. *Journal of Broadcasting and Electronic Media, 42,* 423–434.

Snopes.com. (2004). *The Harris levels.* Retrieved December 13, 2004, from http://www.snopes.com/horrors/madmen/doom.asp

Snow, R. P. (1974). How children interpret TV violence in play context. *Journalism Quarterly, 51,* 13–21.

Sparks, G. G. (2001). *Media effects research: A basic overview.* Belmont, CA: Wadsworth.

Spear, L. P. (2000). The adolescent brain and age-related behavioral manifestations. *Neuroscience and Biobehavioral Reviews, 24,* 417–463.

Sports Illustrated. (2004). *Tyson's Quickest Knockouts.* Retrieved January 14, 2004, from http:www.cnnsi.com/boxing/news/

Stambrook, M., & Parker, K. C. (1987). The development of the concept of death in childhood: A review of the literature. *Merrill-Palmer Quarterly, 22,* 133–157.

Starker, S. (1989). *Evil influences: Crusades against the mass media.* New Brunswick, NJ: Transaction Publishers.

Steinberg, L. (2001). Adolescent development. *Annual Review of Psychology, 52,* 83–110.

Stenberg, C., Campos, J. J., & Emde, R. (1983). The facial expression of anger in seven month old infants. *Child Development, 54,* 178–184.

Steuer, F. B., Applefield, J. M., & Smith, R. (1971). Televised aggression and the interpersonal aggression of preschool children. *Journal of Experimental Child Psychology, 11,* 442–447.

Strasburger, V. C. (1995). *Adolescents and the media: Medical and psychological impact.* Thousand Oaks, CA: Sage.

Strasburger, V. C. (2001). Children and TV advertising: Nowhere to run, nowhere to hide. *Journal of Developmental and Behavioral Pediatrics, 22,* 185–187.

Strasburger, V. C., & Donnerstein, E. (1999). Children, adolescents, and the media: Issues and solutions. *Pediatrics, 103,* 129–139.

Strasburger, V. C., & Wilson, B. J. (2002). *Children, adolescents, and the media.* Thousand Oaks, CA: Sage.

Sun, S. W., & Lull, J. (1986). The adolescent audience for music videos and why they watch. *Journal of Communication, 36,* 115–125.

Susman, E. J., Inoff-Germain, G., Nottelmann, E. D., Loriauz, D. L., Cutler Jr., G. B., & Chrousos, G. P. (1987). Hormones, emotional dispositions, and aggressive attributes in young adolescents. *Child Development, 58,* 1114–1134.

Sutton, M. J., Brown, J. D., Wilson, K. M., & Klein, J. D. (2002). Shaking the tree of knowledge for forbidden fruit: Where adolescents learn about sexuality and contraception. In J. D. Brown, J. R. Steele, & K. Walsk-Childers (Eds.), *Sexual teens, sexual media* (pp. 25–55). Mahwah, NJ: Erlbaum.

Sutton-Smith, B., Gerstmyer, J., & Meckley, A. (1988). Play-fighting as folklore amongst preschool children. *Western Folklore, 47,* 161–176.

Swartz, J. D., & Holtzman, W. H. (1963). Group method of administration for the Hotzman inkblot technique. *Journal of Clinical Psychology, 19,* 433–441.

Tamburro, R. F., Gordon, P. L., D'Apolito, J. P., & Howard, S. C. (2004). Unsafe and violent behavior in commercials aired during televised major sporting events. *Journal of Pediatrics, 114*(6), 694–698.

Tan, A. S., & Scruggs, K. J. (1980). Does exposure to comic books violence lead to aggression in children? *Journalism Quarterly 57,* 579–583.

Thomas, A., & Chess, S. (1977). *Temperament and development.* New York: Brunner/Mazel.

Thomas, M. H., & Drabman, R. S. (1975). Toleration of real life aggression as a function of exposure to televised violence and age of subject. *Merrill-Palmer Quarterly, 21*(3), 227–232.

Thomas, M. H., Horton, R. W., Lippencott, E. C., & Drabman, R. S. (1977). Desensitization to portrayals of real-life aggression as a function of exposure to television violence. *Journal of Personality and Social Psychology, 35,* 450–458.

Thompson, K. M., & Haninger, K. (2001). Violence in E-rated video games. *Journal of the American Medical Association, 286,* 591–598.

Thompson, K. M., & Yokota, F. (2004). Violence, sex, and profanity in films: Correlation of movie ratings with content. *Medscape General Medicine, 6*(3). Retrieved January 15, 2005, from http://www.medscape.com

Thorne, A., & Michaelieu, Q. (1996). Situating adolescent gender and self-esteem with personal memories. *Child Development, 67,* 1362–1378.

Tirodkar, M. A., & Jain, A. (2003). Food messages on African American television shows. *American Journal of Public Health, 93,* 439–441.

Tolan, P. H., Gorman-Smith, D., & Henry, D. B. (2003). The developmental ecology of urban males' youth violence. *Developmental Psychology, 39,* 274–291.

Took, K. J., & Weiss, D. S. (1994). The relationship between heavy metal and rap music and adolescent turmoil: Real or artifact? *Adolescence, 29,* 613–621.

Tremblay, R. E., Boulerice, B., Harden, P. W., McDuff, P., Perusse, D., Pihl, R. O., et al. (1996). Do children in Canada become more aggressive as they approach adolescence? In Human Resources Development Canada & Statistics Canada (Ed.), *Growing up in Canada: National longitudinal study of children and youth* (pp. 127–137). Ottawa: Statistics Canada.

Trzesniewski, K. H., Donnellan, M. B., & Robins, R. W. (2003). Stability of self-esteem across the life-span. *Journal of Personality and Social Psychology, 84*, 205–220.

Turner, C. W., & Goldsmith, D. (1976). Effects of toy guns and airplanes on children's antisocial free play behavior. *Journal of Experimental Child Psychology, 21*, 303–315.

Ubi Soft. (2001). *Ubi Soft licenses Tom Clancy's Rainbow Six Rogue Spear game engine to train U.S. soldiers.* Retrieved June 6, 2003, from http://corp.ubisoft.com/

Underwood, B., & Moore, B. (1982). The generality of altruism in children. In N. Eisenberg (Ed.), *The development of prosocial behavior* (pp. 25–52). New York: Academic Press.

Underwood, M. K. (2003). *Social aggression among girls.* New York: Guilford Press.

Unger, J. B., Schuster D., Zogg J., Dent C. W., & Stacy A. W. (2003). Alcohol advertising exposure and adolescent alcohol use: A comparison of exposure measures. *Addiction Research and Theory, 11*, 177–193.

U.S. Department of Health and Human Services. (2001). Analysis of data from the National Youth Survey 1976–1993, Rochester Youth Development Study, 1986–1999, Denver Youth Study, 1986–1999, and Pittsburgh Youth Study, 1986–1999. *Youth violence: A report of the Surgeon General.* Washington, DC: U.S. Department of Health and Human Services.

U.S. Surgeon General's Scientific Advisory Committee on Television and Social Behavior. (1972). *Television and growing up: The impact of televised violence* (DHEW Publication No. HSM 72–9086). Washington, DC: U.S. Government Printing Office.

Valenti, J. (2001). Valenti testifies that industry's self-regulation best help to parents, not government intervention. Retrieved October 31, 2004, from http://www.mpaa.org/jack/2001/2001_07_25a.htm

Valkenburg, P. M., Cantor, J., & Peeters, A. L. (2000). Fright reactions to television: A child survey. *Communication Research, 27*, 82–97.

Valkenburg, P. M., & Janssen, S. C. (1999). What do children value in entertainment programs? A cross-cultural investigation. *Journal of Communication, 49*, 3–21.

Van Beijsterveldt, C. E. M., Bartels, M., Hudziak, J. J., & Boomsma, D. I. (2003). Causes of stability of aggression from early childhood to adolescence: A longitudinal genetic analysis in Dutch twins. *Behavior Genetics, 33*, 591–605.

Van Goozen, S. H. M., Matthys, W., Cohen-Kettenis, P. T., Thijssen, J. H. H., & von Engeland, H. (1998). Adrenal androgens and aggression in conduct disorder prepubertal boys and normal controls. *Biological Psychiatry, 43*, 156–158.

Van Mierlo, J., & Van den Bulck, J. (2004). Benchmarking the cultivation approach to video game effects: A comparison of the correlates of TV viewing and game play. *Journal of Adolescence, 27*, 97–111.

Vance/Roberson v. CBS Inc./Judas Priest. 1990. No. 86–5844 and 86–3939 (Washoe County, 2nd Judicial District Court of Nevada, August 24, 1990).

Vetro, A., Csapo, A., Szilard, J., & Vargha, M. (1998). Effect of television on aggressivity of adolescents. *International Journal of Adolescent Medicine and Health, 3,* 303–320.

Vidal, M. A., Clemente, M. E., & Espinosa, P. (2003). Types of media violence and degree of acceptance in under-18s. *Aggressive Behavior, 29,* 381–392.

Viemero, V., & Paajanen, S. (1992). The role of fantasies and dreams in the TV viewing-aggression relationship. *Aggressive Behavior, 18,* 109–116.

Vokey, J. R., & Read, J. D. (1985). Subliminal messages: Between the devil and the media. *American Psychologist, 40,* 1231–1239.

Vossekuil, B., Fein, R. A., Reddy, M., Borum, R., & Modzeleski, W. (2002). *The final report and findings of the safe school initiative: Implications for the prevention of school attacks in the United States.* Washington DC: U.S Secret Service and U. S. Department of Education.

Vygotsky, L. S. (1978). *Mind and society: The development of higher mental processes.* Cambridge, MA: Harvard University Press.

Walker, E. F., Walder, B. J., & Reynolds, F. (2001). Developmental changes in cortisol secretion in normal and at-risk youth. *Development and Psychopathology, 13,* 721–732.

Walser, R. (1993). *Running with the devil: Power, gender, and madness in heavy metal music.* Middletown, CT: Wesleyan University Press.

Walsh, D., & Gentile, D. A. (2001). A validity test of movie, television, and video game ratings. *Pediatrics, 107*(6), 1302–1308.

Walsh, D., Gentile, D. A., Gieske, J., Walsh, M., & Chasco, E. (2003). Eighth annual mediawise video game report card. *National Institute on Media and the Family.* Retrieved May 7, 2004, from http://www.mediafamily.org

Ward, S., & Wackman, D. (1972). Family and media influences on adolescent consumer learning. In E. A. Rubinstein, G. A. Comstock, & J. P. Murray (Eds.), *Television and social behavior* (Vol. 4, pp. 554–565). Washington, DC: U.S. Government Printing Office.

Ward, S., & Wackman, D. (1973). Children's information processing of television advertising. In P. Clarke (Ed.), *New models for mass communication research* (pp. 119–146). Beverly Hills, CA: Sage.

Warden, D., & Mackinnon, S. (2003). Prosocial children, bullies and victims: An investigation of their sociometric status, empathy and social problem-solving strategies. *British Journal of Developmental Psychology, 21,* 367–385.

Watson, M. W., & Peng, Y. (1992). The relation between toy gun play and children's aggressive behavior. *Early Education and Development, 3*(4), 370–389.

Wegener-Spohring, G. (1989). War toys and aggressive games. *Play and Culture, 2,* 35–47.

Wenglinsky, H. (1998). *Does it compute? The relationship between educational technology and student achievement in mathematics.* Princeton, NJ: Educational Testing Service. Retrieved November 23, 2003, from //ftp.ets.org/ pub/res/tech nolog.pdf

Werner, E. E., & Smith, R. S. (1982). *Vulnerable to invincible: A longitudinal study of resilient children and youth.* New York: McGraw-Hill.

Wertham, F. (1954). *Seduction of the innocent.* New York: Holt, Rinehart, & Winston.

Wiehe, V. R. (1997). *Sibling abuse: Hidden physical, emotional, and sexual trauma* (2nd ed.). Thousand Oaks, CA: Sage.

Wikipedia. (2004). *The rite of spring.* Retrieved August 17, 2004, from http://en.wikipedia.org/wiki/The_Rite_of_Spring

Williams, T. B. (Ed.). (1986). *The impact of television: A natural experiment in three communities.* New York: Academic Press.

Wilson, B. J., Colvin, C. M., & Smith, S. L. (2002). Engaging in violence on American television: A comparison of child, teen, and adult perpetrators. *Journal of Communication, 52,* 36–60.

Wilson, B. J., Smith, S. L., Potter, J. W., Kunkel, D., Linz, D., Colvin, C. M., et al. (2002). Violence in children's television programming: Assessing the risks. *Journal of Communication, 52,* 5–35.

Windle, R. C., & Windle, M. (1995). Longitudinal patterns of physical aggression: Associations with adult social, psychiatric and personality functioning and testosterone levels. *Development and Psychopathology, 7,* 563–585.

Wingood, G. M., DiClemente, R. J., Bernhardt, J. M., Harrington, K., Davies, S. L., Robillard, A., et al. (2003). A perspective study of exposure to rap music videos and African American female adolescents' health. *American Journal of Public Health, 93*(3), 437–439.

Winkel, M., Novak, D. M., & Hopson, H. (1987). Personality factors, subject gender, and the effects of aggressive video games on aggression in adolescents. *Journal of Research in Personality, 21,* 211–223.

Woodard, E. (1999). *The 1999 state of children's television report: Programming for children over broadcast and cable television* (Rep. No. 28). Philadelphia: University of Pennsylvania, The Annenberg Public Policy Center.

Woolley, J. D. (1997). Thinking about fantasy: Are children fundamentally different thinkers and believers from adults? *Child Development, 68,* 991–1011.

Woolley, J. D., Boerger, E. A., & Markman, A. B. (2004). A visit from the candy witch: Factors influencing young children's belief in a novel fantastical being. *Developmental Science, 7,* 456–468.

World Wrestling Entertainment, Inc. (2003). Retrieved August 4, 2004, from http://www.wwecorporate.com/advert/1_advert.html

Wotring, C. E., & Greenberg, B. S. (1973). Experiments in televised violence and verbal aggression: Two exploratory studies. *Journal of Communication, 23,* 446–460.

Wright, J. C., Huston, A. C., Reitz, A. L., & Piemyat, S. (1994). Young children's perceptions of television reality determinants and developmental differences. *Developmental Psychology, 30*(2), 229–239.

Yankelovich Partners. (1993, May 24). How should we teach our children about sex? *Time,* 60–66.

Yen, S. S., & Laughlin, G. A. (1998). Aging and the adrenal cortex. *Experimental Gerontology, 33*(7–8), 897–910.

Yokota, F., & Thompson, K. M. (2000). Violence in G-rated films. *Journal of the American Medical Association, 283*, 2716–2720.

Yurgelun-Todd, D. (1998). *Physical changes in adolescent brain may account for turbulent teen years, McLean Hospital study reveals* [Press Release]. Retrieved December 1, 2002, from http://www.mclean.harvard.edu/PublicAffairs/Turbulent Teens.htm

Zillmann, D. (1983). Transfer of excitation in emotional behaviour. In J. T. Cacioppo & R. E. Petty (Eds.), *Social psychophysiology: A sourcebook* (pp. 215–240). New York: Guilford Press.

Zillmann, D. (1998). The psychology of the appeal of portrayals of violence. In J. Goldstein (Ed.), *Why we watch: The attractions of violent entertainment* (pp. 179–211). New York: Oxford University Press.

Zuckerman, M. M. (1994). *Behavioral expression and biosocial bases of sensation-seeking.* New York: Cambridge University Press.

Author Index

Subject Index

A

Abnormal aggression,
  effect on youth, 41
Academic television, in early
  childhood, 332
Active learning, 276–277
Active mediation, research on,
  293–294
Adolescents
  advertising and, 335–337
  affective body image, 112, 341
  aggressive cues and, 134
  aggressive-rejected children and, 263
  aggression-related constructs and,
    235–236
  alcohol consumption and
    advertising, 339
  anorexia and, 341
  backlash towards antiviolence
    attitudes, 294
  body image and, 112
  comic book reading and, 145
  controlling negative emotions
    and, 100
  cross-race friendships and, 334
  decision-making processes of GAM
    and, 67
  deviant social networks and, 264
    early adolescents and media
    violence, 282
  eating disorders and, 342
  effects of nonviolent media and,
    325–343
  effects of violent music on, 196–197

functional magnetic resonance
  imaging (fMRI), 257–258
gender differences in media
  consumption, 78
high levels of exposure to sexual
  content, 340
imitative behavior and, 130–132
long-term violent video game
  exposure, 234
media consumption and, 77–78
media statistics and, 76
neighborhood violence and, 265
normative aggression and, 26–31
parental monitoring and, 22,
  259–264, 288–289
peers and, 262
positive mood levels
  (decrease of), 283
sensation seeking and, 84
sexual behavior and, 339–341
social isolation and, 25
television watching vs. classroom
  time, 75
violent video games and, 235
youth programs and violence, 77
Advertising
  alcohol consumption and, 339
  cigarette advertising and, 338
  commercial exposure and increased
    desire, 337
  commercials and aggressive
    acts, 202
  television commercials and
    unsafe images, 202

About the Author

Steven J. Kirsh is an associate professor of psychology at the State University of New York at Geneseo. He received his Ph.D. in developmental psychology from The Pennsylvania State University. Professor Kirsh's research focuses on the influence of violent media on social information processing. He has published multiple scientific articles and chapters and given presentations on this subject. Recent research projects include the effects of violent media consumption on emotion recognition and the influence of violent video game play on emotional Stroop interference. Professor Kirsh has also published research on parent-child attachment relationships and the teaching of psychology. He is on the advisory board for *Annual Editions: Human Development* and serves as a reviewer for numerous journals. He currently teaches courses on child development, introductory psychology, and media violence.